In recent decades, Wordsworth's poetry has been a focus for many of the theoretical schools of criticism that comprise modern literary studies. Don Bialostosky here proposes to adjudicate the diverse claims of these numerous schools and to trace their implications for teaching. Bialostosky draws on the work of Bakhtin and his followers to create a "dialogic" critical synthesis of what Wordsworth's readers – from Coleridge to de Man – have made of his poetry. He reveals Wordsworth's poetry as itself "dialogically" responding to its various contexts, and opens up fruitful possibilities for current criticism and teaching of Wordsworth. This challenging book uses the case of Wordsworth studies to make a far-reaching survey of modern literary theory and its implications for the practice of criticism and teaching today.

Wordsworth, dialogics, and the practice of criticism

Literature, Culture, Theory

❖❖

General editors

RICHARD MACKSEY, *The Johns Hopkins University*

and MICHAEL SPRINKER, *State University of New York at Stony Brook*

The Cambridge *Literature, Culture, Theory* series is dedicated to theoretical studies in the human sciences that have literature and culture as their object of enquiry. Acknowledging the contemporary expansion of cultural studies and the redefinitions of literature that this has entailed, the series includes not only original works of literary theory but also monographs and essay collections on topics and seminal figures from the long history of theoretical speculation on the arts and human communication generally. The concept of theory embraced in the series is broad, including not only the classical disciplines of poetics and rhetoric, but also those of aesthetics, linguistics, psychoanalysis, semiotics, and other cognate sciences that have inflected the systematic study of literature during the past half century.

Titles published

Return to Freud: Jacques Lacan's dislocation of psychoanalysis
SAMUEL WEBER
(*translated from the German by Michael Levine*)

Wordsworth, dialogics, and the practice of criticism
DON H. BIALOSTOSKY

The subject of modernity
ANTHONY J. CASCARDI

Onomatopoetics: theory of language and literature
JOSEPH GRAHAM

Other titles in preparation

Paratexts
GERARD GENETTE
(*translated from the French by Jane Lewin*)

The object of literature
PIERRE MACHEREY
(*translated from the French by David Macey*)

Parody: ancient, modern, and post-modern
MARGARET ROSE

Kenneth Burke: a rhetoric of the subject
ROBERT WESS

Wordsworth, dialogics, and the practice of criticism

DON H. BIALOSTOSKY

Professor of English, University of Toledo, Ohio

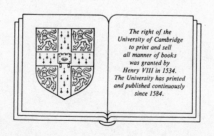

The right of the
University of Cambridge
to print and sell
all manner of books
was granted by
Henry VIII in 1534.
The University has printed
and published continuously
since 1584.

CAMBRIDGE UNIVERSITY PRESS

Cambridge

New York   Port Chester   Melbourne   Sydney

Published by the Press Syndicate of the University of Cambridge
The Pitt Building, Trumpington Street, Cambridge CB2 1RP
40 West 20th Street, New York, NY 10011–4211, USA
10 Stamford Road, Oakleigh, Victoria 3166, Australia

© Cambridge University Press 1992

First published 1992

Printed in Great Britain at the University Press, Cambridge

A catalogue record for this book is available from the British Library

Library of Congress cataloguing in publication data
Bialostosky, Don H.
Wordsworth, dialogics, and the practice of criticism / Don H. Bialostosky.
p.   cm. – (Literature, Culture, Theory; 2)
Includes bibliographical references and index.
ISBN 0 521 41249 8
1.   Wordsworth, William, 1770–1850 – Knowledge – Literature.
2.   English literature – History and criticism – Theory, etc.
3.   Criticism – Great Britain – History – 19th century.
4.   Dialogue.
I.   Title.   II.   Series.
PR5892.L5B5   1992
821'.7–dc20   91–11011 CIP
ISBN 0 521 41249 8 hardback

In memory of

Norman Maclean

Contents

Contents

Contents

Preface

By a "practice" I am going to mean any coherent and complex form of socially established cooperative human activity through which goods internal to that form of activity are realised in the course of trying to achieve those standards of excellence which are appropriate to, and partially definitive of, that form of activity, with the result that human powers to achieve excellence, and human conceptions of the ends and goods involved, are systematically extended.   Alasdair MacIntyre, *After Virtue*

Most of us who have been privileged to profess literature in the 70s and 80s have gotten more than we bargained for. Whatever text or author, whatever practice of reading or writing, whatever pedagogical or political project drew us to literary studies, our professional development of that first interest has taken us places we did not expect to go, put us in the company of people we did not expect to encounter, and confronted us with issues we did not expect to address. In my own case, an undergraduate professor sent me to Wordsworth's *Prelude* to see what it could teach me about my vocational crisis over the choice of a field of graduate study, and I ended up choosing the Wordsworthian enterprise of "English" itself, writing a dissertation on Wordsworth's Preface to *Lyrical Ballads*, assuming the identity of "Romanticist," and discovering that a Romanticist in the 70s and 80s, especially a Wordsworthian, was also singularly implicated in the field of "theory." My author, after all, had authorized a progressive and theoretically self-conscious enterprise of literary study, and his collaborator Coleridge had criticized his poetic theory and promoted a selection of his poetry in terms that became fundamental for New Critical theory and therefore fundamental for its opponents. The principal expositors of nearly every theoretical program for criticism during the past two decades (and of some decades earlier) have found it necessary to take up Wordsworth's poetry along with his and Coleridge's poetic theories, and many of them have been "Romanticists" as well as theorists. Even Wordsworthian critics who have chosen not to highlight their theoretical investments have nonetheless exhibited them to theoretically sensitized readers, and more and more critics have chosen to name their own theories lest they be theoretically characterized by another critic.

The intersection of Wordsworthian, Romanticist, and theoretical interests is by now so well known in England and America that I would expect most readers who pick up this book to recognize it and many to participate in it. A specialization in any one of these interests to the complete exclusion of the others seems impossible to me today, though a comprehensive profession of all three interests combined seems equally impossible. Theorists who have followed the theoretical debates of the last two decades have necessarily encountered only a limited Wordsworthian canon, just as Wordsworthians and Romanticists have been implicated in no more than a selection of the theoretical debates in progress, but I believe that whatever the limits of their knowledge, all who recognize this conjuncture will also recognize that it is one of the places in which the future of literary studies is being imagined and decided.

What brings our intersecting interests together in this conjuncture is a bond of "common enterprise" that Paul de Man mentioned in an early lecture, only to reject it out of hand as the bond to be discovered "at the root of Wordsworth's theme of human love." Though no critic concerned with the intersection of Wordsworth, Romanticism, and theory has played a more important part in the last two decades in shaping our common enterprise of literary studies, de Man did not represent his own work or Wordsworth's as programmatic. He rejected without argument any explanation of Wordsworth's theme of human love that appealed to a common enterprise upon which the poet believed himself and his readers to be embarked and emphasized instead "a common temporal predicament." He found "the key to an understanding of Wordsworth ... in the relationship between imagination and time, not in the relationship between imagination and nature" and not – to complete a thought he does not develop – in the relationship between imagination and common purpose or practice (THW 15–16). De Man predicted a direction for literary studies but did not advocate one, and he presented Wordsworth not as the advocate of a project but as the witness of a condition.

I believe, however, that de Man's disregard for the Wordsworthian common enterprise has misrepresented Wordsworth and interdicted our consideration of Wordsworth's role in founding the enterprise that constitutes us as students and teachers of literature. At the least, evidence of a programmatic Wordsworth can be found to answer the evidence de Man cites for his problematic Wordsworth. De Man repeatedly called our attention to that moment in the Preface to *Lyrical Ballads* where Wordsworth entertains the "illusory analogy" that "'considers man and nature as essentially adapted to each other, and the mind of man as naturally the mirror of the fairest and most interesting properties of nature,'" but we may also recall those moments in which Wordsworth declares that each of his poems "has a worthy *purpose*" opposing a "general evil" which he believed would soon "be systematically opposed by men of greater powers and with far more distinguished success" than his own.[1] De Man characterized Wordsworth's poetry from the perspective of the *Essays upon Epitaphs* as assuming the "temporal perspective" of an "epitaph written by the poet for himself . . . , so to speak, from beyond the grave" (THW 9), but we may also recall Wordsworth's account of the poet in the Preface as "a man speaking to men . . . who rejoices more than other men in the spirit of life that is in him . . . , singing a song in which all human beings join with him . . . in the presence of truth as our visible friend and hourly companion" (LB 255–59). Though de Man's selections from *The Prelude* have emphasized the reflective moments of contemplating the Boy of Winander's death or the French Revolution's failure, we may also recall the closing lines of the poem in which Wordsworth looks forward to working as a joint laborer in the redemption and instruction of his fellow men.

To speak more generally, we may remind ourselves that Wordsworth situated both the writing and the reading of his poetry not merely within nature or time, or even within language — de Man's ultimate critical category — but within a purposeful human enterprise dedicated to the advancement of learning and the sharing of pleasure, even if this purpose was not, as he said, "a distinct purpose formally conceived" (LB 240). The poet accepted the obligation "to extend the domain of sensibility for the delight, the honour, and the benefit of human nature," and the readers incurred the corresponding obligations to apply "to the consideration of the laws of this art the

1. RR 52. LB 246, 149, 250.

best power of their understandings" and to exert within their own minds a "corresponding energy" to that exerted by the poet in order to comprehend his work. The one introduced "a new element into the intellectual universe," and the other, through learning and exertion, brought that element within the domain of the ongoing "'Spirit of human knowledge'" as well as "the sphere of human sensibility" and enjoyment (ES 66, 82–84). These and other affirmations of the "worthy *purpose*" (LB 246) Wordsworth imagined his art to serve drew me to his democratic yet intellectually demanding practice at the outset of my own profession of literature, and the troubling implications and alien representations of that practice I did not bargain for have not yet discouraged me from pursuing my vocation in its terms.

Recent accounts of the genealogy of literary studies would suggest that I am not alone in my investment in the Wordsworthian enterprise. Jonathan Arac has argued that Wordsworth "did more than anyone to establish a vocation of literature in relation to which... our own culture's idea of the literary critic took shape." Clifford Siskin claims that Wordsworth underwrote an enterprise of critical inquiry and literary education in England and America which has produced the classrooms and the vehicles of literary publication in which his poetry has been written about, as well as the very literary critics and students of literature who have written about it. By refusing to accept either a given contemporary readership or a contemporary knowledge of literature as adequate to judging his work, Wordsworth projected into the future a task of learning and reading to which we may imagine what Robert Scholes has called "the English Apparatus" to be an institutional response.[2]

The adequacy of that institutional response and, indeed, the formulation of the task itself have come under increasing scrutiny in recent years. The proliferation of "readings" generated by the institution of criticism has called into question whether the "great Spirit of human knowledge" in literary studies is truly moving, as Wordsworth believed, or just standing still, repeating itself (see graph). The recent questionings of the institutionalized distinction between "literature" and "history" have also called into question the boundaries of the "intellectual universe" in which poets write and

---

2. *Genealogies* 3. *Historicity passim.* Robert Scholes, *Textual Power: Literary Theory and the Teaching of English* (New Haven and London: Yale University Press, 1985), 1–17.

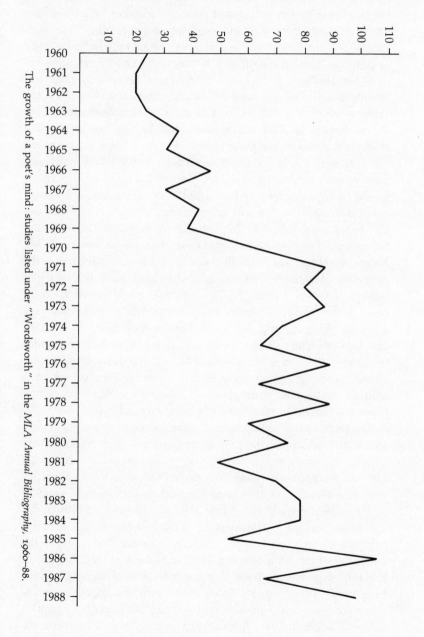

The growth of a poet's mind: studies listed under "Wordsworth" in the *MLA Annual Bibliography*, 1960–88.

readers read, and critics have asked who has been left out and what has been sacrificed in setting that poetical "universe" apart from the world of politics, society, and economy. From another side, both "literature" and "history" have been subsumed by a radical critique of language that has questioned the autonomy and liberating power of either intellectual discipline. And these diverse critiques and agendas have called into question the educational functions of literary study as either a specialized area or a part of liberal education.

For literary scholars and teachers and for the institutions and students that sustain and make claims upon them, these questions call for re-examination of the literary enterprise and of Wordsworth as a founder and continuing object of that enterprise. Readings of *his* poems have proliferated and need to be accounted for. *He* has been held responsible for the anti-historical aestheticization of literature, and *he* has been re-read as "a poet of sheer language" (RR 92) who has provoked some of his followers to self-deluded aesthetic defenses. *He* has been identified as the liberator of oppressed classes and as the oppressor of women in literature. *He* has been made the center of pedagogical experiments. His poems have been chosen to demonstrate the efficacy of almost every critical school of the past fifty years in America, and his name has been invoked to warrant postmodern literary studies as well as to discredit the entire enterprise of "Literature." It is not only possible to address the larger questions of the literary enterprise today by writing about Wordsworth; it is scarcely possible to write about Wordsworth without addressing those questions. I at least have not been able to do so.

The chapters that follow, then, engage the issues of literary studies and liberal education through an engagement with Wordsworth. Chapter 1, "Wordsworth, literary history, and the constitution of literature," engages two recent Foucauldian accounts of Wordsworth's role in the founding of "Literature" and defines the historical situation of the present inquiry in relation to them. Chapter 2, "Displacing Coleridge, replacing Wordsworth," examines the claims of these competing "founding fathers" of modern literary study, probes the difficulties of choosing between them, and works to build the critical tradition that would make Wordsworth's claims more powerful. Chapter 3, "Wordsworth's dialogic art," tests the critical resources that have been used to characterize Wordsworth's poetry against a marginal poem in the Wordsworthian canon and re-examines his canonical poems from the point of view of the margin in terms drawn from the work of Mikhail Bakhtin. Chapter 4, "Dialogics of the lyric: a symposium on 'Westminster Bridge' and 'Beauteous Evening,'" examines how two of Wordsworth's canonical sonnets have been read by critics connected with eight post-war critical schools, introduces a Bakhtinian reading among them, and addresses the problem of how those readings have generally neglected one another and failed to constitute a responsible field of discourse. Chapter 5, "Social action in 'The Solitary Reaper'" criticizes Geoffrey Hartman's paradigmatic reading of "The Solitary Reaper" as a dramatization of consciousness and resists a New Historicist reduction of the poem to an evasion of historical reality. Chapter 6, "What de Man has made of Wordsworth," reviews the roles that Wordsworth has played in Paul de Man's writings. Chapter 7, "The revival of rhetoric and the reading of Wordsworth's *Prelude*," supplements recent rhetorical readings of Wordsworth through a recovery of classical rhetorical distinctions and an application of them to the first book of *The Prelude* and to the venerable topic of Wordsworth's theory of poetic diction. Chapter 8, "Theoretical commitments and Wordsworthian pedagogies," examines the pedagogical implications for Wordsworth's poetry of recent shifts in critical theory. Chapter 9, "Wordsworth, Allan Bloom, and liberal education" marshals Wordsworth as an alternative authority in the recent debates on liberal education.

Throughout this preface I have dwelt upon the common enterprise of literary study and teaching that has enabled the composition of these chapters and linked my work with the work of other participants in that enterprise. Professing literature, as Gerald Graff's recent book of that name has reminded us, is something more than reading it, and those of us who study and teach it professionally cannot leave our own practices, purposes, and projects out of account when we discuss it. I have tried in what follows to highlight those practices and bring those projects and purposes into the foreground of my own writing and the writing of my fellow critics and fellow teachers, emphasizing not just the logical presuppositions of our arguments and practices but also the signs of our affiliations with and oppositions to the others who have provoked us to write and teach as we do. I have tried, as Graff urges, to "teach the conflicts" but also to present the convergences of my own and others' work. Accordingly, matter usually consigned to the footnotes and acknowledgments has regularly taken a place in my text, and topics that often go unmentioned have been mentioned. My own argument has sometimes been conducted through the double-voiced dialogic representation of others' arguments rather than in formal counter-argument, and it has sometimes taken its shape not from a division of any thesis of mine but from the openings and materials they have made available. I have sometimes tested the limits of academic decorum and sometimes experimented with what might be taken as excessive elaborations of uncommon genres, because I am convinced that the enterprise of literary studies can no longer address its authors and its objects without addressing at the same time what its own members have made of them. What Dominick LaCapra has said of the essay-review applies to my own adoption of that genre and of the symposium, as well as to my use of dialogic figures of thought even in the critical essay: "It is a recognition that critical discourse is dialogical in that it attempts to address itself simultaneously to problems ... and to the words of others addressing those problems ... it is an enactment of the humanistic understanding of research as a conversation with the past through the medium of significant texts; it is also an especially vital forum in a contested discipline that is undergoing reconceptualization."[3]

I acknowledge here, as Wordsworth himself did, the experimental character of my departures from the genre in which my readers may reasonably expect me to be writing, and I ask, as he did, that my readers recognize the deliberateness of my experiments and the urgency of the circumstances that have provoked me to them. The quantity and variety of the work we produce has far outrun our capacity to assimilate and respond to it. The paradigms on offer for our common enterprise are many; and their cases for our adherence remain unadjudicated or are decided by fashion or the need for a conveniently vulnerable authority. Our syllabi and teaching techniques frequently reflect old models and habits of literary study that our research and theory claim to have displaced or discredited. If we are to justify our work to ourselves and to the institutions and polities that grant and sustain our professional privileges, and if we are to appreciate and build upon the extraordinary quantity and variety of work our colleagues have already produced, we students of literature must find new ways to assimilate and respond to what our colleagues make of our objects of inquiry, and we must reflect on what it means

3. Dominick LaCapra, *Rethinking Intellectual History* (Ithaca: Cornell University Press, 1983), 20–21.

for us always to meet those objects in the company of those colleagues.

In Wordsworth we must even recognize that a producer of compelling literary objects is at the same time an influential, founding colleague whose sense of purpose has shaped our own purposes and whose account of his own works has helped to guide our accounts of them. If he were alive today, we would have to give him an honorary degree. Though he is not, we must nonetheless grant him the collegial acknowledgment of a critical response. In the common enterprise we share with him and in part owe to him, we meet him not just as an object to analyze or a genius to admire but as a fellow inquirer to question, hear out, and answer in our turn.

Many of my fellow inquirers have heard out and answered parts of this book on its way to its present shape, and many others have provoked and shaped its titular author on his way to writing it. Wayne C. Booth, Winifred Casterline, Norman Maclean, James M. Redfield, Stuart Tave, and Charles Wegener deserve special mention for disciplining and informing the author's intellect in ways that he can still recognize in this text published fifteen to twenty-five years after his formal submission to their instruction has ended. Colleagues at the University of Akron, Ball State University, Columbia University, Indiana University, Michigan State University, Northwestern University, Reed College, Rhode Island College, Siena Heights College, St. John's University, Collegeville, Minnesota, the State University of New York at Stony Brook, and the University of Washington have invited me to produce or present various parts of this argument and responded to my presentations with further provocations. Organizers of sessions at conventions of the College English Association of Ohio (Barry Chabot), the Modern Language Association (Evan Watkins, A. W. Phinney, and Tilottama Rajan), the National Council of Teachers of English (David Laurence), the Northeast Modern Language Association (Charles Rzepka), and the Society for the Study of Narrative Literature have also brought parts of this work into being or provided occasions for its testing and transformation. Bruce Bashford, Peter Elbow, Clint Goodson, Charles O. Hartman, Steven Mailloux, Peter Manning, Wallace Martin, Wendy Olmsted, Gene W. Ruoff, David Q. Smith, Michael Sprinker, and Susan Wolfson have read substantial parts or all of this work in progress and responded to it with collegial tact and intellectual rigor.

If I have not always taken their good advice, I have always been grateful for it.

A number of institutions that play a part in the "English Apparatus" have also enabled the production of this volume. A grant for recent recipients of the Ph.D. from the American Council of Learned Societies and a Summer Study Grant from the National Endowment for the Humanities a decade ago have at last borne some fruit in this argument. The Department of English at the State University of New York at Stony Brook released me from teaching duties to work on this project with the expectation that it would come to fruition much sooner than it has. Academic Vice President William Free, Dean Alfred Cave, and the Chair of the English Department, David Hoch, at the University of Toledo generously provided me with the time to work on this project and with the able research support of Beth Poulos, Lynn Anderson, and Lori Demers, to whom I am also grateful. A Challenge Grant from the Ohio Board of Regents has subsidized the excellent technical assistance of Laurie Cohen. I also thank the Graduate School at Toledo for a Faculty Research Award that has accelerated the completion of the project. The Carlson Library at the University of Toledo and the Harlan Hatcher Graduate Library at the University of Michigan, the latter made available to me through the courtesy of the Graduate School Visiting Scholars program 1987–89 and of Robert Weisbuch, Chair of the English Department, 1989–90, were indispensable to my work. Borders Book Shop and Shaman Drum Bookshop helped, too. The editors who have seen the book through the press at Cambridge, Kevin Taylor, Josie Dixon, and Linda Randall, also deserve special acknowledgment.

I am pleased, in addition, to acknowledge several editors who have accepted or published earlier versions of parts of this book for their encouragement of my work and their generosity in permitting me to publish here revised and expanded versions of those pieces: Kenneth Johnston and his fellow editors of *Romantic Revolutions* at Indiana University Press, Marilyn Gaull, editor of *Wordsworth Circle*, Eugene Garver of *Rhetoric Society Quarterly*, Clint Goodson and Roger Meiners of *Centennial Review*, David Laurence of *ADE Bulletin*, and Michael Macovski, editor of *Textual Voices, Vocative Texts* from Oxford University Press. Without their endorsements at crucial points in the project, I might well have been discouraged from elaborating the whole of which the pieces they published could become parts. I must also acknowledge with thanks the editors of three journals that rejected earlier versions of parts of the book, W. J. T. Mitchell of *Critical Inquiry*, Ronald Schleifer of *Genre*, and John W. Kronik of *PMLA*, for sharing their provocative anonymous readers' reports with me. In choosing, as I have, to call attention to the other voices that have shaped and provoked my own, I cannot ignore them and have, in fact, cited several of their remarks in Chapter 4.

The voices that have challenged standard arrangements in the institutions of literary study during the past decade have not left domestic relations unquestioned. In particular, challenges to male privilege have charged the convention of acknowledging my wife's part in making this book possible with rhetorical dangers that would make me prefer to thank her in private rather than to risk appearing to patronize her in public. She deserves recognition, however, for taking time from managing our home, rearing our children, contributing her energies and intelligence to their schools, and beginning her training for her own career to read every word of this book and give me the benefit of her excellent eye and ear for the English language. Her presence at the center of my life and my secure place in her life for more than twenty-five years have enabled me to discover and pursue projects like the present one, just as she has found and followed her own purposes. I cannot imagine living, let alone writing books, without her. I would not, then, make my theme of "common enterprise" serve, as de Man made his theme of "common temporal predicament" serve, as "the root of Wordsworth's theme of human love," for "love," as Wordsworth declares near the end of *The Prelude*, is "first and chief" (1805 XIII, 144).

Abbreviations used in text and notes

Advancement	Bacon, Francis. *The Advancement of Learning.* Ed. G. W. Kitchin. London: J. M. Dent & Sons, 1973.
ANC	Lentricchia, Frank. *After the New Criticism.* Chicago: University of Chicago Press, 1980.
Approaches	Hall, Spencer, with Jonathan Ramsey. *Approaches to Teaching Wordsworth's Poetry.* New York: Modern Language Association, 1982.
CEA Critic	*College English Association Critic.*
DLDA	Voloshinov, V. N. "Discourse in Life and Discourse in Art," *Freudianism: A Marxist Critique.* Trans. I. R. Titunik. New York: Harcourt Brace Jovanovich, 1976.
DLDP	Voloshinov, V. N. "Discourse in Life and Discourse in Poetry," *Bakhtin School Papers.* Trans. John Richmond. Ed. Ann Shukman. Russian Poetics in Translation, no. 10. Oxford: RPT Publications, 1983.
DN	Bakhtin, M. M. "Discourse in the Novel," *The Dialogic Imagination.* Trans. Caryl Emerson and Michael Holquist. Ed. Michael Holquist. Austin: University of Texas Press, 1981.
EE	Wordsworth, William. *Essays upon Epitaphs, Prose* II.
ES	"Essay, Supplementary to the Preface," *Prose* III.
FF	Arac, Jonathan. "The Function of Foucault at the Present Time," *Humanities in Society* 3 (Winter 1980): 73–86.
FM	Bakhtin, M. M., and P. N. Medvedev. *The Formal Method in Literary Scholarship: A Critical Introduction to Sociological Poetics.* Trans. Albert J. Wehrle. Baltimore: Johns Hopkins University Press, 1978.

Genealogies	Arac, Jonathan. *Critical Genealogies: Historical Situations for Postmodern Literary Studies.* New York: Columbia University Press, 1987.
Historicity	Siskin, Clifford. *The Historicity of Romantic Discourse.* New York: Oxford University Press, 1988.
JEGP	*Journal of English and Germanic Philology.*
LB	Wordsworth, William, and Samuel Taylor Coleridge. *Lyrical Ballads.* Eds. R. L. Brett and A. R. Jones. London: Methuen, 1963.
Marxism	Williams, Raymond. *Marxism and Literature.* New York: Oxford University Press, 1977.
MLA	Modern Language Association.
MLN	*Modern Language Notes.*
MLQ	*Modern Language Quarterly.*
MPL	Voloshinov, V. N. *Marxism and the Philosophy of Language.* Trans. Ladislav Matejka and I. R. Titunik. New York: Seminar Press, 1973.
Making Tales	Bialostosky, Don. *Making Tales: The Poetics of Wordsworth's Narrative Experiments.* Chicago: University of Chicago Press, 1984.
New Organon	Bacon, Francis. *The New Organon.* Indianapolis: Bobbs Merrill, 1960.
NLH	*New Literary History.*
OED	Oxford English Dictionary.
PC	Richards, I. A. *Practical Criticism.* New York: Harcourt Brace and World, 1929.
PDP	Bakhtin, M. M. *Problems of Dostoevsky's Poetics.* Trans. Caryl Emerson. Minneapolis: University of Minnesota Press, 1984.
PMLA	*Publications of the Modern Language Association.*
Prose	*The Prose Works of William Wordsworth.* Eds. W. J. B. Owen and Jane W. Smyser. 3 vols. Oxford: Clarendon Press, 1974.
RI	McGann, Jerome. *The Romantic Ideology: A Critical Investigation.* Chicago and London: University of Chicago Press, 1983.
RMGM	Burke, Kenneth. *A Rhetoric of Motives and a Grammar of Motives.* New York: World Publishing Company, 1962.

RR	de Man, Paul. *The Rhetoric of Romanticism*. New York: Columbia University Press, 1984.
SiR	*Studies in Romanticism*.
SEL	*Studies in English Literature*.
THW	de Man, Paul. "Time and History in Wordsworth," *diacritics* 17 (1987): 4–17.
T&P	Miller, J. Hillis. "Theory and Practice: Response to Vincent Leitch," *Critical Inquiry* 6 (Summer 1980): 609–14.
WC	*The Wordsworth Circle*.

❖❖❖

Wordsworth, literary history, and the constitution of literature

❖❖❖

A constitution is a *substance* – and as such, it is a set of *motives*. There are constitutions of a purely natural sort, such as geographical and physiological properties, that act motivationally upon us. We are affected by one another's mental constitutions, or temperaments. A given complex of customs and values, from which similar customs and values are deduced, is a constitution. And we may, within limits, arbitrarily set up new constitutions, legal substances designed to serve as motives for the shaping or transforming of behavior.   Kenneth Burke, "The Dialectic of Constitutions"

The trope by which I here treat the enterprise of "literature" as grounded in a "constitution" and take Wordsworth as one of its "founding fathers" received remarkable confirmation in the recent exhibition "Wordsworth and the Age of English Romanticism," a widely disseminated public show in the late 80s that generated not only academic books and conferences but wide audiences and comment. It arrived in the United States just as the celebration of the bicentennial of the United States Constitution concluded, and visitors might have wondered whether the British Romantic show continued the American celebration.[1] The topic of revolution and its aftermath was common to them both; the Declaration of Independence in two different printed versions was displayed among the opening documents of the Romantic exhibition; styles of portraiture, printing, and handwriting belonged to the same period; and the mounting and magnitude of the Romantic display bespoke matters of comparable cultural importance. Visitors who took the Romantic exhibition for a part of the American observance would ultimately have noticed images of an unfamiliar revolution and portraits of unfamiliar

---

1 Jonathan Wordsworth *et al.*, eds., *William Wordsworth and the Age of English Romanticism* (New Brunswick and London: Rutgers University Press, 1987).

founders that compelled them to distinguish the American Revolution from the British Romantic revolution, but they might nevertheless have held to their sense of connection between the events and wondered what this Romantic revolution was about, what constitution followed from it, what roles its celebrated founders played, what treasured documents embodied it, what institutions of interpretation perpetuated those documents, what controversies embroiled those institutions, and what consequences, if any, those institutions might have for their own lives.

Two academic books that appeared around the time of the exhibition could be taken to address themselves to those questions and thereby further to instantiate my trope of Wordsworth as a founding father of the constitution of literature. Clifford Siskin's *The Historicity of Romantic Discourse* could be taken to reply that "the society that places Literature at its center" (95) was constituted by the Romantic revolution, and Jonathan Arac's *Critical Genealogies* could add that "Wordsworth did more than anyone else to establish the vocation of literature in relation to which ... our own culture's ... idea of the literary critic took shape" (3). Siskin actually juxtaposes Wordsworth and Thomas Jefferson as founders of their respective constitutions. Arac contrasts Wordsworth and Coleridge as founding fathers of literary criticism in terms that some have used to contrast Jefferson and Madison as American founders. Both critics focus on Matthew Arnold as a major early interpreter of the constitution of literature who plays a role in the history of that constitution analogous to the one Lincoln played as interpreter of the American Declaration of Independence and the U.S. Constitution.

Siskin and Arac join a growing group of critics interested in how modern American critics of Romanticism and of literature generally have adopted their critical forms, stances, words, and authorizations – what I am calling the constitution of their enterprise – from the Romantics themselves. Jerome McGann has combated modern critics' adoption of what he calls this "Romantic Ideology" in the name of a "New Historicism" that reinserts Wordsworth's writing in Wordsworth's historical context.[2] Siskin and Arac identify their projects with Ralph Cohen's "New Literary History" and show how

---

2 R. I. Marjorie Levinson has raised the banner of New Historicism over this project in *Wordsworth's Great Period Poems: Four Essays* (Cambridge: Cambridge University Press, 1986). See also David Simpson, *Wordsworth's Historical Imagination: The Poetry of Displacement* (New York and London: Methuen, 1987).

the historical situation of contemporary American literary culture is constituted for Arac by the Romantic founders and for Siskin by Romantic formal innovations. Both "New Historicism" and "New Literary History" are constitutional projects in the sense I am developing, "an enactment of human wills ... done by *agents* (such as rulers, magistrates, or other representative persons), and designed (*purpose*) to serve as a motivational ground (*scene*) of subsequent actions, it being thus an instrument (*agency*) for the shaping of human relations" (RMGM 323, 341). For both schools Wordsworth is a representative person of the Romantic constitution whose program for poetic production and literary criticism needs to be displaced, revived, or revised in order to enable the actions and shape the human relations they desire.

I will take up McGann's "New Historicism" at several points in subsequent chapters, but I turn here to recount and criticize Siskin's and Arac's arguments because they open constitutional issues of the kind that define my entire project. Seeing, as I do, a fundamental conjunction of Wordsworthian, Romantic, and critical theoretical issues in literary studies at the present time, they give plausibility to my constitutional trope and provoke me to elaborate upon as well as to differ with their constitutional interpretations.

Under the common rubric of "New Literary History" Siskin and Arac share several interpretations of the constitution of literature. Arac holds with Siskin that "only around 1800 did there come into being the notion of 'literature' as we have since known it" and that this notion of literature "formed a new, literary human nature ... that makes psychoanalysis possible" and underwrites "psychological" at the expense of social criticism (*Genealogies* 48–49, 56). Following Foucault, as Siskin also does, Arac sees the "production of 'literature' as a particular social and linguistic space in the nineteenth century, achieved through a series of separations and purifications" as part of "an increasing differentiation of social functions" (264). Arac also sees "the history of criticism [as] ... part of the history of literature" (3); he questions the social uses which "literary criticism" has served and urges connection of the concerns once enclosed within "literature" with the "larger concerns of state and economy" (307–08). Finally, like Siskin, he wishes to "end [the] cycle of repetition" (93) in which modern critics uncritically read Romantic texts in Romantic terms. Siskin's and Arac's constitutional critiques and programs nonetheless differ substantially, and I will discuss them each at some length before returning to my own version of the constitution. I must remind my reader, however, that even my dialogic revoicing of their arguments is beginning the work of my own.

Literature and the power of Romantic Discourse

What I call the constitution of literature Siskin's Foucauldian language calls "Romantic Discourse." He argues that a "Romantic Discourse," typified by Wordsworth, continues to exert "extraordinary power over our professional and personal behaviors" (13), and he attempts to historicize that discourse in order to change our relationship to it, diminish some of its power over us (13), and permit us to "break our own critical habits" (190) of "dependence upon" it (183). Though Siskin historicizes the discourse of addiction as one powerful innovation of Romantic Discourse, he nevertheless relies on it to characterize the way modern "literary professional[s have] addictively returned" (186) to Romantic genres even in their recent revisionary attempts to demystify visionary Romanticism. Sensitized to what he reads as a compulsive repetition of the past by today's doctors of literature, Siskin attempts to make others aware of the power of the Romantic canon in order to avoid "the political mistake of being blind to that power, and of thus facing the inevitable prospect of reproducing ... Romantic relationships that have not yet been written to an end" (14).

"Literature" with a self-conscious capital "L" is one of the principal Romantic inventions Siskin tries to attenuate. "Like America," he writes, "Literature ... is an invention that has obscured its own origins ... [and] dehistoricized a version of the human" that serves coercive political functions (85–86). Dedicated to the Wordsworthian/Arnoldian imperative to "make us feel," Literature prescribes an order in which "every individual ... is supposed to identify sympathetically with the [literary] work" and conform to the psychological norm it establishes (84). Those who fail to do so are doubly damned as lacking the "healthful state of association" Wordsworth required of his readers and as failing to exercise the capacity of being excited "without the application of gross and violent stimulants," whose exercise elevates one being above another (LB 247–48). They are, in other words, sick and inferior – at once needing the cure of literary education because of their illness and deserving their degradation because of their failure to exert themselves. In response to his own

4

presentation of this version of human needs, Wordsworth "sets up the writer as the doctor who can cure [his readers'] 'savage torpor'" (81). At the same time he founds the apparatus of Literature that has proliferated into a system of "creative writers, analytic critics, developing students, and loving readers who have helped to form academic departments, publishing houses, foundations, and governmental bureaucracies" (84) that control us not by imposing direct moral prohibitions but by stimulating our desires for literary works, treating our unhealthy failures to appreciate them, and grading our degrees of appreciation.

If any readers have trouble, as I do, hearing what Siskin hears – the insidious workings of Foucauldian discipline in Wordsworth's programmatic rhetoric – they may better hear what Siskin hears in Wordsworth if they listen to the Wordsworthian echoes in F. R. Leavis's defense of "'English' as a Discipline of Thought."[3] Wordsworth himself may sound to us like a defender of the universal "discriminating powers of the mind" against the causes that threaten to reduce those powers to "a state of almost savage torpor." When he writes that "the human mind is capable of excitement without the exercise of gross and violent stimulants; and he must have a very faint perception of its beauty and dignity who does not know this, and who does not further know that one being is elevated above another in proportion as he possesses this capability" (LB 249), these words may seem universal and ennobling enough. But Leavis sounds (and makes Wordsworth sound) more like an enforcer of class and coterie discipline when he writes in a similar vein that "the reader who cannot see that Tennyson's poem, with all its distinction and refinement, yields a satisfaction inferior in kind to that represented by Wordsworth, cannot securely appreciate the highest poetic achievement at its true worth" (74–75). Wordsworth may come across as worthy and serious when he declares that his sort of poetry is "important in the multiplicity and quality of its moral relations" (LB 272), but Leavis seems more threatening and potentially invasive when he comes "to the point at which literary criticism, as it must,

3 F. R. Leavis, *The Living Principle: 'English' as a Discipline of Thought* (New York: Oxford University Press, 1975). Siskin himself does not cite Leavis in evidence in this connection but, in effect, invents him. John Willinsky hears the same note in Leavis's tone and traces its echoes through the school system in "Literary Theory and Public Education: The Instance of F. R. Leavis," *Mosaic* 21 (1988): 165–77.

enters overtly into questions of emotional hygiene and moral value – more generally (there seems no other adequate phrase), of spiritual health" (75).

Neither Leavis nor Wordsworth, however, is dedicated simply to the imperative Siskin identifies – to "make us feel." Both of them insist on the cultivation of thought *and* feeling in a combination that envisions poetry as a provocation to active critical thought that would enable readers to judge its emotional appeals. But both Wordsworth and Leavis also call attention to and deliberately cultivate what Leavis calls "habits of assumption" (104) which it is easier to condemn in their opponents than it is to recognize in themselves. Neither believes in *"reasoning* [the reader] into an approbation of … particular poems" (LB 242), but both believe in cultivating habits of such appreciation through an intellectual and emotional discipline that can too easily be reduced to the choice between learning to echo the judgments and tones of the teacher or failing the class. No conformity is more insidious than that which imagines itself as critical thought and no social group more elitist than that which imagines itself as the saving remnant of universal human values. Leavis's discipline of English makes the Wordsworthian constitution of literature sound too close to Siskin's disciplinary discourse for comfort.

Siskin's Foucauldian vision of the constitution of Literature and its disciplined subjects thus threatens, as he recognizes, "our assumptions about what we study and why" (67). It presents us and our founding father Wordsworth as addicts, pushers, and quack doctors, our object of study as a controlled and controlling substance, and our function (if not our conscious purpose) as the enforcement of conformity and the naturalization of social inequality. To historicize Literature in this way is to produce an effect of alienation that demoralizes our professional identities without reconstituting them. Siskin acknowledges the need to "provide an alternative" (6) to Romantic Discourse. What alternatives does he provide?

Siskin offers two, one explicit and one implied. Explicitly he offers the practice of "New Literary History" his book exemplifies. That practice addresses our current situation "of conceptual and thus generic transition" (4) by enabling an understanding of change, but it offers no "'cure' for our Romantic addictions." In effect, New Literary History enrolls critics addicted to Romanticism in something like a Romanticists Anonymous where they will hear over and over the "tale of [their] need to be cured" and recognize at each hearing the "ongoing power" of Romantic Discourse. Siskin does not posit any other power that could supplant the insidious and ongoing power of Romantic Discourse, and it is not at all certain that his New Literary History has the power to fulfill his desire "to classify [the Romantic] self as a construct – to put it in the past" (194). At best, it would seem that it might help us become, in the language of Alcoholics Anonymous, "recovering Romanticists."

The second, implicit alternative Siskin offers is the late eighteenth-century discourse that he reconstructs in contrast to Romantic Discourse. Characterized, like Foucault's regime of sovereignty, by sharp differences of social and literary kinds in place of Romantic differences of degree, personified powers in place of mystified individual power, and didactic directness in place of masked Romantic didacticism, this eighteenth-century discourse provides Siskin's instruments of generic analysis and underwrites his direct didactic style. Though presumably this cultural form has been "put ... in the past," Siskin brings it back and effectively identifies himself with it instead of with the Romanticism he deplores. He repeatedly reasserts distinctions of kind against Wordsworth's reductions of kind to degree in a neo-classic correction of Romantic aberration. Like the personifications he analyzes in the poetry of Collins, Gray, and Goldsmith, Siskin's personified figures of Literature, Power, and Romantic Discourse become agents which make "the self ... the subject of their authoritative activities and not an active, authoritative subject" (75). In effect, Siskin repeats the position of what he calls the helpless self of Sentimental verse subjected to the personified Power(s) that dominated it. *This* domination is the reality that makes the active Romantic self seem illusory.

For Siskin, the absolute Powers of the Old Regime still rule from underground in the new, and it is not clear how an exposé of their persistence can lead to their circumscription or productive ordering in any new constitution. Foucauldian discourse performs for Siskin the functions of a constitution (or perhaps what Burke would call the constitution behind the constitution). Romantic Discourse serves as what Burke calls the motivational ground of subsequent actions, shapes human relations, and indeed produces human subjects of various kinds, but what Burke would call the scene/agent ratio is heavily weighted in favor of scene, or Romantic Discourse, and the agents produced by that scene have no relative autonomy in the face

7

of its power and nowhere else to turn to ground their actions or redefine their relations to one another.

Wordsworth and the possibilities of critical discipline

Arac shares some of Siskin's understanding of the Romantic constitution of literature, but he finds more alternatives and more room for active agency within Romanticism and the constitution of literature to which it gives rise. As an inconsistent and incomplete constitution, it has more room for the negotiation of conflicting interests and for the acknowledgment of formerly excluded interests than Siskin's ubiquitous disciplinary discourse allows.

Arac, like Siskin, recognizes repetitive disciplinary effects of Romantic Discourse in contemporary criticism, and he wishes, like Siskin, "to end [the] cycle of repetition" (*Genealogies* 83), but because he recognizes what Burke would call the necessarily "partially representative" (RMGM 371) character of any constitution, he is not confined to repeatedly documenting the repetitive power of a ubiquitous Romantic Discourse. He can appeal instead to an alternative mode of cultural reproduction – the activity of exclusion – that opens up alternative strategies of cultural or constitutional transformation. He calls attention to those authors, texts, and elements of texts that repetitive emphasis overlooks instead of dwelling on the scandal of repetition itself (*Genealogies* 81). This emphasis draws Arac's focus from the centers created by repetition to the excluded margins, from texts to contexts, from dominant precursors to recessive predecessors.[4] Indeed Arac locates literature itself on the margin of a society in which "other technical skills have proved more socially powerful than the mastery of words" (7), while Siskin envisions "the society that places Literature at its center" (95). Arac also sees Wordsworth not as Siskin's (and McGann's) "'normative and, in every sense, exemplary'" (196 n. 15) figure for the Romantic constitution of literature but as an alternative to the still dominant figure of Coleridge. While Siskin exaggerates the power and centrality of Romantic Discourse in order to compel an alienating recognition of contemporary Romantic practices, Arac attempts to displace powerful Romantic figures with other figures that enable

---

4 See Daniel Stempel, "History and Postmodern Literary Theory," in *Tracing Literary Theory*, ed. Joseph Natoli (Urbana: University of Illinois Press, 1987), 89.

other practices. Arac does not try to put a monolithic Romantic past behind us but to "excavate the past that is necessary to account for how we got here and the past that is useful for conceiving alternatives to our present condition" (2).

That present condition for Arac is not Siskin's time of change or transition but rather an "impasse" that requires us to discover alternative routes, discipline our powers to enable us to take those routes, and rouse our wills to determine us to exercise those powers. In search of alternative routes he reviews the history of the constitution of literature, from the Romantic founding to the recent critical revolutions, to find what both Bakhtin and the legal profession would call loopholes – unexploited texts and passages, alternative interpretations of familiar texts and passages, underused authorities and fresh contextualizations of well-used authorities. For discipline, he looks to a "more resolute focus on rhetoric" to provide alternative strategies of interpretation that can "repluralize the figures" of rhetoric in the wake of New Critical and deconstructive reductions of those figures to a small number of tropes (*Genealogies* 75, 78). (I will return to this topic in Chapter 7.) And for inspiration he looks above all to Walter Benjamin, who undertook literary history "as a task for human agency, 'a revolutionary chance in the fight for the oppressed past'" (22).

As one alternative constitutional route, Arac takes Wordsworth around the obstacles to productive criticism posed by the continuing authority of "Coleridge's romantic metaphysics of symbol and imagination" (3). Though this important turn to an alternative constitutional authority is complicated for a number of reasons I will consider in Chapter 2, Arac makes good use of it by selecting Wordsworthian texts that have not commonly been taken as constitutionally significant and reading them in violation of their canonical meanings. He chooses "Nutting" instead of "Tintern Abbey" (34–49), for example, though he might have gone further afield, as those of us have done who have tried to redeem the neglected experimental poems (see my Chapter 3 below) and the works of the later Wordsworth from the "oppressed past." Siskin, for one, advocates attention to neglected Wordsworthian poetry outside the "Great Decade," especially the plentiful sonnets, though he holds Wordsworth at least as responsible as Coleridge and Arnold for the "myth of creativity" (8) that justified the exclusion of these poems from the canon in the first place.

Arac finds Arnold less of an obstacle than Coleridge to the constitution he wants. He discovers more in Arnold's work than the "proverbs of criticism" Siskin identifies him with – the tribute to Wordsworth's ability to "make us feel" and the reduction of Wordsworth's poetic work to the selections from the "Great Decade."[5] Arac reads Arnold's Biblical criticism, studies his career in the schools, and appreciates his importance in the history of the constitution of literature: "Arnold achieved what Johnson and Coleridge, those earlier geniuses of English criticism, did not do: he established the terms of a continuing cultural discipline" (*Genealogies* 129).

Although Arac seeks different goals and different means for that discipline from Arnold's, he affirms the productive, empowering, affirmative aspect of the discipline as such even as he acknowledges the subjected social roles it imposes and the exclusions it necessarily brings into being. Arac cites the later Foucault and through him Arnold's contemporary Nietzsche as the source of this affirmation of discipline; Siskin cites the same Foucault, but he reads Foucault's substitution of productive disciplinary power for repressive sovereign power as the exposure of a more subtle domination, not as what Arac calls an empowering self-subjection.

Arac's view of a contemporary impasse in literary history leads him to seek ways around our prominent contemporary constitutional interpreters as well, but his way around them is through them. He extensively criticizes half a dozen living judges on today's literary supreme court including two important Wordsworthian interpreters – Geoffrey Hartman (see my Chapter 5), who refuses to decide cases but writes ingenious opinions, and M. H. Abrams, who deprecates "'ingenious exegetic[s]'" (*Genealogies* 65) and decides cases without enough difficulty. Arac offers his own combination of ingenious exegesis and confident decision as an alternative to both of them and makes himself a strong candidate for a seat on the bench, which, after all, has no statutorily limited number of seats. Though his involvement with the controlled substance of Romanticism might disqualify him in the eyes of those like Siskin who distrust its power, Arac seems to me to have made that power productive of knowledge without being compulsively dominated by it.

5 The phrase "proverbs of criticism" is from Lionel Trilling, "The Fate of Pleasure: Wordsworth to Dostoevsky," in *Romanticism Reconsidered*, ed. Northrop Frye (New York: Columbia University Press, 1963), 73.

It appears as if the constitutional text from which Arac derives this productive relation between power and knowledge is Foucault's claim that power in a disciplinary society produces positive effects. But it is important to emphasize in my own argument, concerned as it is with the continuing power of Wordsworth's constitution of literature, that Arac also draws upon a Wordsworthian text that raises the same question of the relations between knowledge and power. He is not just a disciple of the late Foucault but also of the mid-career Wordsworth. Arac alludes repeatedly to the figure of "Hannibal among the Alps," and to the distinction between the "Public" and the "People" from Wordsworth's 1815 Essay Supplementary to the Preface, but he never cites the text by name. Nevertheless, the key terms of his argument are also the key terms of Wordsworth's Essay, and the critical role he assumes and the critical discipline he advocates are authorized by it. Without offering an interpretation of the Essay Supplementary, Arac writes in the spirit of this marginal but potentially important constitutional text and draws from it a source of power for criticism understood as the active production of knowledge in response to the enduring power of literature.[6]

M. H. Abrams's misreading of Wordsworth's Essay Supplementary

The constitutional potential of Wordsworth's Essay Supplementary has been obscured, however, not just by Arac's allusiveness but by the most authoritative reading the Essay Supplementary has received.

6 Siskin's argument does not draw on the Essay Supplementary to the Preface, but in the debunking historicist spirit of Siskin's book, Alan Liu reads the text as a "not a little frightening" indication of the imperious and imperialist ambitions of Wordsworth's "Empire of the Poet." Like Siskin, Liu emphasizes the reader's bondage and submission to the poet rather than the poet's provocation of an active reader's response that reveals the reader's autonomous power. See *Wordsworth: The Sense of History* (Palo Alto: Stanford University Press, 1989), 490–91. See also Marlon Ross's critique of the Essay Supplementary in "Romantic Quest and Conquest: Troping Masculine Power in the Crisis of Poetic Identity," in *Romanticism and Feminism*, ed. Anne K. Mellor (Bloomington: Indiana University Press, 1988), 39–42; reprint in Ross, *The Contours of Masculine Desire* (New York: Oxford University Press, 1989), 36–38. Richard Poirier turns to the Essay Supplementary as a constitutional text for the enterprise of literature more in the spirit of Arac's and my appropriation of the text and links it to an American literary tradition in which Emerson and William James are key figures. See his *The Renewal of Literature: Emersonian Reflections* (New York: Random House, 1987), 41–44.

M. H. Abrams's much reprinted reading, which appears in both his introductory essay to his 1972 collection of critical essays on Wordsworth, "Two Roads to Wordsworth," and in a late section of *Natural Supernaturalism* entitled "Transvaluations" (390–99), has canonized what Jon Klancher describes as a "liberal, comforting" and orthodox Wordsworth in a text where Arac and I find a more liberating, demanding, and radical author.[7] The precedent of Abrams's reading must, in effect, be answered and overturned if the Wordsworthian constitution of literature is to enable the activities and shape the human relations I want from it and believe can be warranted by it.

In "Two Roads to Wordsworth," Abrams makes the Preface to *Lyrical Ballads* typify the first road to Wordsworth, the road of simplicity and natural feeling in the language of Enlightenment humanism. Abrams himself took this road to Wordsworth in *The Mirror and the Lamp*. The Essay Supplementary, on the other hand, typifies the second road to Wordsworth, the road Abrams takes in *Natural Supernaturalism*. The Essay Supplementary, he writes, "reiterates in sober prose the claims [Wordsworth] had made, years before, in the verse 'Prospectus' to *The Recluse* ... and in the opening and closing passages of *The Prelude*: claims that it is his task to confront and find consolation in human suffering" (1). In addition, the Essay Supplementary abandons the language of humanism, according to Abrams, to adopt the theological language of Christian paradox, "for Wordsworth claims in this essay that there are 'affinities between religion and poetry,' 'a community of nature,' so that poetry shares the distinctive quality of Christianity, which is to confound 'the calculating understanding' by its contradictions" (2). Abrams goes so far as to claim that Wordsworth's "chief enterprise as a poet is expressed [in the Essay Supplementary] in a Christian paradox – he must cast his readers down in order to raise them up: their spirits 'are

---

7 M. H. Abrams, "Introduction: Two Roads to Wordsworth," in *Wordsworth: A Collection of Critical Essays* (Englewood Cliffs, N.J.: Prentice-Hall, 1972), 1–11. This essay also appears in Abrams's recent collection of essays *The Correspondent Breeze: Essays on English Romanticism* (New York and London: W. W. Norton, 1984), 145–57; as "Transvaluations," in Abrams's *Natural Supernaturalism: Tradition and Revolution in Romantic Literature* (New York: W. W. Norton, 1971), 390–99; and in *William Wordsworth*, ed. Harold Bloom (New York: Chelsea House, 1985). Jon P. Klancher, *The Making of English Reading Audiences, 1790–1832* (Madison: University of Wisconsin Press, 1987), 148.

to be humbled and humanized in order that they may be purified and exalted'" (2).

Abrams, however, makes the Essay Supplementary stand for something that it explicitly rejects, subordinates, and transcends. Wordsworth does indeed write that religious readers of poetry "resort to poetry, as to religion, ... as a consolation for the afflictions of life," and he does note an "affinity between religion and poetry" and a "community of nature" between them. But Wordsworth notes these commonalities only in order to warn against the kind of reading they produce and to reject the religious reader as a reliable judge of poetry: "In this community may be perceived also the lurking incitements to kindred error; – so that we shall find ... no lovers of the art [of poetry] have gone farther astray than the pious and the devout."[8] Wordsworth looks for adequate judgments of poetry not to these religious readers but to "those and those only, who, never having suffered their youthful love of poetry to remit much of its force, have applied to the consideration of the laws of this art the best power of their understandings" (66), to those who read poetry not as a source of consolation but *"as a study"* (62).

Furthermore, Wordsworth does not say that the poetic imagination resembles religion by confounding the calculating understanding with its contradictions; rather he says that certain religionists (the Unitarians)[9] confound themselves when they base their religion on the "proudest faculty of our nature," the calculating understanding itself. Finally, the poet's difficulty in creating taste does not "lie in establishing that dominion over the spirits of readers by which they

---

8 ES 62, 65–66. Kenneth R. Johnston corroborates my judgment in *Wordsworth and "The Recluse"* (New Haven and London: Yale University Press, 1984), 339.

9 Abrams inserts "the imagination" in brackets to gloss the following passage: "For when Christianity, the religion of humility, is founded upon the proudest faculty of our nature [the imagination], what can be expected but contradictions?" ("Two Roads" 2). But this passage immediately follows a sentence that complains of the "excesses ... of those sects whose religion, being from the calculating understanding, is cold and formal" (ES 65). In a letter to Catherine Clarkson, Jan. 15, 1815, Wordsworth identifies these religionists as the Unitarians. He writes, "One of the main objects of the Recluse is, to reduce the calculating understanding to its proper level among the human faculties – Therefore my Book must be disliked by the Unitarians, as their religion rests entirely on that basis" (*Wordsworth's Literary Criticism*, ed. W. J. B. Owen [London: Routledge and Kegan Paul, 1974], 221). Though Wordsworth later in the Essay Supplementary calls the imagination "perhaps the noblest [faculty] of our nature" (ES 81), it is not the proudest.

are to be humbled and humanised, in order that they may be purified and exalted" (ES 65, 80–81). Wordsworth asks whether the problem lies there, but he rejects this alternative and finds the poet's real problem is to inspire the reader's "exertion of a co-operating *power*." The poet's problem is not to subdue the reader's spirit but to invigorate it, not to humble it before the dominion of his own power "by the mere communication of *knowledge*" (81) but to "call forth and bestow power, of which knowledge is the effect" (82).

The consequential differences between the activities enabled and human relations shaped by these two constitutional interpretations may perhaps best be envisioned in the pedagogies that follow from them. Teachers who subdue their students' spirits "by the mere communication of *knowledge*" in the name of humbling, humanizing, purifying, exalting or comforting those students will conduct a different enterprise of literary study than those who see their own role and that of the texts they teach as provoking students to the exercise of powers that lead them to the discovery of knowledge for themselves. The ethical, political, intellectual, and even aesthetic stakes in these differences are high, and Wordsworth, I believe, can be effectively cited not on the side Abrams claims him for but on that which Arac and I maintain.

Power and knowledge in Wordsworth and Foucault

Arac quotes in another text a passage from Foucault that envisions remarkably similar relations between knowledge and power to those I have brought out in Wordsworth. "'What gives power its hold ... [is that] it does not simply weigh like a force that says no, but that it runs through and produces things, it induces pleasure, it forms knowledge, it produces discourse; it must be considered as a productive network which runs through the entire social body'" (FF 78). Power for both Wordsworth and Foucault is thus a precondition of knowledge and pleasure. Wordsworth, however, envisions this knowledge-producing power as a sign and a function of his own genius, whereas Foucault identifies the exercise of this power with disciplined experts rather than with "the 'writer of genius,'" but the difference may be less consequential than it at first appears.[10] Wordsworth, for one thing,

10 Michel Foucault, *Power/Knowledge*, trans. Colin Gordon (New York: Pantheon, 1980), 129.

insists upon his works of genius as a contribution to a cultivated "intellectual universe," a recognizable "advance" which widens "the sphere of human sensibility" (ES 82) in the domain of poetic art, and he further insists, as we have seen, that readers qualify themselves as judges not just through the corresponding exercise of their imaginative powers but through the disciplined expertise that comes from study of the laws of the art. "Wordsworth bases his faith in the ultimate triumph of his work," I have argued elsewhere, "not in the fateful tides of taste or even in the enduring powers of love or the human heart alone but in the disciplined activities of the human mind in the enterprise of literary study" (*Making Tales* 7). Wordsworth's personification of "the great Spirit of human knowledge" (ES 84), in which both the poet's work and the people's active appreciation participate, manifests itself in those disciplined activities just as Foucault's personified power manifests itself in the various intellectual disciplines and produces knowledge and pleasure and discourse through them.

Arac contrasts this knowledge-, pleasure-, and discourse-producing power to "Foucault's polemical redefinition [of a humanism] that elides any difference between humanism and Christianity." Humanism by that definition is "everything that restricts the desire for power in our ways of teaching, learning, and living" (*Genealogies* 78). This definition encompasses the humanism of both of Abrams's roads to Wordsworth, for Wordsworth's desire for productive power can be found down neither of them. Pleasure and joy can at least be found down what Abrams calls Wordsworth's humanist road, but they are oversimplified, idealized, and vulnerable to irony and to political critique. Down the Christian road, the quest for "consolation in human suffering" presumes the frustration of desire and the sense of powerlessness in the face of disappointments that humble and humanize us. Arac shows that Abrams identifies the historical disappointments of his own generation with the historical disappointments to which Wordsworth responds (79); and we might add that Abrams exaggerates the importance of Wordsworth's consoling Christian moments as balm for his generation's suffering those disappointments.

But in the Essay Supplementary, Wordsworth finds even in "*suffering*" not a call for consolation but a "connection ... with effort, with exertion, and *action* ... To be moved ... by a passion, is to be excited, often to external and always to internal, effort" (81). In communicating passion and power, the poet arouses such effort, provokes a response always to the internal effort of maintaining or restoring pleasure and sometimes to the external effort of producing critical discourse, making new poems, discovering literary historical knowledge, or committing political acts. Even the production of consoling discourse may be an active response to suffering, a work of desire, but the acceptance of consoling discourse can easily become an excuse for passivity and a circumscription of desire. Like the complacency of taste against which Wordsworth struggles, the complacency of accepted consolation limits the sphere of human possibilities and rationalizes the acceptance of limitations and the cessation of effort. Such complacency occludes our powers instead of provoking them and erects fixed images of what we and our authors are and can be.

In the spirit of the Essay Supplementary, Arac's project at its best moments opposes such complacent humanism and claims the sphere of active power for disciplined writers and readers alike.[11] "Writing solicits from us our interpretive power," he writes, "the stones we critics and readers throw to shatter the old, fixed images and startle new life in again. The sublime inheres not only in the text, but also in the reader's activity of fixing upon passages, highlighting them in ways that disrupt any equability of composition in favor of intensity of attention, the means by which literary history prolongs itself" (*Genealogies* 155–56). The exercise of power Arac here envisions seems less co-operative and more disruptive than the power Wordsworth hopes to call up in his readers, for the readers here are doing what the poet does there – violating commonplace expectations, disrupting textual continuities, shattering old images and bringing new ones to life.

There is just no telling, however, when poets will be the retailers of commonplaces and when they will be the instruments of liberation, just as there is no way of knowing in principle when critical readers will be the standardizers and regularizers of poetic novelties and when they will be the stone-throwing shatterers of old, fixed images.

11 We should note, however, that what Arac praises as Wordsworth's anti-humanism Frank Lentricchia, another recent critic influenced by Foucault, praises as "the irreducible humanist romanticism of Coleridge and Wordsworth. Rather than locating the origin of expression in a large, all-inclusive system which 'authorizes' the single self, as a mere passive medium, to speak poetic language, Coleridge and Wordsworth instead preserve the active, conscious subject as the triggering force in the poetic process," ANC 13.

The exercise of the power Arac, Foucault, and Wordsworth call for is an act (Foucault calls it an event), not a role or a capacity, and we discover it only in being acted upon and acting in response. It can be informed and cultivated by the disciplines of writing and reading we teach and practice, but it cannot be reproduced by them or regularized in a constitutional distribution of powers to specified functionaries. The exercise of such power is the good for the sake of which we organize disciplines and arrange constitutional functions, but precisely because power is not identical with those arrangements and functions, we resist them when they frustrate our exercise of it or exclude us from it. We thus resist not power itself but in the name of and for the sake of power, and we discover power not only in resisting oppressive arrangements and debilitating functions but also in co-operating with interesting arrangements and in serving demanding functions.

Siskin would resist Wordsworth's call to the reader to exercise a "co-operating *power*" because he reads that call as an inducement to "the sympathetic participation of [the reader] in the supposedly liberating act of 'making' the poem" (55). For Siskin, the reader is deluded into believing he helps create what in fact he reproduces; he has the illusion of mastery that was the object of Foucault's earlier critique of humanism as "everything … which told us that 'acquiescence' made 'mastery' possible" (*Genealogies* 126). But Arac's later Foucault rejects this vision of mystified sovereignty for a vision of productive power. As Arac puts it, "the disciplines extend power to us, and through us to our students, and through our students to us, in the mode of pleasure. Power is productive" (FF 77).

The reader's exercise of a "co-operating *power*" with Wordsworth's literary power, then, even on Foucault's authority, need not be an acquiescent repetition but may also be a counter-action, and the poet's exercise of literary power need not be a coercive imposition but may also be a provocation, even a demand, for productive questions and responses. The constitution of literature need not impose the work of the author or teacher as a norm by which to discipline the sensibility of the reader or student; it may rather cultivate the disciplines through which poets and readers, teachers and students, may recognize and exercise the powers of literature and secure their blessings not only to themselves and their posterity but "in widest commonalty spread."[12]

12 William Wordsworth, Preface to *The Excursion*, in *Prose* III, 6.

The function of literary history at the present time

Both Siskin and Arac block my temptation to conclude with these uninterpreted and uncriticized echoes of the preamble to the U.S. Constitution and Wordsworth's Prospectus to the *Recluse*, but only Arac would encourage me to affirm and elaborate their power. The passages I have repeated are not, after all, concluding gestures but parts of preambulatory declarations, and they do not settle the difficult constitutional questions of how to institute the goods with which they are concerned. The power they would secure and distribute – the textual power Robert Scholes identifies as the ultimate good of literary studies (20) – comes into being within the disciplinary forms not only of language and literature in general but of specific curricular, canonical, pedagogical, and institutional arrangements – what Scholes calls "the English Apparatus" (1–17).[13] What follows the eloquent preamble to a constitution is the determination of those arrangements in some particular form that both enables and restricts the realization of the preamble's aims, and what issues from that determination is a struggle both to fulfill its enabling provisions and to change those arrangements (and sometimes other constitutional provisions, or even entire constitutions) that disable and disenfranchise interested parties.

In these terms, the current struggle over the implications of the Wordsworthian constitution of literature for its gendered subjects may be the most pressing unresolved constitutional question of our day. Was the Wordsworthian constitution established, as Arac argues in a reading of "Nutting," "at the cost of reasserting the inequality between the sexes" (*Genealogies* 49) or, as Siskin argues, by the "centering" *and* the "negation" of the female that produces a pathological subjectivity "for both men and women" (*Historicity* 164–78)? Was its establishment part of a process of "'remasculinization'" (45), as Arac says, or of the "feminization of the writer" that Siskin sees (172)? Again, was it established, as Daniel O'Hara argues against Arac, by Wordsworth's lifting "the burden of primal guilt

13 Though Scholes holds Romantic aestheticism responsible for some of the current problems of the English Apparatus, his book and its related *Text Book: An Introduction to Literary Language*, ed. Nancy Comley, Robert Scholes, and Greg Ulmer (New York: St. Martin's Press, 1988) come closer than any other work I am familiar with to giving practical shape to the program I have been admiring in Wordsworth, Foucault, and Arac.

from the figure of Eve" and freeing the woman for "superior magnanimity of mind" or, as Marlon Ross argues, "by masculine self-questing and visionary conquest" that "sustains sexual and political hierarchies, ... limits the poet's capacity for sympathy, ... limits the readers' capacity for possessing themselves and sharing the visionary experience, ... [and] discourages 'the exertion of a co-operating *power* in the mind of the Reader'"?[14] Does Wordsworth thus assert the sublimity of his own masculine imagination at the expense of the feminine or does he, as Theresa Kelley argues, "re-define the imagination as something more than sublime vision," appreciate "the domestic, civic virtues that belong to the beautiful," and criticize "overweening military machismo"?[15] Does he, as Nina Auerbach claims, transmit "two great enigmas of eternity ... 'nature and the language of the sense' that become in the hands of Emily Brontë's embattled women a poisoned fruit that strangles the soul it is supposed to feed," or could he have provided, as Jan Montefiore claims, some of the unacknowledged and problematic premises that shape contemporary radical feminist poetry?[16] The struggle to resolve these questions will test how wide the commonalty can be to which the goods of the Wordsworthian constitution of literature can be spread, and it will lead, as it has already begun to do, to the re-reading of canonical constitutional texts and authorities and to the re-evaluation of non-canonical ones for evidence and arguments bearing on these cases. Perhaps the greatest test of the breadth of that commonalty will be the test of its ability to accommodate subjects whose racial and cultural identifications place them outside the terrain over which white Anglo-American men and women struggle, as they are also often outside the world represented by Literature and outside the forums in which it conducts its critical debates.

But whatever the determination of the question of gender or race or any other question, its determination and its consequent establishment of authorities, terms, definitions, traditions, situations, schools, canonical selections, and paradigmatic texts will permit the

---

14 Daniel T. O'Hara, *Lionel Trilling: The Work of Liberation* (Madison: University of Wisconsin Press, 1988), 16–17. Ross, "Romantic Quest and Conquest," 49.

15 Theresa M. Kelley, *Wordsworth's Revisionary Aesthetics* (Cambridge: Cambridge University Press, 1988), 126, 76, 155.

16 Nina Auerbach, *Romantic Imprisonment: Women and Other Glorified Outcasts* (New York: Columbia University Press, 1985), 220–21; Jan Montefiore, *Feminism and Poetry: Language, Experience, and Identity in Women's Writing* (London and New York: Pandora, 1987), 8–14.

work of literary studies to proceed only if further questions can be asked that probe the limits of those determinations and inquire into the possibilities they occlude. A constitution sufficient to sustain an enterprise over time cannot merely make its determinations and repeat them to the bitter end; it must build in some institutionalized review of its practices and premises that reconsiders and, when necessary, reopens settled questions or redirects new inquiries. Constitutions that take into account their own "partially representative" (RMGM 371) status and their permanent openness to desires that they cannot formally encompass are more likely to continue to provide productive roles for participants in their activities and to meet the needs of constituencies unanticipated or neglected at their founding than constitutions that pretend to eternal, universal, and strictly interpretable foundations.

When Arac identifies his enterprise of literary history or genealogy with the intention "to excavate the past that is necessary to account for how we got here and the past that is useful for conceiving alternatives to our present condition" or declares that its aim is "to add to our substantive knowledge of the history of literary criticism, and to contribute to a new practice of writing literary history," the second parts of both his formulations take on this function of deliberate constitutional review (*Genealogies* 1–2). Without rejecting the cognitive task that the first parts of his formulations acknowledge, he reintroduces the practical dimension of literary history that the history of criticism, as a purely cognitive specialty, has occluded, and he revives, without recalling, a long forgotten prudential understanding of literary history whose time may at last have come.

Like Gerald Graff, Bruce Robbins, A. C. Goodson, and a number of other recent writers, Arac has thus reconceived the history of criticism and of literary studies more generally as pragmatic constitutional history, an inquiry into precedent texts, authorities, terms, and topics on the premise that they constitute a charter for the present activities of those who inquire into them. Neither Arac nor any of these other new constitutional historians, however, has recognized a precedent for their own conception of literary history in an author who was crucial to Wordsworth's conception of his literary work but who has been generally excluded from our own traditions. When Francis Bacon defines "literary history" in his *Advancement of Learning*, he makes it not a specialized history of what, since Wordsworth, we call literature but a just story of learning, containing the antiquities and originals of knowledges and their sects, their inventions, their traditions, their diverse administrations and managings, their flourishings, their oppositions, decays, depressions, oblivions, removes, with the causes and occasions of them, and all other events concerning learning, throughout the ages of the world ... the use and end of which ... is this in few words, that it will make learned men wise in the use and administration of learning.   (*Advancement* 70)

Literary history in this sense is a practical inquiry into the constitution of learning for the sake of its advancement, not merely a learned specialty that adds its knowledge to the store of learning without, as it were, minding the store. And it is a comprehensive inquiry that does not stop with the "small memorials of the schools, authors, and books" set down by "divers particular sciences, as of the jurisconsults, the mathematicians, the rhetoricians, the philosophers" (69) or, as we might see it, by the diverse schools of criticism and literary study, each with its own Founding Father or Mother, but all inattentive to all the others (see my Chapter 4).

Bacon notes the inquiry into literary history in this sense as "deficient," but I can happily note it as recently extant, though not without need of further cultivation and recognition as a distinctive line of inquiry. Little more than a decade ago, when I first came upon Bacon's definition of literary history and recognized it as a charter for the enterprise I wished to pursue, the history of criticism was still represented by authoritative figures like M. H. Abrams, Bernard Weinberg, A. O. Lovejoy, and R. S. Crane, all of whom shared an ideal of objective detachment and a belief that the texts or statements constituting the history of criticism were given and the task at hand was to get them right and account for their variations from age to age. They did not see the terms on which they carried out their equally given enterprise at stake in their interpretations of the history of criticism, though we can now often recognize the interests that conditioned their interpretations of texts and directed their choice of topics. Their authoritative examples seemed then to require me to make a strident polemical defense of a Baconian project that would declare and pursue its own practical interests in reviewing the constitution of literary studies, even if those interests were distinctively those of learning itself and not those of church or state, both of which, for Bacon, have their own institutional histories. I was not satisfied with the tone or the arguments of the various defenses of Bacon and critiques of the "objective" history of criticism I drafted in the late 70s, and I did not finish them.

That a version of what I see as Baconian literary history has emerged in the last decade in the work of Arac, Gerald Graff, Bruce Robbins, A. C. Goodson, Dominick LaCapra and others has enabled me to imagine my own work in a historical situation in current literary studies and to present it as a contribution that I hope will advance our knowledge of that situation as well as of literature. It will appear in the next few chapters that the contemporary emergence of Mikhail Bakhtin's work and of a school of contemporary criticism growing out of it have played an even greater part in provoking and enabling my work during that period. What I must emphasize is that these emergent enterprises have made it possible for me to identify and shape my professional self as part of more than one collective "we" and to take it upon myself to articulate further these enterprises for "us" and for others. What follows will, I hope, demonstrate how aware I am that each "we" with which I have identified myself does not exhaust the larger field of colleagues and constituents to whom we are responsible, but I would have this ratification of each particular "we" stand at the outset as my placement of myself under or in the constitution I presume to examine here. Believing as I do that all others concerned with this inquiry are similarly situated by equally specific interests, debts, friends, opponents, schools, and critical languages, I give this account of my affiliations instead of seeking, as M. H. Abrams did in *The Mirror and the Lamp*, "to adopt an analytic scheme which avoids imposing its own philosophy."[17] My self-situating gesture (and my call to others to acknowledge their own specific situations) has been learned among the lessons of the last decade in literary study and is, for me, an inescapable feature of literary history at the present time.

17 M. H. Abrams, *The Mirror and the Lamp* (New York: Oxford University Press, 1953), 6.

2

Displacing Coleridge, replacing
Wordsworth

If identities are lost through acts of negation, they are also acquired thereby, and the restoration of what has been denied cannot be accomplished through simple affirmation.　　　　　Barbara Johnson, *A World of Difference*

While scholarly documentation is a generic requirement, it also honors friendships, acknowledges and evades indebtedness, repays favors, and settles affronts, real or imagined. This human unseemliness critical constructions also share with literary constructions.
　　　　　Gene W. Ruoff, *Wordsworth and Coleridge*

Coleridge's role in providing several key constitutional texts for modern Anglo-American criticism has been widely recognized both by historians of criticism pleased by his influence and by those who have opposed it. His definitions of imagination and of the symbol, his metaphor of organic unity, his exaltation of poetic genius have remained important even under recent attacks, which have kept them current by opposing them. Other signs of Coleridge's continuing influence may be that Wordsworth's poems have repeatedly served as demonstration texts for modern critical theories, as they did for Coleridge's theory in the *Biographia Literaria*, while Wordsworth's critical pronouncements on poetry are frequently dismissed in terms derived from Coleridge's critique of them in the same text. As one who entered literary studies partly through the appeal of Wordsworth's democratic, demystifying, and socially consequential pronouncements in the Preface to *Lyrical Ballads*, only to find them still under the shadow of Coleridge's exaltation of the poet over ordinary people and his celebration of the "magical" aesthetic faculty that idealizes and unifies an otherwise fallen world, I welcome Arac's recognition and join his questioning of Coleridge's persistent authority.

In his introduction to *Critical Genealogies* Arac writes,

Contemporary criticism is still significantly determined by its romantic beginnings. From T. S. Eliot and I. A. Richards in the 1920s and 1930s, to Cleanth Brooks, Robert Penn Warren, and F. O. Matthiessen in the 1930s and 1940s, to M. H. Abrams and Paul de Man since the 1950s, one crucial axis of modern criticism is a series of rereadings in Coleridge. In order to displace this Coleridgean fascination, I focus especially on Wordsworth. For Wordsworth did more than anyone else to establish the vocation of literature in relation to which Coleridge's, and our own culture's, idea of the literary critic took shape. Yet as a critic, and self-critic, Wordsworth opposed Coleridge. (3)

Arac's announcement of this intention to displace modern criticism's rereadings of Coleridge and replace them with rereadings of Wordsworth (and, he goes on, of Shelley and Hazlitt) could be taken as part of what Raymond Williams calls the historical work of counter-hegemony to which I imagine myself also to be committed: "the recovery of discarded areas, or the redress of selective and reductive interpretations" (*Marxism* 116). On what for me is the persuasive premise that repetitions of selected Coleridgean topoi have dominated decades of modern critical discussion to the exclusion or misapprehension of more desirable Wordsworthian topoi, Arac declares his will to shift the focus of discussion in contemporary criticism, not, as Vincent Leitch has noted, outside the boundaries of "elitist poetic traditions,"[1] but from a dominant to a neglected (and for me a less elitist) voice within one of those traditions – the Romantic. By constructing named persons ("Wordsworth" and "Coleridge") in identifiable "places" of authority dependent upon where others "focus" their attention, Arac makes the situation he defines seem clear and the change he would work appear to be within his power and ours. If we were to shift our focus as he does, we would help him displace Coleridge from the focal place that has given him authority in modern criticism. To dismiss the "Coleridgean fascination," as Williams says the makers of selective traditions dismiss "'nostalgic'" or "'out of date'" traditional sources they do not want, would appear to make room for Wordsworth to take Coleridge's place at center stage.

Arac's bold opening move appeals to me, because it calls attention

---

1 Vincent Leitch, Review of *Critical Genealogies*, *Modern Fiction Studies* 34 (1988): 321.

to the role of our choices and intentions in actively selecting our critical traditions and dramatizes our alternatives in a way that permits him and us to act immediately and directly upon them. His move also troubles me, however, because it ignores the difficulties to which Williams says all such moves are vulnerable as well as the special circumstances that complicate any attempt to displace Coleridge and replace him with Wordsworth (among others) as a center of critical authority. For one thing, it is not enough, according to Williams, to shift our focus from a hegemonic to a counter-hegemonic figure "unless the lines to the present, in the actual process of selective tradition, are clearly and actively traced. Otherwise any recovery can be simply residual or marginal. It is at the vital points of *connection*, where a version of the past is used to ratify the present and to indicate directions for the future, that a selective tradition is at once powerful and vulnerable" (116). Williams would lead us to ask not just who opposed or preceded whom but what, in our present and future, a Wordsworthian tradition will let us be and do that the Coleridgean tradition has kept us from being and doing.

Arac's later answers to this question are complex, and I would note that his point is not just, as he here declares, that Wordsworth's view of the critic was prior to Coleridge's or that Wordsworth's view is opposed to Coleridge's. For the constitutional purposes of selecting a critical tradition, the point is not primarily about Wordsworth's relation to Coleridge but about both their relations to us, whoever, in the end, we turn out to be. I believe with Arac, and will argue in this and the next chapter, that the choice between these authorities remains consequential for us as teachers and students of literature in a democracy. Our conceptions of language, poems, poets, ourselves, and our students are all at stake in differences between these two authorities that are too easily occluded under the label "Romantic" or ignored under the hegemony of Coleridgean premises. In the case of Wordsworth and Coleridge, however, the choice is complicated by several considerations I must discuss as I try to formulate the opposition between these Founding Fathers and call for a shift in our allegiances. The conflicts and inconsistencies internal to each author as well as their involvements with one another and our selective involvements with them make any program of displacing one and replacing him with the other less easy and less unambiguous than Arac's programmatic statement imagines or than I myself once imagined.

Contradictions of bourgeois authorship

The last section of this chapter will consider one recent critical argument in which "Coleridge" has been divided against himself, but I must acknowledge at the outset what I now see as a division in "Wordsworth" between conflicting impulses and interests which complicate my effort to appropriate him as an authority for a democratic literary enterprise. Peter Stallybrass and Allon White have provided the terms that bring these differences into focus for me. Their analysis of the invention of the modern English "author" from Jonson to Wordsworth demonstrates that the creation of "the symbolic domain of 'authorship'...was produced *over against* the popular, as embodied in the festive scene of the fair and the carnival and as embodied in popular drama."[2] They point to Wordsworth's ambivalent, at moments even horrified, portrait of Bartholomew Fair in *The Prelude* to show how Wordsworth, like his Renaissance and eighteenth-century predecessors, constructed himself as an author through symbolic transcendence of his low subjects and affirmation of "the poetics, and also the politics, of the old classical dispensation" (123) that he elsewhere repudiates.

Stallybrass and White present this gesture in *The Prelude* as a retreat from Wordsworth's "radical programme as a 'man speaking to men'" in the Preface to *Lyrical Ballads* (123), but someone reading the Preface in the wake of reading their book is likely to discover the same ambivalences in its argument. The tensions between the poet's selection of language from low and rustic life and his promise to purify it "from what appear to be its real defects, from all lasting and rational causes of dislike and disgust" (LB 245) have been familiar at least since Coleridge pointed to them as an absurd contradiction that discredited Wordsworth's poetic theories for imagining that low and rustic life and language could be distinguished for anything but their coarseness and derivativeness. Coleridge succeeded in persuading many subsequent critics to resolve Wordsworth's ambivalence through ridicule of his interest in the low and celebration of his imaginative exaltation. In Stallybrass and White's terms, however, this ambivalence is among the many signs in the Preface of a bourgeois author asserting at the same time his attraction to his low subjects and his professional self-exaltation and refinement at their

2 Peter Stallybrass and Allon White, *The Poetry and Politics of Transgression* (Ithaca: Cornell University Press, 1986), 61.

expense. The dynamics of this ambivalence are more interesting for our understanding of his work, his career, and our own situation than Coleridge's repression of them (itself an interesting sign of the same problematic of authorship).

Wordsworth is as repelled by popular entertainments in the Preface as in *The Prelude*, defining his cultivation of the beauty and dignity and elevation of his office against their "gross and violent stimulants" and the "degrading thirst after outrageous stimulation" they satisfy (248–49). He celebrates his own art, on the other hand, in the name of the bodily fluids of tears, blood and "vital juices" (254) that distinguish his subjects and language from those of poets given to "false refinement" (246) and link him with the sweaty masses. He claims to sing a collective and festive song of pleasure in which "all human beings join with him" (259), even though he insists that each reader judge his poems in individualist isolation "by his own feelings genuinely, and not by reflection upon what will probably be the judgment of others" (270). He risks his reputation in choosing to represent "incidents of common life" (244) even as he declares the separation of his work from "the vulgarity and meanness of ordinary life" (254).

Although I would once have tried, in answer to Coleridge's attack, to select or subordinate these opposing attitudes toward popular pleasures and common people in order to construct a consistent position for Wordsworth,[3] I am now persuaded by Stallybrass and White that the poetic and political tensions revealed in them are inherent not only in the creation of the author in bourgeois society but also in the institutionalization of a literary study that has constructed its classrooms and library shelves around the works and careers of such authors. To recognize ourselves as implicated in the same tensions – for example, between identifying with the interests of our students and refining them, or between introducing popular texts into our classrooms and making them theoretically respectable – is to turn to Wordsworth's Preface or his *Prelude* in order to reflect on his response to these tensions, and our own. We cannot have him as a "man speaking to men" without the embarrassment of his talking down to them and the further embarrassment of his failure, in this

---

3 For an admirable attempt to rationalize these conflicting impulses as rhetorical strategies, see Anuradha Dingwaney and Lawrence Needham, "(Un)Creating Taste: Wordsworth's Platonic Defense in Preface to *Lyrical Ballads*," *Rhetoric Society Quarterly* 19 (1989): 333–45.

phrase, to imagine women speaking or being spoken to at all, and we will do better than he only if we can resist, as he sometimes could not, the temptation to purify him, as he wished to purify his subjects and language, of "lasting and rational causes of dislike and disgust" (245). To idealize his democratic gestures to the exclusion or repression of his *"will to refinement"* (Stallybrass and White, *Transgression*, 94) and his disgust at popular culture would be to obscure the paradoxical problematic of literary education in a democratic but divided society and to diminish our chances of thinking it through. If we can nevertheless choose Wordsworth's ambivalence toward popular culture over Coleridge's contempt for it, we will be choosing to address a problem to which an acceptable solution is not yet obvious.

Mutual influences and mediations

If Wordsworth's symptomatic self-division complicates any proposal to choose him over Coleridge as a constitutional authority, so do Coleridge's and Wordsworth's parts in shaping one another's works, projects, and selves. Celebrations of the *annus mirabilis* and accounts of Coleridge's supplying key ideas to Wordsworth's poetry and criticism have long made Wordsworth difficult to separate from Coleridge, and Wordsworth's centrality in Coleridge's *Biographia* has made Coleridge's critical theory hard to separate from his criticism of Wordsworth's poetry and theory, even, as Raimonda Modiano has recently shown, where Wordsworth is not ostensibly Coleridge's subject.[4] But a substantial body of recent work, some of it available to Arac and some of it completed since his book was finished, has made their interdependence as poets and critics seem even more compelling now. What Beth Darlington and Kenneth Johnston have shown about Coleridge's role in shaping Wordsworth's sense of his poetic vocation and his commitment to the *Recluse* project, what A. C. Goodson has made of Wordsworth's part in shaping Coleridge's vocation and agenda as a critic, and what Paul Magnuson and Gene Ruoff have demonstrated about the dialogic interdependence of the two poets' poems make it difficult to speak of shifting attention from one writer to the other without the displaced writer still haunting the discussion.[5] Such selves do not occupy discrete positions from which

---

4 Raimonda Modiano, "Coleridge and Wordsworth: The Ethics of Gift Exchange and Literary Ownership," *WC* 22 (Spring 1989): 113–20.

5 These are only a few of the arguments that have explored what Thomas McFarland calls the symbiosis of the two Romantic writers in his *Romanticism and*

they can be displaced but inhabit and produce one another in many of the texts and passages among which a selective critical tradition would choose.

In his brief critical survey of recent Wordsworthian criticism, Arac faults James Chandler for relying upon a "simple dichotomy between Rousseau and Burke" to locate Wordsworth's position (*Genealogies* 51) and ignoring recent work that would discredit that dichotomy, but Arac himself ignores Chandler's final chapter on "The Role of Coleridge" that complicates Chandler's placement of Wordsworth and would complicate Arac's own "simple dichotomy" between Wordsworth and Coleridge.[6] The habit of posing binary alternatives dies hard, but any recourse to one of these figures for present purposes will unavoidably involve recourse to the other, and the question of their roles in a contemporary critical tradition will never be a question of displacing the one and replacing the other but always of locating ourselves in the field of their likenesses and differences.

Wordsworth and Coleridge have thus complicated our relation to them because they helped to shape one another, but they have also complicated that relation by mediating each other's poetry and theories for us. Wordsworth's critical remarks set the critical topics for much of the subsequent criticism of Coleridge's "Ancient Mariner," and Wordsworth's version of the distinction between imagination and fancy has interacted with Coleridge's in subsequent discussions.[7] The second volume of Coleridge's *Biographia Literaria* has exerted and continues to exert a much larger influence in the reception of Wordsworth's poetry and his poetics. A survey of teachers of

the *Forms of Ruin: Wordsworth, Coleridge, and Modalities of Fragmentation* (Princeton: Princeton University Press, 1981). See also Beth Darlington, *Home at Grasmere: Part First, Book First of "The Recluse"* (Ithaca: Cornell University Press, 1977), Johnston, *Wordsworth and "The Recluse"*, A. C. Goodson, *Verbal Imagination: Coleridge and the Language of Modern Criticism* (New York and Oxford: Oxford University Press, 1988), Paul Magnuson, *Coleridge and Wordsworth: A Lyrical Dialogue* (Princeton: Princeton University Press, 1988), and Gene W. Ruoff, *Wordsworth and Coleridge: The Making of the Major Lyrics, 1802–1804* (New Brunswick: Rutgers University Press, 1985). For further references see Karl Kroeber, "Wordsworth," and Max F. Schulz, "Coleridge," both in *The English Romantic Poets: A Review of Research and Criticism*, ed. Frank Jordan (New York: MLA, 1985), 328–29, 443–44.

6 A. C. Goodson's 1989 MLA conference paper, "Cultural Politics of the 1790s," would further complicate the matter by asking us to examine not just Wordsworth's but also Coleridge's Burke and the effect of Coleridge's on Wordsworth's Burke.

7 See Goodson, *Verbal Imagination*, 227 n. 1, and Schulz, "Coleridge," 435.

Wordsworth conducted in the mid-eighties for an MLA volume on *Approaches to Teaching Wordsworth* (see Chapter 8 below) found that the *Biographia* is "the secondary work most frequently recommended to students by respondents" – an institutional fact not easily "displaced," notwithstanding the surveyors' reservations as to "whether or not Coleridge's remarks constitute, as has often been claimed, the best introduction to Wordsworth ever written" (*Approaches* 14). And if undergraduates reading Wordsworth for the first time cannot escape Coleridge's mediation of Wordsworth in anthologies and syllabi, scholars and critics rereading Wordsworth and his other scholars and critics will find Coleridge's version of Wordsworth everywhere in critical apparatuses, introductions, explications, and argumentative topoi. Coleridge's topics of refutation shaped W. J. B. Owen's expectations as to the topics of Wordsworth's own argument in the most detailed commentary we have on Wordsworth's Preface to *Lyrical Ballads*, and Coleridge's judgments of Wordsworth's virtues and vices as a poet have governed the praise and blame of many critics and provoked the revaluations of many others.

Confessions of an American Coleridge displacer

My own first response to the discovery that standard authorities on Wordsworth regularly and uncritically repeated Coleridge's erroneous judgments of his poetics was to feel a Blakean indignation and energy that fueled the composition of a dissertation demonstrating the intelligibility of Wordsworth's Preface in its own terms and the groundlessness of Coleridge's account of it. The only section of the dissertation to be published argued that Coleridge's widely authoritative interpretation of Wordsworth's Preface had erroneously represented Wordsworth's theoretical position as inconsistent, obscure, and absurd.[8] The effect of my direct attempt to displace Coleridge as an authority on Wordsworth through forensic demonstration is difficult to gauge, for some have praised it, others have attacked it, and many have continued to repeat the judgments it contravenes without answering or acknowledging it. Its treatment in two authoritative sources that have appeared since its publication

8 See my "The Intelligibility of Wordsworth's Preface to *Lyrical Ballads*" (Ph.D. dissertation, University of Chicago, 1977), and "Coleridge's Interpretation of Wordsworth's Preface," *PMLA* 93 (1978): 912–24.

is revealing for my present theme of the ways in which critics' investments in their authors complicate any efforts to displace those authors or persuade those critics to shift their allegiances.

Though Walter Jackson Bate and James Engell do not note my refutation of Coleridge's reading of Wordsworth's Preface in their 1983 Bollingen edition of the *Biographia*, my article's appearance in the profession's most widely circulated journal five years before their edition was published speaks from the margins of their edition. As Raymond Williams observes, "the real record is effectively re-coverable, and many of the alternative or opposing practical continuities are still available" (116), in this case to critics whose inquiries may depend on an estimate of the adequacy of Coleridge's interpretation of Wordsworth. They may judge from the bibliographic record the significance of Bate and Engell's omission and the character of their investments.[9]

The bibliographic record, however, is also not available without the mediation of scholars invested in their subjects. The two listings of my article on Coleridge's interpretation of Wordsworth's Preface in the institutionally important MLA-sponsored bibliography *The English Romantic Poets: A Review of Research and Criticism* both list the article in proximity to their listings of Engell's introduction to the second volume of the Bollingen *Biographia*, though neither directly notes, as only an interested author would, Bate and Engell's failure to mention it. Karl Kroeber's chapter on "Wordsworth" introduces my article as an "extremely important" attempt to distinguish the "true difference" of Wordsworth's ideas from Coleridge's and even echoes my hopeful conclusion that the recognition of that difference could be "'momentous for Anglo-American criticism,'" though Kroeber thinks the similarities between the two writers are finally more important than the differences. Engell's introduction comes up as a relatively judicious instance of what Kroeber calls the "Coleridgean bias" that

9 Samuel Taylor Coleridge, *Biographia Literaria*, ed. James Engell and Walter Jackson Bate (Princeton: Princeton University Press, 1983). For an extensive critique of Engell and Bate's edition arguing that the annotation in the edition reveals "an editorial stance on controversial matters which is unremittingly defensive, evasive, non-committal, or intrusive in ways intended to shape the reader's views along paths congenial to the editors," see Norman Fruman, "Review Essay: Aids to Reflection on the New *Biographia*," *SiR* 24 (1985): 141–73. Both the tone and the reception of Fruman's work since his *Coleridge: Damaged Archangel* in 1971 illustrate the difficulties encountered by anyone who sets out to displace Coleridge in the present critical situation.

has treated Coleridge's criticisms of Wordsworth as admirable and accurate and characteristically failed to "recognize the complexity of Wordsworth's views" (329). Max Schulz's bibliographic essay on "Coleridge" treats my article as an instance of how "militant Wordsworthians still probe the critical ordinances articulated" in the *Biographia*, even as James Engell, "secure in the current esteem in which Coleridge is held," can vigorously defend Coleridge's criticisms of Wordsworth without being as defensive as Thomas Raysor had to be in 1939 (443). Schulz dismisses my argument (he calls it an "attack") for its "spirit of acrimony" and its purported use of the same refutative strategy of reading that it accuses Coleridge of using and contrasts my argument with the "common sense and dispassionate fairness" of another recent interpreter of the controversy between Wordsworth and Coleridge, Paul Hamilton.

The genre of annotated bibliography does not allow either Kroeber or Schulz space to review my arguments and evidence, but their divergent judgments and mutually suspicious characterizations of "Wordsworthians" and "Coleridgeans" reveal the difficulty for any project that would displace Coleridge and replace him with Wordsworth. It is not just that Wordsworth and Coleridge have interpreted each other for us but that we contemporary interpreters of them have been shaped by our identifications with and investments in them and interpret them through those identifications and investments. We cannot displace one another's heroes without displacing one another and reenacting their differences in our own.

Schulz's attempt to isolate me by characterizing my tone as an irrational and ill-tempered violation of the tone appropriate to "the current esteem in which Coleridge is held" – a violation that appeals not even to all Wordsworthians but only to the "militant" ones – illustrates the way in which Williams says that selective privileges and interests assert their investments through "complex elements of style and tone" (*Marxism* 117). Though I believe that Schulz has overstated my bad manners and pathological aggressiveness, he has caught the sense of isolation from which I wrote an argument that I thought needed to be heard not so much by Coleridgeans as by many authoritative Wordsworthians who wrote as if Coleridge had persuaded them, too. I was so preoccupied, in fact, with the power Coleridge's text exerted over Wordsworth's in Wordsworthian circles that I failed to investigate or cite all pertinent Coleridgean interpretations and contextualizations of the *Biographia* and the

Wordsworth–Coleridge controversy – including an earlier article of Schulz's[10] – and was surprised to find the main bibliographic entry for my article in the *MLA Bibliography* under Coleridge rather than Wordsworth. I felt myself to be writing with few allies even in the Wordsworthian camp and consequently had few others whose agreement with my position could warrant a confident and moderate tone.

Schulz's judgment of my tone may also have been affected by the aggressive insecurity of a previously unpublished critical voice, drawing material from a dissertation written without supervision of a mentor identified as either a Wordsworthian or a Coleridgean, and writing from a marginal job (visiting instructor) at a moment when the prospects of regular employment were uncertain and the need to get a hearing in print was great. Such matters, as Williams describes them, "material in substance but often ideal in form" (117), have their bearings on tone – understood as the verbal signs of a subject's relations to his or her heroes *and* his or her readers or auditors in a world of concrete social relations.[11] To displace someone's focus from one hero to another is to dislocate their ideal identifications and their material investments in those heroes and to reorient their relations to their audiences as well. It is to put subjects at the risk of losing the bearings of accepted discourse and sounding notes that may seem false or alien to those who remain "secure" in the "current esteem" of their heroes or the tenure of their positions.

The literary critical community, like all other communities, maintains its established heroes and enforces conformity to its canons partly by ridiculing or condemning or censoring voices whose tones do not acknowledge its unspoken agreements. Williams expresses confidence that the domination of interests enforced by tone and style can be "recognized, demonstrated, and broken" (117), but I do not imagine that they can be displaced simply by a redirection of attention. A revoicing, rather, of their own characteristic notes may expose the participants in a dominant interest enforced by judgments of tone to hear themselves differently, but it probably will not change their minds and will only have effect on others less fully invested in those interests and consequently more able to entertain other

10 Max F. Schulz, "Coleridge, Wordsworth, and the 1800 Preface to *Lyrical Ballads*," *SEL* 5 (1965): 619–39.
11 See my elaboration of the Bakhtin School's concept of tone in "Discourse in Life and Discourse in Art" in *Making Tales*, Chapter 2.

interests and admire other heroes. The story of the Emperor's New Clothes (like Kuhn's *Structure of Scientific Revolutions!*) reveals, among other things, the generational differences between those who will go to great lengths to maintain a tone that preserves the "current esteem" of their heroes and those who, without the same investments, will rudely divest the invested.

That wonderfully subversive story begs a crucial question, however, and sets a trap for anyone who would identify, as I have identified my younger self, with the decorum-violating child, for the story-teller authoritatively declares that the Emperor *had* no clothes on and that everyone knew it, though they were afraid to admit that they did, and readers of the story have no recourse to any other version of the situation. The situation of critical investments in Founding Fathers and Mothers is not the same, however, for "Coleridge's distortions of Wordsworth's Preface" or "Coleridge's authoritative criticism of Wordsworth" are not simply *there* to be seen by all but have been constructed by interested arguments that appeal to controversial evidence that can be judged by variously interested parties. There is no naked state of affairs evident to all, and the task of judgment is not simply to admit such a state despite our resistances to it, henceforth leading a life without illusory investments, but rather to weigh arguments and evidence and tones, remaining open to the persuasiveness of alternative investments.

But no one, under these debatable circumstances, should expect anyone else to abandon a productive investment solely on grounds of its alleged inadequacy to the facts, without supplying hope, promise even, of a more productive investment. We may remain loyal to our loved ones even after they have been convicted of crimes, though we may also decide to divorce them, even when they are found innocent, if someone more appealing comes along. Wordsworth recognized at the end of the Preface to *Lyrical Ballads* that "all men feel an habitual gratitude, and something of an honorable bigotry for the objects which have long continued to please them: we not only wish to be pleased, but to be pleased in that particular way in which we have become accustomed to be pleased. There is a host of arguments in these feelings" (272), he goes on, having explained his earlier renunciation of "the selfish and foolish hope of *reasoning* [the reader] into an approbation" of his poems (242), and he promises "other enjoyments, of a purer, more lasting, and more exquisite nature" to compensate those who would reinvest their poetic interests in his sort of poetry (272). My own refutation of Coleridge's reading of Wordsworth vaguely anticipated "momentous" consequences from its displacement of Coleridge as a critic of Wordsworth's Preface, but its forensic preoccupation with doing justice to Wordsworth offered nothing for Coleridgeans or Wordsworthians to reinvest in to make a future without the discredited Coleridge.

The historical situation and, consequently, the tone of my first intervention into the Wordsworth–Coleridge controversy did not carry over to the second one, for not only had I found a tenure-track job (though not yet tenure) when I wrote *Making Tales* but I also had found other Wordsworthians who contributed to my understanding of Wordsworth's narrative poetics and my ability to take pleasure in his narrative poems, as well as a recognizable classical analog and a recognizable contemporary theoretical expositor for Wordsworth's position. Situated by the work of John Danby, Robert Langbaum, Steven Maxfield Parrish, Paul Sheats and others whose readings they helped to influence, I found it necessary to undertake "a critical examination of the poetic systems of Coleridge and Wordsworth as those systems guide the reading of Wordsworth's experimental poems" and a "systematization of the recent work on *Lyrical Ballads* that has begun to find new interest in them." This work had, I thought, "reached a stage at which the grounds of its successes with some poems can be clarified and from which those successes may be extended to other poems long held in derision or contempt" through the elaboration of an "alternative system [to Coleridge's] that will permit us to account for what we already enjoy and extend our appreciation to Wordsworth's still neglected narrative experiments" (8). The difference between Plato's and Aristotle's accounts of poetic diction permitted me to locate the issue between Wordsworth and Coleridge in terms provided by an enduring and authoritative cultural tradition (though the Platonic locus has been less elaborated and repeated than the Aristotelian). Bakhtin (or the Bakhtin School) offered a then emerging and now widely recognized modern source for what I then called a "poetics of speech" and would now call a dialogic poetics that helps to elaborate Wordsworth's key distinctions and topics and give them cogency and productivity as an alternative to Coleridge's poetics. The Bakhtin School's emphasis on the transition from discourse in life to discourse in poetry opened a way to recuperate Wordsworth's interest in the "real language of men" from Coleridge's strictures, and its elaboration of the problem of reported speech enabled a positive formulation of poetic practices Coleridge could only condemn as lapses of decorum (for a recapitulation of this argument, see Chapter 3 below). My task as I saw it was not to displace Coleridge so much as to elaborate Wordsworth's poetics so that it could take its place beside Coleridge's and demonstrate its efficacy in making Wordsworth's experimental poems available for enjoyment.

The limited focus of my inquiry on Wordsworth's narrative experiments, however, left unexplored the implications of a Wordsworthian/Bakhtinian sociological poetics for Wordsworth's other sorts of poems – those that Coleridge had taught generations of critics to read in his terms – and for a modern criticism that had made a version of Coleridge's poetics (and of Coleridge's criticism of Wordsworth) canonical in its own critical theory and practice. It remains, in the chapters that follow, to indicate what a Wordsworthian tradition and its system might make of the rest of Wordsworth's poetry and, in the next section, to suggest how such a tradition and system might modify a literary critical enterprise which has rationalized a Coleridgean "tradition and its system" and perpetuated itself on the terms that tradition and system have provided.

Towards a tradition for the Wordsworthian system

Chapters 3, 4, and 5 will recapitulate and elaborate the Wordsworthian/Bakhtinian poetic system I presented in *Making Tales* and extend its application from Wordsworth's experimental narratives to his canonical poetry and to one of the central concerns of the Coleridgean critical tradition, lyric poetry. Here I will address the need for a tradition that could function as the "empowering past" for that Wordsworthian system and suggest several sources that might play a part in it.[12] Frank Lentricchia announced a decade ago that the New Criticism, which had institutionalized its version of Coleridgean poetics and the tradition in which that poetics was central, was "moribund" as early as 1957, and he criticized what was, at the time of his writing, the most recent distillation of "the neo-Coleridgean mainstream of modern theoretical criticism," Murray Krieger's *Theory of Criticism: A Tradition and Its System* (1977) – the book from whose subtitle I have taken the title for this section (ANC 4, 215). The New

---

12 The phrase is from Bruce Robbins, "The History of Theory: Starting Over," *Poetics Today* 9 (1988): 779.

Criticism had apparently been breathing its last for at least twenty years when Lentricchia set out to displace it by placing himself and us "after" it, and another decade still left Jonathan Arac with the same historical situation of displacing Coleridge and the New Criticism and replacing it with some other tradition and system. It appears to me that we will continue to pronounce premature obituaries and act out displacements that never quite take place until we have articulated that other system and found a new story to tell of *its* tradition.

Lentricchia declares in *After the New Criticism* that "the great hope for literary critics in 1957, when the hegemony of the New Criticism was breaking, was that the muse would be demystified and democratized and that younger critics would somehow link up poetry with the world again" (7), but he does not elaborate the system of this demystified and democratized muse or link it directly, as I would, to Wordsworth and a Wordsworthian tradition. Wordsworth's Preface to *Lyrical Ballads* seems to me to announce a poetic enterprise continuous with widely shared human motives and interests and capacities, a poetic enterprise not dependent upon special poetic faculties and their "magical" or god-like powers. Despite the ambivalences I have documented above, his democratization of poetic work grounded in the "grand elementary principle of pleasure" and his demystification of a poet who differs from other people only in degree, not in kind, mark for me exactly what, as I put it earlier, "a Wordsworthian tradition [would] let us be and do that the prevailing Coleridgean tradition has kept us from being and doing" with its emphasis on a transcendental faculty of imagination that differentiates poets from other people and a mystified poetic symbol that embodies that faculty. A Wordsworthian tradition would let us teach poetry as a pleasurable verbal and cultural practice that self-consciously cultivates powers inherent in the ordinary verbal and cultural experience of our students. It would let us teach literature/writing to those students without mystifying it or condescending to them (see Chapter 8).

Lentricchia, in his next book, *Criticism and Social Change*, calls for an active remaking of tradition in the wake of New Criticism, but his own argument there stages a battle between two larger-than-life recent critical authorities, Paul de Man and Kenneth Burke, without constructing the democratic and demystifying tradition in which his chosen authority, Burke, might resonate with and be sustained by a story and a historical community of concerns. Wordsworth, who appeared briefly and occasionally in *After the New Criticism* as the advocate of an active, unmystified self committed to "a socially directed ideal of the poetic character" (258) recedes in *Criticism and Social Change* to a voice echoed in occasional allusions to the "savage torpor" of modern industrial society. Lentricchia exposed the premises of Krieger's Coleridgean system, but he did not go very far toward offering an alternative tradition, Wordsworthian or otherwise.[13]

By 1977, however, Krieger was defensively aware that "the tradition is *my* tradition," not "the theoretical tradition" he had originally hoped to present,[14] though this modest stance underestimated the degree to which many others had shared and still shared *his* tradition so that *their* tradition – from Plato and Aristotle to Sidney to Coleridge (and Kant) to the New Critics (and the existentialists) – has remained the only available articulated tradition on the American scene until the dissemination of the Continental Hegelian/Saussurean tradition. Many critics of the last decade have continued to set themselves against Krieger's tradition, to undermine it *as* a powerful tradition, or "to celebrate the present at the expense of [any] monumental or antiquarian" tradition without taking it upon themselves to construct and promulgate an alternative (Robbins, "History of Theory," 778). They have appeared to need to exaggerate (and thereby perpetuate) the continuing domination of the Coleridgean tradition – long after its advocates had retreated to defensive postures – in order to justify their own counter-hegemonic stances in relation to it, even as they have themselves come to occupy positions of power in the universities and colleges and to assume responsibility for establishing curricula and syllabi that will *make* the tradition for the next generation of students.

Bruce Robbins has argued, persuasively to my mind, that the task before us is to "rewrite the history rather than leaving it alone or leaving it to others" because "any history or canon of criticism will become the empowering past for some version of the criticism of the present" (779–80). This task of rewriting the history of criticism is a

13 Frank Lentricchia, *Criticism and Social Change* (Chicago and London: University of Chicago Press, 1983). Lentricchia returns briefly and interestingly to Wordsworth as a constitutionally significant critic in *Ariel and the Police* (Madison: University of Wisconsin Press, 1988), 17–20.

14 Murray Krieger, *Theory of Criticism: A Tradition and Its System* (Baltimore: Johns Hopkins University Press, 1977), xiii, ix.

large one, and, as I have indicated in the previous chapter, I believe
it is already under way in the work of a number of recent critics. It
is not, at this stage in its emergence at least, a project to be
consolidated in a magisterial survey on the order of *The Mirror and
the Lamp* or defended in a last ditch argument like Krieger's *Theory of
Criticism* but must, I think, be the work of many separate inquiries that
may come to recognize their mutual relevancies and common
tendencies.

To the end of provoking more of such inquiries and enabling as
much of such recognition as is presently possible, I shall here sketch
not a history of the Wordsworthian tradition but a syllabus of texts
from which I have begun to construct such a tradition. This partial
and perhaps somewhat idiosyncratic reading list for a Wordsworthian
"tradition and its system" cannot replace or suppress the Coleridgean
New Critical tradition Krieger consolidates, but I hope that at every
juncture it will introduce counter-voices that will limit the claims of
that tradition and provoke inquiry into the possibility of an
alternative. The constraints of syllabi and curricula will compel
choices that reduce the roles played by previously authoritative texts
in order to introduce their critical counterparts, but the tradition I
advocate thrives in a field of contestation and requires the co-
presence of forcefully articulated alternatives to make its own force
felt. It is characterized, in fact, precisely by the preservation and
highlighting of alternative voices that the unifying and idealizing
Coleridgean tradition "dissolves and dissipates."

"Rhetorical" is the name Robbins gives to the tradition I, too,
would revive, and he locates the beginning of that tradition in a text
and context that makes me less uneasy with that name than I have
previously been. As long as rhetoric for me was defined as an
alternative to poetic and dialectic within the Aristotelian disciplinary
system, rhetoric appeared to be too limited an enterprise to
encompass Bakhtin's dialogics and Wordsworth's poetics of speech,[15]
but if one locates the beginning of rhetoric, as Robbins does, in
Gorgias' elaboration of the power of speech, then Wordsworth's and
Bakhtin's perspectives both find a founding father in him. In the
passage from "A Defence of Helen" that Robbins cites – following
Harold Bloom's selection of it to begin his anthology, *The Art of the
Critic* – Gorgias adumbrates a series of Wordsworthian topics and

15 See my "Dialogics as an Art of Discourse in Literary Criticism," *PMLA* 101
(1986): 788–97.

emphases. Like Wordsworth he defines poetry as "speech with meter," takes an interest in "the relationship of the structure of language to the structure of the mind"[16] – especially that between language and the passions – treats language as a cause of pleasure and pain, calls attention to both the deceptiveness and the inescapability of verbal mediation of experience, and links the languages of poetry, superstition, science, oratory, and philosophy (as Wordsworth links the languages of prose and poetry) in a common participation in the powers and limitations of speech. Gorgias thus joins Plato, whom I had previously imagined to be the founder of a poetics that emphasizes speaking rather than Aristotelian making, as one who, like Wordsworth, makes *logos* rather than *mythos*, discourse rather than plot, the fundamental category of poetics. To read Plato and Aristotle after Gorgias would be to read them as imposing disciplinary boundaries that remain fluid in his argument, and to read him and Wordsworth in relation to each other would be to recognize a common perspective in which poetry, rhetoric, history, philosophy, and science are being freshly distinguished as related kinds of discourse dependent upon common verbal powers and related pleasurable interests.

In the broadly conceived field of rhetoric opened by Gorgias, we might also turn to another ancient Greek precedent usually excluded by the disciplinary boundaries of narrowly "poetic" topics and texts. Herodotus' style of narration, with its preservation of alternative stories and its interest in imaginative as well as factual sources, is much closer to Wordsworth's style in *The Prelude* and in many lyrical ballads than Thucydides' monologic appropriation of narrative authority to himself. Occupying a position between the muse-inspired voice of Homer and the purportedly scientific voice of Thucydides, Herodotus, like Wordsworth, takes an interest in apparently superstitious and mythological stories as well as in factual evidence and critical rationality. No longer inside the mythical world view, these writers respect its power and examine its products instead of setting their own rational minds against it. They are alert to the half-created, half-perceived character of narrations – their own and other people's – without accepting the alternatives of pure myth or poetry and pure history or science that Krieger poses from one side and Thucydides poses from the other. Herodotus self-consciously

16 Nancy S. Struever, *The Language of History in the Renaissance* (Princeton: Princeton University Press, 1970), 11.

practices an impure mixed diction and a self-critical inquiry into self-serving story-telling in the light of which Wordsworth's interests and practices do not seem as anomalous as they do in the terms we have routinely drawn from Coleridge. We might also be better positioned to appreciate Alan Bewell's persuasive account of Wordsworth as an anthropological poet if we read Wordsworth and Bewell in a tradition that included the father of anthropology.[17]

In later antiquity, to read Quintilian and Cicero on tropes and figures next to Longinus' *On the Sublime* is again to make possible a different reading of Wordsworth. Instead of dwelling exclusively on the Longinian transcendent greatness achieved through the brilliant images and the power of imagination, which Coleridge too emphasizes, we may discover classifications of necessary though not necessarily impressive figures of thought and forms of argument that Wordsworth relies on to achieve effects other than the sublime. As I shall show at some length in Chapter 7, the workaday instruments of Roman rhetoric – the standard parts of argumentative disposition and the ordinary repertoire of figures of address – inform Wordsworth's poetic practice and his reflections on it, again, as with Gorgias, linking the language of prose and the language of poetry through their common participation in the powers and devices of speech.

From the Middle Ages, my alternative tradition would set medieval rhetoric, as mediated by Robert O. Payne's book on Chaucer, *Key of Remembrance*, against Augustinian (and more recently Robertsonian) orthodoxies that subordinate literary pleasure to truth – another version of the Coleridgean tradition's anxious preoccupation with the opposition of poetry to science.[18] Two passages, one linking Payne's Chaucer to what Wordsworth shares with Gorgias and the other linking him to what John Danby sees in Wordsworth, will suggest wider connections. Gorgias writes,

---

17 For a profoundly consequential revival of Herodotean history and critique of Thucydidean pretensions to scientific authority in history, see Martin Bernal, *Black Athena: The Afroasiatic Roots of Classical Civilization*, vol. I (New Brunswick: Rutgers University Press, 1987). For Alan Bewell's treatment of Wordsworth as an anthropological poet whose poems conduct experiments that depict the workings of the mind at various stages of cultural development, see his *Wordsworth and the Enlightenment: Nature, Man, and Society in the Experimental Poetry* (New Haven: Yale University Press, 1989).

18 Robert O. Payne, *The Key of Remembrance, a Study of Chaucer's Poetics* (New Haven, Conn.: Published for the University of Cincinnati by Yale University Press, 1963).

If everyone had memory of all the past, knowledge of the present, and foresight of the future, speech would not be (? like this). But as it is, we have no facility in remembering the past or viewing the present or divining the future; so that on most subjects most people summon opinion to be the mind's adviser. But opinion is treacherous and unstable, and involves her employers in treacherous and unstable successes.[19]

Payne writes, "The past (and with it, most of knowledge) is lost without a creative act of will – but the will and its creation are human, and so inherently error prone; and memory is not actually the past, but our useful illusion of it – yet who is sure that his *is* the useful illusion?"[20] These self-critical insights into the mind's inescapable role in the construction of its own past, present, and future seem to me entirely congenial with Wordsworth's characteristic awareness of the contingency and constructedness of his own recollections, interpretations, and projections. As I will argue in the next chapter, the self-conscious gestures through which Wordsworth indicates this awareness (like those of many of Chaucer's narrators) are at least as central to his work as the moments of authoritative certainty and imaginative unity that his Coleridgean readers prefer. Again, Payne writes,

Our concern for the poem as a process concurrent with our surrender to its effects, has often been discussed as a function of the self-conscious narrator and thus as a way of adding depth of perspective. But in addition it is a device for creating a self-conscious audience, and thus a way of making the reader's exercise of moral judgment become self-discovery. (231)

John Danby similarly writes that Wordsworth confronts the reader "with the need to be aware of what he is judging with as well as what he is judging."[21] Here the tradition I would construct anticipates Wordsworth's project of producing the active and self-critical reader who corresponds to the active and self-critical poet Payne's first passage envisions, a project to which I return in Chapter 8 on Wordsworthian pedagogy. These affinities, combined with affinities in Wordsworth's and Chaucer's interests in characters and language

19 Gorgias, "A Defence of Helen," in *The Art of the Critic: Literary Theory and Criticism from the Greeks to the Present*, ed. Harold Bloom (New York: Chelsea House, 1985), 5.

20 Payne, *The Key of Remembrance*, 219. See David Simpson's *Wordsworth and the Figurings of the Real* (Atlantic Highlands, New Jersey: Humanities Press, 1982) for a Wordsworthian reformulation of this last question.

21 John Danby, *The Simple Wordsworth* (London: Routledge and Kegan Paul, 1960), 38.

from the lower and middle classes, suggest the possibility of saving Wordsworth from his inclusion among Arnold's "high serious" poets and linking him, along with Chaucer – who did not make Arnold's grade – to Bakhtin's serio-comic writers and their sophistic rhetorical traditions.[22]

In the Renaissance, I would introduce Bacon as a counterpart to Sidney, bringing *The Advancement of Learning* and the expanded doctrine of the idols from *The New Organon* to supplement and criticize Sidney's *Defense of Poetry* – a key text in Krieger's tradition and system. Few Wordsworthians and no historians of criticism that I know have registered the importance of Paul Sheats's placement of Wordsworth in the tradition of Bacon's "great instauration." Sheats shows that

> although he sought to deny the Baconian conception of art as a pleasing and useful fiction, and to shape an art that like natural philosophy buckled the mind to the nature of things, he proceeded in a Baconian spirit that evinces a profound distrust of subjective aberration and a patient humility before the power, divinity, and potential beneficence of nature. He precisely inverted the Neoplatonic [and I would add Coleridgean] distinction between nature's brazen and the poet's golden world, but he did so on behalf of Sidney's faith in the ethically formative power of art.[23]

To follow Sheats's lead and link Wordsworth's poetic project to Baconian commitments can provide us with a proximate source in Bacon's doctrine of the idols for Wordsworth's participation in Gorgian skepticism and permit us to acknowledge the critical and scientific motives of Wordsworth's poetic project along with the artistic and aesthetic motives. If Bacon diminished (though he also recognized) poetry's affinities "with man's nature and pleasure" and conceded poetry's superiority in expressing the passions (*Advancement* 82–85), Wordsworth accepts Bacon's terms but exalts poetry by making the poet a self-conscious representer of the "grand elementary principle of pleasure" (LB 258) and deliberate inquirer into "the history or science of feelings" (*Prose* III, 85). If Bacon set out to repress or at least to correct for the Idols of the Cave of the individual mind, "which refracts and discolours the light of nature; owing either

22 For a Bakhtinian reading of Chaucer, see William T. McClellan, "Dialogic Discourse in *The Clerk's Tale*" (Ph.D. dissertation, City University of New York, 1985).
23 Paul Sheats, *The Making of Wordsworth's Poetry, 1785–1798* (Cambridge, Mass.: Harvard University Press, 1973), 248.

to his own proper and peculiar nature; or his education and conversation with others; or to the reading of books, and the authority of those he esteems and admires; or to the differences of impressions, accordingly as they take place in a mind preoccupied and predisposed or in a mind indifferent and settled" (*New Organon* 48), Wordsworth sets out to represent how each of these variables affects his own perception, making Bacon's cave of the human mind the haunt and main region of his song. As I show more fully in Chapters 6 and 9, Wordsworth depicts his own mind and the minds of others as living with Bacon's idols, as correcting themselves and being corrected by experience, but also as celebrating their capacities to construct contingent perceptions of indifferent things into meaningful lives.

Sheats goes on to describe Wordsworth's intellectual development in 1797 in terms derived from Bacon's doctrine of the idols: "Wordsworth's attention now shifts from the idols of the cave to those of the marketplace and the theater, from private trauma to the solipsism and pride that are the effects of public convention, of language, false doctrines, and what he would call a year later 'our pre-established codes of decision'" (161). These terms, too, are pregnant for a revaluation of Wordsworth's critical project, but in a critical tradition from which Bacon's works have been excluded from our attention by both parties – Krieger does not mention him, while Lentricchia does so only twice in passing – this crucial source has been lost to us. Even Art Berman's recent history of the New Criticism in light of its connection with empiricism begins its story of British empiricism not with Bacon but with Hobbes and Locke.[24]

A rereading of Bacon in the tradition I am constructing would not only recover the roots of Wordsworth's enterprise but would connect it with the beginnings of the progressive institutionalized intellectual enterprise (780) and the "pragmatic, political version of professional activity" (778) to which Robbins aspires, for these projects can find their "empowering past" (779) nowhere more than in Bacon's deliberative, prudential work. A tradition of literary study that had preserved deliberative Baconian prudence as well as epideictic Sidneyan defense would not have found itself as isolated and alienated from the worlds of political action, scientific inquiry, and rhetorical discourse as Krieger's tradition and its system, and it might

24 Art Berman, *From the New Criticism to Deconstruction* (Urbana and Chicago: University of Illinois Press, 1988).

not have found itself so preoccupied with poetry as a futile but beautiful means of escape from those other worlds. Such a tradition would have been better prepared to accept Robbins's invitation to "distinguish particular institutional alternatives from each other rather than condemning (or praising) them all together" (768); it would have been more alert to the resonances of Baconian instauration and enterprise in Wordsworth's experimental, progressive projects for poetry and criticism; and it would have been quicker to recognize the history of rhetoric, broadly understood, as part of its own history instead of excluding that history along with Bacon himself.

A history that had regularly connected rhetoric and "literature" instead of treating them as diverse schools with diverse particular histories would have made it possible sooner to recognize Wordsworth's direct links with the eighteenth-century rhetoricians who immediately preceded him and to avoid the parallel but mutually unread stories that the historians of rhetoric and of criticism tell. If we follow M. H. Abrams's account of the history of criticism in *The Mirror and the Lamp* (1953), as Robbins does, the pragmatic or rhetorical orientation of criticism focused on audience was displaced in the Romantic period and after by the expressive orientation focused on the poet and epitomized by Wordsworth and Coleridge. If we follow Wilbur Samuel Howell's account of the history of the "New Rhetoric" in *Eighteenth-Century British Logic and Rhetoric* (1971), nineteenth-century study of rhetoric and *belles-lettres* narrowed its purview to *belles-lettres* alone and abandoned its "concern with rhetoric as an active literary discipline." Nineteenth-century departments of rhetoric and *belles-lettres* turned into departments of English literature and devoted "all their efforts to the poetic and imaginative forms" that the New Rhetoric had failed adequately to theorize.[25]

In his recent book, *Forming the Critical Mind*, however, James Engell claims in his chapter "The New Rhetoricians: Semiotics, Theory, and Psychology," that "The New Rhetoricians establish a critical theory that becomes the spine of romantic poetics and criticism," that "the New Rhetoricians have more in common with Hazlitt, Coleridge, and Wordsworth" than with their eighteenth-century critical contemporaries, and that the New Rhetoricians profoundly shaped the topics and tastes of the great Romantic critics

25 Wilbur Samuel Howell, *Eighteenth-Century British Logic and Rhetoric* (Princeton: Princeton University Press, 1971), 714.

and poets.[26] This radical and potentially fruitful claim is in danger of getting lost in Engell's genially unpolemical chapter in the midst of a much more wide-ranging book that accommodates what Arac calls the Harvard School of literary history with recent European critical theory. Although Engell cites both Abrams and Howell, he does not highlight how dramatically his view of an intellectual link between eighteenth-century rhetorical theory and nineteenth-century literary theory departs from their widely received views. He declares that the school of Adam Smith, George Campbell, Joseph Priestley, Hugh Blair, James Beattie, Thomas Gibbons, Lord Kames, Thomas Sheridan, and Robert Lowth constitutes the "most important and cohesive group" of English inquirers into "the psychological, semiotic, and linguistic foundations of literature" until the twentieth century, and he shows that both Wordsworth and Coleridge continue the inquiries of this group in their poetry and criticism, but he does not invoke or address the weary weight of institutional inertia and habitual history that have prevented most rhetoricians and literary critics from seeing what he has to show us (195–96). He recalls Saintsbury's radical recognition that "the New Rhetoric is nothing less than 'the Art of Literature, or in other words Criticism,'" and he advocates a "salutary ... return to this basic concept of rhetoric," but he does not register in his own rhetoric the powerful opposition this view would have to overcome. He does not examine whether this new placement of Coleridge and Wordsworth within a common rhetorical intellectual tradition would modify his investment, as a Coleridgean, in Coleridge's criticism of Wordsworth or revise his understanding of Coleridge's critical position, or require a distinction between what Wordsworth and Coleridge learned from their rhetorical sources, but we may nevertheless recognize these questions and their importance for the Wordsworthian tradition I am constructing. The whole tired story of the revolutionary emergence of Romantic expressivist poetics from eighteenth-century pragmatic poetics – a story that has underwritten the study of "literature," separated it from the study of speech, and confused the reception of Wordsworth's critical prose – has to be revised in the light of this new version of the key figures and emphases of eighteenth-century poetics and rhetoric. Here, as in every other historical moment I have touched upon, much more inquiry and argument would be required to make persuasive and

26 James Engell, *Forming the Critical Mind: Dryden to Coleridge* (Cambridge, Mass.: Harvard University Press, 1989), 204.

fruitful connections between these figures and emphases and the Wordsworthian tradition I want to construct, but I hope I have said enough to suggest an agenda for such inquiry and to supply a pretext for such argument, much as Arac, Robbins, and others have provided the pretexts for my present argument.

Engell's account of the New Rhetoricians brings the tradition I have been making down to the texts of Wordsworth and Coleridge themselves, but we must bring it down to ourselves in the present to make it our own. Much of the rest of this book will be engaged in elaborating the Wordsworthian position and working out its affiliations and oppositions in recent criticism, but several more steps in the syllabus may be suggested here. First, if Coleridge is not a satisfactory source on Wordsworth's poetry and poetics, neither is Mill or Arnold, both of whom remain important authorities for current critical voices. Mill underwrites the spontaneous, emotional Wordsworthianism that makes an easier target than Wordsworth himself for Abrams's judgments in *The Mirror and the Lamp*, and Arnold's poet of nature and joy makes too easy a mark for modernist irony (see my discussion of de Man's essay "Wordsworth and the Victorians" in Chapter 6). For all the influence of Wordsworthianism in the nineteenth century and for all its persistence in the present, it is not clear that any rhetorical or critical voices from that century recognized or elaborated the Wordsworth I want to promote. Arac's turn to Pater or Richard Poirier's to Emerson might be explored further as possible exceptions.

In the twentieth century I would set John Dewey's *Art as Experience* (1934) – rich with both Wordsworthian and Coleridgean influence but committed fundamentally to the Wordsworthian continuity between ordinary experience and aesthetic experience – against I. A. Richards's contemporary *Coleridge on Imagination* and his earlier influential appropriations from Coleridge in *Principles of Literary Criticism*, sources whose impact on such crucial mid-twentieth-century constitutional interpreters as M. H. Abrams and Cleanth Brooks can hardly be exaggerated.[27] Brian Caraher's theoretical work on Dewey and Wordsworth will help make a place for Dewey's voice, which, like Bacon's, has been largely ignored by both New

27 John Dewey, *Art as Experience* (New York: Capricorn, 1934). I. A. Richards, *Coleridge on Imagination* (Bloomington: Indiana University Press, 1960), and *Principles of Literary Criticism* (New York: Harcourt, Brace & World, 1925). For a discussion of Richards and his influence see the beginning of Chapter 8 below.

Critics and their recent antagonists. Richard Rorty, another Deweyan who has recently been characterized as a Baconian, has also come, in his flight from philosophy, to places that resonate with Wordsworth's voice.[28]

I will try to show in the next three chapters why the works of the Bakhtin School are still for me the most fruitful elaboration of premises like Wordsworth's, but those works, too, need to be located for Western readers in an intellectual tradition that can help us to trace the tradition they share with Wordsworth. We should recall at a minimum, however, that Bakhtin's relevance to our recent rethinking of the critical tradition is not merely a faddish adoption of a previously unknown critical authority but an appropriate choice of authority for our critique of New Criticism, which recognized in Wellek and Warren's *Theory of Literature* its affinities to the Russian formalist sources the Bakhtin School criticizes and helps us to criticize.[29]

I hope that my remarks in this section will lead other teachers, students, and engaged historians of criticism to see Robbins's Gorgias, Bernal's Herodotus, my Quintilian, Payne's Chaucer, Sheats's Bacon, Engell's New Rhetoricians, Caraher's Dewey, and my Bakhtin as parts of a connected intellectual itinerary whose texts share important critical tendencies. If others were moved to explore that itinerary in teaching and further inquiry, the alternative tradition and system I am calling for might come to provide the shared premises and story for a democratic and demystified common critical enterprise. If I have not single-handedly here brought that alternative tradition and system into being, I hope at least to have made connections that some of my predecessors have missed and pointed the way for some who will follow me.

28 Caraher, *Wordsworth's "Slumber" and the Problematics of Reading* (University Park: Pennsylvania State University Press, 1991). Giles Gunn links Rorty with Bacon in "Rorty's *Novum Organum*," *Raritan* 10 (1990): 80–103.

29 René Wellek and Austin Warren, *Theory of Literature* (New York: Harcourt Brace, 1942). See my "Dialogic Criticism," in *Contemporary Literary Theory*, ed. G. Douglas Atkins and Laura Morrow (Amherst: University of Massachusetts Press, 1989), 214–28. See also A. C. Goodson, "Structuralism and Critical History in the Moment of Bakhtin," in *Tracing Literary Theory*, ed. Joseph Natoli, 27–53.

Proverbs of criticism and metonymies
of critical authority

The establishment of critical systems or traditions or authorities is as complex a matter as their displacement. When A. C. Goodson writes that "it is not the scholars but the leading critics who shape the view of tradition, literary and critical at once, by which we read and learn" (*Verbal Imagination*, 6), his "not ... but" formulation is as misleading as Arac's proposal to turn from Coleridge to Wordsworth, for the scholars are invested in the leading critics and their views of tradition and help to interpret, consolidate, and perpetuate them. Like leading poets, leading critics have some say in how and whether we will read them, but not the final say. Wordsworth's fortunes as leading poet and leading critic have depended upon scholars' interests in his work and Coleridge's, and though his own words have remained available for new interpretation and appropriation, they have waited on us literary scholars and teachers to activate and assign them.

Literary scholars and teachers thus live on and give continuing life to what Bakhtin calls "socially significant verbal performance[s]." These performances can "infect with [their] own intentions" – "sometimes for a long period of time and for a wide circle of persons" – "certain aspects of language that had been affected by [their] semantic and expressive impulse[s], imposing on them specific semantic nuances and specific axiological overtones," thus creating "slogan-words, curse-words, praise-words, and so forth."[30] What Lionel Trilling felicitously called "proverbs of criticism" are the lasting effects of such verbal performances, the tags with which we associate an author's name on qualifying exams, the buzz words we must echo or struggle with to make ourselves heard in a given social formation, the commonplace sediments of critical inquiry or literary journalism that mark the establishment of a literary or critical tradition.

The proverbs through which Trilling thought Wordsworth's Preface "has established itself ... firmly in our minds" he also thought led to deplorable misunderstanding of Wordsworth. "Spontaneous overflow of powerful feelings" and "emotion recollected in tranquillity" held sway, and still hold sway, not because of their centrality to Wordsworth's argument, and not, I should add, because

30 M. M. Bakhtin, *The Dialogic Imagination*, ed. Michael Holquist, trans. Caryl Emerson and Michael Holquist (Austin: University of Texas Press, 1981), 290.

Coleridge emphasized them – their tradition is independent of *Biographia Literaria* – but, Trilling thought, because of their eloquent boldness.[31] "The tenacity with which we hold in our mind our distortions of what Wordsworth actually does say suggests," Trilling writes, "the peculiar power of the essay as a whole … not chiefly as a discourse, but rather as a dramatic action … We are prepared to respond to its utterances less for their truth than for their happy boldness" ("The Fate of Pleasure," 73–74).

Trilling does not explain, however, why these bold and eloquent utterances should have caught on while another – his preferred one (and mine) – on the "grand elementary principle of pleasure" as the foundation of the "naked and native dignity of man"[32] did not. It would appear that even the boldness and eloquence of a leading poet's or a leading critic's utterance is not a sufficient ground for explaining its subsequent appropriation and repetition – its social significance. A study of the cultural interests, whether of Mill or Arnold or Abrams or Babbitt, and the social and institutional forces (including inertia) that have perpetuated the spontaneous emotional Wordsworth would be needed to supplement a rhetorical analysis of Wordsworth's inventive and stylistic departure from the commonplace before we could begin to understand how these Wordsworthian proverbs of criticism have stood for "Wordsworth" for so long for so many. The interests of both his admirers and his detractors in this selective representation would need to be examined, for even Irving Babbitt acknowledges, "I call attention to the Rousseauistic and primitivistic elements in Wordsworth but do not assert that this is the whole truth about Wordsworth."[33] The metonymy whereby an author's name is used to stand for a selection of his work – perhaps the most commonplace metonymy in literary

---

31 The tradition of these proverbs is, I believe, Arnoldian, mediated by Irving Babbitt, M. H. Abrams, and many others. For an argument that "spontaneous overflow" is "not by any means central to [Wordsworth's] own critical theory," see Chapter 1 of Stephen M. Parrish, *The Art of "Lyrical Ballads"* (Cambridge, Mass.: Harvard University Press, 1973), which challenges Abrams's placement of Wordsworth in Abrams's terms. For an effort to interpret what "spontaneity" means for Wordsworth, see Paul Magnuson, "Wordsworth and Spontaneity," in *The Evidence of the Imagination*, ed. Donald H. Reiman *et al.* (New York: New York University Press, 1978), 101–18.

32 Thus in Trilling – "native" and "naked" are reversed in Wordsworth's text.

33 Irving Babbitt, *Rousseau and Romanticism* (1919; reprint New York: World Publishing, 1955), 10.

study – serves both the author's friends and opponents and makes the author's name the word over which they are ultimately likely to wage their struggles.[34]

There are, then, plural "Wordsworths" and "Coleridges" abroad in the divergent appropriations of different schools and traditions of Wordsworthian and Coleridgean criticism. To displace one "Coleridge" may be simply to find another one in place and to call for the replacement of "Coleridge" by "Wordsworth" risks establishing the *wrong* "Wordsworth." The "Wordsworth" criticized by Coleridge has little or nothing in common with the "Wordsworth" enshrined by Trilling's proverbs or with the "Wordsworth" I have recovered from Wordsworth's texts. The "Wordsworth" of *The Mirror and the Lamp* has little in common even with the "Wordsworth" of *Natural Supernaturalism*. And we must ask whether the "Coleridge" we have set out to displace, the "Coleridge" whose criticism has been proverbialized by I. A. Richards and the New Critics, is the only available Coleridge or the "true Coleridge" or the most useful "Coleridge" for our present purposes.

A. C. Goodson has recently argued that "he" is not. He rejects the "Coleridge" constructed by I. A. Richards and American New Criticism from "a handful of poems and a dozen formulaic critical passages" (xvii) concerned with imagination and the symbol. In his place Goodson ventures a Coleridge "buried in marginalia and notes ... who confers the engagement and range which is missing in our sense of the other, the idealizing Coleridge of Chapter XIII of the *Biographia*" (45). Goodson's Coleridge appears not as a figure identified with other proverbs of criticism, however, but as an "exemplary reader" (59), who has informed the criticism of William Empson and Raymond Williams "not as an exemplar of critical method, rather as a model of response to writing in society" (58). Goodson associates Coleridge not with bold utterances but with a terse formulation that is admittedly "not a startling idea," though it is "a crucial one for ... modern criticism": "'Activity of thought in the play of words'" (51), and he presses home the ways in which Empson

---

34 Quintilian identifies this type of metonymy as a way to "indicate an invention by substituting the name of the inventor" and illustrates it with the example of speaking "of 'Virgil' when we mean 'Virgil's poems.'" *Institutes of Oratory*, 4 vols., trans. H. E. Butler (Cambridge, Mass.: Harvard University Press, 1921–22), Book VIII, VI.23–26. Which poems or lines of poems we had in mind would be the next question to ask.

and Williams had Coleridge in mind as they traced and engaged in that activity in their readings. By focusing on "Coleridge's example" (78) instead of his principles, Goodson can claim him as an important and still vital shaping influence for critical programs more social and democratic than those of the Tory aesthetes with whom his name has been most commonly associated.

Having affirmed Lentricchia's hope that "the muse would be demystified and democratized and [that]...younger critics would somehow link up poetry with the world again" (ANC 7), I must welcome a Coleridge who, Goodson writes, "was committed from the outset to the social horizon which Lentricchia would recuperate for critical purpose,"[35] but I must also declare some reservations. I am not confident, in the first place, that Goodson's exemplary reader Coleridge can displace the more familiar metaphysically principled Coleridge whose "formulae for imagination remain the standard version of his position" (xii). The latter figure is concentrated, for one thing, through repeated citations and anthology selections, while the former is dispersed, as Goodson admits, through notebooks, letters, and marginal entries that were never part of the living Coleridge's public utterances, though scholars have now made them available to us. To make his Coleridge prevail, or even take his place, beside the familiar one, Goodson would first have to *produce* him in selections and commentaries that made his example available as his selected principles have been.

It will also be difficult, on the evidence of Goodson's own argument, to put to rest Coleridge's "formulae for imagination" and the reading of Wordsworth they produce. Goodson distances himself at some points in his argument from Coleridge's criticisms of Wordsworth, but at other points he reproduces the Wordsworthian proverbs of criticism that justified Coleridge's judgments and deploys them in his own argument. Goodson focuses on Coleridge's objections to Wordsworth's declaration that the "best part of language" "originally derived" from the "best objects" (LB 245),

---

35 *Verbal Imagination*, 204–05 n. 3. Goodson overstates Lentricchia's opposition to Coleridge in declaring him "against everything associated with Coleridge's name" (xii). Lentricchia affirms the "irreducible humanist romanticism of Wordsworth and Coleridge" that preserves the "active, conscious subject as the triggering force in the poetic process" (ANC 13) and he defends Coleridge against de Man's charges of bad faith (294), even as he attacks the same New Critical Coleridgean proverbs of criticism from which Goodson attempts to distance himself.

making Wordsworth a partisan of the "matter-of-fact" literal image while Coleridge stands for the word shaped by imaginative thought. Goodson properly defends Wordsworth from this characterization (see esp. pp. 106–07), but he also calls upon the very same version of Wordsworth to link Leavis's "naive mimeticism" with "Wordsworth's archaic emphasis on 'the best objects from which the best part of language is originally derived'" (31).

The more familiar figure of Coleridge would appear to continue to exert considerable power over Goodson's judgment of Wordsworth, but I believe that figure also prevents Goodson from recognizing the non-Coleridgean source of his own most powerful critical insights. For me the most powerful and persuasive part of Goodson's argument is his reading of Coleridge's Conversation Poems as "deeply conflicted and problematic" manifestations of a "poetics of response" that "began from the language of the other" and "responded to an existing discourse" (178–79). Goodson shows how the words of identifiable others provoke and produce Coleridge's poetic utterances, making them what I will call in the next chapter manifestations not of poetic imagination but of dialogic sensitivity to what others have said.

Goodson, however, associates Coleridge's example as a critic not with any insight into such conflict of competing languages but with his commitment to a "common language" (80, 201), and Goodson does not register the tension between those Coleridgean formulations and Williams's rejection of "such single vision." Williams, Goodson notes, recognizes the possibilities of "alternative worlds in a single word" and of language that registers "'very interesting periods of confusion and contradiction'" (70) like the ones Goodson demonstrates in Coleridge's Conversation Poems (and the one Stallybrass and White have led me to see in Wordsworth's Preface). Goodson, however, does not see that such dialogic phenomena are excluded from consideration by the Coleridgean hypothesis of common language. Although Goodson quotes Williams as criticizing Leavis's "'idealist accounts of language as a common possession'" (70), Goodson ten pages later celebrates Williams's supposed appreciation of Coleridge as one who judges writing "by the light of a shared experience and a common language," as if such light were not the naturalized light of particular classes in particular historical situations whose "shared experience" and "common language" could not possibly be shared by or common to all.

Goodson represents Wordsworth as one who criticized Coleridge's "poetics of response as an expression of compulsive dependency" (179), but I believe and will show in much of what follows that Wordsworth practiced and theorized a comparable poetics of response, sensitive to the diversity of social languages and the diversity of world views and evaluations they embodied. What I would call Goodson's dialogic reading of Coleridge's Conversation Poems demonstrates to me that Wordsworth and Coleridge practiced, in some cases, the very same poetics – socially responsive, defensive, provoked by the otherness of the words of others. What Goodson's persistence in Coleridge's hypothesis of "common language" suggests to me is that the critical prestige of this hypothesis has obscured and continues to obscure not only Wordsworth's poetry and theory[36] but also Coleridge's poetry. Williams clearly rejects this hypothesis, and Goodson rejects it in practice though not yet in theory. Were he to bring his own theory into conformity with his best practice, it is not clear that the new "Coleridge" he recommends in *Verbal Imagination* would stand as high as Williams, or perhaps even as Wordsworth, in his critical estimation. If such a Coleridge is to serve the purposes I think my present project shares with Goodson's program for "the formation of institutional practices" (xv), that Coleridge will need what Goodson says Wordsworth's dialogic experiments needed – "severe keeping" (113).

But "Wordsworth," too, will need such keeping in a discursive situation in which his name has come to stand for so many different aspects of his work. In the next chapter, I will examine some of the versions of "Wordsworth" that have laid claim to his name in recent criticism and will put forward a dialogic "Wordsworth" as an appropriate and productive alternative to them. My addition of "dialogic" to my Lentricchian litany of "democratic" and "demystifying" values in my "Wordsworth" will be my attempt to establish a memorable – even an alliterative – slogan that could stand for "Wordsworth" in current critical debates. My effort, however, will not be to displace but to place the other versions of "Wordsworth" I consider and to make a place among them for one that I think promises to serve both Wordsworth and us well.

36 See my arguments in both "Coleridge's Interpretation of Wordsworth's Preface" and *Making Tales*.

❖❖

3

Wordsworth's dialogic art

❖❖

For me personally, certain studies in structuralist and post-structuralist theory have led to a particular way of naming and describing my new orientation. Calling it "semiotic" is simply my way of taming it, of trying to obtain textual power over it – which is what naming is all about. Along with the name "semiotics," of course, come new objects of study and new methods of studying.

"Interpretation and Criticism in the Classroom"
Robert Scholes,

If, as I believe, the historical situation of Wordsworthian criticism today is not dominated by a single authoritative voice – not Coleridge's or M. H. Abrams's or Geoffrey Hartman's or Paul de Man's or Jerome McGann's – or by a single name for his art – not "expressive" or "imaginative" or "visionary" or "rhetorical" or "ideological" – then the problem of locating ourselves in that situation, as I have just argued, is not a matter of displacing a dominant voice or name and replacing it with neglected ones. The positing of such a dominant authority has simplified the revisionist stances many of us have taken to insert ourselves into recent critical debates, but I believe that we must imagine another form for those debates and another way to enter them if they are to become productive – I would almost say progressive – dialogues. We need to find a way to imagine the multiplicity of would-be authorities and the multiplicity of competing names they put forward for Wordsworth's art that does not reduce the situation to a struggle against the supposed hegemony of a dominant voice or to a despair at the "chaos" of divergent voices, and we need to find a way to enter that dialogue that not only respects the claims of those who have gone before us but also claims the respect of our contemporaries. If we choose not to magnify our struggles into Oedipal or revolutionary battles with our critical Fathers or to give up struggling altogether in the face of hopeless confusion, how can we think about what we are doing in a way that justifies and dignifies the enterprise to which we would contribute and our contributions to it?

Bakhtin offers an image of the prose writer's situation that may help us imagine both our need for the names others have already given our object and our struggle to make a name for ourselves among them.

> For the writer of artistic prose the object reveals first of all precisely the socially heteroglot multiplicity of its names, definitions, and value judgments. Instead of the virginal fullness and inexhaustibility of the object itself, the prose writer confronts a multitude of routes, roads and paths that have been laid down in the object by social consciousness. Along with the internal contradictions in the object itself, the prose writer witnesses as well the unfolding of social heteroglossia *surrounding* the object, the Tower-of-Babel mixing of languages that goes on around any object; the dialectics of the object are interwoven with the social dialogue surrounding it. For the prose writer, the object is a focal point for heteroglot voices among which his own voice must also sound; these voices create the background necessary for his own voice, outside of which his artistic prose nuances cannot be perceived, and without which they "do not sound".   (DN 278)

Unlike Arac's spatial/visual language of displacement and shifting focus, Bakhtin's auditory language here permits several voices to occupy the same place at the same time and to sound off against each other in a way that they would not sound alone. Voices already in place give new voices a background against which they can define themselves, and multiple voices provide multiple occasions to elaborate the nuances of a new word in a field of other words. If the other voices and their words were displaced or unheard or forgotten, a new voice with its new word would have that much less to say for itself and the overall field of words for the object would be that much less articulated.

Competing names for Wordsworth's art

If we choose not to posit a single dominant voice that has given an authoritative name to Wordsworth's art, the constellation of adjectives naming the most salient quality of his art offers a rich field for further articulation. M. H. Abrams's adjective "expressive," Northrop Frye's term "low mimetic," Coleridge's and Geoffrey Hartman's "imaginative" or "visionary," Robert Langbaum's "dramatic," and John Danby's "ironic" have held larger or smaller parts of the field since the Second World War, representing some of the most significant critical schools and traditions of English studies in that period. In the last decade deconstructive readers have highlighted Wordsworth's "rhetorical" art and New Historicist readers have emphasized his "ideological" art, while Harold Bloom's vocabulary echoes in Clifford Siskin's deconstructive discussion of Wordsworth's "revisionary" art. Thomas McFarland has also spoken up during the same period for his idiosyncratic adjective "diasparactic."[1]

Into this noisy social dialogue – hardly the "still, sad music of humanity" – I and others have been trying to introduce Bakhtin's word "dialogic" and "make it sound" amid its proliferating competitors and users. My work in *Making Tales* was already committed to the phrase "poetics of speech" when translations of Bakhtin under the sign of the dialogic first appeared, though the work of Bakhtin's School figures importantly in my argument there. More recently Tilottama Rajan has suggested the potential fruitfulness of a dialogic reading of Wordsworth, Paul Magnuson has appropriated the term for a major study of Wordsworth's and Coleridge's lyrics, and Gordon Thomas has dared to use the barbarous Bakhtinian phrase "dialogized heteroglossia" in the very heart of the Lake District. Jonathan Arac has called upon the term in passing in his critique of recent Wordsworthian criticism. Most recently, Gene W. Ruoff has explored the dialogic interrelations of Wordsworth's and Coleridge's major lyrics of 1802, though he distances himself from "literary dialogics" along with all other theoretical explication of his practice. Until Magnuson's, Rajan's, Thomas's and Ruoff's work appeared, apparently uninfluenced by my own, two of my graduate students were the only ones I know to have published explicitly dialogic readings of Wordsworth's poetry.[2]

1 Abrams, *The Mirror and the Lamp*. Coleridge, *Biographia Literaria*. Northrop Frye, *Anatomy of Criticism* (Princeton: Princeton University Press, 1957). Geoffrey Hartman, *Wordsworth's Poetry 1787–1814* (New Haven: Yale University Press, 1964). Robert Langbaum, *The Poetry of Experience* (New York: Norton, 1957). Danby, *The Simple Wordsworth*. Clifford Siskin, "Romantic Genre: Lyric Form and Revisionary Behavior in Wordsworth," *Genre* 16 (Summer 1983): 137–55. McFarland, *Romanticism and the Forms of Ruin*.

2 Tilottama Rajan, "Displacing Post-Structuralism: Romanticism after Paul de Man," *SiR* 24 (Winter 1985): 451–74, and "Romanticism and the Death of Lyric Consciousness," in *Lyric Poetry: Beyond New Criticism*, ed. Chaviva Hošek and Patricia Parker (Ithaca: Cornell University Press, 1985): 194–207. Gordon K.

Much still remains to be said for the word. Its users to date have been more eager to demonstrate its power to illuminate various poems than to articulate its place among the competing words for Wordsworth's poetry or to explore the implications of choice of adjectives for our reading of the poet and his oeuvre. The articulation of that place will occupy the bulk of this chapter, but the implications of the choice deserve a moment's attention first.

Each of the competing adjectives I am going to consider carries at least three kinds of implications. First, an adjective takes its meaning from a tradition of critical usage and from the work of individual critics within a tradition. In this context it carries with it a set of related terms, topics, and models of poetic practice that direct and limit the questions we can ask of a poem or a poet's body of works. Second, in consequence of this limited focus, our use of an adjective tends to sort out certain kinds of poems from the poet's works and certain parts of individual poems for special attention, leaving others in the background. Finally, by guiding these selections, our choice of an adjective colors our judgment and enjoyment of both the poems and the art of the poet who wrote them. Our choice of adjectives thus shapes the canon of works and parts of works that the metonymy "Wordsworth" stands for in our minds, as well as the instruments of critical inquiry we bring to them and the judgments we make of them. A new adjective thus has the potential to reshape "Wordsworth," criticism, and us.

In order to show what difference our choice of adjectives makes to our reading of Wordsworth's poetry, I have chosen a poem whose critical fortunes have not been very happy – "The Sailor's Mother." Two of Wordsworth's earliest and most influential promoters singled the poem out for blame: Coleridge dissected its faults in the *Biographia*; Arnold just called it a failure. In showing how earlier critical adjectives guided and confirmed this judgment and how the term "dialogic" challenges it, I will prepare the way for showing that

Thomas, "The *Lyrical Ballads* Ode: 'Dialogized Heteroglossia,'" *WC* 20 (1989): 102–05. Magnuson, *Coleridge and Wordsworth. Genealogies* 51. Gene W. Ruoff, *Wordsworth and Coleridge: The Making of the Major Lyrics, 1802–1804*, 14–15 and *passim*. See also Stephen Bidlake, "'Hidden Dialog' in 'The Mad Mother' and 'The Complaint of the Forsaken Indian Woman'," *WC* 13 (1982): 188–93; and Margaret Garner, "The Anapestic Lyrical Ballads: New Sympathies," *WC* 13 (1982): 183–88. My review of Ruoff's book [in *European Romantic Review* 1 (1990): 99–102] argues that his work can be assimilated to the dialogic theory he resists.

what makes this poem "dialogic" is a property widely shared by
Wordsworth's best-known as well as by his most neglected poems.

> One morning (raw it was and wet,
> A foggy day in winter time)
> A Woman in the road I met,
> Not old, though something past her prime:
> Majestic in her person, tall and straight;
> And like a Roman matron's was her mien and gait.
>
> The ancient Spirit is not dead;
> Old times, thought I, are breathing there;
> Proud was I that my country bred
> Such strength, a dignity so fair:
> She begg'd an alms, like one in poor estate;
> I look'd at her again, nor did my pride abate.
>
> When from these lofty thoughts I woke,
> With the first word I had to spare
> I said to her, "Beneath your Cloak
> What's that which on your arm you bear?"
> She answer'd soon as she the question heard,
> "A simple burthen, Sir, a little Singing-bird."
>
> And, thus continuing, she said,
> "I had a Son, who many a day
> Sail'd on the seas; but he is dead;
> In Denmark he was cast away;
> And I have been as far as Hull, to see
> What clothes he might have left, or other property.
>
> The Bird and Cage they both were his;
> 'Twas my Son's Bird; and neat and trim
> He kept it: many voyages
> This Singing-bird hath gone with him;
> When he last sail'd he left the Bird behind;
> As it might be, perhaps, from bodings of his mind.
>
> He to a Fellow-lodger's care
> Had left it, to be watch'd and fed,
> Till he came back again; and there
> I found it when my Son was dead;
> And now, God help me for my little wit!
> I trail it with me, Sir! he took so much delight in it."[3]

A dialogic view of this poem gives special importance to a feature
that most other critical perspectives would recognize, even if they

3 *Poems, in Two Volumes, and Other Poems, 1800–1807 by William Wordsworth*, ed.
Jared Curtis (Ithaca: Cornell University Press, 1983), 77–78.

would not accord it the importance I do – the distinction between the speech of the poet and the speech of the character in the poem. For Bakhtin, "the boundaries of each concrete utterance as a unit of speech communication are determined by a *change of speaking subjects,*" and the mode of relation between those subjects has much to do with the genre and function of any work that embodies more than one voice. Bakhtin further claims that "the utterance is not a conventional but a real unit, clearly delineated by a change of speaking subjects," and I will presuppose in my analysis that the other critical perspectives I examine would acknowledge its reality, even though they would interpret its significance differently.[4] My dialogic perspective will interrogate the other critical perspectives, then, whatever their other purposes, by asking how they would understand the characters of those two voices and appreciate their relations to one another in the poem.

M. H. Abrams's longstanding account of Wordsworth's "expressive" poetics would make the speeches of the poet and the woman parallel but disconnected instances of the natural expression of feeling. Abrams's well-known formulation allows us to speak of the common psychological genesis of the two kinds of speeches, but when it comes to trying to describe their relation to one another, we can only say that the poet is trying to speak as naturally as the woman, taking her naturalness as a "model" for his own. To read the poem as "expressive" would compel us to try to break it into distinct lyric utterances, ignoring the poet's report of the woman's speech and emphasizing his sentimental reversion to her naive naturalness.

However, because Abrams treats Wordsworth as a theorist of natural expression rather than of poetic art, I may have misappropriated his adjective for use with my noun.[5] Certainly his argument belongs to the Arnoldian tradition that emphasizes the naturalness of Wordsworth's expression, even as it suspects that such expression is insufficient in poetry. When this tradition has described Wordsworth's theory and practice as "expressive," it has usually been to criticize their limits rather than to explore or explain their virtues. It should perhaps not surprise us that this adjective does not go very far toward accounting for the poem in question.

4 M. M. Bakhtin, *Speech Genres and Other Late Essays*, trans. Vern W. McGee (Austin: University of Texas Press, 1986), 71–72.
5 See Parrish's attempt to emphasize Wordsworth's art in opposition to this Arnoldian line of belief in the first chapter of *The Art of the "Lyrical Ballads".*

If Abrams's adjective "expressive" may modify a natural process, Frye's term "low mimetic" unquestionably identifies a kind of art. Ostensibly following Aristotle, Frye invents this term to classify the social level of objects of imitation compared to that of the audience, and he applies it to both Wordsworth's theory of art and to the characters he represents in his poems. Frye's perspective is one of the few I will be considering that allows something good to be said about "The Sailor's Mother." He considers the woman's speech as a successful low mimetic imitation of pathetic inarticulateness and thus values it as an artistic representation, but he does not consider the relation of her speech to that of the poem's speaker. If the poet's representation of the woman's speech is sufficient to characterize the poem as "low mimetic" in its fictional mode, perhaps Frye would have us say that the speaker's more heightened diction makes its thematic mode (the mode in which the poet speaks) "high mimetic," but how from such diverse modes of speaking and representing does one go on, as Frye does, to classify Wordsworth's art as "low mimetic"? And how can he prevent the difference between "high" and "low" from carrying evaluative weight? For all his claims that the scale of modes is descriptive rather than evaluative, he finds the "queer, ghoulish" appeal of pathos less worthy than the appeals of the more elevated modes of high mimetic tragedy, of romance, and of myth.[6]

Coleridge does not even pretend that the distinction of diction he finds in such poems is without evaluative weight. It makes him feel "an abrupt downfall" when the poem shifts from the poet's expression of "the music of his own thoughts" in the second stanza to his imitation of "the *real* and *very* language of *low* and *rustic life*" in the fourth. Coleridge's adjectives for the elevated diction of the former stanza – the ones he thinks are characteristic of Wordsworth's genius – are "imaginative," "visionary," or simply "poetic"; for the inferior diction into which the latter stanzas fall his words are "dramatic," "real," or "prosaic." He can appreciate the qualities of dramatic diction when it is not mixed with the higher diction of the lyric poet's own imaginative utterance, but he finds that the mixture is one of the chief defects of Wordsworth's art. In his list of Wordsworth's faults he cites

6 Frye, *Anatomy of Criticism*, 39.

an undue predilection for the *dramatic* form in certain poems, from which one or the other of two evils result. Either the thoughts and diction are different from that of the poet, and then there arises an incongruity of style; or they are the same and indistinguishable, and then it presents a species of ventriloquism, where two are represented as talking, while in truth one man only speaks.[7]

For the moment we will not concern ourselves with "ventriloquism," which is the alleged vice of *The Excursion*. For Coleridge, "The Sailor's Mother" suffers from incongruity of style and would have been more delightful to him in prose. Having located the essence of poetry and of Wordsworth's art in the elevated passages expressive of the idealizing and unifying work of the secondary imagination, Coleridge cannot appreciate poems that fall from such heights or theories of poetry that declare such fallings off to be deliberate. His account of the poetic, imaginative, or visionary essence of Wordsworth's art has influenced the most persistent and powerful tradition of reading Wordsworth's poetry not only to prefer those poems or parts of poems that manifest these qualities but also to see those poems or parts that lack them as fallings off, lapses, or failures. Readers in this tradition, two of whom I will engage later in this chapter, feel the many interruptions of elevated passages as flaws, whether they are caused by the presentation of others' voices or by shifts in the poet's own voice.

The most fruitful innovation in this line of reading, first convincingly practiced by Geoffrey Hartman, has been to take the failures and fallings off as interesting symptoms of psychological complexes and existential anxieties rather than just as lapses in poetic decorum. One may read the same stylistic evidence either way, but Hartman's "avoidance of apocalypse" is far more compelling than Coleridge's "inconstancy of style" and far more productive of further readings. Like Paul de Man's alternative reading of such stylistic discrepancies as tropological structures that reveal profound truths about language, Hartman's reading of those discrepancies as revealing structures of consciousness has helped make writing about Wordsworth's poetry a central preoccupation of theoretically informed criticism during the past twenty-five years. But Hartman's and de Man's criticism and the criticism they have influenced have generally been concerned with discrepancies in the poet's own style rather than with discrepancies between his style and the style of a character like

7 Coleridge, *Biographia*, II, 69–71, 135.

the sailor's mother, and I reserve my extended engagements with them for Chapters 5 and 6.

Coleridge's distinction between imaginative and dramatic diction in Wordsworth allows not only for such reinterpretations of discrepancies between the two styles but also for explorations of the dramatic style itself. Robert Langbaum was the first to take the low road and persuasively apply the adjective "dramatic" to Words-worth's poems, but even he stops short of valuing Wordsworth's presentation of the speech of his characters. He still finds that the poet's "visual presentations" of his characters, composed under the "visionary stare" of Wordsworth's genius "give more insight into them than their own utterances."[8] Like Coleridge, he prefers the poet's elevated descriptions to the characters' represented words and leaves the connection between them unexamined.

Stephen Parrish, however, takes Langbaum's adjective and reverses his Coleridgean judgment of Wordsworth's art. He turns aside from the visionary passages and makes the "dramatic" elements of Wordsworth's art his principal focus. His reading of "The Thorn" as a dramatic monologue reveals the interest of following the "subtler windings" of one of Wordsworth's character's speeches. His discovery of Wordsworth's theoretical emphasis on drama recognizes the importance Wordsworth placed on the character's words.

Parrish's use of the term "dramatic," however, only shifts the focus from the poet's to the character's utterance and still fails to consider how they might be connected in a single poem. Parrish is as sorry to see Wordsworth adopt his own diction as the Coleridgeans are to see him stoop to imitate his rustic speakers. Though Wordsworth distinguishes between the parts of composition where the poet speaks in his own person and character and the parts where he speaks through the mouths of his characters, Parrish reads him as if he were talking about different *kinds* of composition.[9] He teaches us how to value dramatic poems like "The Thorn" but not poems combining poetic diction and prosaic speech like "The Sailor's Mother."

Through his choice of the adjective "ironic," John Danby addresses himself to the relation between those voices in the idiom of British New Criticism, which differs from American New Criticism in its claim that the "words on the page" are interesting not just as ambiguous words but as "the embodiment of living occasions." The

8 Langbaum, *The Poetry of Experience*, 71–72.
9 Parrish, *Art of the "Lyrical Ballads,"* 138.

ironies he praises in Wordsworth's *Lyrical Ballads* are not the American New Critic's verbal ironies contained in the ambiguous meanings of words themselves; the ironies are rather to be found in shifts of tone among "the narrator, the characters... and the poet himself as the finally responsible assembler" of the poem (38). Here is a formulation that promises to help describe the relations between poet's and character's voices in such poems as "The Sailor's Mother." In practice, however, Danby confines himself to examining shifts of tone within the poet's voice, overlooking shifts among voices of separate speakers. He gives us a Wordsworth whose art is to modulate his own voice to a variety of tones instead of one whose art is to achieve a sustained poetic elevation, but he leaves the relation between the character's voice and the poet's unexplored.

The adjectives I have examined so far represent what I take to be the most significant efforts of our predecessors to characterize Wordsworth's poetics and poems. They reflect the concepts and values of the principal interrelated traditions of criticism that have been current in America and England until recently – the Arnoldian, the Aristotelian, the Coleridgean, and the New Critical. All but the Arnoldian view developed by Abrams have produced interesting readings of selections of Wordsworth's poetry, but all leave unresolved the problem of how to describe and value the relation between the poet's voice and the voices of others he reports in such poems as "The Sailor's Mother."

The failure of all these perspectives to account for the relation of the utterances in "The Sailor's Mother" might tempt us to adopt Thomas McFarland's adjective "diasparactic" to describe the poem, for McFarland claims that Romantic poems generally and Wordsworth's in particular are characterized by incompleteness and disunity. McFarland's adjective would ratify the impression that the poem's parts are incoherent and teach us to recognize incoherence as the thing to be expected in Romantic poems. But this, to echo Wordsworth's response to an easy way out of another interesting problem, would be to encourage idleness and unworthy despair. We have other critical resources available that may reopen our inquiry instead of laying it to rest.

Bakhtin's term "dialogic"

The resource to which I turn has not been neglected by previous critics. Until recently it was just not available, and it does not sound particularly pertinent to an inquiry into Wordsworth's poems either. Mikhail Bakhtin wrote, after all, in the Soviet Union, mostly in the twenties and thirties, and his work has been translated into English only in the last twenty years. He does not write about Wordsworth or English Romantic poetry, except for a few mentions of Byron, and his word (in translation, of course) "dialogic" does not come from a theory of poetry but from a theory of the novel. But when the terms we have available fail us, we will naturally look to other traditions and genres for help. Frye's "low mimetic" category has already associated Wordsworth's art with that of the realistic novel, but as we have seen, this classification did not tell us very much about the relation of voices in a given poem. Bakhtin's work focuses precisely on how to describe and read that relation. The translations of the work of Bakhtin and his close collaborators on reported speech, on poetics understood as the reconstruction of tonal relations among speaker, hero, and listener, and on the dialogic genre of the novel, have given us a new resource for describing the dynamics of voices in Wordsworth's art.

At first glance, Bakhtin's model interestingly resembles Coleridge's. Like Coleridge, Bakhtin develops a contrast between poetic language and the language of prose, but he reverses Coleridge's subordination of prose to poetry. His analysis also resembles Coleridge's in claiming that poetry – always "in the narrow sense" (DN 260, 285) – excludes alien social languages and depends upon the poet's and his tradition's fabrication of a specifically poetic language superior to the languages of common speech, but Bakhtin analyzes not this poetic language in itself but the prose language of the novel that artistically organizes diverse social speech types and diverse languages – including poetic language – into a whole that sets the various languages against and puts them into communication with one another. This orchestrated display of diverse languages creates a dialogue among socially specific ways of "conceptualizing the world in words" (DN 292) and represents them as they coexist with, supplement, contradict, or address one another in people's consciousnesses.

Unlike Coleridge, Bakhtin makes no essential connection between verse composition and elevated language or between dialogic art and prose, though he does recognize culturally determined associations between them. Indeed, he is aware that poetic language becomes only one language among many in the dialogue created by the novel and that in certain times and places verse composition itself can become "novelized" and incorporate the dialogic interplay of the novel into its own diction. When poets cannot speak the elevated diction of their craft without hearing and acknowledging the countervailing accents of other crafts and classes, when they cannot rest in their most inspired utterances without admitting other voices that bring them down to earth, when they objectify their own language instead of dwelling within it, when they anticipate and accommodate their readers' probable responses and modify their descriptions of their heroes to take the heroes' own languages into account, they are novelized poets and their art is dialogic. Though for Coleridge such poets would be poets only part-time, for Bakhtin they are poets of an especially interesting kind whose art reflects the same awareness of ideological diversity and raises the same kinds of questions about it as the art of the novelist.

Bakhtin's notion of the novelized poet provides an alternative not only to Coleridge's view of poets as lyric visionaries but also to his alternative model of poets as dramatists who present diverse other voices from outside and usually above the world they depict. Bakhtin's novelists write from within the world whose voices they represent, and their voices are distinguished from the others not by their superior elevation or by their fingernail-paring silence but by their being the voices within which all the other voices appear. The novelist's is the voice that captures the other voices and refracts them to express an artistic purpose as well as to preserve the intentions of the characters' utterances. Novelists present the characters' speech mediated by their own interests in it and remarks about it. The novelist is never just the maker of a dramatized dialogue that presents the exchange of other voices but is a participant in dialogue with those represented voices, offering versions of their motives and of their significance for other purposes. When Wordsworth in 1815 writes that the distinguishing mark of narrative is the fact that "the Narrator, however liberally his speaking agents be introduced, is himself the source from which every thing primarily flows" (*Prose* III, 27), he has put his finger on the distinguishing mark of Bakhtin's novelistic genre as well, though he has not said how important this mark is to his own poems or what implications it might have for reading them.

"The Sailor's Mother" as dialogic narrative

"The Sailor's Mother" makes sense as a dialogic narrative. The whole poem is presented through the speech of a single speaker who relates not only the speech of the sailor's mother but also his own speech on the occasion of his meeting her and his thoughts upon first seeing her. He now tells how he first saw her, but he tells it having heard what she later said in response to his question. Since he tells of their exchange without anyone's asking, we can imagine that what moves him to speak is his further thought about it. It is as if his telling the anecdote were a continuation of the exchange he reports, addressed to his first impressions from the perspective of someone who has now heard what the woman has had to say for herself. It is by no means obvious that he hears her words as what Coleridge called an "abrupt downfall" from the elevation of his first impression.

The overall question a dialogic reading would ask of the poem is, how does the speaker reaccent his former thoughts and speech and the woman's speech in reporting them? Or to put it another way, how does he now hear himself after hearing her? One thing the juxtaposition of the language of his thoughts with the language of her speech does is to make both of them audible as languages, but it does not yet tell us how the speaker now hears them. If we do not jump to the conclusion that he hears an "abrupt downfall" in his shift from his own words to hers, what other possibilities are there? One is that he is not disappointed but fulfilled in what he hears her say, so that in reporting it as he does he feels that it requires no further comment. The poem's ending with her speech without narratorial comment suggests that the woman's speech somehow "speaks for itself" in answer to the speaker's original expectations, but what does it say?

Here we must listen again to the specific accents of his first impression. They are the accents not merely of a visionary or poetic elevation but of a socially, politically, and philosophically loaded interpretation of the woman's dignified bearing. In associating the woman's demeanor with that of a "Roman matron," with an "ancient Spirit" not yet dead, and with the pride of his country's continuing power to breed such strength and dignity, the speaker had made her an embodiment of his patriotic, historic, and cultural values. His initial vision thus reads her dignity in the light of his conservatism, his low expectations about the present time, and his Stoic theory of dignity. Listen now to just one passage of contemporary prose that will help us confirm and clarify the context of the speaker's values:

I hear, and I rejoice to hear, that the great lady, the other object of the triumph, has borne that day (one is interested that beings made for suffering should suffer well), and that she bears ... the imprisonment of her husband, and her own captivity, and the exile of her friends, and the insulting adulation of addresses, and the whole weight of her accumulated wrongs with a serene patience, in a manner suited to her rank and race, and becoming the offspring of a sovereign distinguished for her piety and her courage; that, like her, she has lofty sentiments; that she feels with the dignity of a Roman matron; that in the last extremity she will save herself from the last disgrace; and that if she must fall, she will fall by no ignoble hand.[10]

That is Edmund Burke's description of Marie Antoinette in captivity. His emphasis on the traditional aristocratic dignity with which his heroine bears her sufferings closely parallels that of Wordsworth's narrator's first internal utterance on seeing the sailor's mother. The narrator seems to have taken his first pleasure in the beggar woman's bearing by interpreting it as self-possessed and grounded in the same traditional sources of dignity Burke admires in the beleaguered queen. The terms of this perception level the distinction between beggar and queen by transferring the terms of admiration from the latter to the former. But the narrator finds a second source of pleasure in the woman's artless account of the bird she carries that compels him to reevaluate his first appreciation of her. Her dignified bearing, it turns out, is supported not by a Stoic ability to bear "accumulated wrongs" but by a hidden source of pleasure, a singing bird associated with the son she loved and lost, because it is something he loved and cared for and enjoyed and left behind for her.

One can imagine how such a discovery would please someone like Wordsworth more than a confirmation of his first vision, if one realizes that it would establish human dignity not on the basis of a traditional philosophic stance but on that of a grand elementary principle of pleasure such as he announced in the 1802 Preface to *Lyrical Ballads*, written within weeks of this poem. To echo the terms Wordsworth himself used in that Preface, the sailor's mother, looking on the complex of pain and pleasure of her relationship to her son,

10 Edmund Burke, *Reflections on the Revolution in France*, ed. Thomas H. D. Mahoney (New York: Bobbs-Merrill, 1955), 85.

finds in it an object that excites sympathies in her which, from the necessities of her nature, are accompanied by an overbalance of pleasure, and the poet, directing his attention to her sympathies and pleasures, discovers in them a confirmation of his disposition to celebrate the grand elementary principle of pleasure. If the joke is on the narrator and his highfalutin first impressions, it is not a painful joke since the impression that replaces the first one is, as he says of another poem, "more salutary" than the one it replaces. He reports his speech and hers, then, in the satisfaction that arises from her correction of his first impression; he hears himself ironically, as he hears her words with continuing pleasure in her pleasure.

"Dialogic," "communicative," and "ideological"

Gene Ruoff's 1972 reading of "The Sailor's Mother" anticipates several key points of the reading I have just presented as dialogic — without benefit of Bakhtin or cover of a thematizing adjective.[11] Beginning from close attention to Wordsworth's own poetic pronouncements, Ruoff argues that "The Sailor's Mother" illustrates Wordsworth's preference for the language of real and substantial action and suffering over the heightened language produced by poets, including Wordsworth himself. Ruoff writes: "The logic of the poem's development argues that the full revelation of the woman's strength and character is to be found in the story which she tells, that her voice is surer and more revealing than the poet's eye, even to the point that any formal closure by the poet would be irrelevant" (206). Ruoff further declares that "the expressive qualities of the woman's story depend largely upon the situation in which she tells it and the predisposition of the poet to whom she tells it" (207). Ruoff has clearly formulated the question I have characterized as dialogic and sketched the answer I have proposed to it without benefit of the adjective I have been recommending or any other foregrounded adjective.

I believe, however, that the adjective "dialogic" accounts for his successful reading better than the adjective Ruoff used along the way to link his reading with the linguistic pragmatics that informs it, namely "communicative," and I believe that a dialogic reading of the poem is likely to specify the "situational contexts" of an utterance

11 Ruoff, "Wordsworth on Language: Toward a Radical Poetics for English Romanticism," *WC* 3 (1972): 204–11.

differently than a reading informed by the characteristic communicative interests of pragmatics. Such a reading, as Ruoff characterizes it, treats poetic discourse as "an act of communication" that stresses the relationship between the poet and his audience (205) or alternatively the relationship between "signs and their users" (207). Neither of these formulations, however, accounts for the power of his reading of the poem. That reading does not emphasize the poet's consciousness of his audience and even less the woman's consciousness of her auditor. The poet-narrator is indeed impressed with the relation of the woman's words to herself and her situation – to her real and substantial suffering, but the power of her words for him comes not just from the authenticity of their relation to her situation but from their capacity to address unwittingly his interests and needs, as the leech-gatherer's words address other such interests and needs in "Resolution and Independence." What is most remarkable about the poem is that the pragmatic situation of begging and giving alms becomes an occasion for the poet to produce a patriotic vision, ask a question, and hear the answer to that question saying something its answerer could never have anticipated or understood. While a reading informed by pragmatics could account for the beggar's polite address to the poet and perhaps for other conventional aspects of their exchange, a dialogic reading can better account for the discrepancy between the awkward language in which the woman accounts for herself and her property and the ideologically charged languages that define the poet's response to her bearing and her words.

A dialogic reading will also direct us to specify, as I have tried to do, the contexts of that ideologically loaded diction by identifying its provenance in a field of other ideologically recognizable languages and even other specific utterances, while a reading informed by pragmatics will be more likely to specify the "situational context" in terms of who is saying what to whom, in the presence of what, and under what historically specifiable circumstances. Pragmatics will tend to emphasize, as Ruoff's theory does, the external "circumstantiality" of "thinking and observing in a particular place and at a particular time" (208) rather than the dialogic circumstantiality of echoing, addressing, and answering particular languages characteristic of particular ideological orientations to the world.

This distinction between dialogic analysis and communicative pragmatics may help to clarify the similitudes and dissimilitudes between my dialogic reading and the sort of ideological reading Jerome McGann advocates in *The Romantic Ideology*. Because a dialogic reading looks beyond this poem as text to the poem as cultural product – in this case, by connecting the voices in "The Sailor's Mother" with Burke's and Wordsworth's voices outside the poem and to the social and ideological values their words involve – I might hope to claim some affinity between my criticism and the criticism McGann advocates. McGann, after all, was the first Romanticist to call attention to Bakhtin's work in his essay on "Keats and the Historical Method."[12]

But McGann was much more interested in those parts of Bakhtin's oeuvre that emphasize the relation of a text to its external social situation than in those parts that emphasize the internal dialogization of texts themselves. McGann's recent argument for a dialectical rather than a dialogic criticism confirms that he rejects the dialogic in favor of the dialectical for the same reason that he earlier criticized the Romantic Ideology itself – that it is internal and self-enclosed, while dialectic confronts the writer with something entirely alien and arbitrarily related to himself. He does not, like Bakhtin, read internal dialogue as a reflection of and response to the words and ideologies of others but as an escape from the material presence of others, and he calls for "a self-conscious response to certain social and historical factors," not just for the dialogic impingement of one person's words on another person. As Anne Mellor has recently complained, McGann links ideology directly to the material situation of a class rather than to the dialogic situation of an individual speaker and collapses "dialogic distinctions" in a hypostatized monologic "Romantic Ideology."[13]

For McGann, I believe, my account of Wordsworth's dialogic art would finally fall short of exposing Wordsworth's ideological art, because it has failed to criticize the language of Wordsworth's grand elementary principle of pleasure itself as ideology or false consciousness. From this point of view Wordsworth's focus on the woman's pleasure in her son's singing bird simply replaces his first illusion about her with a second, all the more seductive because its

12 Jerome J. McGann, "Keats and the Historical Method in Literary Criticism," *MLN* 94 (1979): 988–1032.
13 Jerome J. McGann, "Some Forms of Critical Discourse," *Critical Inquiry* 11 (1985): 414. Anne K. Mellor, Review of Jerome McGann's *The Romantic Ideology*, *SiR* 25 (1986): 282–86.

putative ground is nature rather than history or culture. McGann would further correct the correction of evaluative stance that Wordsworth celebrates, criticizing Wordsworth the narrator's complacent acquiescence in the correction of Wordsworth the character's initial false vision of the sailor's mother. The ultimately ameliorative theme of the narration discredits its presentation of Wordsworth's responsiveness to correction from another person's voice. McGann, I imagine, would not take the woman at her word either, but she would be less responsible for her false consciousness than the sophisticated and once revolutionary poet who should have known better than to have absolved himself of political responsibility for changing the material condition of beggars just because this beggar finds pitiful ideological consolation for herself. He should have been shocked by the fact of her poverty and indignant about its political and economic causes, not exalted by his idiosyncratic interpretation of her words.

Such dialectical certainty would collapse the differences between the voices I have been at some pains to distinguish under the single category of illusion or ideology or false consciousness, as it would break on the hard wheel of history the poetic art whose proper pleasure I have tried to take. The dialogic reading I have offered lacks the dialectical self-assurance to dismiss Wordsworth's pleasure principle and to declare, as McGann declares of "Tintern Abbey" that "what appears to be an immense gain ... is in reality the deepest and most piteous loss" (RI 88), but I as a dialogic reader also cannot prevent McGann's voice from troubling my pleasure in Wordsworth's pleasure. Still, to take comfort at the loss of friends and kindred by cherishing something that one's loved one has cherished does seem natural to me, or if not natural, then at least widely shared by persons of diverse class and political persuasion – and to juxtapose the voice that takes such comfort with a voice that celebrates more conventional nobility and dignity does reveal the value of such comfort in a new way.

Further to juxtapose a critical voice that denigrates attention to such losses and compensations as a distraction from the higher imperatives of political action is to hear an echo of Pericles' call to subordinate mothers' (and, I would add, poets') losses and comforts to heroic action on behalf of the community. The enumeration of unwriteable heroic poems in the first book of *The Prelude* shows that Wordsworth himself heard this voice, and much of the argument of that poem shows that he felt answerable for not meeting its claims. His pleasure, too, is a troubled pleasure, and his compensations, however abundant, are always answers to the losses and lapses that they cannot silence. The claims of political action and the voice of political rhetoric trouble Wordsworth's dialogic conscience and my own.

But the voice of political heroism in *The Prelude* is only one of the numerous recognizable voices through which Wordsworth makes himself heard in that poem, and I cannot confine my interest and commitment to that voice alone. James Chandler has helped us hear Wordsworth's responses to the voices of Burke and Rousseau; Alan Liu has helped us hear the accents of romance, tragic drama, and prophecy. Susan Wolfson has made audible Wordsworth's responses to his own previous formulations of the drowned man episode, as I have tried to do with the several versions of the episode of the discharged soldier (*Making Tales* Ch. 5). The interaction of the many voices these readings reveal within Wordsworth's voice makes a stronger claim on my interests than the self-indulgent single voice of the ideologue to which McGann would reduce them.[14]

Dialogic aspects of Wordsworth's oeuvre

I would add that the readings that have made these many voices audible bespeak a widespread interest in Wordsworth's dialogic art that might be consolidated and clarified by a recognition of the adjective I am proposing. These readings also demonstrate that dialogic features are not confined to canonically peripheral poems like "The Sailor's Mother" but characterize Wordsworth's greatest long poem as well.[15]

These features in fact are common in Wordsworth's narrative poetry. In *Lyrical Ballads* more than half the poems include reported speech either directly or indirectly. In the mid-length narratives from *Peter Bell* to *The White Doe*, reported utterance is again a crucial device. *The Excursion*, probably the least read and least written about

14 James K. Chandler, *Wordsworth's Second Nature* (Chicago: University of Chicago Press, 1984). Alan Liu, "'Shapeless Eagerness': The Genre of Revolution in Books 9–10 of *The Prelude*," *MLQ* 43 (1982): 3–28. Susan Wolfson, "The Illusion of Mastery: Wordsworth's Revisions of 'The Drowned Man of Esthwaite': 1798, 1805, 1850," *PMLA* 99 (1984): 917–35.

15 For an elaboration of the dialogic hypothesis applied to *The Prelude*, see my "On First Looking into Norton's Wordsworth," *CEA Critic* 52 (1990): 53–61.

major poem by a major poet in English, is again dialogic, and the understanding of its development depends on our learning to hear the relation among voices that we have only just begun to distinguish.[16] The list of poems congenial to dialogic analysis thus might include the collection on the basis of which Wordsworth made his claim to the public's approval for fifteen years, his two significant long poems, and a large group of relatively overlooked narrative poems.

With confirmation from Magnuson's and Ruoff's recent books, I would also add to it Wordsworth's two acknowledged lyric masterpieces, for as Rajan has suggested, Romantic lyric poetry, insofar as it is "open from within to contestation" may be productively read as dialogic art.[17] On the old assumption that lyric poetry expresses "an ideal, integrated consciousness,"[18] Wordsworth's lyrics continue to disappoint his critics. Recently "Tintern Abbey" and the "Intimations Ode" have both been criticized again, on the Coleridgean ground of their unevenness of style, by Thomas McFarland. In language revealing from a dialogic perspective, he complains of Wordsworth's interruption of "great currents of statement with parenthetical expressions" and his introjection of "an alien element of thought into his most typical utterance."[19] Jonathan Wordsworth has also criticized "Tintern Abbey" in terms that prick up our dialogic ears. At the point where William Wordsworth acknowledges that his eloquent tribute to the forms of beauty may be "but a vain belief," Jonathan Wordsworth hears "a sudden paltry taking into account of other people's views."[20]

Both McFarland and Jonathan Wordsworth hear voices other than the one they identify with the true Wordsworth intruding on that true voice to assert something unWordsworthian or to compel Wordsworth to answer. Both critics imagine that a poet's voice, perhaps especially a lyric poet's voice, is properly single, sustained in its characteristic ideas, flowing without provocation from outside in

---

16 David Q. Smith, "The Wanderer's Silence: A Strange Reticence in Book IX of *The Excursion*," *WC* 9 (1978): 162–72.

17 Rajan, "Displacing Post-Structuralism," 451; "Romanticism and the Death of Lyric Consciousness."

18 ANC 109, quoted in Rajan, "Romanticism and the Death of Lyric Consciousness," 195.

19 Thomas McFarland, "Wordsworth's Best Philosopher," *WC* 13 (Spring 1982): 59, 62.

20 Jonathan Wordsworth, *William Wordsworth: The Borders of Vision* (Oxford: Clarendon Press, 1982), 25.

what McFarland calls "a broad and deep current of Wordsworthian certainty" (McFarland, "Best Philosopher," 62). Neither allows that "other people's views" or "alien elements" might be the provoking and sustaining and shaping conditions of lyric utterance, the necessary voices constituting the dialogic situation of the lyric speaker. Both critics sensitively detect the signs of those other voices, but, like Coleridge, they judge those voices and the speaker's response to them as defects in the poems characteristic of this poet, not as provocations and resistances that shape the utterances for which we admire him.

But what would be left of "Tintern Abbey" without its speaker's hidden dialogue with those other voices? Take the voice that in the first stanza hears him name "hedge-rows" and corrects it in "hardly hedge-rows, little lines of sportive wood run wild." Without that correction we would not hear the difference between the voice of desire pressing his perception of the scene toward wildness and the voice of matter-of-fact description resisting that desire and calling a hedge a hedge. The speaker's desires in this poem cannot reveal themselves without acknowledging the claims of that skeptical, matter-of-fact voice. Or what of the voice that sets the rest of the poem in motion, the one that must impinge on the speaker between the first and second stanzas to suggest that "these forms of beauty" *have* been to the speaker "as is a landscape to a blind man's eye"? Without this voice accusing the speaker of ignoring his beloved forms of beauty in his absence from them, there would be no stanza (and no poem) denying the accusation and affirming what those forms have meant to him. If the speaker did not hear this accusation, there would be no crescendo of affirmation rising to suggest the "serene and blessed mood" he may have owed to them. But if he could simply affirm this mood and ignore the skeptical voice that makes him admit that it might "be but a vain belief," then he would have answered the accusing question and could rest his case. When he responds, however, to the "other person's view" that his eloquent claims might be just a vain belief, he reopens the question that sustains his discourse to its final reaffirmation of his love of Nature – not, of course, without interruption from other voices, but with new questions, new affirmations, new doubts, and new sources of hope.

Richard Matlak has recently gone as far as to specify who some of these other people are who impinge on Wordsworth's language in the poem, as I have specified Burke as a dialogizing other of "The

Sailor's Mother." Matlak hears Dorothy Wordsworth's voice in the matter-of-fact other person's view to which Wordsworth repeatedly responds even before he addresses Dorothy directly, and he hears Coleridge's voice in the orthodox religious view against which Wordsworth carefully defines his unorthodox half-creating and half-perceiving. Though I would prefer to rename Matlak's "rhetorical" reading dialogic, his analysis, whatever we would call it, confirms my judgment that if Wordsworth's voice were not shot through with "other people's views," "Tintern Abbey" would be a stillborn descriptive poem or a catechistic recital of Wordsworthian doctrine.[21]

McGann's reading of "Tintern Abbey" in *The Romantic Ideology* represents the poem as just such a recital. Calling for a reengagement with doctrine in Romantic poetry, McGann quotes without its subjunctive introduction the passage where Wordsworth explores the possibility that he may have owed a "sense sublime" to the forms of beauty he experienced on his previous visit, and he reaccents Wordsworth's "If this be but a vain belief" by accenting – contrary to the meter and the context – the *if* rather than the *this* to weaken the force of Wordsworth's doubts. He ignores all the evidence of resistance to desire in the poem and reads it as if it consummated a wish to erase or displace other voices that it repeatedly acknowledges and struggles to answer.[22] This reading, like my hypothetical ideological reading of "The Sailor's Mother," reduces the evidence of dialogic differences to a single declarative voice whose false consciousness is obvious and exemplary.

Close attention to Wordsworth's dialogic art resists both the aesthetic demand for unity of consciousness and the ideological projection of a unified doctrine in "Tintern Abbey" and in Wordsworth's other poems. If we expect Wordsworth's voice to be involved with other voices, if we hear how his voice is indeed

21 Richard E. Matlak, "Classical Argument and Romantic Persuasion in 'Tintern Abbey,'" *SiR* 25 (Spring 1986): 97–129.

22 For an alternative response to this passage by a critic McGann has set himself against (59–76), see L. J. Swingle's remark: "When Wordsworth writes in 'Tintern Abbey,' 'We see into the life of things' (line 49), he immediately turns our attention from dogma to inquiry by adding in the next phrase of the poem, 'If this / Be but a vain belief' (lines 49–50). Accurate thinking about the nature of Romanticism would appear to demand investigation of the implications of this odd artistic maneuver: what does it mean for a writer to assert and undercut assertion in the same breath?" This investigation or inquiry is the burden of Swingle's interesting *The Obstinate Questionings of English Romanticism* (Baton Rouge and London: Louisiana State University Press, 1987), 8.

constituted in and as an interplay of voices, we will stop complaining of interruptions or condescending to ideologies and move on to examine interactions and resistances.[23] We may even discover that even the poems the critical tradition has all along valued sustain our interest not by flattering our own unacknowledged Romantic ideology but by admitting questions to their highest affirmations, by allowing alternative interpretations of their most cherished beliefs, sometimes by changing their minds in response to other people's views.

But "dialogic" may not be the only adjective that can characterize these interactions or guide our inquiry into them. An essay by Clifford Siskin, published before the book I discussed in Chapter 1, uses the adjective "revisionary" to talk about the same passages in "Tintern Abbey" I have just been describing as dialogic, and his account is impressive. In calling Wordsworth's art "revisionary," he calls attention to the poet as a reader of what he has just written who reinterprets and corrects it in what he writes next. Each part of the poem, Siskin writes, "is itself potentially a whole ... that, when placed in revisionary relationship to the others ... both reinterprets them ... and is itself reinterpreted."[24]

"Revisionary" differs from "dialogic," as deconstruction generally differs from Bakhtin's theories, by positing writing rather than speech as its paradigm and by imagining the poet composing a text rather than a speaker uttering the words inscribed in the poem. Once we admit these two perspectives I do not think we can easily make one of them go away. The problem they pose for us as critics is the counterpart of the problem Siskin says Wordsworth set for himself in writing *Lyrical Ballads*: "to write experiences into poetry without losing the supposedly natural power of the original (speech) acts" (149). We must read the experiences back out of poetry without losing the power of the voices that those texts represent, but without forgetting that they are always textually represented voices. "Dialogic," then, may not be the only or the last word for Wordsworth's art, but it is a word of sufficient precision and power to take its place among the others I have reviewed. It allows us to

---

23 David Simpson has paid close attention to these aspects of Wordsworth's poetry in his recent *Wordsworth's Historical Imagination*, but he has treated them less as signs of dialogic art than as symptoms of cultural pressures and tensions. See my review in *Clio* 19 (1989): 77–79.
24 Siskin, "Romantic Genre," 139.

treat the imaginative and dramatic aspects of Wordsworth's poems under a single critical rubric instead of choosing between them, and it allows us to treat his great lyric as well as his experimental narrative works in a common frame of reference. It directs our attention toward internally divided voices in Wordsworth's poems and to historically informing and provoking voices in his world, while resisting both aesthetic and ideological reductions of Wordsworth's voice to monologic utterance. At the same time it provides us with an image of our own critical prose that welcomes other critics' words as the necessary condition of our own words and leads us to expect that whatever we have said will give others more to say.

4

Dialogics of the lyric: a symposium on "Westminster Bridge" and "Beauteous Evening"

The critical colloquy is at times marked as much by vacuity as acuity; literary critical exchange can represent not so much a conversation of the deaf as a series of harangues, issuing from isolated voices in scattered telephone booths.   Nancy S. Struever, "Topics in History"

Two juxtaposed utterances belonging to different people who know nothing about one another if they only slightly converge on one and the same subject (idea), inevitably enter into dialogic relations with one another ... on the territory of a common theme, a common idea.

Mikhail Bakhtin, "The Problem of the Text"

A dialogic orientation that opens our critical inquiries to the multiple voices of other critics instead of focusing our energies on the single voices of dominant authorities could be a mixed blessing if we lack the generic resources to organize that multiplicity and enter into it. Karl Kroeber properly fears the "suicide-through-plenitude" that might befall Wordsworthian criticism were we to become swamped by "the accelerating increase in the quantity of writing about the poet" and "lose track of our most useful lines of inquiry," but he may not have led us all the way out of the swamp in his survey of Wordsworthian criticism by "reporting selectively, not compre-hensively" and "defining clearly [his] own point of view through frank expressions of opinion" (256). The genre of comprehensive narrative bibliography of *all* Wordsworthian criticism, however selective and opinionated, may simply be no match for the hundreds of articles and books it must review in a little over eighty pages, even if it is an indispensable point of entry to them.

Our comprehensive genres may thus not be up to what they must comprehend, but our typical genres of critical production may pose the opposite problem of not demanding that we comprehend enough.

In his afterword to the recent collection of essays, *Lyric Poetry: Beyond New Criticism*, Jonathan Arac remarks with some impatience that "so many essays from such diverse concerns agree to ignore so much important work" (346). Arac's complaint about these essays could be applied to many others that have accumulated on the topic of "the lyric" or "the poem" since the New Critics discovered how to produce critical essays as responses to isolated lyric poems. Such critical essays have exhibited "the stability of organization and the capacity to engender successors" that M. H. Abrams takes as the marks of a genre in his essay on the greater Romantic lyric, and they also share with the lyric genre he describes a model of the relation between a speaker and the object that provokes his discourse: put a Romantic poet in front of a natural scene or a New Critic in front of a lyric poem and discourse will be produced without need to posit any prior conversations or any other interlocutors.[1]

The genre of the New Critical essay, then, like the lyric genre it typically interprets, tacitly agrees to ignore precedent utterances and to stage the encounter of an already informed mind with its object. Were it to polemicize with previous views or to shape itself as a contribution to a discussion already under way, it would be less likely to meet New Critical criteria like those set by the editors of the volume going beyond New Criticism – "that each essay work from at least one specific text" (353) and that the essays "bring contemporary theoretical questions to bear on the interpretation of specific lyric traditions and poems" (14). Critics with their given theories, like poets with whatever notions they happen to carry with them, will produce characteristic kinds of utterances when they respond to the poems before them and "agree to ignore so much important work."[2]

This agreement about genre will produce many interpretations of

---

1 "Structure and Style in the Greater Romantic Lyric," in *From Sensibility to Romanticism*, ed. Frederick W. Hilles and Harold Bloom (New York: Oxford University Press, 1965), 527–30.

2 National isolation as well as generic habit contribute to this ignoring of precedent work. Writing in London for publication in 1976, Harvey Peter Sucksmith can declare that "Westminster Bridge" "has so far received almost no scrutiny at length" despite several substantial American readings of the sonnet including Cleanth Brooks's in *The Well Wrought Urn* and J. Hillis Miller's lengthy 1971 reading (see note 6 below). Sucksmith's celebration of "spiritual illumination" and "affirmation" in the poem might have been sharpened or modulated had he answered the Americans' emphasis on its paradoxes. See Sucksmith's "Ultimate Affirmation: A Critical Analysis of Wordsworth's Sonnet 'Composed upon

poems without clarifying theoretical disagreements or adjudicating their diverse consequences in practice. The accumulation of essays produced on this model will testify to its generic "capacity to engender successors," but it will not result in an articulated conversation. The pile may be added to, but it won't add up. Arac notes that the New Critical emphasis on the isolated lyric poem has been replaced in the recent collection with emphasis on the "intertextual" relations between poems or poets, but the critical practice he describes and criticizes seems not to have taken this emphasis to heart as it applies to the intertextual relations among critics.

Arac tries to supplement this lack by providing some of the history of the discussion the essayists neglect in their "tactical" (352) deployment of ideas of the lyric. He reconstructs, for example, the intertextual relations between Bakhtin and Kristeva out of which the term "intertextuality" itself emerged, and he highlights the differences between personalizing and impersonal uses of the term (348–50). His afterword produces a history and imagines a potential context for essays that typically apply theories to poems.

But while the genre of the "afterword," in which Arac has more than once written,[3] makes its writer responsive to the essays that precede it as they need not have been responsive to one another or to other previous work, its limits prevent it from overcoming the inarticulateness of accumulations of critical essays. It must characterize trends rather than responding to specific arguments, call attention to omissions instead of working out their implications, and depend on prior reading of the other essays instead of revoicing them as they figure in its own argument. An afterword can call attention to the inarticulateness of the collection of essays it follows, but it cannot make it fully articulate.

These limits are shared, with few exceptions, by all the genres available for articulating and addressing what has already been written. Introductions, afterwords, annotated bibliographies, reviews, and review essays are all much smaller and much less prominent than the works they respond to. A situating paragraph at the beginning of

Westminster Bridge,' and the Image of the City in *The Prelude*," *Yearbook of English Studies* 6 (1976): 113–19.

3 See his "Afterword" to *The Yale Critics: Deconstruction in America*, ed. Jonathan Arac, Wlad Godzich, and Wallace Martin (Minneapolis: University of Minnesota Press, 1983), 176–99.

an essay (what one colleague of mine has called the "turkey shoot"), a three-page review of a three-hundred-page book, or Arac's ten-page response to over three hundred pages containing twenty-one essays fairly represent the usual proportions. The reviewing genres are also typically set apart from the "original contributions" in opening chapters or paragraphs, review sections (sometimes in smaller print) or notes, even though both "originality" and "contribution" make sense only in a conversation that can remember what has already been said and recognize what now needs saying.

Bakhtin's emphasis on the dialogic character of all discourse ("intertextuality" is Kristeva's word, not his) can perhaps help us to restore not only the lyric poet but also the critic-essayist to awareness of the conversation from which their generic habits have abstracted them. If, as he claims, *all* utterances are shaped as responses to and anticipations of other utterances, then the lyric poet singing in splendid isolation and the critic closeted with the poem alone will both be found to have company. If, as he also claims, all objects of discourse are always already invested with discourse, then the lyric poet's beloved and the lyric critic's poem do not wait speechlessly for the poet and critic to articulate them; they themselves have already spoken and been spoken for. J. Hillis Miller, who has raised the New Critical essay's neglect of prior critics into a principle and carried it out in his practice, characterizes the tradition of one text's interpretation by others as "an opaque mist or ... an impenetrable thicket of thorns around the sleeping beauty"[4] through which the critic-prince, in effect, penetrates to a direct encounter with the text itself. Bakhtin, who uses the same figures of "obscuring mist" and entanglement to describe the object of discourse already involved in previous discourse, also admits the contrary figure of the "'light' of alien words," and he does not imagine that either the critic or the work can be separated from the conflicting discourse in which they have been constituted (DN 276).

Bakhtin's premises can lead us to recognize in both poems and essays the hidden dialogues that shape their discourse, but they can also guide us toward critical (perhaps by way of poetic) genres that integrate responses to our object of discourse with responses to the others who have spoken about it and articulate those responses more comprehensively and self-consciously than the New Critical essay

4 J. Hillis Miller, *The Ethics of Reading* (New York: Columbia University Press, 1987), 15.

allows. The symposium, one of the dialogic genres Bakhtin associates with the tradition of Menippean satire, offers itself for these purposes (PDP 120). It is not to be imagined, however, as a group of essays solicited for oral presentation and published as a collection but, on the model of Plato's *Symposium*, as an *account* of previous utterances on a topic selected from a larger field of available utterances by a narrator. Involved with the topic and affiliated with or opposed to previous speakers, narrators of symposia may tell what they think "most worth remembering" and respond to it in their own terms or in the terms of their heroes.

This generic model informs my present discourse, which constructs a symposium from among a number of critical essays that have chosen to demonstrate their theories of lyric or of poetry in readings of one or both of two canonical Wordsworth sonnets, "Composed Upon Westminster Bridge" and "It is a beauteous evening, calm and free."[5] These two poems have provoked characteristic readings from critics representing most of the major schools of thought in modern American criticism, just as the topic of love in Plato's *Symposium* provoked typical responses from representatives of the principal intellectual professions of Socrates' day. Cleanth Brooks turned to both poems in the opening gambit of his New Critical classic, *The Well Wrought Urn*; Norman Maclean chose one of them to illustrate his Chicago School analysis of a lyric poem; Kenneth Burke used both to take dramatistic exception to Maclean's reading; Charles Molesworth chose "Westminster Bridge" for a rhetorical reading; J. Hillis Miller selected it for a deconstructive one; and Michael Riffaterre used it to illustrate his intertextual semiotics. Most recently Judith W. Page has made "It is a beauteous evening, calm and free" the chief exemplar in her feminist analysis of Wordsworth's "Calais sonnets," and Alan Liu has made "Westminster Bridge" the exemplary instance in the concluding chapter of his New Historicist argument.[6] Though all but Liu's essay remain true to form in paying

5 The sonnets are widely anthologized. I am using the texts of these sonnets as they appear in *The Poetical Works of William Wordsworth*, 5 vols., ed. Ernest de Selincourt, rev. Helen Darbishire (Oxford: Clarendon Press, 1952–59).

6 Cleanth Brooks, *The Well Wrought Urn* (1947; reprint New York: Harcourt Brace Jovanovich, 1975), 3–7; Norman Maclean, "An Analysis of a Lyric Poem," in *Discussions of William Wordsworth*, ed. Jack Davis (Boston: D. C. Heath & Co., 1964), 130–38 (originally published in *University of Kansas City Review* 8 [Spring 1942]: 202–09); RMGM 465–84; Charles Molesworth, "Wordsworth's 'Westminster Bridge' Sonnet: The Republican Structure of Time and Perception," *Clio*

little or no explicit attention to precedent utterances on the poems, their complex potential interrelations may be brought, as Bakhtin says, "by means of a dotted line to the point of their dialogic intersection" (PDP 91).

In bringing out those points of connection among them, however, I will not be standing outside their dialogue but within it, organizing my presentation of their words and responding critically to their claims in order to bring out the value of the position with which I myself identify. As Apollodorus comes forward as an unabashed lover of Socrates and arranges his account of the symposium to bring out the superiority of his hero's discourse on love, so I here identify myself with Bakhtin's dialogics and shall attempt to demonstrate its value in interpreting lyric poetry, even as I represent the views of the other symposiasts. Bakhtin has not addressed himself to the poems that concern me, and his most extensive published comments on the lyric (narrowly conceived) treat it as a monologic foil to the dialogic novel.[7] But his works and those of his school on language, literary form, poetic discourse, and the novel repeatedly supply me with comments and perspectives that inform my criticism of the critics and my readings of the poems.

Unlike Plato's Apollodorus, however, I do not save my hero's discourse for last but draw on it repeatedly as I report and respond to what each of the others has said. And I cannot, as Plato himself does, invent the speeches of my symposiasts to enhance their interest and persuasiveness. Working from written texts rather than from oral tradition, I am bound by what my several symposiasts have in fact written, though my presentations select and order their views to my purposes. I hope and believe that my representations, however

6 (1977): 261–73; Michael Riffaterre, "Intertextual Representation: On Mimesis as Interpretive Discourse," *Critical Inquiry* 11 (September 1984): 141–62; J. Hillis Miller, "The Still Heart: Poetic Form in Wordsworth," *New Literary History* 2 (1971): 297–310. (Miller republished his essay with a few modifications as the second chapter of *The Linguistic Moment: From Wordsworth to Stevens* [Princeton: Princeton University Press, 1985]. Page references here are to the version in *NLH.*) Judith W. Page, "'The Weight of Too Much Liberty': Genre and Gender in Wordsworth's Calais Sonnets," *Criticism* 30 (Spring 1988): 189–203. Alan Liu, "The Idea of the Memorial Tour: 'Composed Upon Westminster Bridge,'" in *Sense of History*, 455–99, 633–43.

7 DN 275–88. Caryl Emerson reports, however, that an as yet untranslated essay on one of Pushkin's poems "demonstrates Baxtin's thorough appreciation of the complexity and multi-voicedness of lyrical form." See her "Problems with Baxtin's Poetics," *Slavic and East European Journal* 4 (1988): 504.

critical, have been fair to their texts, and I know that my readers may, as Plato's could not, return in each case to those texts and judge the adequacy of my representation for themselves.

Dialogics of paradox: Cleanth Brooks and New Criticism

Cleanth Brooks opens *The Well Wrought Urn*, a book that, for better or worse, has come to stand for the New Criticism, with readings of the two Wordsworth sonnets I have focused on. It may facilitate what follows to place both sonnets before my readers:

Composed Upon Westminster Bridge, September 3, 1802

Earth has not anything to show more fair:
Dull would he be of soul who could pass by
A sight so touching in its majesty:
This city now doth, like a garment, wear
The beauty of the morning; silent, bare
Ships, towers, domes, theatres, and temples lie
Open unto the fields and to the sky;
All bright and glittering in the smokeless air.
Never did sun more beautifully steep
In his first splendour, valley, rock, or hill;
Ne'er saw I, never felt, a calm so deep!
The river glideth at his own sweet will:
Dear God! the very houses seem asleep;
And all that mighty heart is lying still!

It is a beauteous evening, calm and free,
The holy time is quiet as a Nun
Breathless with adoration; the broad sun
Is sinking down in its tranquillity;
The gentleness of heaven broods o'er the sea:
Listen! the mighty Being is awake,
And doth with his eternal motion make
A sound like thunder – everlastingly.
Dear Child! dear Girl! that walketh with me here,
If thou appear untouched by solemn thought,
Thy nature is not therefore less divine:
Thou liest in Abraham's bosom all the year;
And worshipp'st at the Temple's inner shrine,
God being with thee when we know it not.

Brooks begins with these poems, because Wordsworth – poet of direct self-expression and simple poetic diction – is a hard case for Brooks's now familiar thesis that "the language of poetry is the language of paradox." Brooks claims, nevertheless, that both sonnets are "based upon ... paradoxical situation[s]" and that the Westminster Bridge sonnet gets its power from "the paradoxical situation out of which [it] arises" (3–5), but he does not say what he means by "the language of paradox" or "paradoxical situation." Whatever he means, he makes the situations in Wordsworth's sonnets sound paradoxical in the language in which he describes them.

In the one, "the poet is filled with worship, but the girl who walks beside him is not worshiping ... yet ... the innocent girl worship[s] more deeply than the self-conscious poet who walks beside her" (4). Brooks here presents "Beauteous Evening" as if its paradox were in the situation itself, not in the perspective of the speaker, as if the paradoxical contrast between the speaker's worship and the girl's lack of it were impersonally reversed by a revelation of the truth of the girl's deeper inner worship. In the other poem, Brooks makes the paradox one that the speaker himself registers as a surprising discovery: he expects that only nature can "wear the beauty of the morning," but he declares in what Brooks calls "almost shocked exclamation" that "'*Never did sun more beautifully steep / In his first splendour,* valley, rock, *or* hill'" than now he steeps London, of all things (6).

These ways of talking suggest a distinction between paradox as an utterance taken to be inconsistent or self-contradictory on its face and paradox understood as an utterance contrary to someone's opinion, i.e. between impersonal or "objective" paradox intelligible in itself, and socially relative or dialogical paradox intelligible only to one who knows the "dox," or opinion, against which the paradox plays. In his eagerness to demonstrate the pervasiveness of paradox, however defined, Brooks does not examine the distinction implied by his descriptions of the two poems between these interpretations of paradox, and he takes for granted the objective understanding. The dialogical view of paradox, however, would question the objective understanding and the distinction itself. It would insist that *some* "dox," either tacitly assumed as dialogizing background or verbally represented within the poem itself, is the necessary ground of a dialogic phenomenon like paradox. There is no reversal of or play on expectation without an expectation, and no expectation without *someone* to expect it, even if *everyone* expects it and the expectation therefore goes without saying.

Because Brooks does not reflect on the dialogical model of paradox implicit in his description of "Westminster Bridge," he also does not consider the various ways that paradox relates to "dox," that is, the ways in which by-opinions respond to or relate to the opinions they play on. Bakhtin analyzes a large class of discourse oriented to other discourse, as paradox is oriented to "dox" or even to "orthodox," but he recognizes also both "diverse forms of interrelationship" and "various degrees of deforming influence exerted by one discourse on the other" (PDP 199). Brooks's position gains what power it has by calling attention to all kinds of by-play in poetry under the rubric of "paradox," but it gives little help in discriminating those forms and degrees of by-play – those relations of dox and paradox – that Bakhtin elaborates.

Brooks's reading of "Westminster Bridge" thus recognizes a speaking person who feels compelled by a striking impression of London to reverse his usual opinion of it. But Brooks underestimates the radical relation of dox to paradox that the poem depicts. The speaker expresses not just Brooks's "sense of awed surprise" at the discovery that "man-made London is a part of nature too" (6); he gives unreserved testimony to the power of the scene before him against the claims of anything else the earth has to show or of any moment he has known of natural illumination. Indeed the shock to the speaker's usual assumptions is so great that he seems to cast off his usual identity and to stand for the moment outside it, ecstatically rejecting that dull-souled perspective that could pass this experience by and testifying to an experience of calm in this vision deeper than any he has ever seen or felt. If the position he declares stands paradoxically toward his usual opinion, the tone in which he declares it is that of the convert who has turned decisively away from blindness toward the light of revealed truth. He preserves the memory of his former view not as a standard to which the new experience unexpectedly conforms but as a reminder of the dullness of soul from which the present revelation has freed him. The speaker's paradoxical utterance in this case *supplants* the dox against which it shaped itself but preserves that dox as the reminder of what he imagines he has transcended.

A different relation between dox and paradox holds in "Beauteous Evening." If we set aside Brooks's impersonal description of it and read it dialogically as a speaking person's utterance, the relation of the speaker's dox and paradox is mediated by his failed attempt to share his sense of the evening's holiness with the child with whom he is walking. The dox, the initially posited declaration of God's immanence in the evening, meets a resistance in the child's indifference to the invitation to listen to the sound of the "mighty Being" the speaker hears. In the paradoxical sestet, the speaker finds a way to preserve his own sense of that Being's power by positing a secret inner relationship between God and the child to explain away the child's outward nonparticipation in the worshipful posture the evening provokes in him. Here the paradox is not a *replacement* of the posited dox but a *supplement* to it, a compensation for its failure to include the child. It can be taken, I think, neither as a simple continuation of the poem's initial worshipfulness nor as an unexpected reversal of the speaker's and child's apparent relations to God but as a recovery from embarrassment. The speaker, carried away with his sense of the evening, has invited the child to enter into something unsuited to her, and, like the father in "Anecdote for Fathers," he covers his embarrassment at the awkward discovery of his mistaken manner of address with affectionate declarations and compensatory imaginings. The speaker's appeal for "choral support" from his child-companion is disappointed;[8] the assurance of his worshipful tone is threatened. But with a pause in his discourse lasting for perhaps several moments beyond the fulsome full stop of "everlastingly," he reasserts himself in his affectionate condescension toward the child and his exalted recuperation of her failure to share his evaluation of the evening. He does not adopt a view that she could share but reasserts the presence of the power she has not acknowledged and even exalts her relation to that power over his own in a delicate self-abasement in keeping with his initial worshipfulness.

If, as one Bakhtin School essay claims, "the fundamental condition of lyric intonation is *unhesitating confidence in the sympathy of the listeners*," then this lyric poem moves in the direction of what that essay calls "'lyric irony,'" which expresses "social conflict" through the "meeting in one voice of two embodied evaluations, and their interferences and interruptions" (DLDP 25). Though the child says nothing, her lack of response registers her implicit evaluation of the

8 The phrase is from a work that some critics have attributed to Bakhtin but that others continue to attribute to its titular author, V. N. Voloshinov, "Discourse in Life and Discourse in Art" (DLDA 103). I will also refer to a second translation of the essay, "Discourse in Life and Discourse in Poetry" (DLDP).

situation and provokes a changed tone from the speaker. Furthermore, the relation of religiously sophisticated adult and unsophisticated child is a social relation, like the one in "We Are Seven," that calls the sophistication itself into question and provokes the adult to offer a sophisticated account of the child to explain away its apparent unorthodoxy. The adult's religious paradox here, like the adult's physical explanation of the child's ignorance in "We Are Seven," functions to protect his orthodoxy.

The paradox in "Beauteous Evening," then, works to preserve the speaker's fundamental opinion, while the paradox in "Westminster Bridge" gains its power by contradicting the speaker's expectation. Both relations of paradox to dox could be given rather ponderous abstract names from Bakhtin's taxonomy of discourse types: "Beauteous Evening" would be uni-directional double-voiced discourse, the second part of which is an active type of discourse in hidden dialogue with the child's implied contradictory evaluation of the evening. That is to say that the sestet continues the evaluative direction of the octave by attributing to the child a standpoint consistent with the narrator's desires, even as it implicitly answers the child's implied contradictory standpoint. "Westminster Bridge" in these terms could be called vari-directional double-voiced discourse parodically representing and rejecting the speaker's now transcended view of London as a successfully exorcized dullness of soul (PDP 199). Both poems are double-voiced in that they enact a relation between two opinions, but the voices are in agreement despite resistance in "Beauteous Evening" and in opposition in "Westminster Bridge." The awkwardness of Bakhtin's terms compared to the grace of Brooks's unexamined "language of paradox" should not obscure the gain Bakhtin's locutions make in precise discrimination over Brooks's blanket term.[9]

9 Bakhtin's terms achieve an even greater gain in discrimination over F. R. Leavis's critical terms "movement" and "complexity." Leavis resists defining the terms, but his use of them in relation to the two sonnets discovers a complete absence of both qualities in "Beauteous Evening" (which he calls *Calais Beach*) – "it contains no surprises, no turns, imposing a readjustment in the delivery, but continues as it begins, with a straightforwardness at every point and a continuity of sameness." "Westminster Bridge," on the other hand, demonstrates its "superiority over *Calais Beach*" through its organization around the adjective "smokeless," which "conveys, in fact, both its direct force and its opposite" and reveals "the duality of consciousness out of which the sonnet is organized." Leavis grasps the "complexity" of "Westminster Bridge," noting that "the calm is so preternaturally deep because of a kind of negative co-presence ... of the characteristic urban associations" and that "the stillness of the 'mighty heart' is

My dialogic reading has not rejected Brooks's claim that paradox operates in these poems but has instead reinterpreted the grounds of paradox as social and recognized the functions of paradox as varied. These lyric poems, like "Tintern Abbey" as I discussed it in Chapter 3 and "The Solitary Reaper" as I will discuss it in Chapter 5, work not as the expression of single or simple voices but as responses to other voices within or outside the speaker. The experiences of London or of the beauteous evening reveal their power not just in the speaker's direct response to them but in his response to other opinions of them. The speaker's impassioned paradoxical utterances are provoked not just by things but by the social world of other utterances that evaluate them, not just by the phenomenal world of nature or nature-like London but by the doxical world of social relations, values, and words.[10]

Dialogicality and intertextuality: Michael Riffaterre and semiotics

The statement with which I have just concluded sounds like the premise of a recent essay by Michael Riffaterre that also takes up the "Westminster Bridge" sonnet and Brooks's reading of it. In that essay Riffaterre explores the kind of literary mimesis that refers not from "words to things" but "from words to words, or rather from texts to

so touching because of the latent sense of the traffic that will roar across the bridge in an hour's time." But he finds in "Beauteous Evening" not "even this measure of complexity; it has no structure, but is just a simple one-way flow of sentiment." I do not know whether Leavis misses the paradoxical structure in "Beauteous Evening" because of the looseness of his critical terms, his distaste for the religious language of the poem, or the assignment he has given himself "to compare these two sonnets of Wordsworth's and establish a preference for one of them." Brooks's New Criticism assigns the discovery of paradox, loosely defined, in any given poem, but Leavis's assigns a comparative judgment between selected poems in which one will have the valued properties in question and the other will likely prove to be deprived of them. See *The Living Principle*, 113–20.

10 For an early response to Brooks that claims that he places "too much emphasis on the poetic force of the paradoxical situation" and argues that "harmony, not surprise, is the keynote of the Westminster Bridge sonnet," see Charles V. Hartung, "Wordsworth on Westminster Bridge: Paradox or Harmony?," *College English* 13 (1952): 201–03. For an effort to resolve the difference between Brooks's "surprise" and Hartung's "harmony" as a New Critical "tension," see Charles G. Davis, "The Structure of Wordsworth's Sonnet 'Composed Upon Westminster Bridge,'" *English* 19 (1970): 18–21.

texts" (142). Riffaterre emphasizes the reference of words to words over the reference of words to things just as I emphasize the shaping of words "not just by things but by the social world of other utterances." But despite the similar language and similar structures of our assertions, several important differences compel me to distinguish my dialogics from Riffaterre's semiotics of the lyric.[11]

Most important is a difference like the one Arac observes between impersonal and personalizing understandings of "intertextuality." Both Bakhtin and Riffaterre posit other words necessary to understand the words of any given poem, but Riffaterre imagines those words as an intertext – "a corpus of texts, textual fragments, or textlike segments of the sociolect that shares a lexicon and, to a lesser extent, a syntax with the text we are reading" (142). Bakhtin, on the other hand, posits the dialogic figure of the speaker whose words sound against the dialogizing background of other people's words. In the same way, Riffaterre's term "sociolect" appears to emphasize the same social understanding of language that I have emphasized, but again his definition objectifies and depersonalizes the dialogic social world of interacting opinions and voices when he defines a "sociolect" as "language viewed not just as grammar and lexicon but as the repository of society's myths ... themes, commonplace phrases, and descriptive systems" (160 n. 2). Riffaterre's "sociolect" here treats social myths and commonplaces on the same linguistic model it uses for grammar and lexicon, again without imagining the dialogic world of speakers *appealing* to those commonplaces and *invoking* those myths in specific social situations.[12]

11 In looking for a theoretical position and a critical practice capable of challenging Riffaterre's, Paul de Man suggests that Bakhtin's theory and practice would pose a challenge of some magnitude, "for the reader/text relationship, in Riffaterre, is dialectical rather than dialogical." See de Man, "Hypogram and Inscription: Michael Riffaterre's Poetics of Reading," *diacritics* 11 (Winter 1981): 27. De Man does not develop the Bakhtinian challenge he anticipates but presents his own deconstructive critique of Riffaterre, 27–35. For de Man's most extensive engagement with Bakhtin see "Dialogue and Dialogism," in *The Resistance to Theory* (Minneapolis: University of Minnesota Press, 1986), 106–14.

12 Though Riffaterre recognizes the "I" in the poem, he judges it as finally "superfluous" to what he calls the "parallelism of text and intertext" that suffice "to make representation into an interpretation" ("Intertextual Representation," 159–60). The "I" of personal experience "must be generalized," he writes, so that "the beholder's 'I' is but the grammatical tool of the semiosis itself" (154). The speaker becomes a mere means to the reader's decoding of signs. In an earlier essay, Riffaterre asserts not just the precedence of reader over speaker but the

When Riffaterre describes "Westminster Bridge" as the kind of text that "owes its descriptive power to an intertext that it negates while compelling the reader to remain fully aware of that intertext" (149), his point once again resembles my claim that "the speaker's paradoxical utterance supplants the dox against which it shaped itself but preserves that dox as the reminder of what he imagines he has transcended." Riffaterre's "intertext" has the same role in his model as "dox" has in my terms or "dialogizing background" has in Bakhtin's, but, while Bakhtin and I imagine the represented speaker interacting in his utterance with the opinions of others, Riffaterre's impersonal formulation imagines a text acting on an actual reader by means of an intertext.

Riffaterre's reader interprets the poem, then, not by re-creating a speaker's utterance as it responds to other utterances but by recognizing how the idiolect – which he defines as the "individual's specific semiotic activity" (160 n. 2) – interacts with the sociolect. In "Westminster Bridge" the reader discovers the poem's idiolectic evaluations of London in two ways. First, the poem uses "positive markers" in the "extolment lexicon" (151) to transfer to London the "descriptive features characteristic only of Nature herself" (152). In addition, the poem negates one negative marker in the usual language applied to the city – the "smoke" whose negation in the word "smokeless" preserves what Riffaterre calls a "trace left by the intertext at the surface of the text displacing it" (153). For Riffaterre, the words work on the reader, without reference to anyone's use of them and without reference to the things they describe, because they have unambiguous places in textual codes that necessarily operate in the reader's mind (cf. 142, 154, 159). Riffaterre, then, treats evaluation as if it were a matter of a word's place among other words in a social lexicon, as, for instance, "'garment' has the plus sign, as opposed to *cloak*, with its minus sign" (151). He treats "surprise," which, like

complete dispensability of the speaker, whom Riffaterre identifies with the biographical poet. Riffaterre writes, the poetic "act of communication ... is a very special act, however, for the speaker – the poet – is not present; any attempt to bring him back only produces interference, because what we know of him we know from history; it is knowledge external to the message, or else we have found it out by rationalizing and distorting the message. The message and the addressee – the reader – are indeed the only factors involved in this communication whose presence is necessary" ("Describing Poetic Structures: Two Approaches to Baudelaire's *les Chats*," in *Structuralism*, ed. Jacques Ehrmann [1966; reprint Garden City, New York: Anchor Books, 1970], 202).

Brooks, he finds in the poem, not as the speaker's response to the reversal of his expectations but as an objective relation the reader must recognize between the connotations of the city in the sociolect and its connotations in the idiolect. He attributes "emotion" not to the speaker's response to London but to the poem's use of a device like repetition, which he calls a "codified, well-established sign for emotion" that the reader must decode as such (156).

Riffaterre does not specify the emotion to be decoded from the repetition he points to in the line, "Ne'er saw I, never felt, a calm so deep!" To do so I think he would have to go beyond decoding. He would need to acknowledge the "I," which appears for the first time in the poem in this line, as significant for more than the fact that it is a pronoun "not repeated" (156). It is a pronoun that is unprecedented, like the experience it acknowledges. The "I" in this line evokes a specific person testifying that his experience of London at this moment surpasses in the depth of its calm any other experience of calm he has ever known. The tone of this testimony – conveyed more by word order in relation to metrical stress and by position in the line than by *choice* of words – is emphatic and unequivocal. The reversed word order of "Ne'er saw I" with "Ne'er" at the head of the line, the repeated "Ne'er...never," the stress on "saw" and "felt" as well as on "calm" and "deep" make this experience for the one who exclaims it more than the transfer to London of Riffaterre's "descriptive features characteristic only of Nature herself" (152). What this speaker emphatically declares he sees and feels is more intense and less "obvious" than Riffaterre's statement of "the lesson we are supposed to learn...that London has beauty...equal to nature's" (150).

A "semiotic mechanism" (150) that can account for the poem's communication of no more than this is inadequate, and a reader who can be satisfied that this is all there is to communicate has let his theory reduce the poem to a commonplace. Brooks, who fails to mention the line I have been concerned with, misses, as Riffaterre does, the emphatic point that the speaker experiences this moment's calm as surpassing anything he has known in nature, or anywhere else for that matter, but he at least imagines a speaker and hears his tone of "almost shocked exclamation" (6). The very looseness of Brooks's terms and the slippage they permit between "the language of paradox" and "paradoxical situation" leave him free to abandon his apparently objective linguistic model when a poem like this one seems to demand attention to the tones of its speaker's utterance. Riffaterre's more systematic linguistic approach leads him to diminish the speaker to a superfluous grammatical feature appropriated by the reader and to diminish tone to an objective plus or minus relation between sociolect and idiolect. Riffaterre provides an emblem for this impoverished notion of tone in the photographic metaphor he chooses for the relation of sociolect to idiolect. He writes, "The complementarity of sonnet and sociolect resembles the correspondence between a photograph and the negative it has been developed from: developing requires a reversal of tones, an exchange of black for white" (153). Brooks can hear, though he does not account for, the tones that mark the speaker's profound response to the scene before him and to his own and others' mistakenly low expectations of its value. Riffaterre finds the "power" of the poem, such as it remains for him, in its objective substitution of what he calls "a positive structure for its negative homologue," and he admires the simple mechanical beauty of its shift of minuses to pluses, of black tones to white (154).

A Bakhtin School account of tone preserves objectivity without abstracting itself from the speaker's situation and identifying with a mechanically decoding reader's perspective. For Bakhtin and his colleagues, an utterance, like an enthymeme, always has two parts, the verbally realized part and the implied part, the speaker's words and the understood situation they respond to and resolve. Sounding much like Riffaterre, Bakhtin's collaborator Voloshinov asserts that "implied evaluations" of these understood situations "are not ... individual emotions, but socially determined and necessary acts," but he goes on to find a place for the "I" that Riffaterre minimizes when he adds, "*Individual* emotions can only accompany the *fundamental tone of the social* evaluation as *overtones* – the 'I' can realize itself in discourse, only when dependent on the 'we'" (DLDP 12).

The "we" here that provides the dialogizing background for a given individual utterance is not, however, an "it," a "sociolect" abstracted to represent the stereotyped values of a society, but a specific community of others whose prior utterances and potential responses provoke, situate, and make the utterance intelligible, a "dialogized heteroglossia, anonymous and social as language, but simultaneously concrete, filled with specific content and accented as an individual utterance" (DN 272). However commonplace or conventional those individually accented utterances may appear to the observing linguist or historian, they will have impinged on the speaker as the words of significant precursors and listeners, and they will have shaped the speaker's tones (and the properly situated reader's interpretation of them) more subtly than Riffaterre's theory allows. The contrast between Voloshinov's metaphors for tone and Riffaterre's photographic trope can stand for the difference between their theories. Voloshinov's musical trope of "overtone" permits the intonation to "freely undergo deployment and differentiation within the range of the major tone" (DLDA 102). And his visual trope epitomizes, in its difference from Riffaterre's, the difference in the range of values his theory permits us to recover. He writes, "*The commonness of assumed basic value judgments constitutes the canvas upon which living human speech embroiders the designs of intonation*" (DLDA 103). Even if Riffaterre let his photographic trope transfer shades of gray from negative sociolect to positive idiolect, it would still be less nuanced and interesting than the intricate and colorful tonal designs to which Voloshinov's trope and his theory direct our attention.

Theme and meaning: Norman Maclean and the Chicago School

It is not accidental that the Bakhtin School's dialogics has something to say to Riffaterre's semiotics and Brooks's poetics: Bakhtin and his collaborators shaped their arguments in response to the tradition of abstract objectivist linguistics Riffaterre follows and to the related tradition of Russian formalist poetics Brooks's New Criticism resembles.[13] It should not surprise us, then, that the Bakhtin School's criticism of language conceived apart from its functioning in utterance and of a poetics too exclusively preoccupied with literary language

13 Though I consider Riffaterre together with other linguistic formalists here, I must note that the early essay on "Describing Poetic Structures" itself begins as a critique of the poetic application of the formal linguistics of Jakobson and Lévi-Strauss along lines similar to those Bakhtin follows in MPL. Riffaterre too sees the indeterminateness of purely grammatical elements in poetic usage, though he distinguishes poetic usage from everyday speech more radically than Bakhtin does. I include him nevertheless among the formalists he criticizes because his account of what he, like Bakhtin, calls "the whole act of communication" ("Describing," 202) in a poem does not go beyond treating invariant linguistic structures or other cultural structures conceived on the model of invariant linguistic structures. He does not posit a variable unifying category like Bakhtin's "theme" as a dialectical counterpart to the invariant structures Bakhtin calls "meaning."

should itself resemble the Chicago School's attack on the New Criticism's linguistic assumptions – the Bakhtin School and the Chicago School offer analogous critiques of analogous formalisms.

As we will see, however, the different unifying principles the two schools invoke and the different conceptions of genre they depend on make their different responses more consequential than their similar situations. Bakhtin and his collaborator Voloshinov frame their criticism of formal linguistics and poetics in terms of what their translator calls the difference between *theme* and *meaning*. "Theme" or "thematic unity" is Bakhtin and Voloshinov's name for the "significance of a whole utterance ... *taken in its full, concrete scope as an historical phenomenon*"; it is not in this usage reducible merely to the subject or topic of discourse. "Meaning" is their term for those abstract linguistic elements "of the utterance that are *reproducible* and *self-identical* in all instances of repetition," elements like phonemes, dictionary definitions, or Riffaterre's "texts" that are invariant across the linguistic system and tonally indeterminate in any instance of their use.[14] In their critique of formalist poetics, Bakhtin and Medvedev formulate the relation between theme and meaning in this way:

The thematic unity of the work is not the combination of the meanings of its words and individual sentences ... Theme always transcends language. Furthermore, it is the whole utterance as speech performance that is directed at the theme, not the separate word, sentence, or period ... The theme of the work is the theme of the whole utterance as a definite sociohistorical act. Consequently, it is inseparable from the total situation of the utterance to the same extent that it is inseparable from linguistic elements.[15]

The thematic unity of an utterance, then, is its generic unity as an utterance of a given kind in a specific situation, and we do not make sense of it merely by identifying independently reproducible linguistic elements or relatively constant common topics of discourse.

To account for how we *do* grasp the themes of utterances in life or in literature, Bakhtin posits speech genres and our capacity to invent and re-create them. If we cannot grasp themes as we identify phonemes or topoi out of context, then we must have not only a

14 MPL 99–101. *Marxism and the Philosophy of Language* was published under the name of V. N. Voloshinov but has been attributed by some authorities to Bakhtin.
15 FM 132. *The Formal Method* was published under the name of Bakhtin's collaborator P. N. Medvedev.

repertoire of familiar situations and the utterances they provoke but also a capacity to imagine unfamiliar situations and the utterances that resolve them. We come to literature in possession of "a series of inner genres for seeing and conceptualizing reality," a repertoire of familiar themes. We may be "richer or poorer in genres, depending on [our] ideological environment." But literature itself "occupies an important place in this ideological environment," and its genres can "enrich our inner speech with new devices for the awareness and conceptualization of reality" (FM 134), for the re-creation and discovery of the themes of utterances.[16]

These questions of genre and of a unifying principle of the poetic whole not reducible to its linguistic elements also arise in R. S. Crane's Chicago School critique of Brooks's New Critical theory. Crane's Brooks indeed comes closer to the theoretically consistent Riffaterre in his reliance on a "single principle, essentially linguistic in its formulation" than to my own theoretically inconsistent but practically insightful Brooks.[17] But the position Crane opposes to the one he attributes to Brooks shares the emphases on genre and on the poem as finished whole that I have just drawn from Bakhtin. Here is Crane coming to his point:

A poet does not write poetry but individual poems. And these are inevitably, as finished wholes, instances of one or another poetic kind, differentiated not by any necessities of the linguistic instrument of poetry but primarily by the nature of the poet's conception, as finally embodied in his poem, of a particular form to be achieved through the representation, in speech used dramatically or otherwise, of some distinctive state of feeling, or moral choice, or action, complete in itself and productive of a certain emotion or complex of emotions in the reader. (96)

Everything in this passage before the phrase "in speech" agrees with Bakhtin and Medvedev's critique of the "formal method" of the Russian formalists, but in that phrase Crane shows his Aristotelian colors and goes on to subordinate speech as medium to a nonverbal object of imitation — feeling or moral choice or action. Crane does not

16 See also Bakhtin's "The Problem of Speech Genres," in *Speech Genres and Other Late Essays*.

17 R. S. Crane, "The Critical Monism of Cleanth Brooks," in *Critics and Criticism: Ancient and Modern*, ed. R. S. Crane (Chicago: University of Chicago Press, 1952), 92–93. Crane, to be sure, acknowledges occasional insights and even notes "promising" inconsistencies in Brooks's argument, but needing a consistent opponent to place in his more comprehensive scheme, he quickly finds the promise "dimmed" (94).

recognize *utterance* or "speech performance" (FM 132) as itself an object of imitation. He recognizes only plot and its analogues as organizing principles of a poetic whole, and he denigrates an explanation of a poem that resorts to "an inconsequential and unmoving 'theme.'"[18]

Crane quotes with contempt the same word "theme" that Bakhtin and Medvedev's translator chooses as the name for their valorized unifying principle, but these conflicting evaluations of a single word would not surprise the dialogic theorist, who expects "a constant struggle of accents in each semantic sector of existence" (MPL 106). Crane himself, however, might have been surprised or displeased by the more positive tone one of his Chicago colleagues gives the word. Norman Maclean offers a paradigmatic analysis of Wordsworth's "Beauteous Evening" as one of several "poems by Wordsworth that treat much the same 'theme' – poems in which Wordsworth represents what he believes is involved in the discovery of God" (138). Maclean, too, places the word "theme" in quotation marks that betray his uneasiness in using it, but theme nevertheless plays a significant part in Maclean's "Analysis of a Lyric Poem."[19]

Maclean's attempt to discuss "the whole poem as some kind of unit in itself" (131) links his effort with both Crane's and Bakhtin's emphasis on unifying principles. Like Bakhtin, he situates his reading by distinguishing it from reductions of the poem to language or to subject matter. Maclean defines himself against a formal analysis preoccupied with prosodic rules and "individual figures of speech," on one hand, and a biographical criticism that reads the poem as a discourse in the poet's life, addressed to his illegitimate child Caroline and through her to her mother Annette, on the other. The biographical reading to which Maclean objects not only diminishes the dignity of the poet and the sublimity of his experience but also turns on an "'imaginative disagreement'" between the poet and his daughter that spoils the harmonious portrayal of their relationship Maclean values.

18 Crane, "Critical Monism," 100. For an extended discussion of the difference between the Aristotelian poetics of plot and the Platonic poetics of speech Bakhtin adheres to, see my "Narrative Diction in Wordsworth's Poetics of Speech," *Comparative Literature* 34 (Fall 1982): 305–29, the substance of which is included in Chapter 1 of *Making Tales*.

19 Maclean's essay appeared in an early Chicago School manifesto along with a theoretical essay by Crane and an essay by Elder Olson on Yeats's "Sailing to Byzantium." See *University of Kansas City Review* 8 (1942). It was not reprinted in the definitive Chicago School volume *Critics and Criticism*.

For Emile Legouis, to whom Maclean is responding, it seems in the line "If thou appear untouched by solemn thought" that the child, like its mother, "'was ill-made for prolonged ecstasies before aspects of nature'" (131–32), but for Maclean the line has "none of the import Legouis suggests" when joined to the "subsequent lines, which affirm the child to be at least equal to the poet in sensitivity and divinity" (137). There is no hint in Maclean's reading that the affirmation could be a response to a felt deficiency in the child's response to the scene and no hint either that the poet's "Listen!" (treated by Maclean as an exalted apostrophe to an unspecified other) might be taken as an invitation to the child to share the speaker's response.[20]

In his answer to purely formal readings, Maclean divides his own analysis of the poem into two parts that correspond closely to Bakhtin's division of meaning from theme. First he attempts to discover the poem's parts at the material levels of prosody, syntax, and signification of its words. Then he turns to account for the relationship of those parts as both an imitation of a developing course of feelings and thoughts and as a treatment of a recognizable Wordsworthian theme. Although Maclean does not pretend that he can recognize the poem's unifying principle in the same way that he can identify its syntactic and prosodic parts, he does not see how much his account of the meanings of the parts already depends upon his thesis about the theme of the whole. He points, for example, to the poem's departure in its second quatrain from normal Petrarchan rhyme scheme and to the poem's division into "three syntactic entities" as signs that the plot of the poem divides into three parts, but neither rhyme scheme nor syntax yields unambiguous divisions. This syntactic division of the poem further suggests to him an intimation of plot movement from "breathlessness, to exaltation, to meditation" (134), because he finds "breathlessness" in the four independent clauses without conjunctions in the first part, "exaltation" in the "apostrophe" of the second part (though not in the apostrophe of the third part) and a "more cognitive" meditative tone in the dependent clauses and participial phrases of the last part (133–34). But apostrophes are figures of thought, not syntactic devices, and it must be clear that the other speculations drawn ostensibly from syntax are again, like the division of the poem Maclean proposes, tonally indeterminate in themselves without an

20 Maclean, "An Analysis of a Lyric Poem," 131–33. For an analysis parallel to Legouis's, see the discussion of Judith Page's reading below.

implicit hypothesis concerning the utterance in this particular context. Unconjoined clauses are not necessarily breathless any more than dependent clauses and participial phrases are necessarily reflective.

Just how far his hypothesis about the whole guides Maclean's account of its parts becomes clear in his reading of its semantic elements, of the words not only as indices of the shifting objects of the poet's attention but also as evidence of his response to those objects, of his feelings and thoughts about them (134). Maclean draws on such evidence most crucially in his account of the first part of the poem in which he argues, for reasons I will make clear in a moment, that the poet responds to the evening "as a sensory being" (135). His argument hangs on the claim that "'beauteous' in its strict meaning is to be distinguished from 'beautiful' in that it is more sensory in its connotations." But it is hard to imagine a "strict meaning" for such a word in the first place and impossible to find warrant for this connotation in the OED, where "beauteous" is distinguished not as sensory but as poetic or literary in its usage. In defense of his claim, Maclean goes on to argue still more implausibly that the remaining lines of the first part, even after its speaker's characterization of the evening as "holy" and his comparison of its quiet to that of a Nun, "as yet...record only the poet's sensory impressions" (135). Only when the sun, at the end of the first part, is said to "brood" does Maclean admit an "activity the course of which cannot be traced by sensory perception" (136). Though he acknowledges the religious connotations mobilized in this part by the words "heaven" and "holy," he insists that it "is improper as yet to read the lines as affirmations on the part of the poet that the evening literally has religious signification" (135).

Why, though the utterance is shaped by a reverent response to the evening from the outset, should Maclean press the connotations of "beauteous" into such unlikely service while he minimizes the mutually reinforcing connotations of "holy" and "heaven" as well as the religious provenance of the simile? Because, as his introduction of "Tintern Abbey" at this point makes clear, he has abstracted a Wordsworthian plot movement "from sensation, to thought, to an understanding of the powers and limitations of thought" (138) from his reading of that most Wordsworthian of poems, and he tries to fit this sonnet's movement into a similar pattern. His syntactic and prosodic divisions of the poem and his tonal interpretation of its syntax follow from this model of its genre.

The generic repertoire to which Maclean has turned for his model of the poem's overall movement is a doctrinal plot pattern abstracted from "many other poems by Wordsworth that treat much the same 'theme'" of what the poet "believes is involved in the discovery of God" (138). My own recourse to generic analogues in "Anecdote for Fathers" and "We Are Seven" locates the thematic similarity not in the divisions of their common religious subject matter but in the participants of their common discursive situations. These poems depict adults who give accounts of exchanges between themselves and children similar to the exchange depicted in the sonnet between speaker and child. In both the poems I look to, the adult's attempt to bring a child to share his adult view is met with frustration, and the frustration is itself resolved by compensatory explanations in the retelling of the encounters. The theme that defines these verbal interactions as a whole is, like the theme of the sestet of "Beauteous Evening," the adult speaker's response to his abortive effort to bring a child to share his adult perspective.[21]

Unlike the personal anecdotes in which the speaker recapitulates his exchange with the child in responding to it, however, the sonnet depicts the response as a final stage in a continuing exchange. Accomplished with less effort and with only the briefest pause after the provoking encounter, the speaker's response in the sonnet resolves his embarrassment smoothly, without the need to dwell on the exchange and go through it again as the speakers in the anecdotes must do. But the effectiveness and ease of the compensatory gesture do not diminish its compensatory force.

A generic hypothesis about the poem shapes not only Maclean's but my own reading of its elements, but his attempt to describe the movement of the poem as an internally necessary plot development revelatory of a familiar Wordsworthian "theme" finally reduces the sonnet to a reproducible Wordsworthian meaning, though he had wished "to explain as exactly as possible its uniqueness" (138). The

21 The variant lines 10 and 11 of the sonnet found in MS 44 confirm my claim that the "Listen!" in 6 should be taken as addressed to the child and that the speaker registers her failure to hear what he hears in the sestet.

> Thou dost not seem to heed these things one jot
> I see it, nor is this a grief of mine

The diction of these lines, especially the "heed these things one jot" strengthens the generic link between the poem in this version and lyrical ballads like "We Are Seven" and "Anecdote for Fathers" and weakens the association with the other sonnets. *Poems, in Two Volumes*, ed. Curtis, 151.

sonnet's theme, in the Bakhtin School sense, escapes him because he is committed to distinguishing the poem's unifying action from its verbal embodiment, while Bakhtin and Medvedev, as we have noted, look for a unifying theme in the embodied verbal interaction itself. Maclean's Wordsworthian genre posits an internal plot of sensation, feeling, and thought externalized in language; the dialogic genre I have suggested recognizes in the speaker's utterance an emotional and thoughtful verbal response not just to God in the evening but to the child at his side.

Dialogics and dialectic: Kenneth Burke and dramatism

Kenneth Burke's response to Maclean's essay and to the Chicago School mini-manifesto of which it was a part is both a model for and an admonition to my own symposium. Burke responds more explicitly to the Chicago position than any of my other critics except Liu responds to any of the other positions against which they define their own. His dialectical program commits him to make his way "through the cooperative competition of divergent voices" (RMGM 253), much as my dialogic practice commits me to engage the other voices that constitute the "social dialogue surrounding" (DN 278) the two sonnets and the lyric genre that concern me. But Burke's dialectic also proceeds, as he himself recognizes, by "reduction of one terminology to another." If, as he says, "any word or concept considered from the point of view of any other word or concept is a reduction" (96), then Burke's reading of philosophy, poetry, and criticism in terms of his dramatistic pentad is clearly a reductive project, and I am compelled to ask myself whether the dialogic reading of other critics I have undertaken is reductive in the same way.[22]

To give a dialogical account of how one terminology affects the terms of another terminology it represents, we must supplement Burke's premise that "any word or concept considered from the point of view of any other word or concept is a reduction" with Bakhtin's and Voloshinov's assertion that "the dissolution of the reported utterance in the authorial context is not – nor can it be – carried out to the end ... The body of the reported speech remains detectable as a self-sufficient unit." The addition of this premise makes the relation between reporting and reported speech not an unresisted reduction of

22 For Bakhtin's contrast of dialogic and dialectic, see PDP 25–26.

one word to another's terms but an "*active relation* of one message to another" in which, though the reporting context has power to distort or diminish or reduce the reported word, the reported word "preserves (if only in rudimentary form) the initial autonomy (in syntactic, compositional, and stylistic terms)" sufficient to permit itself to be distinguished from the language that reports it and even, in some cases, to influence that language (MPL 116). Though dialectical reduction of another's words to one's own terms is a possible move, perhaps even a strong temptation, in dialogic exchange, even the least acknowledgment of another's words as such – even summary of another's argument "in one's own words" – leaves a residue of the other's words that can still be heard and reactivated by a subsequent participant in the discussion. Even would-be dialectical reducers may recognize the resistance of the words they would reduce and the likelihood that those words' users (or their users' students) will talk back.[23]

Burke himself shows some such uneasiness at his own reductive treatment of the Chicago critics when he acknowledges that he may appear to have invoked them merely to insist that "these authors ply their trade under the trade-name of 'dramatism' rather than 'Aristotle'" (481–82). But he nevertheless declares that he could affirm "nearly every particular observation that Mr. Maclean makes about the sonnet ... if he but gave it the pointedness that would derive from an explicit recognition of the 'dramatistic' element in his vocabulary" (476), and he takes the occasion of Maclean's analysis of the sonnet to submit it and the lyric genre to his own dramatistic analysis.

Wordsworth's two sonnets figure in Burke's analysis of the lyric at two levels – as illustrations of the dialectical opposition of the lyric to the dramatic and as illustrations of the "scene–agent (or lyric) ratio" (233) within Burke's dramatistic terminology itself. In Burke's dialectic, if action is the essence of drama, stasis or rest is the essence of lyric. Burke points to both Wordsworth sonnets to illustrate this claim. Anticipating Geoffrey Hartman's figure of the "halted traveler" that I will examine in the next chapter, Burke writes that

a typical Wordsworthian sonnet brings out this methodological aspect of the lyric (its special aptitude for conveying a *state* of mind, for erecting a moment

23 Raymond Williams's account of the way the hegemonic is limited and affected by irreducible "alternative political and cultural emphases" in *Marxism* (113) is analogous to the Bakhtin School's account of the way reporting discourse is limited and affected by the integrity of the discourse it reports.

into a universe) by selecting such themes as in themselves explicitly refer to the arrest, the pause, the hush. However, this lyric state is to be understood in terms of action, inasmuch as it is to be understood as a state that sums up an action in the form of an attitude,

whether the attitude is taken as incipient action, as a culmination of action, or as a substitute for action (475–76). Of "Westminster Bridge" he writes,

The imagery is of morning, so there is incipience. But it is not the incipience of the internal debate, arrested at the moment of indecision prior to a decision from which grievous consequences are inevitably to follow. Nor is it a retrospective summary. It just *is*, a state of mind that has come to rest by reason of its summarizing nature ... It has conveyed a *moment of stasis*.
(246)

But in both sonnets, as we have seen, the speakers acknowledge opinions different from the ones they assert, and they deny those opinions forcefully. If this is not the debate of a dramatic character on the verge of tragic action, it is surely the dialogue of a mind with its own opinions or with the opinions suggested by the behavior of others. Who said that earth *had* anything to show more fair than the beauty the speaker sees in London? Who suggests that the child's lack of solemn thought *should* be interpreted as a sign of her nature's distance from divinity? The speakers' active answers to the voices that suggest these opinions make their "states of mind" dynamic engagements with resistant opinions rather than static expressions of "perfect lyric mood."[24] The child's presence with the speaker in the scene of "Beauteous Evening" and the effect of her behavior on his utterance bring this lyric so close to dramatic monologue that it seems less to exemplify "lyric mood" than dramatic interaction. The dialectical opposition of genres Burke proposes seems, in the examples he has chosen, to collapse into an extension of the dramatic domain.[25]

At the level of dramatistic analysis itself, Wordsworth's sonnets figure for Burke as illustrations of "the scene–agent (or lyric) ratio"

---

24 RMGM 246. In another argument informed by Bakhtin that came to my attention when mine was in press, Dick Leith and George Myerson independently confirm my reading of "Westminster Bridge," calling the sonnet "a *rejoinder*" that presents a mind responsive "partly to sights and feelings but also to other voices." See their *The Power of Address: Explorations in Rhetoric* (London: Routledge, 1989), 105–12.

25 A similar dialectic of genres, subject to a comparable collapse, appears in Bakhtin's opposition of novelistic and poetic discourse in DN (275–88).

(233). In this ratio, the quality of the background or setting or situation is transferred to the agent contained in that setting. Burke uses "Beauteous Evening" as a

> perfect instance of the scene–agent ratio treated theologically ... The octave is all scene, the sestet all agent. But by the logic of the scene–agent ratio, if the scene is supernatural in quality, the agent contained by this scene will partake of the same supernatural quality. And so, spontaneously, purely by being the kind of agent that is at one with this kind of scene, the child is "divine." (8)

Though he claims to be convinced by Maclean's three-part division of the sonnet, Burke twice describes it in this two-part pattern that conforms to the scene–agent ratio (8, 474–75). Both times he emphasizes the spontaneous, unproblematic character of the transfer of divinity from scene to agent, completely ignoring the speaker and the speech performance through which he accomplishes it. He takes the scene as it is *described* in the octave as given rather than as thematized in someone's utterance and takes the transfer of divine qualities from scene to child as an impersonal grammatical pattern rather than as an active invention uttered to counter a contrary impression. It is true that such an invention might more properly fall, not under the grammatical analysis to which the scene–agent ratio belongs, but under Burke's rhetorical analysis, for it seems to be one of those rhetorical devices that have what he calls "a 'you and me' quality about them, being 'addressed' to some person or to some advantage" (xix). But Burke offers the grammatical analysis itself in its artificial separation from his other analytic perspectives as if its terms and their ratios were more "basic forms of thought" (xvii) than the speaker or listener of rhetoric and dialogics. "Scene" in Burke's grammar tends to be as patent, impersonal and objectively constraining as "sociolect" in Riffaterre's, and the mediating work of a speaker on which my dialogics rests is in principle reducible for both of them to abstract grammatical categories. From my point of view, however, rhetoric and dialogics are more fundamental than grammar, and even the most "objective" grammatical categories always carry more casuistical baggage in any instance of their use than Burke will here allow.

In Burke's grammar, for instance, the category of "scene" is meant to be an open functional place that does not beg the question of how a given philosophical casuistry interprets it, but it tends in Burke's actual use to be opposed to agent as the *non-verbal in general* is to the "*verbal in general.*" Though he recognizes that "the ground of any particular verbal action must be a complex of verbal and non-verbal factors" (103), and he calls for attention to words both in their "'nature as words in themselves *and* [in] the nature they get from the non-verbal scenes that support their acts'" (482), it is clear even from this passage that Burke thinks of "scene" or situation as primarily extrinsic and non-verbal, while he attributes to words in themselves a nature of their own apart from their relation to scene or situation.

Bakhtin and Voloshinov's dialogics places utterance in a different relation to a differently understood "*'non-verbal context'*" than Burke's dramatism (DLDP 11). Most importantly, it focuses not on an agent acting alone in a scene but on a speaker whose speaking is the "*product of the social interaction of three components:— the speaker* (author), *the listener* (reader), and *the one of whom* (or of which) *they speak* (the hero)" (DLDP 17). Speaker and listener share (and author and reader must create and re-create) an unspoken context of common "*spatial purview*," "*common knowledge and understanding of the circumstances*," and "*common evaluation* of these circumstances" (DLDP 11). They share these factors, however, not as a commonly recognized "external cause of the utterance" but as "*essential constituent part*[s] *of its sense structure*" (DLDP 12), not merely as an external visible scene but as an intelligible utterance, part of which is verbally realized and part of which is unspoken but implied.

Bakhtin and Voloshinov's common "spatial purview," then, is not the manifest scene of drama that would be there even if the action were not taking place, but a taken-for-granted aspect of the material world that the speaker's utterance responds to and resolves for both speaker and listener – the world implied by the speaker's deictics, assumed in the speaker's pronouns, and taken for granted in the speaker's enthymemes. The listener for whom the utterance is intelligible does not sit in the position of the objective dramatic spectator outside the action and the scene in which it takes place (and outside Burke's dramatistic pentad as well) but participates in the situation that provokes the speaker's utterance and shares the speaker's understanding of what need not be said.[26]

Though Burke intends his dramatistic perspective to recover a properly human interpretation of human action against those scientistic perspectives that reduce action to motion, it preserves the

26 For Bakhtin's contrast of dramatic and dialogic situations, see PDP 17–18.

external and objectified stance of those scientistic models and fails to account for the place of spectators (or listeners) in relation to the scenes they observe or the actions they interpret. The dialogic model of utterance, on the other hand, not only places speaker and listener in *"real, material participation in one and the same section of being"* (DLDP 11); it also makes the object of discourse participate in that world. The hero belongs to the same social world as speaker and listener either as a speaker in his or her own right or as a topic of the discourse of other speakers in the same world. The situation provocative of utterance includes the hero not just as part of a non-verbal scene in which the speaking agent acts but as an already articulate or articulated other whose words provoke the speaker's words.

The religious language of "Beauteous Evening" may be understood in these terms not just as a Burkean terminology, an agency manipulated by the speaker to describe the evening, but as a voice of religious power shaping the speaker's perception of it. What makes the speaker perceive a calm evening and call it "holy" is a social language of holiness associated with his belief in God, whose power the speaker registers, asserts and preserves in his utterance. Even when we take the speaker and the child his listener into account, as Burke does not, we still cannot account for the speaker's utterance as a relation between him, the child, and the evening scene. It is God whose felt presence in the evening moves the speaker to describe it as he does and whose power, even as it is not acknowledged by the child, compels him to assert His unapparent presence for her. God is the hero of the sonnet and the religious language in which He is known to believers like the speaker makes the "scene" expressive for the speaker as it would not be to one who did not share that belief and its language. That the child who shares his spatial purview does not share the religious language in which he evaluates the scene provokes him to draw further on the resources of that language to account for her obliviousness. For the speaker the religious language of his utterance celebrates the power of God not only to inform the scene but even to account for the child, who does not recognize God's power explicitly or respond to the language in which the speaker invokes Him. Again, in another Burkean context – that of "the rhetoric of religion" – this account of the poem might be perfectly acceptable, but it nevertheless challenges the terms of his dramatistic grammar and the reading he has derived from them.

A good dramatistic casuist might still try to reduce the speaker's religious language under the heading of "agency" to an instrument with which the speaker describes the scene and resolves his problem about the child, but the speaker would not imagine himself manipulating a "God-term" so much as he is responding in socially appropriate language to evidences of God's presence. Whereas Burke's dramatism would reduce such languages to manipulable terminologies and demote their sources to "agents," Bakhtinian dialogics acknowledges the power of those languages to shape our individual uses of them and personifies the sources of those languages as relatively autonomous "heroes." Dialogics will direct our attention toward the irreducible otherness in those languages, where dramatism would teach us to perform their reduction to familiar ratios. In practice we will always be choosing to follow one of these lessons, as I have chosen in this section to hold Burke to the idiosyncrasies of his readings and the habitual interpretations of his terms instead of "placing" him and Bakhtin in his (or someone else's) grammatical terms.

Rhetoric and dialogics: Charles Molesworth and the ideological horizon

Had Burke chosen to treat Wordsworth's sonnets in his rhetoric rather than his grammar of motives, that engagement would surely have been different from the one I have just worked through, but another critic provides a rhetorical reading of "Westminster Bridge" that can stand in for Burke's and provoke an engagement in its own right as well. Charles Molesworth, without explicit reference to Burke, shares important terms and interests with him as indeed he implicitly shares terms and interests with the other three critics I have so far introduced into my symposium.

He situates his argument, however, not in a tradition of critical arguments but in a context of biographical and historical information on the personal circumstances surrounding the sonnet's composition and the changing character of Wordsworth's political views. Though at one point he mentions a "formalist criticism" (272) to which he opposes his own inquiry, he does not call his overall position "rhetorical." Instead he repeatedly characterizes specific topics and observations in his discourse as "rhetorical," and I have chosen to highlight them as his characteristic moves to bring out his distinctive contribution to the critical symposium I am constructing. More than any of the other critics I have considered in this chapter (and like Ruoff in the previous one), Molesworth allows the theoretical implications of his essay to emerge from his practice rather than thematizing his theory and illustrating it (or failing to illustrate it) in his practical criticism. He does not, then, announce, nor can we hold him to, a theoretical agenda, but even as I have tried to preserve Burke's idiosyncrasies from identification with his theory, I want to bring out a theoretical theme for my own purposes from Molesworth's rich polytopic responses to the sonnet.

The theme Molesworth does announce – "The Republican Structure of Time and Perception" – does not subordinate all of his responses to the sonnet, but it does subsume his principal observations on both the rhetorical devices in it and their function in its overall rhetorical "argument." Molesworth argues that the poem is not just an observer's response to an uncommon visual scene but a citizen's response to an image of his city, resonant with "civic tones" (269). The terms in which the speaker sees London show traces of "Wordsworth's republican sentiment" (269) that reveal not the city made over in terms of natural beauty, as Brooks and Riffaterre read the poem, "but natural spectacle redrawn in the terms of civic grandeur" (269). Though he concedes that "we do not come away from the poem with a sense of its argument" (266), his accomplishment is to highlight its argumentative features and to define its "fullest argument" for its "fullest audience" (273) as a citizen's "'pointing with pride'" (270) to the revealed majesty and power of his city. The speaker's utterance described in this way not only bears witness to his regenerated view of his city but also teaches "a propaedeutic lesson" to his fellow citizens (272) – it also, we may note, allows itself to be characterized as a Bakhtinian speech genre with the city as its hero and fellow citizens as its listeners.

Though Molesworth enumerates his share of formal devices without clear rhetorical functions, he emphasizes the poem's argument in a way that permits him to notice and account for "devices" beyond the reach of Riffaterre's sociolexical analysis or Maclean's prosodic, semantic, and syntactic categories. He can hear "civic tones" in the regal diction of "majesty" (269). He can point out several "rhetorical negation[s]" (264) in the poem and see them "in the earnest service of forcefully stating [the poem's] higher affirmations" (263). He can recognize in the second line that "a virtual viewer is disposed of in order to establish the correct audience for the scene, and, presumably, for the poem as well" (264). He can account for the "figure of speech" of the "mighty heart" in the last line, in which he says "the city is not only...humanized but individualized, made over into a single subsistent agent, and one, furthermore, as the adjective 'mighty' tells us, with heroic scope and power" (266).[27]

This last formulation resonates in our context with overtones suggestive of both Burke and Bakhtin. Indeed, Molesworth's restatement of the point could lack nothing of the dramatistic explicitness Burke found wanting in Maclean's reading: "What ordinarily is witnessed as the scene of heroic action has taken over the role of heroic agent" (269). The effect of scene on speaker has transformed the scene into an agent whose "mighty heart...lying still" is felt as power or incipient action. That the city as agent is a personified hero recalls Bakhtin's autonomous hero as a participant in the speaker's discourse. The "civic tones" Molesworth hears in the speaker's description are to this poem what the religious tones are to "Beauteous Evening." They are the expression of a social language of "republican sentiment[s]" impressed upon the speaker by the power of the city as the language of religious reverence was impressed upon the speaker in the other poem by the sense of God in the evening (269).

In characterizing the speaker's sentiments as a "republican structure of feeling" (269), Molesworth attempts to ground his reading of the poem in a historical ideological formation that will permit us to recognize its resonance, but he has some difficulty constructing what Bakhtin and Medvedev call "the ideological horizon" (FM 17) in which the poem participates. He reaches toward a reconstruction of Wordsworth's "political views," on the one hand, and toward an ideal construction of "the republican imagination," on the other, combining Wordsworth's historical party affiliations with classical Roman stereotypes of republican virtue (268–69). Molesworth attempts here to identify an objectified non-verbal "structure of time

27 For an amplification of the city in the poem as a figure of "power in repose" and the details in the poem as "embodiments of London's majesty and power," see Patrick Holland, "The Two Contrasts of Wordsworth's 'Westminster Bridge' Sonnet," *WC* 8 (1977): 32–34. Holland's New Critical discovery of a poem that "reconciles and unifies two visions" situates itself in response to W. J. B. Owen's prior contrast between *The Prelude* and "Westminster Bridge," "The Sublime and the Beautiful in *The Prelude*," *WC* 4 (1973): 67–86.

and perception" characteristic of the republican position that accounts for the verbal devices of the poem, but he misses an opportunity to identify a *language* of political sentiment in Wordsworth's explicitly political poetry that helps to locate the language of "Westminster Bridge" within the same ideological horizon those poems define.[28]

Molesworth begins his essay by calling attention to Wordsworth's composition in 1802 of political sonnets he published in 1807 under the heading "Sonnets Dedicated to Liberty," but he places "Westminster Bridge" among a group of "other sonnets not on directly political subjects" composed at the same time (261), and he barely returns to the political sonnets to discover evidence not just of Wordsworth's political ideology at the time but of the language in which that ideology appears. Instead he turns to the poet's life and opinions to construct his account of the "immediate situation" (262) of the poem's composition, but the contemporary composition of those political sonnets is potentially an important part of that situation, and the public voice they assume and the language they deploy can be shown to be more significant to the dialogic situation of "Westminster Bridge" than the poet's marriage plans, his magnanimous settlement of an old debt or even his identification with the Girondist platform some years before. Wordsworth indeed suggests an association between "Westminster Bridge" and the regularly dated and situated sonnets of the "Liberty" group by making it the only dated sonnet of the "Miscellaneous Sonnets" in the 1807 gathering and one of two to specify its place of composition.[29] Molesworth cites one passage from one of the political sonnets, "To Toussaint L'Ouverture," to show Wordsworth making "political heritage" become "natural environment" (271), but this rather abstract figurative move is not as close to the language of "Westminster Bridge" as several passages from other poems.

In "Composed by the Sea-side, near Calais, August 1802" Wordsworth says that the Evening Star that shines on England should look "on her banners, drest / In thy fresh beauty," using a trope close to "This City now doth like a garment wear / The beauty

---

28 Liu's argument, discussed in the final section of this chapter, goes far toward remedying this lack in Molesworth's. My own comparison of the language of "Westminster Bridge" with that of the political sonnets in the following paragraphs was written before Liu's argument appeared and has not been altered to take it into account.

29 The date in 1807 was mistakenly given as 1803 rather than September 1802.

of the morning" in an utterance that overtly glorifies the nation. The opening and closing terms of "Westminster Bridge" – "Earth" and "mighty heart" – are brought together in another sonnet reminding his former companion Jones of the experience they shared of the festival in Calais on the anniversary of the fall of the Bastille: "The antiquated Earth, as one might say, / Beat like the heart of Man."[30] Here the transfiguration of Earth into a human heart marks the apogee of the poet's political hopes for the French Revolution, and the recapitulation of that vital trope in the overall development of "Westminster Bridge" marks a recovery of those hopes now revealed not in action in France but in potential in the transfigured capital city of England. The evocation of Milton's great patriotic contemporaries in "Great Men have been among us" portrays them as knowing how to recognize the national virtues the poet recognizes in the London of "Westminster Bridge": "They knew how genuine glory was put on; / Taught us how rightfully a nation shone / In splendor: what strength was, that would not bend / But in magnanimous meekness." Here the capacity to recognize national glory and splendor is what the great patriots knew and have taught their later countrymen like the poet. It may even be that the capacity to recognize national strength not in its martial exercise but in its voluntary self-restraint may resemble the speaker's capacity in "Westminster Bridge" to recognize that strength in its utter repose.

One might wish to locate the ideological horizon of these political poems, as I did that of the speaker of "The Sailor's Mother" in the last chapter, in relation to the discourse of other ideological spheres of contemporary social life – political debate or patriotic harangue or party manifesto – or even in relation to the republican discourses of a classical education, but one would not reach a point at which one could abstract a republican ideological formation or structure independent of those discourses with which one could then explain the poems. The dialogic perspective finds confirmation for Molesworth's reading of "Westminster Bridge" in the voices of Wordsworth's political sonnets and might lead us to discover wider resonances of his political language in other social discourses, but it would urge Molesworth to change his title from "The Republican Structure of Time and Perception" to "The Republican Voice in 'Westminster Bridge'" and to seek his evidence not in the facts of the

30 "To a Friend, Composed Near Calais, On the Road Leading to Ardres, August 7th, 1802."

poet's life but in his other poetic and prose voices and the social languages they embody. The evidence I have gathered from Wordsworth's political sonnets would suggest a further change of title to "The Patriotic Voice in 'Westminster Bridge'" or even "The Nationalistic Voice in 'Westminster Bridge,'" for the poem's language celebrates the nation without specifying its constitution.[31]

By locating the poem in "the tradition of epideictic verse" (269), Molesworth's rhetorical perspective reveals the city as the hero the speaker celebrates, not just in visual but in political glory, but it also raises the question, "To whom is the poem on the bridge addressed?" Molesworth hears in the mixing of the poem's lyric and political voices a "conflict in the poet's sense of audience" (271). Because the speaker, unlike the speaker of "Beauteous Evening," is alone, the poem's rhetorical genre is a problem. It contains "more than a hint of a moral suasion" and yet it seems closest in genre to the "diary entry," a kind of counterpart to Dorothy's journal entry on the experience from which the poem is drawn (271). The speaker seems to speak "to all the occupants of these 'very houses'" he describes (271), but his utterance in "its fullest argument" for "its fullest audience ... speaks to citizens as well as observers, ... to the ages as well as to the moment" (273).

Molesworth does not look to the one direct address of the poem – the exclamatory "Dear God!" in the thirteenth line – to locate the poem's addressee and situate its utterance (he ignores it in his close reading of the line on 266 and cites it as evidence of something else on 270). But the speaker's testimony, his bearing witness to the vision of London he beholds, seems properly addressed to God by Whom the speaker swears to what he beholds. The utterance gains its authority for any humbler witness, any fellow citizen, partly by neglecting to address him or her. It is not, as Molesworth suggests, that "the poet escapes from the demands of suasion by the pellucidity of his observations" (271) but that he reveals the power to which he attests by his complete attention to it and his appeal to God as his witness. An address to any particular others would, as the speaker in "Beauteous Evening" discovers, open his testimony to question, neglect, or contradiction. But the address to God certifies the utterance on the highest authority instead of attempting to share it or to confirm it from another's experience.

31 For further evidence of Wordsworth's nationalism, see Chandler, *Wordsworth's Second Nature*, 203–04.

As Bakhtin and Voloshinov recognize in talking about the "specific gravity of rhetorical speech," "the stronger the feeling of hierarchical eminence in another's utterance, the more sharply defined will its boundaries be, and the less accessible will it be to penetration by retorting and commenting tendencies from outside" (MPL 123). The rhetorical perspective, then, will be particularly suited to an utterance like this one in which the alternatives of retort and comment are closed off and the speaker presents himself and his experience for admiration or emulation. But the dialogic perspective, whose affinity to the rhetorical Bakhtin clearly recognizes (see DN 268–69, 280), encompasses not only this hierarchical "*declaratory* word" (MPL 159) but also the more vulnerable and responsive dialogized word. Dialogics can learn much from the "great external precision" (DN 269) of rhetorical analysis of conventional speech forms and figures and much from the analysis of determinate rhetorical situations as well, but it cannot limit its purview to those situations or accept those forms as fixed. The voices of the Western lyric tradition are closely allied to the rhetorical tradition, whose terms have shaped not only the criticism but the production of lyric poetry from classical times even to those recent Romantic times in which the tradition has been feared lost.[32] Indeed, in Chapter 7 I will argue for the powerful persistence of rhetorical forms and devices in some of Wordsworth's most "Romantic" poems. But a rhetorical criticism of lyric utterance remains likely to reduce precedent voices to objectified structures or responding voices to silence unless it is conversant with the dialogic possibilities it traditionally rules out.

Dialogics and feminist critique: Judith W. Page and the women in Wordsworth's life

Judith W. Page's feminist reading of "Beauteous Evening" calls attention to the voices of silenced women in that sonnet and reveals the affinity that others have noted between dialogic criticism and feminist critique.[33] Unlike Brooks and Maclean and Burke, who affirm

32 See W. R. Johnson, *The Idea of Lyric: Lyric Modes in Ancient and Modern Poetry* (Berkeley: University of California Press, 1982), for an interesting account of the rhetorical tradition of the lyric. Johnson, however, relying too much on standard accounts of the Romantic lyric like Abrams's "Structure and Style" essay, underestimates the continuation of that tradition into the Romantic period.

33 On Bakhtin's pertinence for feminist criticism and his own neglect of the category of gender see Wayne C. Booth, "Freedom of Interpretation: Bakhtin and the

the uninterrupted lyric unity of the speaker's perspective, Page points, as I would, to the interaction between the poem's speaker and the child at his side. Like Molesworth, Page situates the poem she is reading in a context of biographical and historical information, and also like him, she does not emphasize the theoretical implications of her critical terms.[34] In examining the relations between Wordsworth's "public and private concerns" (189), however, she does not, like Molesworth, use private information to substantiate public rhetorical stances but reads public language as a refiguring of private conflicts, reviving without recalling biographical readings like those that Maclean resisted in his Chicago School reading. By focusing not on a single sonnet but on what she calls the "Calais Sonnets," written in August of 1802 during a critical month in Wordsworth's domestic life, Page reads the languages of both public and private poems as utterances determined by the same domestic situation.

Page opens her argument with a synopsis of this situation: "In August of 1802, when Wordsworth was about to marry Mary Hutchinson, he went to France with his sister Dorothy to settle affairs with his former lover Annette Vallon and their illegitimate daughter Caroline" (189). To read "It is a beauteous evening, calm and free" as an utterance provoked by these circumstances is to specify the social relations represented in the poem not just as those between an adult male and a female child but rather as those between a father and his illegitimate and soon-to-be abandoned daughter. It is also to wonder about her mother, "Annette, the woman who has temporarily impeded his [the father's] marriage ... [as] an unacknowledged presence in the poem" (197).

These specifications – drawn, it should be remembered, not from the text of the poem alone but from an entry in Dorothy

Challenge of Feminist Criticism," *Critical Inquiry* 9 (September 1982): 45–76; Laurie Finke, "The Rhetoric of Marginality: Why I Do Feminist Theory," *Tulsa Studies in Women's Literature* 5 (Fall 1986): 251–72; Dale M. Bauer, *Feminist Dialogics* (Albany: SUNY Press, 1988); Myriam Diaz-Diocaretz, "Sieving the Matriheritage of the Sociotext," in *The Difference Within: Feminism and Critical Theory* (Amsterdam: John Benjamins, 1988), 115–47; and Anne Herrmann, *The Dialogic and Difference* (New York: Columbia University Press, 1989). See also Diaz-Diocaretz, "Bakhtin, Discourse, and Feminist Theories," and Clive Thomson, "Mikhail Bakhtin and Contemporary Anglo-American Feminist Theory," *Critical Studies* 1 (1989): 121–39, 141–61.

34 She does recognize the provenance of those terms, however, in the recent feminist work of Elaine Showalter, Anne K. Mellor, Margaret Homans, Gayatri Chakravorty Spivak, and Mary Jacobus.

Wordsworth's journal that reveals the circumstances of its composition – reconfigure the tone and theme of the utterance and heighten perception of it as a social interaction. The adult speaker becomes a father evading "his particular responsibilities to his illegitimate daughter Caroline," his religious language becomes "patriarchal religious language," and his closing gesture becomes one of placing "Caroline in the hands of God – a substitute father for the father Wordsworth knows he will never be" or even, in consigning her to "Abraham's bosom," symbolically killing the child. The tone of "Listen!" in the sixth line of the poem becomes not a generalized apostrophe as Maclean suggested or an invitation to the child to share the speaker's perception, as I earlier suggested, but a "command" to the child to attend to her father and her Father. The closing account of her relation to God is not just the speaker's compensation for his embarrassed failure to get the response he sought from the child but the father's "appropriating the authority of voice to himself" and telling "the girl who she is and where she lives and what her limitations are" (199). As an utterance addressed in specified circumstances to an auditor who does not speak in the poem, the poem takes on generic affinity not to Maclean's model of "Tintern Abbey," or to my own models of "We Are Seven" and "Anecdote for Fathers," but to the "dramatic monologue."

Page's version of the dramatic monologue stops short, however, of attributing significance to the child's *response* to the speaker's "command," for it characterizes the genre as one "in which the auditor, of course, is allowed no response." This account of the genre goes along with Page's judgment that the girl is not "given any voice in the poem" (199) and with her choice of "My Last Duchess" and "Dover Beach" as generic exemplars, but it misses what are for me more interesting and pertinent exemplars like "Andrea del Sarto" or "The Eolian Harp" in which the auditor's responses are *registered* by the speaker but not reported or recorded in the poem. In these poems, and I would argue in "Beauteous Evening" as well, the addressee's response crucially deflects the speaker's utterance from its course and requires him to make corrections and reinterpretations of his topic. Even if, in this sonnet, the child does not voice her failure or refusal to hear what the speaker urges her to hear, his change of direction in the sestet shows that he has noticed his own failure to involve her in his high-flown version of the scene. His command has not been obeyed (or his invitation has not been accepted), and he shows that he knows it. He is not precisely an obtuse patriarch who "tells the girl who she is and where she lives and what her limitations are" (199) without paying attention to how things affect her but, rather, is sensitive enough to her to see that she does not hear things or him as he does. He is also embarrassed enough by his failure to connect with her that he proposes another line of explanation to patch up the hole she has made in his balloon, but the poem lets the hole show.

Page finally values the poem not for its rhetorical suppression of Wordsworth's "private self and anxieties" but for its powerful revelation of them (199–201); her interpretation of those private motives and feelings, however, is more judicial than judicious. Her indictment calls for a condemnation and depends for its power upon the stability and primacy of the monologically defined scene in which Page places the agents in the poem. The ocean-side scene must become "Calais," the speaker "Wordsworth," the child "Caroline"; Dorothy, Annette, and Mary must be standing in the wings. "Wordsworth" must furthermore be the father who, knowing "the pain of growing into adolescence without a father[,] was now abandoning his child and her mother" (197). Stephen Gill imagines a figure of less certain meaning for the child and for us – "a 32-year-old foreigner, an enemy of her country who spoke rusty French, whom she had been taken to meet as her father," for the man Page represents as cruelly "abandoning" his child had never lived with her during her nine years of life and had chosen to come to see her and her mother the first time events had permitted.[35]

Page's paternity case against Wordsworth is an understandable response to sentimentalized biographical readings of the poem that vindicate, as she says, "Wordsworth as a father to Caroline,"[36] but her case might have been tempered by the knowledge of still earlier biographical readings like Legouis's that anticipate her own findings and further tempered by a willingness at least to entertain a distinction between biographical situation and poetic situation. As discourse in art rather than discourse in life, the poem allows the construction of an ambivalent dialogic relation between its speaker and the child he addresses that calls the speaker's authority and his religious language delicately into question; as discourse in the life

35 Stephen Gill, *William Wordsworth: A Life* (Oxford: Clarendon Press, 1989), 207.
36 See the passage she quotes from Mary Moorman's biography that Page says "vindicates Wordsworth as a father to Caroline" on p. 197 of "Wordsworth's Calais Sonnets."

re-created in Page's argument the poem seems wholly determined by the circumstances that occasioned it, and the poet appears discredited by his determinate response to those circumstances. If the dialogic reading I propose cannot rest content with these determinacies, it remains to be seen whether its only alternative is the cultivation of indeterminacy offered by J. Hillis Miller's deconstructive reading.

Responsibility and indeterminacy: J. Hillis Miller, deconstruction, and the ethics of reading

No recent critic has argued more vigorously against the determinacy of poetic language, or indeed of language in general, than J. Hillis Miller. He has promoted his deconstructive celebration of indeterminacy under the banners of both the "rhetorical" and the "dialogical," though he does not make either term explicit in the essay in which he deconstructs "Westminster Bridge." Nevertheless, I shall query him in that essay about how his ideas and his practices of rhetorical and dialogical criticism compare with those I have already presented, because his demonstration of the sonnet's indeterminacy involves the same methods and effects he elsewhere calls by those names. In another essay he calls "rhetorical" analysis "the investigation of the role of figurative language in literature";[37] the effect he names "dialogical" involves, among other things, the production of indeterminate "vibrating resonances" between alternative meanings "which can never be stilled in a single monological narrative line."[38] Since his reading of the sonnet both focuses on figurative language and discovers indeterminate resonances, an approach to his theory through his practice in this essay is not inappropriate.

Miller's recent work also enters the purview of my symposium at another level. The "ethics of reading" he has recently advocated has made neglect of other critics into an ethical principle that gives precedence to the "imperative" of "the words on the page" over his "ethical responsibilities toward students and colleagues, and the whole institution of literary studies" (T&P 610). If we find Miller's

---

37 "On Edge: The Crossways of Contemporary Criticism," *Bulletin of the American Academy of Arts and Sciences* 32 (November 1978): 18. Reprinted in *Romanticism and Contemporary Criticism*, ed. Morris Eaves and Michael Fischer (Ithaca: Cornell University Press, 1986), 96–111.

38 J. Hillis Miller, "Ariachne's Broken Woof," *Georgia Review* 31 (1971): 58.

ethics of reading compelling, we will respect the imperatives of language he posits and have no ground for complaint at critics' neglect of previous critics' work and no need for the Bakhtinian dialogics of criticism I have been elaborating in this symposium. Miller has enacted his ethics of reading in solo readings of a number of Romantic lyrics that have previously been widely discussed by other critics. His reading of "A slumber did my spirit seal," which has provoked a strong rejoinder from M. H. Abrams, does not invoke the widely known critical controversies surrounding the poem,[39] and his reading of Wordsworth's sonnet "Composed Upon Westminster Bridge" does not notice any of the previous engagements with it. His staged encounter between himself and the sonnet does not explicitly register any relations between his voice and the voices of other critics who have written about it, but it does appropriate the authority of Wordsworth's voice and reiterate an earlier New Critical reading of the sonnet; in so doing, it fails to demonstrate either the power of Miller's deconstructive criticism or the necessity of his ethics of reading.

In his reading of "Westminster Bridge" the only other voice Miller engages is Wordsworth's, as Miller constructs it from two of his other sonnets that make their form their explicit theme. What gives this stage of Miller's argument special interest is the difference between the reading practice he follows when he construes this pair of sonnets as reliable sources of Wordsworth's views and those he follows when he deconstructs "Westminster Bridge" as a poem that enacts the indeterminacies they only describe. Miller's readings of "Nuns fret not at their convent's narrow room" and "Scorn not the sonnet" are as centripetal or centering as his reading of "Westminster Bridge" is centrifugal or decentering.

Miller makes two characteristic kinds of constructive or centering moves in his readings of the thematic sonnets. First, he determines the meaning of Wordsworth's use and theory of the sonnet in these poems by asserting that they "must be understood in the context of [his] theme of poetic impotence" as it appears in the language and the history of composition of *The Prelude* (300). Though he elsewhere will

---

39 Miller's reading of "A slumber" appears in "On Edge: The Crossways of Contemporary Criticism." Abrams's rejoinder appears along with Miller's response to it in *Romanticism and Contemporary Criticism*, ed. Eaves and Fischer. See also Karl Kroeber's remarks in his review of Eaves and Fischer, *SiR* 27 (Summer 1988): 341–42.

assert that "the concept we so blithely name *context* for a given text...can nowhere be fully identified or fully controlled" ("Ariachne's Broken Woof," 58–59), he here asserts the compelling power of the context he suggests and cites corroborating evidence from Wordsworth's letters. Had Miller chosen a comparable strategy for his reading of "Westminster Bridge," some of its indeterminacies might have been determined.

Second, and more revealingly, Miller pulls the diverse metaphors of the two sonnets toward a center instead of probing them for the "radical ambiguity" (306) he discovers in "Westminster Bridge." He tries to make all the metaphors in "Nuns fret not" illustrate a unifying and impersonal Brooksian paradox – that small size allows for a kind of largeness – but his explication can make this point stick only to the figures of the first quatrain. He asserts of "Scorn not the sonnet" that "a coherent system of thought underlies [the] metaphors" in the image of "something small and enclosed which is nevertheless articulated or structured," but he must concede that Spenser's "glow-worm lamp" does not quite fit the pattern and he must imagine as "reticulated" a myrtle leaf that only glitters gaily in the poem (301).

Miller clips and adjusts the tropes in these poems to fit a single determinate "system of thought" instead of highlighting their differences and celebrating the indeterminate oscillations they set up. He constructs these poems to bring out his theme of the "paradoxical relation of the sonnet to its origin" (302) in order to claim Wordsworth's authority for his deconstruction of "Westminster Bridge"; he reduces them to a determinate pattern, comprehends them as if their meaning were unambiguous, the better to show how "Westminster Bridge" illustrates "the incompatibility between meaning and the meaningless" (299).

Miller's reading of "Westminster Bridge" first acknowledges an aspect of apparent unity and straightforward meaning in the poem, what Miller calls "an undeniably mimetic dimension [that]...is not to be dismissed or transcended by further interpretation" (304). In this aspect the poem represents the objects of the cityscape in the smokeless air and the poet's "subjective reaction" (304) of calm corresponding to the calm he perceives. Like Maclean, Miller imagines what is imitated not as utterances but as "extra-linguistic realit[ies]..., whether mental or physical, [that] are presumed to have existed outside that language and not to depend on it for their existence" (305).

Miller goes beyond this mimetic reading to bring out the indeterminateness of the language of "Westminster Bridge" in what he would call a rhetorical analysis of its use of negatives and its pattern of metaphors. He attends to the negatives, explicit and implicit, more closely than any of the other readers I have considered, claiming that each negation "creates a shadowy existence for what is denied," even an evocation of "such dullards" as would not be moved by the beauty of the city (305). Like Riffaterre, however, Miller consigns the figure of the speaker to his mimetic reading and so does not take the interplay of the negations and what they negate as a speaker's gestures situating his utterance in a field of other utterances, its paradox as a response to some dox. But he does not go on as Riffaterre does to read the negations as the idiolect's determination of its relation to a sociolect. Instead, Miller believes the negations create "the presence of what they deny" as "a shimmering mirage lying over their explicit assertions" (306), an unresolved "'suspens vibratoire'" (303) that contributes to the overall "dialogical" effect of irresolution in the poem. Miller represents the negations not as Bakhtinian signs of hidden dialogue with other utterances in the dialogizing background but as language that has the power to call up in the foreground other language that interferes with what it is saying – what he elsewhere calls the "interference of the dialogical with the monological" ("Ariachne's Broken Woof," 60).

Miller's "rhetorical" analysis reads the metaphors in the sonnet to the same "dialogical" effect. He concentrates on the "personification of the city as a sleeping human figure" and discovers a "point of radical ambiguity" in the discrepancy between what he makes of the last two lines – that the city appears to be asleep in the thirteenth line but dead, "like a corpse," in the final one. Having suggested this reading, Miller accepts it as the basis for further implications. First he reasons that the city is "like a corpse because there are no human consciousnesses present within it," and then he notices that the speaker's own consciousness paradoxically violates the condition of human absence that gives the scene a calm like nature's. The "oscillation" that arises between this "rhetorical" reading and the mimetic one that it supplements but does not transcend is for Miller "the characteristic endpoint of any careful reading of Wordsworth's best poems" (306–07). In this "dialogical" suspense "between mimesis and emblem, between imitative form and creative form," he writes, "the images of the poem hang balanced" (309). Miller has produced this suspended "dialogical" effect without voices, dialogue, and meaning by using a "rhetorical" criticism that lacks concepts of speaker, audience, and occasion. He creates indeterminacy by choosing not to inquire into determinants, dialogical or historical.

But he also creates unwarranted determinacies by choosing (or being compelled by linguistic imperatives) not to inquire into alternative readings. He does not answer Burke's or Molesworth's sense of incipience in the poem, for example, a reading that might point toward the awakening of the mighty heart that now lies still. Nor does he entertain the common metaphorical senses of "heart" as the vital center of the nation or as the seat of courage and feeling or simply as a person, senses for which lying still would not necessarily imply morbidity. He does not look for verbal parallels in Wordsworth's other poems, where he would have found these lines that question the inevitability of his reading: "Yet pure and powerful minds, hearts meek and still, / A grateful few, shall love thy modest Lay."[40] These still hearts are alive, just not agitated.

Indeed the crucial move of Miller's reading is to literalize the vehicle of the heart as an individual person's physical organ whose stillness may seem relatively unambiguous and to take this *possible* reading for the necessary and *actual* one. But even without the technology of cardiac stimulation, we may recognize that a heart lying still *may* suggest various states of suspended animation – the love-song convention is but one example. Miller, whose critical principles open his reading to language without contextual limits, creates the final indeterminacy of the poem by uncritically determining this trope and then reasoning from the determination he has made to paradoxical conclusions. He has not made his reading answerable to the specific linguistic diversity he repeatedly celebrates in general.

But has this inattention to alternative meanings and readings "made possible new insights into what is going on" in this particular work (T&P 610)? When Miller's ethics of reading gives precedence to the "imperative" of "the words on the page" over his "ethical responsibilities toward students, colleagues, and the whole institution of literary studies," has he retrieved anything for those students and colleagues and for that institution that they would otherwise have lacked (T&P 613)?

40 "To the Poet, John Dyer," in *Poetical Works*, ed. de Selincourt, III, 10.

In the case of "Westminster Bridge," Miller gives us very little that David Ferry did not give us in his 1959 reading of the sonnet.[41] Not yet having heard of the deconstruction of metaphysics, whose effects Miller illustrates with his reading of the poem, Ferry arrives at a reading that anticipates Miller's main insights by exaggerating the New Critical "tension" between "'surface' and 'deeper' meanings" into a "hostility" (12). Just as Miller preserves the difference between mimetic and emblematic or imitative and creative readings of the sonnet, so Ferry offers "dramatic" and "symbolic" readings. In his "dramatic" reading Ferry touches first on the description of London, focusing on the same details Miller does in his mimetic reading, and then presents the speaker's attitudes toward these objects, Miller's "subjective reaction." Ferry's symbolic reading overlooks the negations Miller emphasizes in his "creative" reading, but it zeroes in on the same figure of the heart lying still in the last line and reads it to very much the same effect, choosing the same shocking word, "corpse," to make the point memorable.[42]

Ferry writes, "The last line of Wordsworth's sonnet suggests that the city is not merely sleeping but dead, its heart stilled. The poet looks at London and sees it as a sort of corpse and admires it as such, welcomes a death which is the death of what the city has come to stand for in his symbolic world" (14). Like Miller, Ferry takes the death of the city as the absence of human beings from the scene, and like him also, Ferry catches the ironic twist this reading produces: "The 'death' the poet is so pleased to witness is the death even of those properties in himself by which he responds so wonderfully to the city at this particular moment" (14–15). Miller writes, "The poet shares in a calm which can only exist if he is absent. He is both there and not there, as if he were his own ghost" (307). Finally, like Miller, Ferry does not permit this symbolic reading to supplant the dramatic one; instead he juxtaposes them to produce a paradox – "that one of

41 *The Limits of Mortality* (Middletown, Conn.: Wesleyan University Press, 1959), 12–15.
42 Brooks, it should be noted, introduces the topos of the "city under the semblance of death," though he does not use the word "corpse" or discover the same paradox as Miller and Ferry. See *Well Wrought Urn*, 6–7. G. M. Harvey, in a reading later than Miller's but without reference to it or any other prior reading, follows a similar New Critical trajectory, discovering a dialectic between a mimetic "rhetoric of sympathy" and a paradoxical "rhetoric of irony" in the poem and claiming that "the calm is, after all, in reality only the serene majesty of a corpse" ("The Design of Wordsworth's Sonnets," *Ariel E* 6 [1975]: 78–83).

the great representatives of our human powers of articulation should be himself a lover of silence" (15). Miller phrases a comparable paradox in somewhat more elaborate terms: "The forms of articulated speech or melody make the unworded blast of the original word available by turning it into definite tones or speech, and at the same time they limit it, transform it, obscure it, veil it over, traduce it by translating it" (302). Both these paradoxical formulations set the articulated against the inarticulable, devaluing the mimetic "surface" of the poem in the light of the depths revealed in Ferry's symbolist "'aspect of eternity'" (12) or Miller's deconstructionist abyss.

I have pressed home the closeness of Miller's reading to Ferry's not just to assert Ferry's claim to precedence and to discredit Miller's claim to novelty; nor do I imagine that Miller has consciously or unconsciously plagiarized Ferry's reading. Two men trained at Harvard at the height of New Criticism's influence in the late 40s and early 50s might well have assimilated the same critical languages and reading strategies and brought them to bear on the same exemplary poem.[43] In any case my point is not just to reaffirm the scholarly obligation of doing one's homework. This obligation sends one to the critical archive to give due credit to others who have anticipated one's own reading or idea, but it does not urge one to formulate one's reading or idea in response to the voices that have already spoken or to discover its affinities and oppositions in the public discourse one is proposing to enter. It is a conservative duty of respecting established intellectual properties rather than a radical enterprise of producing new intellectual property through active appropriation of and contention with others' words and ideas. Dialogics calls attention to critics' neglect of their predecessors not to convict them of failure to meet their obligations but to provoke them to become self-conscious contributors to the critical community that enables and challenges their cultural practices.

The issue that provokes me near the end of my own engagement with the critics I have addressed (knowing that I have still left others out of account altogether)[44] is that Miller's neglect of other critics in

43 See Paul de Man's account of the experience of sitting in on Reuben Brower's course in "The Interpretation of Literature" at Harvard in the 1950s in "Return to Philology," in *The Resistance to Theory* (Minneapolis: University of Minnesota Press, 1986), 23–25.

44 See especially on "Westminster Bridge," Geoffrey H. Hartman, "The Unremarkable Poet," in *The Unremarkable Wordsworth*, ed. Donald G. Marshall (Minneapolis: University of Minnesota Press, 1987), 207–19. See also, on both

his deconstructive practice is as programmatic as attention to other critics in my dialogic practice. Miller ignores the work of others not just because he tacitly accepts the generic limitations of the New Critical essay but because he explicitly believes that their work is irrelevant to his ethical obligation to the text itself.

I have already quoted from a passage in Miller's response to Vincent Leitch in which Miller opts for his obligation to the language of the text in preference to his responsibilities to students, colleagues, and institutions (T&P 613). In a recent conference on the Yale School several remarks by and about Miller suggest a similar opposition of the text to the critics.[45] After offering his unsubstantiated judgments of the readings of several critics in a recent symposium on Matthew Arnold, Miller writes,

Adjudication of differences here is of course possible only by a response to that call, "Back to the texts!," which must be performed again and again in literary study. Nothing previous critics have said can be taken for granted, however authoritative it may seem. Each reader must do again for himself the laborious task of scrupulous slow reading, trying to find out what the texts actually say rather than imposing on them what she or he wants them to say or wishes they said. ("Grounds," 28).

At first listening, these may sound like unexceptionable scholarly commonplaces, hardly deconstructive paradoxes. But they suggest what the transcript of the discussion following the talk confirms, that the texts to be scrupulously reread are only those of what his questioner will call the "primary source," not those of the critics whose disputes are to be adjudicated. If what those critics have said

sonnets, Dell H. Hymes, "Phonological Aspects of Style: Some English Sonnets," in *Style in Language*, ed. Thomas A. Sebeok (Cambridge, Mass.: M.I.T. Press, 1960), 119–20; and on "Westminster Bridge," William A. Bennett, "An Applied Linguistic View of the Function of Poetic Form," *Journal of Literary Semantics 6* (1977): 35–37; and, for comments on Bennett's generative grammatical approach, see David Birch, *Language, Literature and Critical Practice* (London and New York: Routledge, 1989), 135–37.

45 The "Oklahoma Conference on Contemporary Genre Theory and the Yale School" was held in Norman, Oklahoma, May 31–June 1, 1984. Papers from the conference are published in a double issue of *Genre* 17 (Spring and Summer, 1984). I make reference to Miller, "The Search for Grounds in Literary Study," 19–36; "Marxism and Deconstruction: Symposium at the Conference on Contemporary Genre Theory and the Yale School 1 June 1984," 75–97. See also Robert Markley, "*Tristram Shandy* and 'Narrative Middles': Hillis Miller and the Style of Deconstructive Criticism," 179–90. The collection has been reprinted with the same pagination as *Rhetoric and Form: Deconstruction at Yale*, ed. Robert Con Davis and Ronald Schleifer (Norman: University of Oklahoma Press, 1985).

cannot be "taken for granted," it may be that it does not have to be taken into account at all.[46]

Miller's remarks at this conference and my own reading of Miller's essay on "Westminster Bridge" add new force to the question William E. Cain asked of Miller's critical practice in 1979: "What is the responsibility of the critic towards a text, and *what kinds of judgments does he or she render on those who are also engaged in the interpretation of texts*?"[47] The premises on which I have constructed this symposium call into further question the answers Miller gives to this question. "Subjecting oneself to the words on the page" (T&P 613), as Miller proposes to do, does not take precedence over social relations to persons and institutions, for reading is a social act and both the language of the text and the capacities with which we respond to it are socially involved, whether we acknowledge it or not. Any text, as Bakhtin claims, is already "overlain with qualifications, open to dispute, charged with value, already enveloped in an obscuring mist – or, on the contrary, by the 'light' of alien words that have already been spoken about it" (DN 276), and any reader reads such a text with linguistic expectations shaped at least in part by his or her experiences of languages in every social context with which they are familiar, from family to critical school.

Miller's idea of "a linguistic imperative which shapes what a critic or teacher says about a text" distinct from and prior to ethical responsibilities is a dangerous mystification that discourages critical reflection about the linguistic resources one brings to the act of reading and about the social context in which the publication of that act takes place. To imagine that when one has submitted to that "linguistic imperative" then "the ethical operation will already necessarily have taken place" is to abdicate responsibility not only for one's relation to "students, colleagues, and the whole institution of literary studies" but also, finally, for the text and the social text of which it and the critic are part.[48]

46 See "Symposium," 92–93.
47 "Deconstruction in America: The Recent Literary Criticism of J. Hillis Miller," *College English* 41 (December 1979): 374–75. Revised and reprinted in Cain, *The Crisis in Criticism* (Baltimore: Johns Hopkins University Press, 1984), 39.
48 T&P 613. Miller's account of "what deconstruction is about" in "Symposium" (92) continues to talk about the coercion of the reader by the text. Appealing again to de Man's authority, he says "that what takes place in any act of reading is what has to happen because of the words, not what one wishes to happen or expects will happen. When you read, in a way it's a no-lose situation;

Critics who believe in this imperative will imagine the text "forcing" them to report readings that they share with forgotten sources, and they will take as necessary or beyond discussion readings to which significant alternatives already publicly exist. They will depend for their persuasiveness upon an audience ignorant of much that has been said and uninquisitive about much that might be said about the text. They will set themselves apart from the give and take of critical exchange, just as they set the texts with which they engage apart from public conversation in which amateur and professional readers reappropriate their meanings.

Like lyric speakers, literary critics shape their utterances in communities where available languages already assert their power, where much has already been said, and where others who have not yet spoken or not yet been heard have potential to concur or demur. Though these other languages and voices are sometimes represented as dispensable "experts" or intimidating precursors, as chaotic logomachies or discredited establishments, they are also the necessary provocations, formative influences, and enabling others of poetic and critical utterance alike. To ignore them is to be doomed to repeat them or be blind-sided by them; to engage them in the fullness of their power and diversity is to articulate our topics and ourselves comprehensively and responsibly among the others who share our world and time and to advance our common, or at least interrelated, inquiries.[49]

Dialogics and history: Alan Liu, formalism, and New Historicism

The dialogic alternatives to the isolated speaker of the Romantic lyric and the isolated author of the New Critical essay are poetic speakers and critical authors situated in worlds of others who provoke and constrain and contextualize their utterances. Further, as my point of departure from Arac's critique indicated, critical writing conscious of the intertextuality of the poems about which it writes should itself take some form which acknowledges its own intertextuality. Critics cannot persist in writing New Critical essays about poems they now

something's going to happen to you, the text is going to make a necessary occurrence take place even in the worst reading. That has nothing to do with subjectivity. It has to do with the language and your response to it."
49 See my "Dialogics as an Art of Discourse."

understand as parts of more comprehensive dialogic fields without appearing to be unconscious in their own writing of contexts like those they call attention to in the writings of their authors. We cannot dialogize or historicize them without self-consciously dialogizing and historicizing ourselves.

The risks and difficulties of writing with such self-consciousness may already be evident in the magnitude of this chapter and in the diversity of its lines of argument with various interlocutors. They would be even more evident to those who had seen readers' reports on earlier versions of the chapter – submitted as an essay to two journals – that complained that the essay "has gone a little out of control" or that "Molesworth does not belong here" or that "Ferry and Maclean fit in only loosely" or that "Bialostosky has a salient argument with Riffaterre and Miller, but hardly at all with Burke and the others" or that "elaborate recapitulations of all these well known critical essays" are "too much machinery altogether." The pressures to conform to more economical and pointed critical genres – if not the New Critical essay, then at least the polemic with one or two current critical authorities – came from anonymous readers who disagreed entirely on which authorities were worth arguing with and which arguments were important to make.

Recently, the risks and difficulties of writing with such self-consciousness, as well as the critical power of doing so, have also become manifest in Alan Liu's *Wordsworth: The Sense of History*, the final chapter of which chooses to read "Westminster Bridge" to advance the cause of yet another modern critical movement, the New Historicist criticism of power. Published when the previous sections of this chapter were already complete (except, of course, for their added mentions of Liu), Liu's chapter provokes me to reopen my symposium because it departs significantly from the critical practices of my other symposiasts by building upon and accounting for their arguments, historicizing its own discourse as it historicizes Wordsworth's poem, and even acknowledging Wordsworth's anticipation of the critical standpoint it brings to bear upon him.

Liu's self-consciousness in the chapter manifests itself not in his choice of a genre like my symposium but in his repeated and extended reflections – in both text and notes – on his relations to the positions of others and to the changing standpoints of Wordsworth himself (in his carefully precedented dialogic epilogue an uncommon choice of genre does play a part). He makes himself and his place among others an issue even as he makes an issue of Wordsworth's relations to the others the poet sometimes acknowledges and sometimes denies. If the economy of my symposium is bloated by "elaborate recapitulations of all these well known critical essays" – my dialogismus with or prosopopeia of absent critics' voices – the economy of Liu's chapter (which is as long or longer than my own or than the whole collection of essays on "Westminster Bridge" I have analyzed) is swollen by many of the species of self-referential prolepsis, or anticipation, that Quintilian catalogues among the figures of thought – confession, self-correction, preparation, qualification. If I elaborate my reading of the poem by incorporating the voices of others into my own, Liu elaborates his reading by responding to the less frequently and extensively quoted voices of others and to the other voices of the self that call him to account for himself or distinguish himself or locate himself in ideological affiliation and historical precedence with them.

Liu's self-dramatizing self-consciousness still resembles the sole self of the New Critic in making its own responses the focus of attention, yet it responds not just to the "poem itself" but to everything others have said or might say about the poem and about Liu's critical strategies, to all the poem's variant editions, to other texts that contextualize the poem, and even to Liu's own words in his own text. Like Wordsworth's *Prelude* – the work Liu treats at greatest length – Liu's critical argument expands a lyric stance to epic scope by responding not just to one or two voices but to all the other voices that impinge on it from within and outside the critic, and his writing may need the indulgence of the same sort of friendly reader that Wordsworth's poem projects.

My narrative genres of essay review and symposium, on the other hand, dramatize and organize what others have said to advance the plots and themes in which I have tried to engage my readers, but I am always in danger of losing progress and point in what appear to be local skirmishes with no apparent relation to the issue. Both of us risk trying our readers' patience by expanding our own dialogic responsiveness to correspond to the responsiveness we call attention to in Wordsworth himself – even at our readers' expense of time and thought.

Readers who have patiently (or impatiently) followed my symposium this far, or those who have done its work for themselves and engaged the critical literature on "Westminster Bridge," would be rewarded by patient attention to Liu's reading of the poem and its critics, for they would be in a position to recognize his affinities, discover his confirmations or elaborations of points made by others, and appreciate his substantial original contribution to our understanding of the poem. Liu's account of the critical alternatives, informed by knowledge of all the sources on the poem I have cited except Burke and Riffaterre and by several sources I was not previously aware of, boils down the possibilities to two, though each is not entirely at one with itself: Yale formalism (New Critical and deconstructive) against New Historicism (following McGann or Greenblatt). Liu amplifies the "indeterminacy, ambiguity, paradox" (464) of the readings produced by the former school – to which he indicates he owes a considerable debt (xv) – only to turn on it the particularizing critique of the latter school – about which he declares certain reservations (457, 466). In the formalist camp he places Brooks's and Ferry's readings along with Miller's deconstructive reading, understood as a continuation of the New Critical "thesis of paradox" (464), though he does not note the parallel I have demonstrated between Miller and Ferry. He brings all "modern readings of the poem" (460) a bit too hastily under the "High Street arch in New Haven" (464) without recognizing the Harvard Yard origins of Miller's and Ferry's readings and without placing Burke or Riffaterre (or Maclean – who admittedly reads another poem) on the map at all.[50]

Liu inserts his own New Historicist reading *avant la lettre*[51] between two favorable mentions of Molesworth's even earlier anticipation of New Historicism and of some of Liu's argument, but Liu does not locate Molesworth under the High Street arch or anywhere else on a map of modern critical schools or available critical disciplines. He takes an "initial hint" (465) and a closing topos from Molesworth without working through the significant resemblances

---

50 Liu notes that Page's reading – also of the other poem – came to his attention too late to incorporate into his argument (638 n. 21).

51 He declares that he "began this work in 1979–80 before the advent of a recognizably New Historicist method" and has "therefore not been able to engage with the method as centrally or fully" as he "would have liked" (634 n. 2). One would think that nearly a decade of work on the book during the period of the emergence of the New Historicist method would have been long enough to work out this relationship. It might be more accurate to say that Liu maintained an ambivalent relation of identification with and resistance to the New Historicism during this period; hence the book we have.

between their positions or identifying where he builds upon or corrects Molesworth's emphases. Molesworth's essay touches upon the biographical evidence and the political sonnets of the Calais trip that Liu forcefully amplifies as contexts for "Westminster Bridge," and Molesworth introduces the rhetorical categories of analysis Liu drives home in one part of his argument.

In his principal thesis, Liu differs from Molesworth as I do in emphasizing not republican values but *"national power"* (466) as the hero celebrated in the sonnet, but in execution of his argument he leaves behind Molesworth's sketchy biographical information and my own selective attention to the language of Wordsworth's "Sonnets Dedicated to Liberty" to construct a more fully documented and richly articulated version of that thesis that places the poem in at least four related contexts, each of which brings out different relations between the speaker and his hero. Exploiting the ambiguities between the date of the vision on the bridge (July 31, 1802) and the date of composition of the poem (September 3, 1802) and relations between the poem and the political sonnets composed during the same period, Liu reads what I would call the poem's speech genre as an ambivalent combination of "lover's valediction" and "proleptic epitaph" in the context of Wordsworth's vision of the scene on his way to France (477) and as "epithalamial rather than valedictory" (479) upon his return. Against the background of the "great Anarch" France (478), Wordsworth courts and fears for his nation on leaving her and weds her upon his return home, talking *"with the nation about the nation's power"* (485).

Similarly exploiting inconsistencies in the dates Wordsworth attached to the published poem and changes in his placement of it in his various collections of poems, Liu shows, first, how the misdating of the poem as composed September 3, 1803, and the placement of it among the Miscellaneous Sonnets rather than with the political sonnets in connection with which it was written "displaced 'Westminster Bridge' out of the historical world" and made it a poem that invited the indeterminate formal analyses it has received, "a poem embracing all places and times indeterminately... a poem about no place and time at all" (489) spoken by an "'I'... empowered to step forth at last free of all worldly responsibility except imagination" (490). Liu then argues that Wordsworth's restoration of the date "'Sept. 3, 1802,' which [he] first entered informally in his sonnet's title in the densely annotated copy of *1836–37* he used to prepare future revisions ... and then – with increasing fidelity – in the printed titles of the ensuing principal editions" indicated that "the intensely private lyricism it had come to express after 1807 finally returned to the world of the public and topical" (492); "Wordsworth's imagination at last knew its place. Phrased critically: imagination was put in its place" (497). Thus "the later, imaginatively 'dead' Wordsworth ... sacrifices part of his original self – his imagination – to redeem part of history" (456) and that same late Wordsworth anticipates later historicist critics of his earlier lyric self.

The power of Liu's emplotment here, like the power of his contrast between formalist and historicist criticism, depends upon the maintenance of an opposition between history and imagination in which history gives rise to an imagination that first occludes its origins but, in the end, submits to them. This opposition corresponds to that between narrative and dramatic action, on the one hand, and lyric "sinking all dialogic tension into monologue" (313), on the other – an opposition my own argument has been at pains to deconstruct. Liu writes that "if drama is the discourse of inter-locutors, ... then lyric transforms drama into a discourse in which there are no true interlocutors, only the locution that is the self and certain mute circumlocutions (e.g. Coleridge, Dorothy) standing in place of the chorus" (309). I have argued, however, that neither of the exemplary lyric selves in the two sonnets (or, in the last chapter, the self in "Tintern Abbey") can be reduced to such monologic isolation. Interlocutors – other people's words or responses or lacks of response or the self's own internalized others – provoke lyric utterances, too. Coleridge and Dorothy, as Matlak has shown, do more than stand in place of the chorus in "Tintern Abbey"; the child at Wordsworth's side does more, too, in "Beauteous Evening"; and Wordsworth's own previous judgments and expectations, his opinions about nature and the city, on one reading, or his earlier alienation from his country, on another, become the opinions of another person, dull of soul, in "Westminster Bridge" against which Wordsworth defines his new self.

Instead of "sinking all dialogic tension into monologue," the dialogic conception of lyric I have elaborated with the help of the Bakhtin School reads lyric monologue precisely for signs of the dialogic tensions that have provoked and shaped it, even as that conception reduces the dialectical tension between "imagination" and "history" on which the drama of Liu's argument depends. Like

McGann's critique of the "Romantic Ideology," Liu's historicist debunking or demystifying of lyric imagination must preserve, even exaggerate, the mystified formalist notion of isolated lyric consciousness it opposes in order to demonstrate the force of its own historical critique;[52] my dialogics of the lyric reconceives lyric consciousness and lyric form as functions of a dialogic imagination that is not opposed to history but in it.

52 For a parallel critique see my reading of Jeffrey Robinson's teaching of the Immortality Ode in Chapter 8 below.

5

Social action in "The Solitary Reaper"

[T]he great issues posed about Wordsworth in the nineteenth century remain unresolved. I mean above all the issues between Hazlitt and Coleridge as to which was the appropriate totality that defined Wordsworth's poetry: social or metaphysical.   Jonathan Arac, *Critical Genealogies*

Wimsatt and Pottle ... do not treat Wordsworth as a simple celebrant of the natural world. They are as interested as Hartman in the poet's consciousness, but for them consciousness is inseparable from relationships with other people, the natural world, and the poet's earlier self. I see the reorientation in Wordsworthian studies during the sixties, therefore, as founded not on a new appreciation for the poet's complexities but, rather, on a fundamental simplification: an assumption that alienation, not relation, is essential to Wordsworth, as to all human existences.   Karl Kroeber, "Wordsworth"

Liu's loyalty to the dialectical tension between imagination and history – his very constitution of himself as critic in the preservation and elaboration of that tension – can be historicized as part of his acknowledged heritage from the Yale English Department, which has also promulgated powerful dialectical readings of Wordsworth based on the tensions between imagination and nature and imagination and time. Liu, indeed, opens his argument by defending the champion of one of those dialectical readings, Geoffrey Hartman, against historicist critics who would inquire into "'the representation of reality as historical process'" without reference to "the apocalyptic or visionary imagination" that for Liu is "the very threshold, the 'sublime,'" of that representation.[1] And Liu notes that his chapter on "Westminster

---

1 *Sense of History*, 32. Paul de Man, as I have noted in my preface and will discuss at length in Chapter 6, was the champion of the dialectic between imagination and time. His institutional affiliation was with the Yale departments of French and Comparative Literature, but his influence touched students and faculty of the English Department.

Bridge" "stands in what might be called a correspondent relation with Hartman's 'The Unremarkable Poet' in his *Unremarkable Wordsworth,*" a relation sustained in personal contact and exchange of manuscripts.[2]

In the quarter century since the publication of *Wordsworth's Poetry 1787 to 1814,* Hartman has been an enabling authority to many students, colleagues, and Wordsworthian critics of diverse convictions. His image of Wordsworth as the "halted traveller" encountering and avoiding the apocalyptic power of his own imagination and his reading of Wordsworth's poetry under the phenomenological sign of "consciousness" have continued to affect our understanding of the poet even as Hartman himself and many of us have turned to other themes (1–30). The authority of Hartman's book has come not just from the congeniality of his themes to Wordsworth's genius, but also from Hartman's own engagement in major traditions of Wordsworthian criticism and from his attentiveness to features of Wordsworth's poetry that do *not* always fit his chosen themes. Hartman registers poetic figures and effects that resist his arguments as well as those that serve them, and his text opens numerous opportunities to think further and in different terms about Wordsworth's poetry.

Hartman's traveler and Cooke's enforcer

Hartman begins his book with a paradigmatic reading of "The Solitary Reaper" that opens one such opportunity for thought.[3] I shall place the poem in evidence here for the reader's convenience in subsequent discussion:

The Solitary Reaper

Behold her, single in the field,
Yon solitary Highland Lass!
Reaping and singing by herself;
Stop here, or gently pass!
Alone she cuts and binds the grain,
And sings a melancholy strain;
O listen! for the Vale profound
Is overflowing with the sound.

2 Liu, *Sense of History,* 638 n. 20. I have not taken up Hartman's reading of "Westminster Bridge" in "The Unremarkable Poet" in order to focus on his more influential paradigmatic reading of "The Solitary Reaper" in *Wordsworth's Poetry.*
3 Liu's argument makes no reference to "The Solitary Reaper."

No Nightingale did ever chaunt
More welcome notes to weary bands
Of travellers in some shady haunt,
Among Arabian sands:
A voice so thrilling ne'er was heard
In spring-time from the Cuckoo-bird,
Breaking the silence of the seas
Among the farthest Hebrides.

Will no one tell me what she sings? –
Perhaps the plaintive numbers flow
For old, unhappy, far-off things,
And battles long ago:
Or is it some more humble lay,
Familiar matter of to-day?
Some natural sorrow, loss, or pain,
That has been, and may be again?

Whate'er the theme, the Maiden sang
As if her song could have no ending;
I saw her singing at her work,
And o'er the sickle bending; –
I listened, motionless and still;
And, as I mounted up the hill,
The music in my heart I bore,
Long after it was heard no more.

The second sentence of Hartman's first paragraph introduces a fruitful ambiguity in his interpretation of the poem that his subsequent argument does not close. Hartman writes:

Wordsworth records in "The Solitary Reaper" his reaction to an ordinary incident. What others might have passed by produces a strong emotional response in him, therefore the imperatives: Behold, Stop here, O listen! His response rather than the image causing it is his subject, yet he keeps the latter in mind and returns to it, especially in the last stanza, so that our attention is drawn to a continuous yet indefinite relationship between mind and image, each of which retains a certain autonomy.   (3)

In Hartman's second sentence the comma-spliced "therefore" with no verb attached to the phrase "the imperatives" leaves it unclear whether the imperatives are caused by the strength of the poet's emotional response to the image that moves him or whether they are caused by the poet's awareness that "others might have passed by" what produces that response in him. Can these commands be explained solely in terms of the "relationship between mind and image" to which Hartman immediately turns, or do they require us to posit another party to that relationship, the inattentive listeners whose attention to that image the commands may seem to require? Can the imperatives be explained in terms of "mind" and "image" alone, or must the "others" too be granted "a certain autonomy" to account for them?

Hartman's Yale colleague Michael Cooke gives a forceful answer to this question in his 1976 book, *The Romantic Will*. Cooke argues that the energy of the poem is found in a "latent drama...taking place between speaker and subject, and reflexively between speaker and audience...The speaker is not just sharing his reaction with an amorphous audience – the social dimension Hartman points out – he is enforcing a reaction upon an audience whose susceptibility he himself determines" (42). Cooke hears a coercive summoning in the opening "Behold," a "deep coercion" in the "Stop here, or gently pass" that enforces an attitude of reverence whichever alternative is chosen, and "the freedom to confirm the involuntary commitment with a practical choice" in the "O listen" that opens the fifth line of the stanza (42–43). Cooke further suggests that the speaker's assertion of will is not restricted to his relation to his audience but also involves the "passing on to the audience the possession of will he himself experiences" in relation to the reaper (43). Cooke wonders at both the origin and character of the community of response the speaker evokes and at the "troubled forces [that] congregate and are resolved around the solitary reaper" (44).

Cooke's articulation of the speaker–audience and speaker–subject dynamics in "The Solitary Reaper" distinguishes him not just from Hartman but from a tradition of post-war Yale-affiliated critics who have privileged that poem without attending to those dynamics. W. K. Wimsatt used the poem to illustrate the concrete universal in poetry; Frederick Pottle chose it to typify the relation of eye and object in Wordsworth's poetry; and Frederick Garber selected it to model the encounter of Wordsworthian observer and his object of attention. Cooke alone in this tradition gives due weight to the speaker–audience relations Hartman notices but does not account for in his argument.[4]

4 Michael Cooke, *The Romantic Will* (New Haven and London: Yale University Press, 1976). Frederick Garber, *Wordsworth and the Poetry of Encounter* (Urbana: University of Illinois Press, 1971). Hartman, *Wordsworth's Poetry*. Frederick A. Pottle, "The Eye and the Object in the Poetry of Wordsworth," in *Romanticism and Consciousness: Essays in Criticism*, ed. Harold Bloom (New York: Norton, 1970), 273–287. W. K. Wimsatt, "The Structure of Romantic Nature Imagery," in *Romanticism and Consciousness*, ed. Bloom, 77–88. A Harvard Yard reading of

Cooke's argument also aligns him with two schools of critical inquiry that have come to prominence since he wrote it. Formally it shares its awareness of speaker/hero/audience interactions with the Bakhtinian dialogic or sociological poetics I have been elaborating in the last two chapters, and thematically it raises questions about power and social forces in Romantic poetry that have received more explicit development in recent New Historicist critiques of Romantic ideology. Cooke's reading of the poem in light of what Wordsworth called the human and dramatic imagination as opposed to the enthusiastic and meditative or poetical imagination invites us to ask who is doing what to whom in this poem, not just what the poet's imagination is doing with its objects. Both these critical schools offer additional resources for conducting (or perhaps prosecuting) this inquiry.

Dialogic interaction in "The Solitary Reaper"

The premises of the Bakhtin School's dialogic or sociological poetics may help us to pursue that inquiry more systematically. Their model of the utterance posits *"three participants"* to make any utterance intelligible, the speaker, the hero, and the listener (DLDA 105), and it explains the poetic utterance as the speaker's "active expression of evaluation in these two different directions – toward the listener and toward the object of utterance, the hero" (DLDA 107). One additional remark from the Bakhtin–Voloshinov essay "Discourse in Life and Discourse in Art" may head off misunderstanding of their position and also direct our attention toward those elements of the poem to which it pertains. They write,

The author, hero, and listener that we have been talking about ... are to be understood not as entities outside the artistic event but only as entities of the very perception of an artistic work, entities that are essential constitutive factors of the work. They are the living forces that determine form and style and are distinctly detectable by any competent contemplator.

(DLDA 109)

The signs of these entities are the figures of thought that invoke or evoke or entail the relations of speaker, listener, and hero: the commands Cooke emphasizes, the questions, first-person declarations,

the poem contemporary with Hartman's book does call attention to the way in which the commands in the poem invoke "a companion" and involve the reader. See David Perkins, *Wordsworth and the Poetry of Sincerity* (Cambridge, Mass.: Harvard University Press, 1964), 161–62.

offerings of reasons, and many other moves and gestures that take their interactive coloring from the strong presence of these more obvious figures.[5] In poetic utterances these moves and gestures are emphasized by prosodic resources, choices of words, and the order of the utterance's unfolding.[6]

In "The Solitary Reaper" these signs point to a situation different from that which Cooke's predecessors imagined. The three imperatives of the first stanza, all in emphatic first position in their respective lines, call a listener's attention to the reaper, on whom the speaker of the stanza seems already to have his mind fixed. Though Hartman writes of the speaker's "surprise" at the outset of the poem (6), and Frederick Garber talks of the speaker's growing awareness of the girl's isolation (4), the gestures of the stanza bespeak not a developing perception but an emphatic call to share a present perception from an established point of vantage. The opening lines, "Behold her, single in the field, / Yon solitary Highland Lass!" are not only imperative but deictic, pointing to "her" over yonder where the speaker sees her and the listener is to look. "Stop here, or gently pass" carries the same double force, issuing its command and taking for granted the listener's presence with the speaker "here" in the place where it is to be obeyed.

What the speaker sees and hears makes it urgent for him to call the listener to share his focus of attention or at least to refrain from disturbing it by passing rudely and perhaps making the lass conscious that others are watching or hearing her. The solitary unselfconscious activity that captivates him would be ruined were she to realize that she is not in fact alone but is instead the object of another's hearing. Though the call to "Stop here" resembles the opening gesture of an epitaph, as Hartman suggests (12), the "gently pass" gives the whole gesture in this situation a different tone. I hear an urgent whisper intended to protect the living and sensitive object of the speaker's attention from annoyance, to prevent the lass who sings so beautifully from stopping by calling the others nearby not to disturb her. Hartman nicely catches the force of the final imperative, "O listen! for the Vale profound / Is overflowing with the sound" in this gloss: "Even the vale seems to be moved: and should not a passerby,

---

5 See Chapter 7 below for further elaboration of the category of figures of thought and of Wordsworth's uses of them.

6 For a fuller elaboration of this poetics and its implications, see *Making Tales* Chapter 2.

therefore, stop and respond?" But he appears to suggest that the passerby in question is the speaker rather than the listener to whom the speaker, himself already stopped and responding, addresses himself, just as he suggests that the call to "Stop here, or gently pass" is said "by the poet to himself" as well as to "the reader"(7).

I will continue to pursue the hypothesis that the speaker's exhortations, here as in "Beauteous Evening," arise from the desire to share his experience with particular auditors rather than from a need to master himself to stop, look, and listen. Though I will argue, as Hartman does, that the poem shows evidence of a reflexive consciousness, I do not find the evidence in these purported self-exhortations but in a more manifestly self-conscious shift in the poem's manner of presentation. I will return to this topic when I take up the final stanza of the poem.

Once the hortatory note of the opening stanza is registered, it does not disappear in the succeeding stanzas even though the imperatives that establish it do not recur. Hartman, who follows "the overflow of the poet's feelings and the pleasure he takes in each new mood or thought," does not carry over the force of the opening exhortations; he imagines that the poet "in the second stanza...has already traveled, as through a magic casement, beyond the immediate scene" (7–8). But the rhetorical force of the two comparisons that constitute the stanza is to emphasize how "welcome" and "thrilling" the reaper's song is and thus to give reasons for so imperiously calling a listener's attention to it. The speaker presents these birdsongs in terms that suggest not only the human value that makes them comparable to the reaper's song (welcome, thrilling) but also the human contexts that give them this value, the situations of the weary traveler who hears in the nightingale's song the rest and refreshment of an oasis and, I imagine, the situation of the isolated inhabitant of the distant Hebrides thrilled to hear the familiar voice of the cuckoo after a long silent winter. The welcome of rest and refreshment and the thrill of the first signs of renewal and of the arrival of companionship in silent isolation recommend the reaper's song to the listener's attention.

In addition, the negative form of these comparisons asserts not just the identity of girl, nightingale, and cuckoo, as Wimsatt claimed, but the superiority of the reaper's human song to the songs of two highly valued natural singers. Like the lines from "Westminster Bridge" that assert "Never did sun more beautifully steep / In his first splendour, valley, rock, or hill," these lines gain special argumentative force from their reversal of a Wordsworthian expectation that natural beauty will exceed human beauty.

It is not just the beauty of these birdsongs, however, but the meaning that they convey to a properly situated person that makes their qualities comparable for the speaker to those of the Highland Lass's song. And the situations and qualities the speaker emphasizes suggest he feels in his own situation or imagines in his listener's situation comparable weariness to that of the desert traveller or comparable loneliness to that of the Hebridean. But the question he addresses to his listeners in the first line of the third stanza suggests that he is not sure what her song says to his or their situation: "Will no one tell me what she sings?" Garber, who, like Hartman, imagines that the speaker has gone somewhere else in the second stanza, hears in this question a return to "the immediate moment and cir-cumstances" and "the high point in the intensity of [the speaker's] desire to understand [the girl's] song" (7). Hartman hears "a sociable gesture revealing how the song has spread beyond itself to cause this appeal he whimsically makes ... to the reader" (8).

But there is no need to imagine a "return" if the argument of the second stanza continues to address the listeners posited in the opening stanza and if the question continues the address to those listeners. And there is no reason to take the tone as "whimsically" addressed to the actual readers of the poem if instead it pursues a question raised by the comparisons just addressed to the internally constitutive listeners. The desire to understand the song is provoked not just by the foreign language (Erse) in which it is supposed to have been sung but by the unresolved situation in which it has had such a profound effect. The speaker wants to discover what it portends or what it brings to those who feel that effect, and he suddenly reaches out to his listeners to find help in interpreting it.

But the tone of his question suggests to me not whimsy but impatience and irritation that the help has not already been proffered and is not likely to be. The metrical weight on "no, tell, what, sings" suggests not the positive appeal of "Won't someone tell me what she sings?" but the more negative force of "'Will no one [then] tell me what she sings? Then I will tell me what she sings myself,' said the little red hen." The question has less the form and force of a polite request than of an exasperated response to someone who has already refused to answer. The prominent word "will" at the beginning of the line attributes a power of refusal to the others over whom the speaker has attempted to assert his power in the commands of the first stanza.

The dash that marks the end of this question marks the end also of the speaker's listener-focused discourse, for the surmised answers to the question that follow are offered up in the absence of someone else's response – in spite of that absence, if you will. The attempt to compel or urge the listener(s) into a position to share the experience of seeing and hearing the solitary reaper and to contribute to the interpretation of that experience appears to have failed, and the speaker, without anyone's evident cooperation, suggests two possible genres for her song, the historical ballad and the complaint, both of which might account for the "plaintive numbers" he hears and responds to without understanding them. The question he asks in the last four lines of the stanza focuses not on potential answerers – the "no one" of the first line – but on possible meanings of the song itself – the "is it" that occupies the same metrical place in the fifth line.

The final stanza of the poem changes the subject of the previous stanza by professing that the answer to the speaker's question is irrelevant to the main point to be made: "Whate'er the theme, the Maiden sang / As if her song could have no ending." But this stanza changes more than the subject of the previous three stanzas from what she sang to how she sang, for it also suddenly resituates the utterance of those stanzas in the past and so resituates their speaker's discourse as quoted or recreated discourse and their listener's position as different not only spatially but also temporally from the situation of the readers of the poem. As in a number of Wordsworth's other poems – "Old Man Travelling," "Expostulation and Reply," "Resolution and Independence," and Book I of *The Prelude*, a passage that seems a present outburst reveals itself as "recorded" (*Prelude* I, 1850, line 50) or recreated and a speaker whom we had up to then taken to be the speaker of a lyric poem is revealed as a self of whose previous state of mind the present narrator of the poem is conscious.[7]

This formal evidence of self-consciousness is far more convincing to me than Hartman's suggestion that self-consciousness is evident in the self-addressed character of some of the poem's imperatives. And it explains Hartman's observation that the poet "uses the 'I' more overtly than before"(8) in the final stanza, for when the narrator turns

---

7 William Wordsworth, *The Prelude: 1799, 1805, 1850*, ed. Jonathan Wordsworth *et al.* (New York: W. W. Norton, 1979). Citations will be to the 1805 edition unless otherwise noted.

from recreating what he said to talking about himself and his response to the situation in which he said it, he represents himself with "I" as an agent in the situation instead of just presenting himself as a speaker.

In fact, he has not used the "I" at all until the final stanza, and he uses it now as the emphatic subject of the last four actions the poem relates: I saw her, I listened, I mounted up the hill, and I bore the music in my heart (the first two propositions begin the third and fifth lines and the final one concludes the penultimate line of the poem). What strikes me about this sequence of actions is that it focuses entirely on the speaker's relation to the maiden and her song and makes no overt reference to any attempt to get others to notice her or to explain what she was singing. I saw, I listened, I mounted, I bore – the self-sufficient sequence carries an almost triumphant Caesarean air of coming upon the scene, finding something of value and carrying it off successfully with no help from anyone, thank you.[8] But the encounter recreated in the first three stanzas focuses on trying to get others to stop, to listen, and to explain what they have heard, and it ends in apparent failure.

"The Solitary Reaper" and the "present state of public taste"

In the school of reading I have been following, the common way to handle this seeming contradiction between the concluding gesture of the poem and the sequence of gestures it concludes has been to ignore either the shift to past tense in the final stanza or the evidence of address to listeners in the first three, or both, treating the poem as if it were an unbroken present development of the speaker's relation to the image of the maiden with no one else to interfere (see Garber, *Poetry of Encounter*, 7; Hartman, *Wordsworth's Poetry*, 7–8). Though Hartman does acknowledge the evidence of address in the poem, he does not integrate it successfully into his reading of the relation between mind and image. Cooke grasps the speaker–audience interaction with unprecedented clarity, but like all the others, he ignores the shift to past tense, indeed ignores the entire final stanza. From the Bakhtinian dialogic perspective I have been developing,

8 Liu invokes the same Caesarean passage to compare its form – asyndeton – with the asyndeton "Ne'er saw I, never felt" in "Composed Upon Westminster Bridge," but I think his notion of "imaginative imperialism" applies more forcefully in the present context. *Sense of History*, 463.

however, the shift from the present imperative you–her discourse of the opening to the past declarative I–her/I–it discourse of the final stanza is the most notable fact about the poem, and we must try to imagine its force.

After recreating his encounter with his listeners before the singing girl, why does the speaker declare that he at any rate saw her, heard her, and carried her music in his heart "long after it was heard no more"? I think his point is that his apparent failure to share his experience or to get help in interpreting it was still a success. Though others did not help him say what the song meant, it still, "whate'er the theme," made a difference to him, long after it ceased or after there were no others there to hear it and have it make a difference to them. He is testifying to his own power to appropriate the encounter for himself regardless of his failure to engage others in it, declaring its value and his independent power in defiance of his previous listeners' nonparticipation and without bothering to address his present listeners directly. *He* beheld, *he* stopped "motionless and still," *he* listened, and in addition he carried off something of lasting value. He presents himself, in effect, as invulnerable to the resistance of his present listeners not because he won over his previous listeners to confirm his experience but because he managed single-handedly to carry it off without them. Take it or leave it; I already have it in either case – this is the gesture the speaker seems to make to a potential audience indifferent or resistant to sharing his experience.

The poem, in this reading, enacts a response to the crux Hartman raises immediately after introducing it – the tendency of Wordsworth's readers from Coleridge and Jeffrey on to blame his poems for their "excessive involvement in random, personal experience." The self-consciousness it embodies is not exhausted, as Hartman seems to suggest, in the recognition of a disproportion in the poet's emotional response to the maid (6) but includes and is perhaps impossible without the poet's awareness of how others might judge that response. The assertion of the value of the response is not just an "overflow of the poet's feelings" (7) but an answer to other judgments that would deny or diminish its value. The self-consciousness manifested in the poem is more than a spiritual fact reflecting the poet's "access of emotion (inspiration) vis-a-vis nature" (5); it is a social fact reflecting his judgment "of the present state of public taste in this country" and of "how far this taste is healthy or depraved" (LB 243).

I confess that I am troubled by Hartman's image of a poet "so totally 'spiritual' that the most insignificant mood is weighed because it should be significant of something beyond itself, of some actual or hidden relation to the possibilities of self-renewal" (6). As one who has loved the Preface to *Lyrical Ballads* more than the apocalyptic moments of Wordsworth's lyrics, I want (and believe Wordsworth wanted) the significance he is concerned with to include significance for others and the renewal he recommends to include social renewal as well as self-centered evidence of election.

Though the speaker in "The Solitary Reaper" asserts the value of his experience for himself even if no one else shares it, the structure of the poem introduces each reader at first to the position of the listener, who is urged to share the speaker's experience and even to help explain its meaning (see Perkins, *Poetry of Sincerity*). A simulacrum of the experience is open to a reader's imaginative participation even though the speaker relates an instance in which listeners in a position to share it did not fully accept the invitation. Furthermore, the meanings the speaker himself surmises for the girl's song touch upon "the general passions and thoughts and feelings of men" in whose spirit "the Poet thinks and feels" (LB 261), not upon that more specialized poetic feeling of *consciousness of self raised to apocalyptic pitch,*" to which Hartman's surmises ultimately trace the source of the poem. The self-assertion of the concluding stanza is powerful, but it too falls short of apocalyptic self-consciousness.

To read the "Behold" which opens the poem, as Hartman does, as a signal of "the influx of an unusual state of consciousness which is quickly normalized" (16) rather than as a gesture inviting the participation of listeners in the speaker's valuable experience is to reduce (or perhaps exalt) its social action to a spiritual-psychological allegory. To read the poem as the "synthesis of a mind in conflict with itself" (16) rather than as a gesture of a mind in conflict with others is to overlook its ideological struggles and focus instead on the fascinating but illusory struggle between "imagination" and "nature" that New Historicist critics have called the "Romantic Ideology."

The New Historicism and "The Solitary Reaper"

Those critics remind me, however, that to substitute "will" and "society" for "imagination" and "nature" is to open the poem to the world and to challenge my Bakhtinian premise that speaker, hero, and listener are not "entities outside the artistic event" but only entities constitutive of the artistic work itself. Those "entities outside the artistic event" are social beings with wills and interests of their own, historically and politically specific individuals and classes who have a stake in how they are represented; the struggles and actions represented in poems reflect and affect their real social relations and actions.

Marjorie Levinson, who has recently carried the banner of "New Historicism" and the critique of the Romantic ideology into readings of several major Wordsworthian poems, though not "The Solitary Reaper," argued at a reading of an earlier version of this chapter that my Bakhtinian analysis of "The Solitary Reaper" did not go far enough. It neglected, she said, to consider the narrator's social and historical relations to the "solitary Highland Lass" in the poem. The Lass is a peasant at work in the fields, he a bourgeois poet on a tour; she is a Highlander, he is English; she is a woman, he is a man. What sort of social relation, Levinson asked, was the speaker establishing with the Lass whose image he depicts and whose song, untranslated, he carries off with him in the first decade of the nineteenth century? What is he making of her, what version of her is he urging his contemporaries to accept, and what political motives inform that urgency?

Levinson's questions have provoked me to further questions and reformulations of the action of the poem. What, after all, is involved in the social relation between a Highland female farm laborer in 1803 and an English male poet who never speaks to her but presents himself as having seen her, listened to her song, and carried it off in his heart to offer his account of it somewhat insistently and perhaps even defiantly to his middle- and upper-class English readers in 1807? An Englishman's tour of Scotland in 1803 was still a visit to something like a third-world colonial territory or a carpetbagger's tour of the defeated postbellum South. The military and political independence of the Highlanders had been subdued decisively in 1746, but they remained foreign in language, backwards in economy, residually tribal in social organization. Our poet's "solitary Highland Lass" was probably alone working her small subdivision of her landlord's estate, cutting and binding oats for oatmeal or barley for eating or distilling. By 1803 it is surprising that she is not digging potatoes instead of reaping grain, for that crop had come more and more to dominate agriculture among crofters like her, because it could support a larger population on the smaller and smaller plots that repeated subdivision of the land had produced. The generalized plural "battles long ago" of which she sang might most recently have been the one specific battle of Culloden, in which the last hopes of some Highlanders to restore the Stuart monarchy were defeated. Her more familiar contemporary sorrows, losses, and pains might well have included chronic hunger, the departure of loved ones to America, or the loss of them in Britain's wars against Napoleon. The Gaelic language in which she sings was under pressure from educational efforts to supplant it with the English in which Wordsworth celebrates her song. Whate'er the theme, as our poet says, his description of her and his speculations about her theme do not seek for such specifics. His representation of her abstracts her from the probable conditions of a life such as hers and universalizes the suffering that her song might express.[9]

If he had been William Cobbett instead of William Wordsworth, he might have seen her very differently, as Cobbett, for instance, sees a solitary woman bleaching homespun in the following passage:

Today, near a place called Wesborough Green, I saw a woman bleaching her *home-spun* and *home-woven linen*. I have not seen such a thing before, since I left Long Island. There, and, indeed, all over the American States, North of Maryland, and especially in the New England States, almost the whole of both linen and woollen, used in the country, and a large part of that used in towns, is made in the farm-houses. There are thousands and thousands of families who never use either, except of their own making. All but the *weaving* is done by the family. There is a loom in the house, and the weaver goes from house to house. I once saw about three thousand farmers, or

9 It also abstracts Wordsworth himself, as Peter Manning argues, from the "contemporary sociopolitical field" (242) in which the poem functions, the recovery of which reveals its "definable conservative significance" (267). Himself a Yale-affiliated critic who defines his recovery of the contexts of Wordsworth's poem against the dialogizing background of Hartman's work, Manning situates the poem in relation to the ideology of its source in Thomas Wilkinson's *Tours to the British Mountains* and of Wordsworth's larger poetic project to elaborate "a nationalist myth" in *Poems, in Two Volumes* (259). In the one context, "The Solitary Reaper" offers a "vision of a serenely traditional way of life" that reflects "the antagonism of the old land-based society to the new commercial elements that were disrupting it" (248–49). In the other the poem embodies "the values underlying Wordsworth's patriotism" (256). See Peter J. Manning, "'Will No One Tell Me What She Sings?': *The Solitary Reaper* and the Contexts of Criticism," in *Reading Romantics: Texts and Contexts* (Oxford: Oxford University Press, 1990). I am grateful to Peter Manning for sharing this essay with me in manuscript and galley proofs.

rather country people, at a horse-race in Long Island, and my opinion was, that there were not five hundred who were not dressed in *home-spun coats*. As to *linen*, no farmer's family thinks of *buying linen*. The *Lords of the Loom* have taken *from the land*, in England, *this part of its due*; and hence one cause of the poverty, misery, and pauperism, that are becoming so frightful throughout the country. A national debt, and all the taxation and gambling belonging to it have a natural tendency to *draw wealth into great masses*. These masses produce a power of *congregating* manufacturers, and of making the many work at them, *for the gain of a few*. The taxing Government finds great convenience in these congregations. It can lay its hand easily upon a part of the produce; as ours does with much effect. But, the land suffers greatly from this, and the country must finally feel the fatal effects of it. The country people lose part of their natural employment. The women and children, who ought to provide a great part of the raiment, have nothing to do. The fields *must have men and boys*; but, where there are men and boys there will be *women* and *girls*; and, as the Lords of the Loom have now a set of *real slaves*, by means of whom they take away a great part of the employment of the country-*women* and *girls,* these must be kept by poor-rates in whatever degree they lose employment through the Lords of the Loom.

Jon P. Klancher quotes this passage from Cobbett's *Rural Rides* in *The Making of English Reading Audiences, 1790–1832*, and he admires it for

the extraordinary concreteness of language that weaves its way through narrative, descriptive, and argumentative modes. The concrete detail becomes a representative point that his own language will then give a history, a greater social pattern, a means of grasping historical movement. The simplest quotidian act – bleaching linen, for example – can be made the sign of a vast historical transformation from rural artisanal labor into the emerging industrial order...Cobbett's stance allows the radical reader to make connections between hitherto separate orders of experience, affording him a strategic position between cultural utterance and concrete act, quotidian experience and structural change.   (126–27)

Has Cobbett, then, really helped his readers to see what is going on while Wordsworth makes aesthetic capital at the expense of necessary political and economic analysis? Should Wordsworth have been explicit about who did what to whom in those "battles long ago" and who or what might be causing the Lass's present "sorrow, loss, or pain"? Does he not here, as in so many other places, deflect his readers' attention from historically specific conditions on which they might act to what "has been, and may be again," a universalized human condition of suffering, yet another song in the "still, sad music of humanity" that calls not for action but for pleasurable melancholy contemplation? Should he not be aware that he may be contributing to her sorrow, loss, or pain by urging his upper- and middle-class readers to share his complacency before the lovely image he has produced and to overlook the suffering they themselves have produced and exploited?

These criticisms seem as misplaced to me as the corresponding criticism of Cobbett that Klancher cites. In an 1828 review in the *Athenaeum*, the reviewer complains that Cobbett's writing lacks

imagination, a faculty that can only exist as the organ and interpreter of deep feelings and much-embracing thoughts ... But in the author whom we are now considering, as there are none of these expansive and pregnant convictions, none of these consciousnesses of the master laws of the universe; so is there none of that power whereby they might be embodied and made palpable ... He scarcely ever takes us away from those wretched and trivial tumults of the hour, in which our feelings come in contact with nothing but the follies and selfishness, the outward accidents and unhappy frivolities of our kind. (Quoted in Klancher, 128)

Clearly this reviewer would welcome Wordsworth's imaginative vision of the solitary reaper on the same ground that he complains of Cobbett's circumstantiality, just as Klancher welcomes Cobbett's attention to social circumstances on the same ground that he later criticizes Wordsworth's tendency to efface them.

We might do well to question the claims made for both kinds of writing before we are caught in an unproductive opposition between the political lucidity of the one and the Romantic ideology of the other or, from the other side, between the prosaic triviality of the one and the imaginative superiority of the other. Cobbett's account of the solitary bleacher may well draw connections between "the simplest quotidian act" and "the emerging industrial order," but it is not clear to me that he provides his reader with a "strategic position" from which to act to change that order. His trope of "the Lords of the Loom" provides a melodramatic focus for resentment but not a program for action, and his sentimentalization of the "natural employment" of women in subsistence weaving for their families is as nostalgic for a vanishing economic order as Wordsworth's "renewing of the traditional image of the peasant" in "The Solitary Reaper."[10]

We should also remember that Wordsworth's poem – far from

10 Manning, *Reading Romantics*, 256.

removing us from "those wretched and trivial tumults of the hour" to consciousness "of the master laws of the universe" – has been accused of elevating "random, personal experience" to an idiosyncratic importance entirely out of keeping with any universally valid law. The poem does not enforce a Romantic ideology that exalts universalizing imaginative idealizations and occludes everyday people and experiences; rather it re-enacts a failed attempt to share an everyday experience felt to be especially significant in a narrative that testifies to the importance of that experience to the one who experienced it, even if no one else can be brought to see its importance and share in its interpretation.

What strikes the speaker of the poem about the Highland Lass might especially strike a poet, for she (unlike Cobbett's solitary bleacher) is "reaping and *singing*" (my italics), and Wordsworth fancies himself, too, a singer by profession, one who sings "a song in which all human beings join with him" (LB 259). There's the rub, though, for the poem presents a speaker who struggles unsuccessfully to persuade others to "join with him" in his appreciation of the solitary reaper's song. She sings unselfconsciously, and even as she sings by herself, she also sings as part of a tradition of song that binds her to the past and to the common experiences of her community. He, on the other hand, sings only by conventional ascription. He writes poems, and he writes them in controversial relation to both the tradition he inherits and the readers he addresses. He is alone, isolated from the reaper's community (he does not know its language) and from the listeners whom he invokes and tries to bully into sharing his experience; she is in community, even as she reaps and sings alone. His testimony that hearing her has made a difference to him is as unconfirmable by others as the lover's testimony in "She dwelt among th'untrodden ways" that Lucy's death has made "the difference to me." She takes for granted the social confirmation he demands and renounces.

What Michael Cooke says of her song, then, might be better attributed only to the poet-speaker's utterance. Cooke derives her song from a source in "will" and "self." He writes: "The singing conveys a triumph over the very melancholy it reminds us of; and it is not going too far to take it as a tacit activity of will and self, as what the Highland Lass makes of what befalls her" (46). The song itself, however, most likely a ballad or lament, bespeaks not self but community, not will but participation, not making but tradition. The speaker's appropriation of it in the final stanza, on the other hand, is willful self-assertion in spite of his inability to participate in the community it comes from or to share it with the community he belongs to.

Though conservatives and British nationalists in the latter community might have drawn comfort from the poem's image of a Scottish peasant singing at her labors, I find the power of the poem elsewhere — in the urgency of the speaker's appeal to others to share his experience and the violence of his claim to have taken it and kept it for himself. To me these gestures do not sound like the complacent rationalizations of a ruling class sympathizer who ideologically justifies that class's living off the labor of others. They sound more like the intense efforts of a precariously marginal individual to win social confirmation of his pleasurable experience or, lacking that, to announce his unconditional seizure of a source of pleasure upon which his personal and professional being somehow depends. The poem confronts us in a dialogic reading, not with a too easy image of the solitary reaper, but with an almost too difficult image of the deracinated bourgeois poet caught between a traditional society he cannot recover and a contemporary society he cannot persuade.

6

❖❖

What de Man has made of Wordsworth

❖❖

I am always startled by the vehemence of de Man's critics ... Why is this theory of the resistance of language to intentionality so hotly resisted?

Barbara Johnson, *A World of Difference*

The work of de Man should receive the close critical attention he demanded with respect to other difficult texts.

Dominick LaCapra, *Soundings in Critical Theory*

The power of Paul de Man's intervention into Wordsworthian criticism in the last three decades has been out of proportion to the works he has commented upon or the works he has written. He has not, like Geoffrey Hartman, "covered" the Wordsworthian canon or produced an authoritative book-length study on Wordsworth. A few familiar passages from *The Prelude*, two sonnets outside the usual set selected for commentary, "A slumber did my spirit seal," and a few passages from the *Essays upon Epitaphs* and the 1815 Preface comprise the de Manian canon of Wordsworth's works. The only extended reading he has produced is of the sonnet "Composed by the Side of Grasmere Lake." Wordsworth is the sole subject of only one essay de Man chose to publish ("Wordsworth and the Victorians") and one lecture that his students published after his death ("Time and History in Wordsworth"). Wordsworth figures in de Man's other essays as a touchstone alongside Rousseau and Hölderlin and, sometimes, Baudelaire. The citation of a few passages, a sketchy reading, or sometimes even the mention of Wordsworth's name is enough to mobilize his significance.[1] Altogether de Man has published perhaps only sixty-five pages on Wordsworth in seven essays, one review,

---

1 Arac notes that de Man's repeated attention to "the shift in rhetorical registers within the small space of a short text of a few pages of a longer text" is "almost a new version of Matthew Arnold's touchstones" (*Genealogies* 82).

one introduction to another poet's works, and one posthumously published lecture.

Nevertheless, it is no surprise to find de Man displacing Hartman as the chief antagonist in the closing arguments of Karl Kroeber's recent bibliographical survey of Wordsworthian criticism or to find him presiding as the tutelary spirit in Cynthia Chase's and Andrzej Warminski's recent special issue of *diacritics* on "Wordsworth and the Production of Poetry."[2] Nor is it surprising to find Kroeber aggressive – accusing de Man of "indifference to rudimentary standards of scholarship" and himself violating scholarly decorum by playing on de Man's name ("the de Maniacal approach") (336–37) – or to find Chase and Warminski defensive – highlighting de Man's placement of poetry in history and diminishing the "echoes of Heidegger" in his critical vocabulary (3) – and even pious – defending him against heterodox readings of his work (46–48). As Dominick LaCapra has observed, "De Man's writing invites quasi-theological exegesis and projective reprocessing, by both his detractors and admirers, and it is extremely difficult to engage his texts critically through accurate reconstruction and dialogic exchange."[3]

I can think of no writer on Wordsworth since Coleridge who has so divided and provoked his readers, in part, I believe, because de Man offered a radical displacement of Coleridge's Wordsworth and of the Romanticism and the criticism grounded on that Wordsworth at a moment when many critics had become dissatisfied with both. De Man took on the dominant "symbolic" readings of Wordsworth by Abrams, Wimsatt, and Wasserman in "The Rhetoric of Temporality" and offered an allegorical alternative. He also, as Arac shows, offered an "antidote" to the New Critical echoes of "phrases from Coleridge's *Biographia Literaria* that resound in T. S. Eliot, I. A. Richards, F. O. Matthiessen, Cleanth Brooks, and M. H. Abrams" (240–53). Although, as I believe the following analysis shows, de Man's Wordsworth was constructed by doing as much violence to Wordsworth's texts as Coleridge himself had done, de Man's construction, like Coleridge's, had its own internal coherence and its

---

2 Kroeber, "Wordsworth"; Cynthia Chase and Andrzej Warminski, eds., "Wordsworth and the Production of Poetry," special issue of *diacritics* 17 (Winter 1987).

3 Dominick LaCapra, "The Temporality of Rhetoric," in *Soundings in Critical Theory* (Ithaca: Cornell University Press, 1989), 131.

own poetic power to move its adherents and opponents. Many recent critics have found that violence and the new construction in which it issued warranted in their fruitfulness, but like Arac, I will hold that they (both the critics and the construction) rest on an error from which we can and should "preserve ourselves" (259).

For all the intensity of their responses, neither friends nor foes of de Man's vision of Wordsworth have surveyed "the de Manian corpus" on Wordsworth either to gauge its extent or to mark the spots which are the hiding places of its power.[4] Arac, who might well have done so, treats de Man in a context separate from that in which he engages recent critics of Wordsworth. Though I will here conduct such a survey in the chronological order of Tom Keenan's "Bibliography of Texts by Paul de Man," inserting de Man's posthumously published lecture on Wordsworth and its revisions at the times of their presentations rather than the time of their publication, I do not aim to give this sequence what Deborah Esch calls "an aesthetic unity, a pseudohistorical totalization," but rather to take the collection as what she calls "an enumeration of positional acts of reading."[5] I will try to be alert not only to assertions that appear, as Esch puts it following de Man, not "in conjunction with or

4 The quoted phrase is from Deborah Esch, "The Triumph of Reading," in *Reading de Man Reading*, ed. Lindsay Waters and Wlad Godzich (Minneapolis: University of Minnesota Press, 1989), 68. Tilottama Rajan has, however, usefully surveyed and critiqued de Man's significance for Romantic studies in "Displacing Post-Structuralism." Frank Lentricchia works through three of de Man's early essays on Romanticism in chronological order in ANC 284–98, but he leaves the adequacy of de Man's treatment of Romanticism to "another kind of study," 293. Arac makes no connection between his critique of de Man in Chapter 10 of *Critical Genealogies* and his focus on Wordsworth in Chapters 1 and 2. Jonathan Culler (*Framing the Sign: Criticism and Its Institutions* [Norman: University of Oklahoma Press, 1988], 107–35) offers a "general survey of [de Man's] writing, from the essays of the 1950s to the work left unpublished at his death in 1983" (110), but there is no thematic focus to this survey, which follows the order of de Man's published books rather than the order of his essays. Cyrus Hamlin traces the development of de Man's views on Romanticism from de Man's critique of Heidegger's reading of Hölderlin in 1955 to "the seminal text for Paul de Man's work on the poetics of Romanticism," that is, "The Rhetoric of Temporality." See Hamlin's "Literary History after the New Criticism: Paul de Man's Essays on Romanticism," in (*Dis*)*continuities: Essays on Paul de Man*, Postmodern Studies 2, ed. Luc Herman, Kris Humbeeck, and Geert Lernout (Amsterdam: Rodopi, 1989), 144.

5 Esch, "The Triumph of Reading," 74. Tom Keenan, "Bibliography of Texts by Paul de Man," in Paul de Man, *Resistance to Theory* (Minneapolis: University of Minnesota Press, 1986), 122–27.

in reaction to anything, but with an unmediated violence and 'of their own unrelated power'" (69), but also to the repetitions with and without differences and the relations and reactions that coexist with such violence. My survey will try to locate the mines de Man lays in the midst of his otherwise unexplosive arguments, to defuse and examine them instead of blowing up over them.[6]

My own trope here, with its suggestion of the dangers of death, maiming and disfigurement (as well as of emotional violence), picks up one of de Man's verbal instruments of power and reveals how his writing raises the stakes of reading. Stanley Corngold notes de Man's "uninhibited readiness to pronounce on the first and last things in the life of the mind," but he does not go on to observe that de Man often figures the life of the mind or the life of reading and writing as a struggle in which life and death, bodily integrity, the functioning of the senses, the possibility of breathing, and the physical loss or preservation of face are on the line.[7] Even to substitute his words – killing, dismemberment, blindness, drowning, defacement, or disfigurement – for my cooler locutions is to feel the heat of his writing. Such words activate glands, turn stomachs, win converts with their force, make enemies with their violence, and burn themselves into the memories of friends and enemies alike, as the old rhetors well knew. They belong to the gothic register of "gross and violent stimulants" that Wordsworth deliberately avoids (LB 248). They produce immediate effects that are hard to dissipate even with distancing quotation marks and dashes that mark their mention rather than their use. But de Man does not use these words with anything like the frequency that my *accumulatio* has just produced, and in my survey, duly warned of their danger, I will try to cool them off by spreading them out instead of heating them up by piling them together.

6 LaCapra sees the need for an "intricate general account of [de Man's] writing that would attempt to elicit its historicity in terms of a complex interaction of repetition and change over time" ("The Temporality of Rhetoric," 132). I am attempting to provide such an account for the selection of de Man's texts that touch on Wordsworth.

7 Stanley Corngold, "Error in Paul de Man," in *The Yale Critics*, ed. Arac, Godzich, and Martin, 91.

Wordsworth and the dialectic of nature and consciousness 1960–66

Five pieces in several different genres, first published between de Man's completion of his dissertation in 1960 and his delivery of a Christian Gauss lecture on Wordsworth in 1967, invoke de Man's ruling idea in this period of a dialectical contradiction between nature and consciousness, giving Wordsworth's poetry several different relations to that contradiction. It is not clear, however, whether de Man changes his mind about Wordsworth in the course of these essays, reviews, lectures, and introductions or just changes his tone in response to shifting occasions and audiences.

The first piece, "Intentional Structure of the Romantic Image,"[8] focuses primarily on Hölderlin's wish that poetry should originate as natural organisms (flowers) do and Mallarmé's self-conscious interrogation of the unbridgeable difference between the natural world and conscious poetic language. Both poets for de Man illustrate the unchallenged "priority of the natural object" in nineteenth-century European poetry (9). Wordsworth appears in this essay, along with Rousseau and Hölderlin, as one of the "early romantics" (16) who have not yet closed off alternative possibilities for poetry that later nineteenth-century Romantics no longer considered. All of them write texts that describe not nostalgia for the object but "the passage from a certain type of nature, earthly and material, to another nature that could be called mental and celestial" (13), texts that "uncover a fundamentally new kind of relationship between nature and consciousness" (14). This new possibility for consciousness is that it could "exist entirely by and for itself, independently of all relationship with the outside world, without being moved by an intent aimed at a part of this world" (16).

De Man discovers a tendency toward this "new kind of relationship between nature and consciousness" (14) in three passages from Book VI of *The Prelude* – eleven lines from the Grand Chartreuse passage of the 1850 text that invoke "another nature which could be called mental and celestial" (13), the Gondo Gorge passage from the 1805 text where "one feels everywhere the pressure of an inner tension at the core of all earthly objects, powerful enough to bring them to

8 De Man, "Intentional Structure of the Romantic Image," in RR 1–17. This essay was originally published in French in 1960 and twice anthologized in English translation in 1970 and 1972.

explosion" (14), and the preceding apostrophe to imagination from the same text in which "'imagination' has little in common with the faculty that produces natural images born 'as flowers originate'" (16).[9] De Man declares, however, that the "violence" of the explosive inner tension of the second passage "is finally appeased by the ascending movement ... from a terrestrial nature ... toward [the] 'other nature' mentioned by Rousseau, associated with the diaphanous, limpid, and immaterial quality of a light that dwells nearer to the skies" (14). This essay is the last place de Man entertains the possibility that the potentially explosive violence might be appeased or the hope that poetry could escape the dialectical opposition of mind and nature into a poetry of pure mind.[10]

Wordsworth makes his next appearance in de Man's published writing not as one of the vanguard of poets who anticipate a "fundamentally new kind of relationship between nature and consciousness" (14) but as "a 'natural' romantic" whose "imagination remains patterned throughout on the physical process of sight." In "Symbolic Landscape in Wordsworth and Yeats" (RR 125–43), it is Yeats whose frame of reference – like Wordsworth's, Hölderlin's, and Rousseau's in the previous essay – that "by the very nature of his statement, originates from experiences without earthly equivalence" (143). In this contrast between "Wordsworth's involved but persistently reverent 'look(ing) at the subject'" and "Yeats's intermittent contempt for 'natural thing(s),'" Wordsworth plays the role of nature poet who "appreciates the complexity of what happens when eye and object meet" (126), whereas Yeats writes a poetry in "a more or less fixed symbolic system which is not derived from the observation of nature" (138–39), though it cannot escape from sensuous embodiment. De Man reads closely Wordsworth's "Composed by the Side of Grasmere Lake," insisting that "all the action in the poem [even its "transcendental dimensions"] stems from visual

9 Kroeber, in "Wordsworth," notes with irritation that de Man "switched texts" here from 1850 to 1805 without indicating that he had done so, but it must be noted that the change of texts would not affect what de Man makes of these passages.

10 Rajan notes that the ending of "The Intentional Structure" "appears peculiarly utopian." It seems to imagine "that the problem of intentionality can be sublated (or rather sublimated) by deferring the poetic project from the realm of the natural to an internalized supernature." She recognizes that this move "will not be repeated" in de Man's later work, "Displacing Post-Structuralism," 455. See also Kroeber's paragraph on "Intentional Structure" in "Wordsworth," 337.

events and obeys the logic of the eye," in contrast to Yeats's "Coole Park and Ballylee, 1931," which can be read both naturalistically and in terms of esoteric symbolism. Wordsworth balances the "mimetic and symbolic" whereas Yeats juxtaposes incompatible styles. Wordsworth's poem "comes to rest" in the tranquillity of a "complex act of pure vision" (132–33); Yeats's poem "could certainly never end, like Wordsworth's sonnet, in a promise of 'tranquillity'" (143).

Geoffrey Hartman notes the "remarkably balanced" quality of this contribution to Richard Poirier's and Reuben Brower's collection *In Defense of Reading*.[11] De Man's essay is devoted roughly half and half to its readings of Wordsworth and Yeats, but I think the appearance of "balance" comes from its muting of any dialectical judgment of the difference between the two poems in favor of a nuanced account of each one compatible with the American New Critical program of the collection in which it appears. Instead of subordinating Wordsworth's poetry of perception to Yeats's poetry of "symbolic meaning prior to... natural appearance" (138), as he might well have done in an essay like "Intentional Structure," addressed in the first instance to a dialectically initiated European audience, de Man here appreciates "the delicate interplay between perception and imagination" (126) in Wordsworth's poem. Instead of heightening the failure or the contradiction in Yeats's juxtaposition of "sensuous 'loveliness'" with "antinatural uses of language" as he might have done elsewhere, de Man here celebrates the "almost miraculous skill" of "Yeats's masterful hands" that hold these divergent elements together (143). Instead of heightening the distinction between Yeats and Wordsworth, de Man treats both poems as movements "from material to spiritual insights" (143). Hartman characterizes de Man's essay with the same term, "balance," with which that essay characterizes Wordsworth, but de Man's other essays and the Wordsworth they project are more radical, antinatural, and allegorical – more like Yeats in this essay.

Even in a review of Harold Bloom's *The Visionary Company* that appeared the same year as the essay on Wordsworth and Yeats, de Man brings Wordsworth closer to Yeats and to the "dialectical mind."[12] In this review de Man takes exception to Bloom's Blakean

---

11 "Looking Back on Paul de Man," in *Reading de Man Reading*, ed. Waters and Godzich, 7.
12 "A New Vitalism: Harold Bloom," in Paul de Man, *Critical Writings 1953–1978*, ed. Lindsay Waters (Minneapolis: University of Minnesota Press, 1989),

reading of Wordsworth's "highly complex attitude toward nature."
De Man contrasts Bloom's "vitalist" interpretation of the "continuity...in passing from an objective to a humanized nature" to his
own understanding of a "dialectical mind" in whose passing "there
has to be a discontinuity somewhere, a renunciation, or a sacrifice, at
any rate a delicate and obscure point of development that cannot be
merely crossed by means of the sheer stamina of a blind *élan vital*,"
and he objects to Bloom's understanding of Wordsworth as a
naturalist who strives "'to find the unfallen Eden in nature, to read in
her a more human face.'" Wordsworth's nature "always contains an
element that can be called divine precisely to the extent that it
entirely escapes the possibility of being humanized. No dialogue
could ever be possible between man and the profound otherness, the
'it-ness' that is always a part of Wordsworth's nature." Wordsworth's
imagination, de Man goes on to say in terms close to those of the
essay on Wordsworth and Yeats,

is an extended mode of seeing, originating in the act of visual perception and
not in sexuality. Instead of humanizing nature, Wordsworth creates
increasingly dehumanized entities, a world in which it is hard to tell men and
women from rocks and stones. He may be indeed "a man talking to men,"
but he is talking to them about nonhuman beings. And the "face" that his
memory tries to recapture is not the innocent Adam in Beulah, nor the
"human form divine," but more closely akin to Yeats's "looking for the face
I had / Before the world was made."

De Man's review of Bloom is interesting not only for its formulation
of de Man's dialectical reading of Wordsworth but also for its
reflections on the tone of Bloom's critical argument. De Man notices
"the tone of lecture notes...aimed at the general public rather than
the specialist" with its "gentle praise for all his authors and politeness
toward his readers," but he observes that

Bloom's criticism has a much deeper virtue than the polite tone of his latest
work suggests. It is the product of a genuine intellectual passion that actually
has little patience with balanced judgments and strikes out for absolute
positions. The outward moderation is only a concession to urbanity, or
perhaps a device to lure the reader into the author's camp. What counts in
this book is the general thesis.   (91–95)

90–96. Both the review and "Symbolic Landscape in Wordsworth and Yeats" are
listed in Keenan's bibliography as published in 1962. My presentation of them
has reversed the order in which they are listed in the bibliography.

This depreciation of "balanced judgments" in favor of "absolute positions" marks de Man's awareness of the difference in decorum between a polite and balanced essay like "Symbolic Landscape in Wordsworth and Yeats" and his more uncompromising dialectical works, even as it anticipates, perhaps even provokes, a shift in the decorum of Bloom's work toward a more absolute and less accommodating stance.

In "Wordsworth and Hölderlin," his inaugural lecture for the chair of Comparative Literature at the University of Zürich first published in German in 1966 (RR 47–65), de Man addresses the problem that modern scholars have in thinking about Romanticism – that "we [scholars] carry it [Romanticism] within ourselves as the experience of an *act* in which, up to a certain point, we ourselves have participated" (50), so that when we make "a conscious effort to think of our own historical situation in relation to the romantic movement" (48) we are not thinking about something from which we have "the illusion of detachment" (50). This involvement in Romanticism explains, perhaps, why scholars have "avoided or evaded" (47) "the question" of Romanticism that "seems continually to resist interpretation" (49). It also explains why the Romantic poets themselves may provide a helpful example, for the poets write about the same "experience of the temporal relation between the act and its interpretation" that the scholars are involved in, and their example may show scholars "why the interpretation of romanticism remains for us the most difficult and at the same time the most necessary of tasks" (50). The Romantic poets represent the problematic movement from unmediated act to interpretive consciousness of temporality that is for de Man the modern critic's situation as well.

De Man turns to Wordsworth for examples of this problematic movement from both "the private sphere of personal memory" and "the world of history" (55). In the first category, he reads "There was a Boy" and a brief analogous passage from *The Prelude* II (the flute-playing on the lake). The dialectical movement he traces in both passages is a "transition from one world to another," from an "inauthentic past" (55) in which we experience an "illusory" (52) "analogical correspondence between man and nature" (51) to a "precarious knowledge of its [poetic language's and presumably the poet's] future" mortality (55). Unlike "Intentional Structure," which noted in passing that "entities engendered by consciousness" begin and imply "a negation of permanence, the discontinuity of a death"

(4), this lecture notes not just the death of products of consciousness but "the fine mixture of anxiety and consenting submission with which consciousness admits mortality" (55). The consciousness of death in this lecture redefines the consciousness of consciousness; temporality replaces intentionality in de Man's account of "our situation" and our authentic understanding of it.

In the second category of the problematic he examines, "the world of history," de Man follows a series of passages from *The Prelude* VI, from Wordsworth's joy at celebrating the anniversary of the French Revolution through the Grand Chartreuse to the Simplon Pass and the Gondo Gorge. Again the movement is from "the intoxication of the act" to "reflection [that] must negate the act that nonetheless constitutes its origin" (56). History at once "is an act, a dangerous and destructive act, a kind of hubris of the will that rebels against the grasp of time. But on the other hand it is also temporally productive, since it allows for the language of reflection to constitute itself" (57–58). Imagination, it appears, is involved in both these moments, the "active" and the "interpretive" stages (58). It is both involved in the act, in its "danger and failure," and beyond the act, in a consciousness of having "escaped destruction thanks to an effort of consciousness to make sure of itself once again" (58). De Man identifies Wordsworthian imagination with the act but even more with the reflection: "For Wordsworth there is no historical eschatology, but rather only a never-ending reflection upon an eschatological moment that has failed through the excess of its interiority" (59).

Like Yeats and Wordsworth in "Symbolic Landscape," Hölderlin and Wordsworth here exemplify "one and the same problematic" (60), but de Man's Hölderlin starts from a more advanced position in the same dialectic – the overcoming of "a correspondence between nature and consciousness" that Wordsworth comes to only at "a highly advanced point in his thinking" (59). The "same problematic" we have seen in Wordsworth as an excess of interiority takes the form in Hölderlin of an exploration of the relation between men and gods, exploring the human "excess issuing from a fullness which causes us to transgress our own limits" (61). Poetry here again, however, is not to be identified solely with the excess. It "never allows this power to rush blindly to meet the unknown future of death. It turns back upon itself and becomes part of a temporal dimension that strives to remain bound to the earth and that replaces the violent temporality (*reissende Zeit*) of action with the sheltering temporality (*schützende Zeit*) of interpretation" (63).

Coming back to his opening reflection on the situation of the literary historian, de Man suggests that "the poet and the historian converge in this essential point [of "preserving memory, even the memory of the heroic act that throws itself into the future and destroys itself in this project"] to the extent that they both speak of an action that precedes them but that exists for consciousness only because of their intervention" (65). Poetry and history thus share a reflective complicity in the heroic actions whose memory they both preserve, and literary history may learn from the poets to persevere in that reflection that "lends duration to a past that otherwise would immediately sink into the nonbeing of a future that withdraws itself from consciousness" (64). If literary historians "would achieve a historical significance," they must pursue not action but difficult interpretation, against their own evasions and resistances, in order that "the poetic magnanimity to which our consciousness owes tribute [not] sink into forgetfulness" (65).

In drawing this programmatic lesson for (post-)Romantic literary history from Romantic poetry, de Man forgets, however, to inquire into the differences between poetry and history, even as they have been formulated by the Romantic poets from whom he draws them. Wordsworth's analysis of those differences in the Preface to *Lyrical Ballads* would complicate de Man's account by re-aligning the poet with precisely the "illusory analogy" between mind and nature that de Man says Wordsworth goes beyond (52). Wordsworth's poet differs from the biographer and historian only in writing under one restriction, "that of the necessity of giving immediate pleasure to a human Being," and his acceptance of that restriction leads the poet to accept, as a condition of his professional activity, the very premise de Man goes beyond – that "considers man and nature as essentially adapted to each other, and the mind of man as naturally the mirror of the fairest and most interesting qualities of nature" (LB 257–59).

The poet, we might say, remembers actions only insofar as he can represent them pleasurably for his fellows, whereas the historian, like the scientist interested in truth as a specialized acquisition that distinguishes him from others, remembers actions in painful and alienating detail, sacrificing immediate pleasure and overcoming the resistances of immediate pain for the sake of the mediated pleasures of intellectual achievement and avoidance of greater harm. The poet cultivates and preserves the "lively, pleasurably entertaining" strategies by which human beings ameliorate direct acknowledgment of a "destructive world" (RR 55); indeed he does not acknowledge a "destructive world" himself as a privileged viewpoint but chooses, as it were, what de Man calls "the aspect of renewal" over the aspect "of danger" that the world presents. The historian, on the other hand, not restricted as the poet is, may choose to bring out the aspect of danger and pain or to dwell upon the "infinite complexity of pain and pleasure" (246) without, like the poet, resolving that complexity in favor of pleasure.

But asking the poet to instruct the historian, as de Man does, runs the risk of turning the poet into a historian in order to make him suitably instructive. If, as de Man claims with characteristically dire hyperbole, "the future is present in history only as the remembering of a failed project that has become a menace" (58–59), the future remains open in poetry for Wordsworth, not perhaps as a "historical eschatology" of ultimate purposes or ultimate fulfillments but nevertheless as a series of pleasurable works, each of which "has a worthy purpose" even if it is not always "a distinct purpose formally conceived" (246). Though it may brace the historian in his difficult undertaking to imagine the poet in "a never-ending reflection upon an eschatological moment that has failed through the excess of its interiority" (59), such an image serves better to assure the historian that no one else is having any fun than it does to describe the poet's own self-description or to come to terms with the challenge poetry makes by continuing to exist as distinct from history. De Man here explores the similitude in dissimilitude between poetry and history, but he does not think through the dissimilitude in similitude.

De Man also makes Wordsworth a witness of pain rather than a celebrant of pleasure in his "Introduction to the Poetry of John Keats," published in the United States the same year de Man delivered his inaugural lecture in Switzerland.[13] Wordsworth figures in the introduction, as he did for Keats himself in one famous passage, as the explorer of "the 'dark passages'" (190) of self-awareness Keats comes to explore only at the very end his life. De Man finds Keats's historical consciousness fully developed in *The Fall of Hyperion*. That full development consists in understanding what de Man called the

13 *Critical Writings*, ed. Waters, 179–97.

"dialectical mind" in his review of Bloom – "the sacrificial nature of all historical movement" and

> the deeper theme of man's temporal contingency. The poet is the chosen witness of the damage caused by time; by growing in consciousness he gains no new attributes of beauty or might, merely the negative privilege of witnessing the death of those who surpassed him in greatness ... every step in the progression [of history] takes on the form of a tragedy beyond redemption, though not beyond the power of understanding.   (187–88)

De Man claims that until the end Keats exempts himself from this tragic vision. He "does not remain in the barren, impoverished world of human contingency, the world of gray rocks and stones that is the landscape of Wordsworth's *Prelude* ... because Keats's self is in fact dissociated from the suffering mankind with which he sympathizes" (194). De Man's repetition here of his elided allusion to the last line of "A slumber did my spirit seal" without mention of ameliorating trees, his transference of the color gray from the name Lucy Gray to the landscape, and his application of that description to the landscape of *The Prelude* which de Man himself epitomized in "Symbolic Landscape" with "a 'gentle breeze' blowing 'from the green fields and from yon azure sky'" (125) show de Man here writing not literary history but tragic poetry of his own. In the end, according to de Man, Keats reaches the insight characteristic of Wordsworth and Rousseau and, at times, of Blake and Coleridge – "a philosophical generality rooted in genuine self-insight," where "'philosophy' in the later Keats" is "the power that forces a man to see himself as he really is" (196–97). For these philosophical poets (unlike "us" whose "sense of self-hood hardly ever rises above self-justification"), "consciousness of self was the first and necessary step toward moral judgment" (197), and consciousness of self is tragic consciousness of temporality and mortality. Though de Man notes at the beginning of his essay that in the wake of the outmoded Victorian image of Wordsworth, his image "is far from having been fixed and determined by a poetic or critical itinerary that went beyond him" (179–80), de Man draws in this essay upon a fixed image of Wordsworth as a dialectical philosopher bearing witness to "man's temporal contingency" and the contingency of his own sole self (187).

"Time and History in Wordsworth" (1967/1987)

This image does not become unfixed in de Man's 1967 Christian Gauss lecture, "Time and History in Wordsworth," but it is developed with what de Man calls "the subtle nuances of temporality and intent that a valid commentary should bring out" (THW 4). Responding to Geoffrey Hartman's then recent *Wordsworth's Poetry*, which he admires for its ear "finely attuned to the slightest nuances of Wordsworth's language" (5), and addressing a less specialized audience more like the one he addressed in "Symbolic Landscape," de Man adopts the stance of "gentle praise for all his authors and politeness toward his readers" he had commented upon in Bloom's *Visionary Company* (91). He did not publish the lecture, though it would have been his most developed and extensive commentary exclusively devoted to Wordsworth's poetry.

Lindsay Waters in "Paul de Man: Life and Works" believes that "it is all too apparent why de Man failed to publish" this lecture. "He was in the process at just this moment of changing his thinking about a number of key issues, and the Wordsworth lecture was indicative of where he had been rather than where he was going." It is "most remarkable for its adherence to a metalanguage derived from Heidegger."[14] In introducing the lecture, which they published for the first time in a special issue of *diacritics* on "Wordsworth and the Production of Poetry," Cynthia Chase and Andrzej Warminski are more interested in the future to which it points than in the past from which it comes. Accordingly, they twice minimize "its use of a vocabulary of 'authentic temporality' and 'finitude' with echoes of Heidegger" in favor of its turn to "language," "the question of reading," and "explicitly rhetorical terms" in several notes from a 1971 or 1972 presentation (I will comment on these notes at the appropriate point in my chronology). Chase and Warminski do not mention that the lecture incorporates de Man's reading of "There was a Boy" from his lecture the year before on "Wordsworth and Hölderlin," where the Heideggerian language is at least as prominent (3).

De Man resituates his reading of "There was a Boy" here as the first reading in a series that leads to a claim, contra Geoffrey Hartman, that "the key to an understanding of Wordsworth lies in the

14 *Critical Writings*, ed. Waters, liv.

relationship between imagination and time, not in the relationship between imagination and nature" (16). He also adds to it a turn that identifies the poem as a proleptic autobiography whose first part was in first person in an early draft and whose fictional anticipation of reflection on the poet's own death "can only exist in the form of a language" (9). "This temporal perspective" of speaking "from beyond the grave," de Man writes, "is characteristic for all Wordsworth's poetry" (9) – an assertion we might describe, as de Man later describes "the language of imagination," as "privileged in terms of truth; it serves no empirical purposes or desires other than the truth of its own assertion" (16). The assertion asserts itself (or, to use a subject-centered language, de Man asserts himself in this assertion) but by no means asserts a true generalization about Wordsworth's poetry.

De Man goes on to read the *Essays upon Epitaphs* as a commentary on "The Boy of Winander" and "a meditation on the temporality that characterizes the consciousness of beings capable of reflecting on their own death" (10) and to read a sonnet from the River Duddon sequence, "Not hurled precipitous from steep to steep," as an examination of Wordsworth's understanding of temporality in "its more empirical mode of manifestation, namely history" (11). Similar to his move from personal memory to history in the essay on Wordsworth and Hölderlin but less evidently concerned with political history, this move from awareness of individual death to contemplation of "history" develops the same point in two different phases: "Like the boy experiencing the foreknowledge of his death, history awakens in us a true sense of our temporality, by allowing for the interplay between achievement and dissolution, self-assertion and self-loss" (13). In this first phase we still have the movement from action or excess to interpretation or reflection whose burden is the recognition of mortality. The second phase, a "move backwards, against the current of the movement" of the first phase, "does not exist in nature but is the privilege of the faculty of mind that Wordsworth calls the imagination; asserting the possibility of reflection in the face of the most radical dissolution personal or historical" (14). History, understood as "the retrospective recording of man's failure to overcome the power of time," becomes a bond among human beings, but it is "not one of common enterprise, or of a common belonging to nature: it is much rather the recognition of a common temporal predicament that finds its expression in the individual and historical destinies that strike the poet as exemplary" (15).

De Man nuances his description of that predicament in this lecture with an acknowledgment of "a certain form of hope" and the "affirmation of a possible future" that "made it possible for man to pursue an enterprise that seems doomed from the start, to have a history in spite of a death which Wordsworth never allows us to forget" (13). De Man at least rarely allows us to forget it. He goes on immediately to assert that the temporality that recognizes the "loss of self into death" is "more originary, more authentic" than the temporality that sees the "progression [from nature] towards history" because "it reaches further into the past and sees wider into the future." The more authentic temporality "envelops the other, but without reducing it to mere error. Rather it creates a point of view which has gone beyond the historical world...but which can look back upon this world and see it within its own, relative greatness, as a world that does not escape from mutability but asserts itself within the knowledge of its own transience" (13). The knowledge of death thus encompasses and colors the form that the "form of hope" can take and the possibilities that the "possible future" can include: "The imagination engenders hope and future, not in the form of historical progress, nor in the form of an immortal life after death that would make human history unimportant, but as the persistent, future possibility of a retrospective reflection on its own decay" (14).

If, as de Man acknowledges, the "restorative power [of mind and language after nature and history have failed]" is "the main assertive power in Wordsworth's poetry," we might say that the negation of this restorative power is the main assertive power of de Man's prose at moments like this one. To declare the limits of "future possibility" so absolutely as "retrospective reflection" and to name the object of that reflection so certainly and sickeningly as the imagination's "own decay" is to exert the power of assertion for the sake of "authenticity" rather than "accuracy," in terms de Man uses later in the essay: "A truth about a self is best described, not in terms of accuracy, but in terms of authenticity" (16–17). De Man asserts himself authentically in these terms by asserting that Wordsworth, despite his apparent assertions to the contrary, exemplifies what de Man is asserting. The test of de Man's assertions is not their accuracy either to Wordsworth's poetic oeuvre or to anyone's empirical experience of the human predicament, because a "predicament" itself *is*, as the OED points out, "that which is predicated or asserted" as well as "a state of being; condition, situation, position; *esp.* an unpleasant, trying, or dangerous situation." The self is defined or posited by its "predicament" or that which it asserts, and the test of it is its power to persist in its assertion without yielding to weaker and easier assertions or being compelled by stronger and more difficult ones. The Wordsworth de Man here creates in his own image is the strongest and most authentic Wordsworth de Man can imagine, a Wordsworth who, in his sonnet "Mutability," can assert "mutability...as an *unfailing* law that governs the natural, personal, and historical existence of man. Thus to name mutability as a principle of order is to come as close as possible to naming the authentic temporal consciousness of the self" (17). The forcefulness of de Man's assertion of this image of Wordsworth is an effect in and of de Man's language, a "poetic language" as he characterized it in "Intentional Structure," "able to posit regardless of presence but...unable to give a foundation to what it posits, except as an intent of consciousness" (6). The power of de Man's absolute assertions, in his own terms, is poetic power.

"The Rhetoric of Temporality" (1969)

Though for Lindsay Waters de Man's "most fully achieved essay" (lvi), "The Rhetoric of Temporality," marks a decisive turn in de Man's thinking that explains why he did not publish his backward looking lecture on "Time and History in Wordsworth," the image of Wordsworth de Man asserts remains unchanged from the lecture to the essay. Waters believes that "with his title 'The Rhetoric of Temporality,' de Man gestured two ways, backward with the Heideggerian word 'temporality' and forward with the word 'rhetoric'" (lii), but the new (or at least newly emphasized) rhetorical terminology of allegory, symbol, and irony does not substantially modify de Man's texts, themes, or assertions about Wordsworth. Indeed, the continuation of those assertions about Wordsworth may modify the rhetorical terminology.

The essay divides into two sections, "Allegory and Symbol" and "Irony," the first a historical argument, the second a structural one. Wordsworth plays key roles in both sections. In the section on "Allegory and Symbol" Wordsworth first appears as Abrams's and Wasserman's "radical idealist," based on their both quoting his remark: "'I was often unable to think of external things as having external existence, and I communed with all that I saw as something not apart from, but inherent in, my own immaterial nature.'" With this passage de Man illustrates one side of the confusion in critical representations of the Romantics, the other side of which is the emphasis on "an analogical imagination that is founded on the priority of natural substances over the consciousness of the self." As he asks further on, "Is romanticism a subjective idealism ... or is it instead a return to a certain form of naturalism ... ?" De Man's Wordsworth

is more clearly conscious [than his critics] of what is involved here when he sees the same dialectic between the self and nature in temporal [as opposed to spatial] terms. The movements of nature are for him instances of what Goethe calls *Dauer im Wechsel*, endurance within a pattern of change, the assertion of a metatemporal, stationary state beyond the apparent decay of a mutability that attacks certain outward aspects of nature but leaves the core intact.

These are the same terms in which de Man characterized "mutability as a principle of order" at the end of his lecture on "Time and History in Wordsworth."

Citing the *Prelude* passages from the Grand Chartreuse and the Gondo Gorge that he has cited often since "Intentional Structure" as well as the passage on the beginning and ending of the river from *Essays upon Epitaphs*[15] that he cited in "Time and History," de Man goes on to assert that "such paradoxical assertions of eternity in motion can be applied to nature but not to the self caught up entirely within mutability." Others (Coleridge and the critics) yield to the "temptation" to borrow this temporal stability for the self, thereby "escaping from 'the unimaginable touch of time'" – a quotation from the Wordsworth sonnet with which he concludes "Time and History in Wordsworth." "Wordsworth [, however,] was never guilty of thus reducing a theocentric to an interpersonal relation" that identifies, as Wasserman put it, "'the phenomenal world of understanding with the noumenal world of reason.'" This whole "pseudo-dialectic between subject and object," de Man concludes, "originates ... in the assumed predominance of the symbol as the outstanding characteristic of romantic diction" (196–98). At this point his argument shifts from Wordsworth to Rousseau and *La Nouvelle Héloïse*.

15 For a critique of de Man's reading of this passage see *Historicity* 32.

When it returns to conclude the section on allegory, Wordsworth too returns as an allegorical poet whose landscape poetry extends the significance of locale to "include a meaning that is no longer circumscribed by the literal horizon of a given place." De Man quotes the same passage on the river from *Essays upon Epitaphs* that he quoted in his lecture on "Time and History" and points as well to the passages on crossing the Alps, climbing Mount Snowdon, and the River Duddon sequence as evidence that Wordsworth goes beyond locodescriptive poetry to the rhetorical topoi of "'a traditional and inherited typology,'" "with this distinction, however, that the typology is no longer the same [as that of the seventeenth-century meditative poem] and that the poet, sometimes after long and difficult inner struggle, had to renounce the seductiveness and the poetic resources of a symbolical diction." This "allegorization of the geographical site ... corresponds to the unveiling of an authentically temporal destiny ... [that] takes place in a subject that has sought refuge against the impact of time in a natural world to which, in truth, it bears no resemblance." This allegory is "not decreed by dogma" but is instead "a relationship between signs in which the reference to their respective meanings has become of secondary importance" to the non-coincidence of the allegorical sign with the sign that precedes it. "The secularized allegory of the early romantics thus necessarily contains the negative moment which in Rousseau is that of renunciation, in Wordsworth that of the loss of self in death or in error." Allegory thus understood "prevents the self from an illusory identification with the non-self, which is now fully, though painfully, recognized as a non-self. It is this painful knowledge that we perceive at the moments when early romantic literature finds its true voice." The customary picture of Romanticism is a defensive strategy against this painful "negative self-knowledge," a "regressive" and "tenacious self-mystification" of the "lucidity of the pre-romantic writers" like Rousseau and Wordsworth (206–08).

Wordsworth and Rousseau (and Hölderlin) do not exemplify the trope of irony that is the topic of the essay's second section (208). Baudelaire's "De l'essence du rire," considered out of historical sequence, is de Man's chief source on the structure of this trope.[16] The structural analysis of irony leads, however, to a "dangerously

---

16 See Dominick LaCapra's critical examination of de Man's reading of Baudelaire's text in "The Temporality of Rhetoric," 116–24.

satisfying" historical conclusion that the "regression" from the eighteenth-century ironic novel to nineteenth-century realism is parallel to the regression from late-eighteenth-century allegorical poetry to nineteenth-century self-mystified symbolic poetry – "a coherent historical picture [rescued] at the expense of stated human incoherence" (222).

Going beyond this analogy between Romantic allegory and Romantic irony, de Man raises the question of whether certain "'allegorical'" texts could be thought of

as being truly meta-ironical, as having transcended irony without falling into the myth of an organic totality or bypassing the temporality of all language?... Would some of the definitely non-ironic, but, in our sense of the term, allegorical, texts of the late Hölderlin, of Wordsworth, or of Baudelaire himself be this "pure poetry from which laughter is absent as from the soul of the Sage?"

De Man introduces a reading of what he calls Wordsworth's "Lucy Gray" poem, "A slumber did my spirit seal," not directly to answer this question but to "approach [it] in a less exalted mood, by making a brief comparison of the temporal structure of allegory and irony."

De Man, however, does not take the time that would be necessary to show that the poem "falls under the definition of what is here being referred to as 'allegorical' poetry" except to introduce the new criterion that it has the "fundamentally prefigurative[17] pattern," and he simply declares that "the text clearly is not ironic." The argument that follows does clarify somewhat the differences in "temporal structure" between the two modes and the sense in which the temporal structure of this poem is more allegorical than ironic, but only because it associates allegory with the more general categories of diachrony and narrative rather than holding to its specific definition as *"repetition... of a previous sign with which [the allegorical sign] can never coincide"* (207). If, as de Man asserts, "irony is a synchronic structure" (an "instant at which the two selves, the empirical as well as the ironic, are simultaneously present, juxtaposed within the same moment but as two irreconcilable and disjointed beings") and "allegory appears as a successive mode capable of engendering duration as the illusion of a continuity that it

---

17 I have corrected "profigurative" in the University of Minnesota Press edition with "prefigurative" from the Singleton edition of the essay.

knows to be illusionary" (226), then the poem described as a "successive description of two stages of consciousness, one belonging to the past and mystified, the other to the *now* of the poem, the stage that has recovered from mystification of a past now presented as being in error," is more like allegory than irony. But allegory as a successive mode may be like other successive modes without all successive modes of poetry being allegorical. De Man's reading of Wordsworth's poem serves as his final example of the "temporal structure of allegory" at the cost of sacrificing his precise definition of allegory.

This reading of the poem as allegory also compels de Man to fend off a reading of it as irony – to claim that the word "thing" in lines three and four is free of irony and to argue that from the point of view of the speaker of the poem "there is no real disjunction of the subject ... [who] fully recognizes a past condition as one of error and stands in a present that, however painful, sees things as they actually are" (224). This denial of the poem's irony, like the assertion of its allegory, is again purchased at a cost to his earlier account of irony, for the poem would appear to illustrate that account by revealing how man painfully learns that "Nature can at all times treat him as if he were a thing and remind him of his factitiousness" (214), thereby opening a disjunction between a naive and a demystified self. Further, the association of irony with synchrony goes back on his earlier remark that "irony engenders a temporal sequence of acts of consciousness which is endless" (220).

It is almost as if de Man wrecks or (to use a cooler word) deconstructs the rhetorical analysis of allegory and irony that has organized his essay in this perverse reading of Wordsworth's poem, preserving the image of Wordsworth from his earlier essays even at the price of confusing the distinctions he has labored to produce in this one. He thus goes on to claim (with his reading of "The Boy of Winander" as autobiography in "Time and History" silently behind him) that "Wordsworth is one of the few poets who can write proleptically about their own death and speak, as it were, from beyond their own graves," offering "an eternal insight into the rocky barrenness of the human predicament" (224). The Wordsworthian "gray rocks and stones" of the "Introduction to the Poetry of John Keats" and the Wordsworthian temporal perspective of speaking from beyond the grave of "Time and History in Wordsworth" persist in clear outline in the penultimate section of "The Rhetoric of

Temporality" even as the definitions of irony and allegory blur.[18] One further point reasserts a perspective which, though it does not clarify the confusion produced by the reading of Wordsworth's poem, does make that empirical confusion over the application of definitions to an example less important. The "temporality" of the poem, whether allegorical or ironic, is an "ideal self-created temporality engendered by the language of the poem, but it is not possible within the actual temporality of experience." The temporality of the poem "does not exist within the subject" but is "exclusively that of the poem itself" (225).

Revisions of "Time and History in Wordsworth" (c. 1971–72)

The assertion of a similar radical disjunction between what exists in language and what exists in actuality has recurred in the essays I have been considering ever since de Man's remark in "Intentional Structure" that "critics who speak of a 'happy relationship' between matter and consciousness fail to realize that the very fact that the relationship has to be established within the medium of language indicates that it does not exist in actuality" (8). In the revisions de Man made to "Time and History in Wordsworth" for presentation to an unspecified audience "around 1971 or 1972," this disjunction, reformulated as a disjunction between "thematic and ... rhetorical structures" or between "theme and figure," becomes de Man's principal theme. It is here rather than in "The Rhetoric of Temporality" that de Man first sets "rhetoric" against "temporality" in his account of Wordsworth, though even here he does not revise the readings that thematize temporality but only reframes them and appends to each new remarks that emphasize the "question of Wordsworth's rhetoricity" (5 n. 4).

De Man's introductory notes to the revised lecture bring in Wordsworth as "the anti-rhetorical, natural poet (i.e. thematic) par excellence, not only because he explicitly attacked the use of figure

18 LaCapra liberates himself from de Man's "eternal insight into the rocky barrenness of the human predicament" by abasing it as a "purplish pop existentialism," and he reopens de Man's reading of "A slumber" by noting that "rocks and stones seem redundant as mineral forms of antilife, but with trees one returns – however faintly and with a 'shock of mild surprise' – to life and the promise of renewal." See "The Temporality of Rhetoric," 113–16.

as *ornatus*, but also because the thematic seduction is particularly powerful, in its transparency and clarity" (5 n. 4); de Man's appendices to his readings counteract that powerful seduction by naming the figures that produce it. Thus, at the end of his reading of "The Boy of Winander," the "temporal perspective" of speaking "from beyond the grave" that de Man earlier declared "characteristic of all Wordsworth's poetry" is re-presented as the effect of a metaleptic substitution that defies what is, "thematically speaking, a radical impossibility" through a "linguistic sleight-of-hand." What was previously a point about the relation between consciousness and time becomes a point about "a leap outside thematic reality into the rhetorical fiction of the sign," and a new, equally bold assertion replaces de Man's claim about the "temporal perspective" of "all Wordsworth's poetry": now "the poem does not reflect on death but on the rhetorical power of language that can make it seem as if we could anticipate the unimaginable" (9–10 n. 8). The object of reflection changes, but Wordsworth again turns out to be reflecting on what de Man is reflecting on.

De Man's reading of the metaphor of the voyage from *Essays upon Epitaphs* is similarly "'deconstructed'" by his reading of "The Boy of Winander" (11 n. 13), and his reading of "Not hurled precipitous ... " reveals the "de-constructive rhetoricity" of the sonnet as a "metonymy of a content becoming a container ... that does not correspond to a thematic, literal reality" (13 n. 14). The theme of time de Man privileged in his earlier version of the lecture is displaced by the theme of rhetoric in his last revision, which asserts: "In this least rhetorical of poets in which time itself comes so close to being a theme, the theme or meaning turns out to be more than ever dependent on rhetoric" (16 n. 16). The notes that make available these revisions to de Man's lecture do not indicate that he cuts the body of the lecture, in which time does more than come close to being a theme, but they do reveal de Man's intruding upon that theme an unprecedented attention to Wordsworth's rhetorical means that interfere with his, and with de Man's own earlier, thematic utterances.

"Autobiography as De-Facement" (1979)

De Man's next extended reading of Wordsworth in "Autobiography as De-Facement" (RR 67–81) appears seven or eight years after the delivery of the revised lecture on "Time and History in Wordsworth," ten years after his last published remarks on Wordsworth in "The Rhetoric of Temporality," and the same year as *Allegories of Reading*, his book on "Figural Language in Rousseau, Nietzsche, Rilke, and Proust."[19] The essay returns to the texts of the earlier lecture, *Essays upon Epitaphs* and "The Boy of Winander," but its tone departs from that lecture's "gentle praise for all his authors and politeness toward his readers" (*Critical Writings*, ed. Waters, 91) for a tone, even a behavior, toward his author and his readers that I would call, using the words de Man applies to the tone of Wordsworth's *Essays*, "aggressive" and "anything but gentle" (79). The violence to Wordsworth's texts and to de Man's readers I find in this essay makes it hard to resist, as I have committed myself to do, the explosive return of violence for violence by throwing back at de Man's text the words he applies to Wordsworth's and indignantly refusing the position of uncritical and unknowledgeable reader he appears to prepare for me.

De Man turns Wordsworth's criticism of Pope's epitaphs in the *Essays upon Epitaphs* into an "aggressive" act by quoting Wordsworth's assertion that "'I cannot suffer any Individual, however highly and deservedly honoured by my Countrymen, to stand in my way'" (79), as if Wordsworth and Pope were two gunslingers and English literature weren't big enough for both of them. But de Man leaves out the first part of Wordsworth's sentence that qualifies this assertion: "I vindicate the rights and dignity of Nature, and, as long as I condemn nothing without assigning reasons not lightly given, I cannot suffer any Individual ... to stand in my way" (EE 80). Both the positive principle asserted in this sentence and the serious commitment to give reasons for his criticism make Wordsworth's severe judgments of Pope critical but not violent, if rational criticism can be distinguished from violence. Both the practice and the claims of de Man's essay call that fundamental distinction into question, but I shall reaffirm it as the working premise of my reading of de Man's essay and let my readers judge whether that reading itself succeeds

19 Paul de Man, *Allegories of Reading: Figural Language in Rousseau, Nietzsche, Rilke, and Proust* (New Haven: Yale University Press, 1979).

in giving the premise plausibility. I must ask those readers' patience, as Wordsworth himself does, in pursuing a "minute criticism" that "is in its nature irksome; and as commonly practiced in books and conversation, is both irksome and injurious. Yet," as Wordsworth continues, "every mind must occasionally be exercised in this discipline, else it cannot learn the art of bringing words rigorously to the test of thoughts; and these again to a comparison with things, their archetypes; contemplated first in themselves, and secondly in relation to each other; in all which processes the mind must be skilful, otherwise it will be perpetually imposed upon" (148). It is only by putting de Man's words to the test of such Wordsworthian critical rigor that we will avoid being imposed upon by them.

De Man introduces his reading of Wordsworth's *Essays upon Epitaphs* in the second part of "Autobiography as De-Facement" to "illustrate" the "abstraction" with which he concludes the first part. As an "exemplary autobiographical text," the *Essays* will illustrate how such texts are subject to "the necessity to escape from the tropology of the subject and the equally inevitable reinscription of this necessity within a specular model of cognition" (72). Rather than work backwards to try to unpack this abstraction in terms of previous abstractions, I shall move forward through de Man's reading of the *Essays*, showing what he makes of them and what they reveal about this abstraction.

De Man first acknowledges the need to defend his description of the *Essays upon Epitaphs* as "an exemplary autobiographical text" by denying it: "It requires no lengthy argument to stress the autobiographical components in a text which turns compulsively from an essay *upon* epitaphs to being itself an epitaph and, more specifically, the author's own monumental inscription or auto-biography" (72). We must remind ourselves that the first place one might think to turn for an exemplary Wordsworthian autobiography would be *The Prelude* and that the *Essays upon Epitaphs* are not obviously an epitaph or an autobiography but a series of critical essays that themselves contain exemplary epitaphs to illustrate their abstractions. It does, then, require some argument to justify de Man's reading them not just as autobiography in the sense in which he earlier declared that "any book with a readable title page is, to some extent, autobiographical" (70) but as an essay that turns into an epitaph that is an exemplary instance of autobiography. Neither the metamorphosis of essay into epitaph nor the identity of epitaph and autobiography is self-evident. But to say that something "requires no lengthy argument" is to imply its self-evidence or near self-evidence to one's readers. To declare that an apparently indefensible, or at least doubly unobvious, claim "requires no lengthy argument" is to put one's readers in the position of going along uncritically with such a claim, or of puzzling over why what appears obvious to de Man is not obvious to them, or of wondering whether de Man is joking, or of taking him seriously and raising a marginal objection as his prose continues on its way.[20]

What his prose goes on to do is to provide not an argument but a series of substitutions that transform the *Essays* into the required exemplary autobiography. Surveying the various sorts of epitaphs Wordsworth cites in the *Essays*, de Man focuses on the concluding epitaph by Wordsworth himself that "tells, in the starkest of languages, the story of a deaf man who compensates for his infirmity by substituting the reading of books for the sounds of nature." Describing this epitaph (which, "as the exemplary conclusion of an exemplary text," has come to stand for the *Essays* as a whole) in terms that link it to several "famous passages of *The Prelude*," de Man turns the *Essays* into this epitaph and turns this epitaph into autobiography. First, the concluding epitaph is said to share with the Blessed Babe passage, the drowned man, and "The Boy of Winander" passages a "general plot...very familiar to readers of *The Prelude*...of a discourse that is *sustained* beyond and in spite of *deprivation*." Then, partly on the strength of "verbal echoes" that link the concluding epitaph to "The Boy of Winander," de Man transfers his autobiographical reading of the latter poem (a variant of which was written in first person) from the boy who shouts to the owls to the deaf man who cannot hear the cuckoo's "shout." Having made (1) the synecdochic substitution of the concluding epitaph for the essays that contain it and (2) the metaphorical transfer of the first person (and thereby of autobiography) from the textual variant to "The Boy of Winander" to the concluding epitaph of the *Essays*, de Man makes that same variant evidence "for the assumption that these figures of deprivation, maimed men, drowned corpses, blind beggars, children about to die, that appear throughout *The Prelude* are figures of Wordsworth's own poetic self." The *accumulatio* of "these figures"

20 Lentricchia sees fewer alternative possibilities in de Man's "rhetoric of authority": "He tells us, in effect, that we all know thus and such is the case and, therefore, wise reader, I shall not bore you by belaboring the obvious." See ANC 293.

(which share not the plot de Man earlier outlined but only the trait of deprivation with the deaf man in the epitaph) warrants the ascription to the poet of "this near-obsessive concern with mutilation." This last phrase introduces an attribution of motive that picks up the earlier assertion that Wordsworth's text turned "compulsively" from essay to epitaph and substitutes the stronger word "mutilation" for "deprivation," one whose primary sense points not just to the state of having a good taken away but to the action of depriving a person or animal of a limb or part of its body (72–73). The essays have become the concluding epitaph; its subject, the deaf man, has become Wordsworth; and his deafness (described in the epitaph in the passive voice as a withdrawal of the gift of hearing) has become a mutilation with which Wordsworth is obsessed. De Man turns similitudes into identities instead of reflecting on "similitude in dissimilitude, and dissimilitude in similitude."[21]

Having thus transformed the *Essays upon Epitaphs* into an "exemplary autobiographical text," de Man raises the question about "autobiographical self-restoration" with which the remainder of his essay will be concerned: "the question remains how this near-obsessive concern with mutilation...is to be understood and, consequently, how trustworthy the ensuing claim of compensation and restoration can be" (74–75). De Man addresses this question through a two-stage argument characteristic of many essays of his deconstructive or rhetorical period. First he argues that "the claim for restoration in the face of death, in the *Essays upon Epitaphs*, is grounded in a consistent system of thought, of metaphors, and of diction" (74), and then he shows that "despite the perfect closure of the system, the text contains elements that not only disrupt its balance but its principle of production" (76) with the effect, for the question at hand, that "the restoration turn[s] out to be a worse deprivation" (80).

De Man's construction of "the perfect closure" of "the most encompassing system of tropes conceivable" in Wordsworth's *Essays* requires the same critical scrutiny as his subsequent deconstruction, for it is again not self-evident that Wordsworth's various local uses of metaphors and other tropes in any way purport to be systematically

---

21 LB 265. These terms of Wordsworth's are similar to LaCapra's Derridean preference for "the 'impure' terms of supplementary differences and similarities" as contrasted to de Man's frequent production of "either/or" binary oppositions in "The Temporality of Rhetoric," 121, 108.

consistent or that they can be construed to be so.[22] Perhaps following Derrida's elaboration in "White Mythology,"[23] de Man constructs them as consistent under "the overarching metaphor for this entire system ... that of the sun in motion," which is not only a "natural object ... powerful enough, as such, to command a chain of images that can see a man's work as a tree, made of trunks and branches, and language as akin to 'the power of gravitation or the air we breathe[,]' ... the parousia of light" but also "a figure of knowledge as well as of nature, the emblem of what the third essay refers to as 'the mind with absolute sovereignty upon itself'" (74–75). In what sense does the sun – a "natural object" that figures in Wordsworth's extended comparison of its motions, from setting to rising to setting again, with the contemplative Soul's movements from mortality to "everlasting life" and back to "the land of transitory things" – in what sense does this natural object "command" other images as they arise in other comparisons in other contexts? Must we supply a biological (or perhaps a Platonic) context that makes the "tree [seen] through a tender haze or a luminous mist, that spiritualises and beautifies it" and makes only its "trunk and ... main branches" visible (EE 58) depend upon the sun for its life, or an optical (or again Platonic) context that makes it depend upon the sun for its visibility? Does the use of the one extended comparison necessarily entail or delimit the other? On what premise of reading do all the metaphorical vehicles of a given category (natural objects) in a given text cohere systematically regardless of their tenor and context?

These questions already loosen the "chain of images" de Man confidently links under the command of the sun as a natural object, but the sequence he connects under the sun as "figure of knowledge" is more important to his argument and thus requires more extensive scrutiny. The very first link that moves from the comparison of sun and Soul in the first essay to the sun as an emblem of "the mind with absolute sovereignty upon itself" at the beginning of the third will

22 In this connection see Tilottama Rajan's remark: "De Man's assumption that rhetorical microstructures and thematic macrostructures form a systematic totality remains an oddly structuralist notion, despite the crucial role played in his analysis by the post-structuralist notion of undecidability," "Displacing Post-Structuralism," 472.

23 "White Mythology: Metaphor in the Text of Philosophy," in *Margins of Philosophy*, trans. Alan Bass (Chicago: University of Chicago Press, 1982), 209–71. Originally published in French in 1971 and first translated into English in 1974. Thanks to Wallace Martin for calling this connection to my attention.

not hold. For one thing, the sun is nowhere in evidence in Wordsworth's text near this phrase but, rather, is brought there by de Man. Just as importantly, the word "itself" in the phrase in question refers not to "the mind" but to an earlier phrase in the sentence from which de Man excerpts his supposed emblem of the sun as a figure of knowledge. Wordsworth writes: "A lovely quality, if its loveliness be clearly perceived, fastens the mind with absolute sovereignty upon itself; permitting or inciting it to pass, by smooth gradation or gentle transition to some other kindred quality" (EE 81). "Itself" here is the "lovely quality," which exercises the power to permit or incite the mind ("it") to pass to other related qualities, as Wordsworth says in the next sentence the thought of meekness can lead to the thought of magnanimity. Not only is the mind not compared to the sun here, it is also not the active sovereign of knowledge but the passive object of a sovereign "lovely quality." The chain of tropes does not hold even in its first link.

The next link in de Man's broken chain declares that "knowledge and mind imply language and account for the relationship set up between the sun and the text of the epitaph: the epitaph, says Wordsworth, 'is open to the day; the sun looks down upon the stone, and the rains of heaven beat against it.' The sun becomes the eye that *reads* the text of the epitaph" (75). Here at least the sun does figure in the passage de Man cites, where Wordsworth argues that "an epitaph is not a proud writing shut up for the studious; it is exposed to all." But the sun only "looks down" in this figure on the stone; an old man "cons" the epitaph, a child "can read it," and a stranger "is introduced through its mediation to the company of a friend" (EE 59). Here, even if we grant the relevance of linking the figure of the sun in this passage to that in the earlier passage in the first essay, de Man and not Wordsworth introduces the crucial figure of the sun *reading* the text of the epitaph.

De Man goes on, "And the essay tells us what this text consists of, by way of a quotation from Milton that deals with Shakespeare: 'What need'st thou such weak witness of thy *name*?' In the case of poets such as Shakespeare, Milton, or Wordsworth himself, the epitaph can consist only of what he calls 'the naked name'... as it is read by the eye of the sun" (75, de Man's silently added italics). But the quotation from Milton comes two pages later in Wordsworth's text with no connection to the figure of the sun looking down upon the stone, although de Man's last phrase strongly implies the continuation of this figure in the passage. Wordsworth uses the quotation not to explain "this text" that the sun is supposedly reading but to make one exception to the "notion of the perfect epitaph" he has elaborated throughout the essay. In the special case of certain "mighty benefactors of mankind" an epitaph may consist of

their naked names, and a grand comprehensive sentiment of civic gratitude, patriotic love, or human admiration – or the utterance of some elementary principle most essential in the constitution of true virtue; – or a declaration touching that pious humility and self-abasement, which are ever most profound as minds are most susceptible of genuine exaltation – or an intuition, communicated in adequate words, of the sublimity of intellectual power; – these are the only tribute which can here be paid.   (EE 61)

Wordsworth's series of "or"s shows that even in this case the naked name is not the whole epitaph, just as his list of possible readers in the previously considered passage showed that what de Man calls the "eye of the sun" is not the only reader of such epitaphs, if it is to be thought of as a reader at all.

De Man forges the next link in his tropological chain with another transition that suggests he is following the stages of Wordsworth's argument: "At this point, it can be said of 'the language of the senseless stone' that it acquires a 'voice,' the *speaking* stone counterbalancing the *seeing* sun. The system passes from sun to eye to language as name and as voice" (75). Wordsworth's text, however, has already passed by the phrases on which this elaboration of de Man's system is based. In the course of a discussion of the burial practices of the ancient Greeks and Romans, especially their practice of interring the dead "by the way-sides," Wordsworth reflects that such practices "must have given, formerly, to the language of the senseless stone a voice enforced and endeared by the benignity of that nature with which it was in unison" (EE 54). The speaking stone is not here counterposed with the seeing sun – the sun is nowhere to be seen – and the systematic passage from "sun to eye to language as name and as voice" takes place only in de Man's construction, which goes on to "[complete] the central metaphor of the sun and thus ... the tropological spectrum that the sun engenders" by identifying

the figure of prosopopeia, the fiction of an apostrophe to an absent, deceased, or voiceless entity, which posits the possibility of the latter's reply and confers upon it the power of speech. Voice assumes mouth, eye, and finally face, a chain that is manifest in the etymology of the trope's name, *prosopon poien*, to confer a mask or a face (*prosopon*). Prosopopeia is the trope of autobiography, by which one's name, as in the Milton poem, is made as intelligible and memorable as a face. Our topic deals with the giving and taking away of faces, with face and deface, *figure*, figuration and disfiguration. (75–76)

This sequence arrives at the second term of de Man's title, "defacement," as the paragraph I examined earlier moved from the *Essays upon Epitaphs* to the first term, "autobiography." Just as the first sequence closed with "mutilation," so this one ends in "disfiguration." In both cases, a series of associations and substitutions departs from something in Wordsworth's text and ends in shocking language that is not there but is nevertheless presented as the logical and necessary implication of what is. In both cases, however, the necessity of this outcome rests upon strong assertions (in both cases the *accumulatio* and the shocking word come in at the end) and specious transitions that will hold up only as long as one does not read de Man's text too closely and return to Wordsworth's text to examine the evidence on which it is supposed to rest. The audacious description of the "perfect closure of the system" de Man has just pieced together is so much at variance with the disconnected and arbitrary series of steps I have traced that it might well convince or at least impress readers who had not followed the steps and tested them against Wordsworth's text. I submit, however, to readers who will follow those steps for themselves, who need not take my assertion for the fact, that Wordsworth's text provides no warrant for the construction of such a system, that de Man's text provides an unconvincing case for such a construction, and that de Man's deconstruction of the "encompassing system of tropes" he has constructed out of fragments of Wordsworth's text proves nothing about Wordsworth's *Essays upon Epitaphs* and very little about the trope of prosopopeia, which is supposed to be the key to the system of that text.

De Man defines that trope in the broadest possible way as not only the giving of voice to the normally unvoiced, but also as the speaking to the inarticulate, the "apostrophe to an absent, deceased, or voiceless entity" (75). But he goes even further than this collapse of a commonly respected distinction to include, in order to complete his account of Wordsworth's "system" under the single trope "prosopopeia," "the art of delicate transition," even though no rhetorical handbook I know of has ever made this association. Because de Man claims that "the *Essays upon Epitaphs* are a treatise on the superiority of prosopopeia...over antithesis" and because Wordsworth also advocates "delicate transition" over antithesis, de Man, it appears, includes "delicate transition" under prosopopeia. It would be more accurate and logical, however, to assess the place of both prosopopeia and delicate transition in Wordsworth's argument than to set up a dominant trope for Wordsworth's text under the name "prosopopeia" in order to show how "the text counsels against the use of its own main figure" (78), as de Man goes on to do.

De Man points to three passages in Wordsworth's text as evidence of this "inconsistency," but he distorts the context of the one phrase he elaborates upon. De Man writes that Wordsworth finds "such chiasmic figures [as the prosopopeia of the "Sta Viator"], crossing the conditions of death and life with the attributes of speech and of silence [,]...'too poignant and too transitory'" and goes on to create a mystery about Wordsworth's use of this phrase (77). But Wordsworth is not concerned with chiasmus at all in the passage in which he uses the phrase; instead he is concerned with his criterion that the inscription of the epitaph is "intended to be permanent" (EE 59) and should therefore not include an utterance like the apostrophe "*Speak! dead Maria breathe a strain divine!*" because it is "too poignant and too transitory" for an epitaph (EE 83).

De Man, however, needs the mystery he creates about Wordsworth's resistance to the trope he supposedly advocates in order to suggest a hidden motive for that resistance. Uncritically accepting another critic's reading of two lines from Milton's sonnet on Shakespeare that Wordsworth omitted in the midst of the passage he does quote in the *Essays*, de Man finds

> the latent threat that inhabits prosopopeia, namely that by making the death [*sic*] speak, the symmetrical structure of the trope implies, by the same token, that the living are struck dumb, frozen in their own death. The surmise of the "Pause, Traveller!" thus acquires a sinister connotation that is not only the prefiguration of one's own mortality but our actual entry into the frozen world of the dead. (78)

Milton's lines, however, need not be read as de Man, following Isabel MacCaffrey,[24] reads them; furthermore, they certainly need not be

24 The lines from Milton's sonnet "On Shakespeare" as de Man cites them are, "Then thou our fancy of itself bereaving / Dost make us marble with too much conceiving"; the paraphrase he accepts from MacCaffrey (without citing his

the key to Wordsworth's ostensible resistance to the figure he supposedly advocates; and finally, de Man's reading of them does not capture the spirit of the *Essays*, in which Wordsworth celebrates "the wholesome influence of [the] communion between living and dead" (EE 66) and values the "Pause, Traveller!" for bringing the traveler into contact with "admonitions and heart-stirring remembrances, like a refreshing breeze that comes without warning, or the taste of the waters of an unexpected fountain" (EE 54). Such invigoration in the contemplation of epitaphs and health in the communion with the dead hardly bespeaks de Man's hyperbolic "actual entry into the frozen world of the dead" – a phrase that allows the transition from language to actuality de Man is usually so careful to deny, but only from language to the actuality of death.

De Man's paradoxical conclusion suggests, however, that this exception may be inconsequential because "death is a displaced name for a linguistic predicament" (81). This declaration issues from de Man's presentation of the "main inconsistency in the text" of Wordsworth's *Essays*, which "occurs in a related but different pattern" to the one that reveals Wordsworth's alleged inconsistency over prosopopeia. It manifests itself, according to de Man, in the discrepancy between the "lucid language of repose, tranquillity, and serenity" Wordsworth advocates for the epitaph and the violent language he uses to attack Pope and "language itself" in the *Essays upon Epitaphs* (78–79). I have already called attention to the critical principles and rational criteria that distinguish Wordsworth's criticism of Pope from violence, but it remains to examine de Man's claim that Wordsworth saves his "most violent language ... for language itself."

The passage on which de Man bases this claim denounces

a certain misuse of language ... in the strongest of terms: "Words are too awful an instrument for good and evil to be trifled with: they hold above all other external powers a dominion over thoughts. If words be not ... [de Man's ellipsis] an incarnation of the thought but only a clothing for it, then surely they will prove an ill gift; such a one as those poisoned vestments, read of in the stories of superstitious times, which had power to consume

source) declares "'our imaginations are rapt "out of ourselves" leaving behind our soulless bodies like statues.'" But in the context of the sonnet it seems more likely to me that the "marble" Shakespeare makes of us is not a soulless statue but an engraving on which his "Delphic lines" leave a "deep impression" on each heart and make our very minds his "livelong Monument" by taking possession of our minds and depriving us of our own imagination by imagining for us.

and to alienate from his right mind the victim who put them on. Language, if it do not uphold, and feed, and leave in quiet, like the power of gravitation or the air we breathe, is a counterspirit ... " (79, de Man's ellipsis)

De Man reads this passage as a violent condemnation of language rather than a critical distinction between kinds of language because he deconstructs the distinction between "incarnate thought and 'a clothing for thought'" on the ground that "incarnate flesh and clothing have at least one property in common ... namely their visibility, their accessibility to the senses," so that "the language so violently denounced is in fact the language of metaphor, of prosopopeia and of tropes, the solar language of cognition that makes the unknown accessible to the mind and to the senses." Since all language depends upon these tropes and upon the sensory qualities they draw upon, there is no difference between the "evil language" Wordsworth condemns and "all language," and so there is no critical distinction between kinds of language in Wordsworth but only a general and violent condemnation of language (79–80).

Again de Man's argument depends upon acceptance of a similitude (in this case between clothing and the body) to the complete disregard of dissimilitudes between, for example, the artificial, changeable, and inessential connection between clothing and the body and the natural and essential connection between the body and the living spirit. I do not deny that these figures are problematic both in their vehicles and in their application to the tenors of different literary styles, but I do deny that these problems go away or that thought about them is advanced by de Man's undiscriminating denial of consequential difference between them. De Man's writing in this essay repeatedly collapses such distinctions instead of investigating them and, like the "gross and violent stimulants" of the gothic diction Wordsworth criticized in the Preface to *Lyrical Ballads*, uses violent language to "blunt the discriminating powers of the mind" (LB 248–49).

The labor of exerting those powers in the face of de Man's powerful writing is considerable and might be overwhelming if one did not share in some way Wordsworth's faith in "certain inherent and indestructible qualities of the human mind, and likewise of certain powers in the great and permanent objects that act upon it which are equally inherent and indestructible" (LB 249–50). De Man takes it upon himself, almost as an embodiment of Wordsworth's language as "counterspirit," in a phrase he does not quote, "to derange, to

subvert, to lay waste, to vitiate, and to dissolve" (EE 85) both
Wordsworth's argument and our confidence in our own minds' ability
to understand it and test each other's understanding of it. But that
argument itself articulates and exemplifies a discipline of critical
discrimination that we can emulate, and it provides evidence against
de Man's misrepresentation of its content and purport to which we
can appeal. We need not be "eternally deprived of voice and
condemned to muteness" as de Man says we are in the face of our
"linguistic predicament" (80–81) or in the face of de Man's corrosive
writing; we may, with Wordsworth, exert the discriminating powers
of our minds, assert the distinctions as well as the likenesses we
perceive, and give reasons and evidence that permit others to retrace
our steps and test our assertions.

De Man's writing in "Autobiography as De-Facement" poses the
most stringent test that the Wordsworthian literary enterprise has yet
encountered, for the "de-facement of the mind" (81) that de Man
declares to be our inevitable and necessary predicament is for
Wordsworth the consequence of a contingent historical situation that
his self-critical poetry and criticism set out to counteract and call
others to counteract. De Man represents as inescapable the evils of
language Wordsworth saw as criticizable and ameliorable. The
conflict between these positions is fundamental, but we must not
mistake the difference between them as that between a rigorous de
Manian intellectual power and a seductive Wordsworthian imaginative power. If my reading of "Autobiography as De-Facement"
is any indication of what is at stake here, the imaginative power,
unchecked by rational self-criticism, belongs to de Man's visionary
misreading of Wordsworth's *Essays*, and the critical intellectual rigor
belongs to Wordsworth's discriminating *Essays* themselves.[25]

"Wordsworth and the Victorians" (c. 1979/1984)

De Man's last published essay on Wordsworth – the first essay
published in his lifetime whose titular subject is Wordsworth – was
probably written around the same time as "Autobiography as De-

25 For an extended argument linking de Man with a modern tradition of "visionary
 criticism," see Daniel T. O'Hara, *The Romance of Interpretation: Visionary Criticism
 from Pater to de Man* (New York: Columbia University Press, 1985), 18, 203–35.
 O'Hara hints at but does not develop Wordsworth as an alternative to this
 tradition (8).

Facement,"[26] but, probably because of the purpose for which it was written and the audience to which it is addressed, it observes a much more polite, tentative, and moderate academic decorum than the essay I have just examined. "Wordsworth and the Victorians," a text that seems, according to Neil Hertz, "to have been intended to serve as a preface to a reissue of F. W. H. Meyers's 1881 volume in the English Men of Letters Series" on Wordsworth ("Lurid Figures," 83), reviews the history of Wordsworthian criticism from Keats and De Quincey through the Victorians to twentieth-century "phenomenological and existential" readings and beyond (RR 86). De Man's survey of his fellow critics of Wordsworth – his only effort of this kind apart from brief self-situating gestures toward M. H. Abrams, Earl Wasserman, and Geoffrey Hartman in earlier essays – is relatively gentle, his treatment of Wordsworth and his texts is generally appreciative and comparatively respectful, and his own tone is more qualified (with expressions like "It is possibly the case ... " [89] and "This all too hasty reading shows ... " [92]) and far less sensational than that of the essay I have just examined. Even de Man's conclusion positions itself "somewhere in between" two extreme positions he identifies with others instead of striking out for an absolute position.

"Anxieties" still "threaten" here (85), "maiming, death, [and] the wear and tear of mutability" (87) are mentioned, and "we risk to drown, can find no surface" (92), but what Hertz calls the "pathos" of "lurid figures" in de Man's writing is much less in evidence here than in "Autobiography as De-Facement": "face," for example, is a key figure in de Man's argument but "de-facement" is not mentioned. It is curious, then, that Hertz nevertheless chooses to organize his remarks on de Man's "lurid figures" around a reading of this essay, where those figures must be brought out through intertextual connections with de Man's more overtly lurid writings, instead of focusing on those writings directly.

De Man argues here that Wordsworth's Victorian critics protected themselves from something puzzling and threatening in Wordsworth's writing by following "the strategy of denegation that calls a threat a shelter in the hope of laying it to rest" (86), and by reading Wordsworth himself, the source of the threat, as if he provided a moral philosophy that "had the power to console, to edify, and to

26 See Neil Hertz, "Lurid Figures," in *Reading De Man Reading*, ed. Waters and Godzich, 102 n. 1.

protect from the anxieties that threaten life and reason" (85). "All subsequent Wordsworth interpreters" – a group whose extraordinary inclusiveness is perhaps most important for including de Man himself – have attempted "to domesticate" this threatening "unnamed and undefined" "something to which Wordsworth's poetry...gives access...by giving it at least a recognizable content." Thus, "with the development of phenomenological and existential modes of thought, Wordsworth becomes, in the twentieth century, a poet of the self-reflecting consciousness rather than a moralist" (86), but what Hertz calls the "lurid thematics" of this existential Wordsworth is still "strangely consoling" compared to something more radically incomprehensible in Wordsworth ("Lurid Figures," 85).

Without explicitly referring to his own earlier work on Words-worth, de Man here recapitulates its themes and arguments in his account of how "the best contemporary criticism" has recognized Wordsworth's "lucidity" in his "absolute refusal to cope with the powers of negation otherwise than by the rigorous acknowledgment of their manifestation." De Man's earlier themes of "maiming, death, the wear and tear of mutability...the predicaments of 'the unimaginable touch of time'" become "in this version of Words-worth...the very substance of the self-reflecting, recollecting mind," and Wordsworth's poetry becomes exemplary of "the power of pure mind" that de Man admired as early as "Intentional Structure." De Man characterizes Wordsworth's "figural diction" in his account of this view as a "miracle" that "recovers the aesthetic in the process of its refusal" (87–89), using a word that he has chosen only once before in the sequence of essays I have followed to characterize the "almost miraculous skill" with which Yeats holds his composite style together (RR 143).

De Man goes on, however, to suggest that "the very alacrity with which Wordsworth's major texts respond to this approach" and, I imagine, the appearance of the miraculous within it, "should make one wary," and he raises the critical question of whether there are "elements in the work that refuse to fit within the uncompromising order of Wordsworth's philosophy of the experience of con-sciousness" (88). In other words, he asks whether there remains in Wordsworth's poetry something "enigmatic," "puzzling," "threat-ening," "unnamed and undefined," that resists not only Victorian thematics but also de Man's own earlier existential thematics. The simple answer, of course, is "yes," and the name of that unnameable is "language," or the "linguistic predicament" for which "death," as de Man said in "Autobiography as De-Facement" "is a displaced name" (RR 81), but even thus to name it is to diminish its mystery and danger. The remainder of de Man's argument in "Wordsworth and the Victorians" reasserts that mysteriousness with an undertow of dangerousness by presenting his own analysis of "the word 'face'" "in the corpus of *The Prelude*" (89) in the context of two prior linguistic analyses of Wordsworth's poetry, William Empson's essay, "Sense in the Prelude," and Wordsworth's own analysis of the figurative uses of "hangs" in the Preface of 1815.

It is not surprising that de Man exaggerates the consistency of the results of these two prior essays in order to introduce the complexity of his own discovery. Though he depicts Empson's interesting essay as showing that "it is impossible ... to make sense out of Wordsworth's 'sense'" (88), whose uses, according to de Man, lead "to near-total chaos" (92), Empson shows only that Wordsworth uses "sense" in several familiar senses and in an unfamiliar and equivocal sense that "means both the process of sensing and the supreme act of imagination."[27] Empson's measured conclusion is that Wordsworth "induced people to believe he had expounded a consistent philosophy through the firmness and assurance with which he used equations ... whose claim was false, because they did not really erect a third concept as they pretended to; and in saying this I do not mean to deny that the result makes very good poetry, and probably suggests important truths" (305); "Wordsworth," after all, "was much better at adumbrating his doctrine through rhetorical devices than at writing it out in full" (300).

It is hard to see how this analysis would threaten any of Wordsworth's commentators except those who had been "induced to believe" such doctrines or, perhaps, to construct them *as* doctrines outside the similitude in dissimilitude of Wordsworth's poetic utterances, but de Man characteristically ignores other rhetorically sophisticated readers of Wordsworth such as Danby and highlights instead the defensiveness of the much diminished but still faithful sect of modern believers in Wordsworthianism. De Man avails himself of the same sort of rhetorical power Empson analyzes through the "firmness and assurance" of his declarations that Wordsworth's use of the word "hangs" in his poetry is "entirely meaningful" and that

27 William Empson, *The Structure of Complex Words*, 3rd edn. (1951; Totowa, New Jersey: Rowman and Littlefield, 1979), 304.

the word is "by Wordsworth's own avowal, *the* exemplary metaphor for metaphor" (89). De Man offers no walk through the concordance on "hangs" such as Empson offers on "sense" to substantiate his claim, and Wordsworth says only that Milton's use of the word "hangs" in a passage from *Paradise Lost* shows "the full strength of the imagination involved in the word *hangs*" (*Prose* III, 31). But de Man now has produced a dialectical opposition between the "perfectly coherent" continuities of Wordsworth's text and the "near-total chaos" of Empson's analysis into which he can insert his own demonstration of "linguistic complexities" "somewhere in between, at the interface of these contradictory directions" (92).

Neil Hertz offers a close reading of de Man's reading of the three passages from *The Prelude* de Man selects to examine the word "face," the one from Book V in which Wordsworth speaks of his mind's having up to now "look'd / Upon the speaking face of earth and heaven" and two passages in which the word "face," as de Man says, remains implicit: the "Blessed Babe" passage in Book II and several lines from Book III just before the moment when Wordsworth has traced his life up to an "eminence" (see "Lurid Figures," 98). Hertz shows how de Man has forced these texts, particularly the "Blessed Babe" passage, through elisions of parts and suppressions of possible meanings. He does not note, however, three further difficulties in de Man's reading. First, de Man quotes the following passage: "The Babe, Nurs'd in his Mother's arms, the Babe who sleeps / Upon his mother's breast, who, when his soul / Claims manifest kindred with an earthly soul, / Doth gather passion from his Mother's *eye!*" (de Man's italics), and he claims that "'Eye' ... is prominent enough to displace 'breast' where one would most naturally expect it" (90). But do we expect "breast" here, where the word has already appeared two lines previously, and where the word "soul" and the mention of "passion" have already prepared us for some other kind of communion than physical nurturance? "Breast" in place of "eye" in this position sounds wrong to my ear. Second, de Man reads the phrase "claims manifest kindred" as "an active verbal deed, a *claim* of 'manifest kindred' which is not given in the nature of things" (de Man's italics), but again it seems absurd to me to make the communion in question verbal or to make, as de Man does, the construction of the mother's face dependent on language. Infants from birth respond to "faces," anything with two "eyes," as fish respond to the colors and patterns of other fish, immediately and "naturally." I am not convinced that this "claim" or bond is not "given in the nature of things," at least to the extent that it is given before language. Perhaps this is part of what Hertz means when he speaks of de Man's "suppressing the figure of the maternal." Third, de Man writes of the final passage he cites that "this same face-making, totalizing power is shown at work in a process of endless differentiation correctly called perpetual 'logic,' of which it is said that it 'could find no surface where its power might sleep'" (92), but in the passage from which de Man quotes it is not the "logic" which "could find no surface" but an "eye," the same eye "which spake perpetual logic to my soul" (1805 III, 160–65).

Hertz writes of de Man's reading of Shelley's *Triumph of Life* in "Shelley Disfigured" that "de Man has shown how and why readers cannot help forcing their texts, but (or rather: *and*) this awareness in no way prevents him from forcing his text" (95). We might strengthen his claim by recalling my own earlier demonstrations of how two of de Man's most powerful antagonists in reading Wordsworth, Coleridge and M. H. Abrams, have also forced Wordsworth's texts. But the inevitability of such forcing should not lead us either to imagine that we cannot detect it in comparing interpretations with what they purport to interpret or that we cannot restrain ourselves or be restrained by others from doing it. The authority all three of these writers have made for themselves over others' readings of Wordsworth suggests that unrestrained "forcing" of others' texts may sometimes be especially interesting and powerful when that forcing makes the texts conform to familiar models or defy those models in paradoxical reversals. But for me, and I expect for others, that authority is diminished when a pattern of forcing is revealed. Such a revelation shifts attention from the text in question to the undeclared motives and interests of the critic; it takes us, as Hertz's argument does, from concern with the language and purposes of de Man's text to speculation about his obsessions.

Hertz points to two sentences at the end of the next-to-the-last paragraph of de Man's essay that intrude into de Man's text distinctions and threatening diction for which the reader has not been prepared. Immediately after presenting the quotation I have just examined from *The Prelude* Book III, de Man writes, "The face, which is the power to surface from the sea of infinite distinctions in which we risk to drown, can find no surface. How are we to reconcile the *meaning* of face, with its promise of sense and of filial preservation, with its *function* as the relentless undoer of its own claims?" (92). Hertz shows how what he calls "this strange irruption" introduces into "Wordsworth and the Victorians" not only the "thematics of drowning" from de Man's "Shelley Disfigured" but also verbal patterns and associations connected with that much more overtly violent essay. He reads its appearance as "a moment of madness, that 'madness of words' that de Man names as such in 'Shelley Disfigured,'" an "obsession, ... the repeated filling-in of unavoidable structures with images drawn from a limited set of anxieties." But again Hertz treats de Man's giving way to compulsion in the face of "questions of intelligibility" as unavoidable and universal: "He can neither avoid falling into it, nor – and this is his stronger claim – can he or any other reader make do without it" (99–100).

I would argue, however, that the evidence of such a pathology of reading is not uniform either from one of de Man's essays to another or from one of his essays to a text of someone else's. "Wordsworth and the Victorians" is, as I have shown, less given to violent diction and uncontrolled pathos than "Autobiography as De-Facement," and Hertz's "Lurid Figures" is less given to them than either of de Man's essays. That Hertz has chosen the less likely essay in which to exemplify such figures makes his case more interesting and surprising, but it does not make the two essays come to the same thing. That de Man has decided or been compelled to act out such violence more in the one essay than in the other is evidence that his pathology or his "pathos," to use the term from the art of rhetoric Hertz uses, is affected by causes or considerations besides the "'madness of words.'" De Man somehow takes audience and occasion into account despite the "'madness of words,'" and even his violent and unanticipated verbal acts appear, as Hertz himself says earlier, to have been done "deliberately" (83). The power they produce to persuade some, provoke others, and compel a few to examine them makes them stick in all three cases, even when they have been analyzed and shown to be inappropriate to what they represent. For me, they reveal de Man exercising the verbal power he also analyzes more than they show him subject to the verbal pathologies he also diagnoses. I am not convinced that his own writing should be subsumed under his account of a "linguistic predicament" that necessarily and inevitably produces such effects; I hold him responsible for his misreadings and exaggerations and excesses as I would expect to be held accountable for my own. Even when we have been compelled by passion or interest or unconscious motive or language itself to produce such effects, there is nothing to stop us or others from checking and correcting them. If they irrupt into our writing, as Wordsworth presents voices as rising up against him in *The Prelude*, we have the choice, as he did, to decide whether or not to let them stand.

Analytic rigor and poetic persuasion in Wordsworth and de Man

At an early moment in the argument of "Wordsworth and the Victorians," de Man uses Wordsworth's poetry to call into question a distinction that I used at the end of my analysis of "Autobiography as De-Facement" when I linked Wordsworth's writing to rigorous intellectual power and de Man's writing to visionary imaginative power. De Man writes:

Common sense tells us that poetry and philosophy are modes of discourse that should be kept distinct: to couple such power of seduction with such authority is to tempt fate itself. Hence the urge to protect, as the most pressing of moral imperatives, this borderline between both modes of discourse. Many poets can easily be enlisted in the service of this cause but others are more recalcitrant, though not necessarily because they are formally involved with philosophical systems. Wordsworth, rather than Coleridge, is a case in point. It is as if his language came from a region in which the most carefully drawn distinctions between analytic rigor and poetic persuasion are no longer preserved, at no small risk to either. (85)

I shall argue in conclusion that de Man is mistaken in this judgment of Wordsworth, that Wordsworth is distinguished as a poet by his preservation of a distinction between "analytic rigor" and "poetic persuasion," and that de Man's own writing often tempts fate by exploiting the combination of seduction and authority that the confusion of this distinction produces.

I shall begin indirectly by returning to what Hertz calls de Man's "thematics of drowning" with a couple of texts de Man does not cite. Francis Bacon tells more than once an anecdote that depends on this thematics. Analyzing in *The Advancement of Learning* the first of several "fallacies in the mind of man," the one he will later name the "idols of the tribe," Bacon points to one example, "*That to the nature of the mind of all men it is consonant for the affirmative or active to affect more than the negative or privative*," and tells, both to illustrate and counteract this tendency, a response of "Diagoras to him that showed him in Neptune's temple the great number of pictures of such as had escaped shipwreck, and had paid their vows to Neptune, saying, *Advise now, you that think it folly to invocate Neptune in tempest*: Yea, but, saith Diagoras, *where are they painted that are drowned?"* (*Advancement* 132–33). Bacon presses his point against natural philosophers who generalize from the instances that fit their theories and ignore those that do not, but he goes further at the end of the paragraph to call attention to the fallacy of the mind that accounts for such false discoveries of conformity between the mind's expectation and nature and to declare that nature and the human mind are out of harmony: "so differing a harmony there is between the spirit of man and the spirit of nature" (133). Bacon's cautionary notice of our tendency to ignore evidence that does not fit the patterns we wish to make nature fit almost turns into a contrary, and equally un-substantiated, generalization – that nature never fits human expectations. We might almost be led to expect that more people would be drowned than saved, or, that we should expect to be drowned rather than saved, since nature is out of harmony with our wishes rather than just untested for conformity to our wishes until all the evidence has been considered.

Bacon would recognize, I think, the workings of another idol of the tribe in his own move to reverse rather than just criticize the tendency of human beings to jump to affirmative conclusions. He holds, as de Man does, that such tendencies are "inseparable from our nature" (*Advancement* 134), but he also believes, as de Man in his more radical skepticism may not, that it is possible to "supply helps" for the understanding and the senses (*New Organon* 47) or to observe cautions that can assist the "true conduct of human judgment" (*Advancement* 134). One help he proposes for the related idols of the cave is that "whatever [the student's] mind seizes and dwells upon with peculiar satisfaction is to be held in suspicion, and that so much the more care is to be taken in dealing with such questions to keep the understanding even and clear" (*New Organon* 56), but we can see from Bacon's own leap how easy it is even for such a caution to turn into a contrary belief that whatever pleases us must be wrong.

De Man states a similar maxim when he declares that "the very alacrity with which Wordsworth's major texts respond to this approach should make one wary" (RR 88), and his wariness and suspicion are subject to the same tendency to become contrary beliefs rather than careful examination of the evidence of Wordsworth's texts. As Hertz shows in his analysis of de Man's reading of *The Triumph of Life*, de Man imposes as beyond doubt an image of drowning on lines in Shelley's poem "that contain no demonstrable images of drowning" ("Lurid Figures," 92), in effect, erecting a counter-temple of images of the drowned instead of following up Diagoras' skeptical question with an investigation of the records of shipwrecks that might settle it. Bacon's generalization that "it is the peculiar and perpetual error of the human intellect to be more moved and excited by affirmatives than by negatives" (*New Organon* 51) should probably itself be investigated, since the appeal of negations seems in many cases as strong as that of affirmations. Murphy's law and de Man's hyperboles would be what Bacon would call prerogative instances for such an investigation.

My second text for the thematics of drowning comes from the beginning of Wordsworth's second *Essay Upon Epitaphs*, though de Man does not cite it. In an anecdote that suggests its affiliation with Bacon's through both its structure and its ultimate recourse to imagery of drowning, Wordsworth says that "a Stranger [who] has walked round a Country Church-yard" and read the eulogistic epitaphs they contained "will be tempted to exclaim..., 'Where are all the *bad* People buried?' He may smile to himself an answer to this question, and may regret that it has intruded upon him so soon." Wordsworth declares that he has found himself in the situation of this reluctant Diagoras in a country churchyard and forgives himself, as "a Man, who is in the habit of suffering his mind to be carried passively towards truth as well as of going with conscious effort in search of it," for having "sometimes insensibly yielded to the delusion of those flattering recitals, and found a pleasure in believing that the prospect of real life had been as fair as it was in that picture represented." He imagines that others will forgive him easily for this indulgence of what he recognizes as "delusion" because, it appears, they will recognize themselves to be subject to a similar delusion – we could call it an idol of the tribe – "namely, how apt, in a series of calm weather, we are to forget that rain and storms have been, and will return, to interrupt any scheme of business or pleasure which our minds are occupied in arranging." Using a "solar" figure to which de Man does not call attention, Wordsworth goes on to compare his experience of the churchyard, "shining, if I may so say, in the light of love," with "a smooth Sea, on a Summer's day," shining in the light of the sun, both of which make him feel a happiness "to have, in an unkind World, one Enclosure where the voice of detraction is not heard." But, juxtaposing the image of the smooth sea over the image of the churchyard, Wordsworth goes on to declare that

I have been rouzed from this reverie by a consciousness, suddenly flashing upon me, of the anxieties, the perturbations, and, in many instances, the vices and rancorous dispositions, by which the hearts of those who lie under so smooth a surface and so fair an outside must have been agitated. The image of an unruffled Sea has still remained; but my fancy has penetrated into the depths of that Sea – with accompanying thoughts of Shipwreck, of the destruction of the Mariner's hopes, the bones of drowned Men heaped together, monsters of the deep, and all the hideous and confused sights which Clarence saw in his Dream!

Diagoras' skeptical question has here become a poetic countervision which with the additional imagery provided by the allusion to Clarence's dream in *Richard III* calls up the whole de Manian catalogue of dark imagery – not just drowning but disfigurement and dismemberment and "ugly death" (EE 63–64).

But Wordsworth does not rest in this reversal in which a tragic vision has replaced an Arcadian one. "Nevertheless," he declares, "I have been able to return, (and who may not?) to a steady contemplation of the benign influence" of the eulogistic rural epitaphs on their readers. Still, he declares, those epitaphs are "a far more faithful representation of homely life as existing among a Community in which circumstances have not been untoward, than any report which might be made by a rigorous observer deficient in that spirit of forbearance and those kindly prepossessions, without which human life can in no condition be profitably looked at or described." Here Wordsworth specifies limiting conditions in both the observer (prepossessions) and the observed (circumstances) which would have to hold to make his judgment good, and he goes on to offer a series of "reasons for believing that the encomiastic language of rural Tomb-stones does not so far exceed reality as might lightly be supposed." This qualified judgment of "an experienced and well-regulated mind" depends not upon an avoidance of delusions but upon a judicious indulgence in them, not just upon a standpoint of rigorous observation from a position unidentified with the objects it observes, "indifferently disposed," as Bacon puts it (*New Organon* 51), but from one of kindly participation in the motives and circumstances of "objects" like oneself. Such judgment does not leap to believe a negative "dream" out of disillusionment with an affirmative "delusion," but instead considers the reasons why appearances might *both* reflect and conceal reality (EE 64–65).

Wordsworth goes on to offer a parallel analysis of the metaphorical language of tombstones in a churchyard by the seacoast to show that their uniformity is not evidence that "the words are used of course without any heart-felt sense of their propriety" (EE 65), or, as he puts it later, that the "words [were] doing their own work" (EE 79). This topic, too, has both a Baconian and a de Manian provenance, in the Baconian analysis of idols of the marketplace, where "words plainly force and overrule the understanding" (*New Organon* 49), and in the de Manian theme of language's silently baffling our speech and our understanding. Wordsworth has again learned his Baconian lesson in knowing how language can take over from and substitute for thought, but he has learned it in the context of the Baconian project of correcting for this tendency, sometimes even himself correcting Bacon's tendency to substitute a skeptical hermeneutics of suspicion for a critical hermeneutics "forewarned of the danger" and fortified against the power of the idols (*New Organon* 47).

The habits of such a mind – critically forewarned and fortified though by no means exempt from error – are evident not just in thoughtful essays like those upon epitaphs but in Wordsworth's poetry as well. The figures of concession, qualification, self-correction, and hesitation that abound in Wordsworth's verse all bespeak a mind alert to the possibility that things may be otherwise than it imagines. The matter-of-factness that Coleridge objected to and the "paltry taking into account of other people's views" that Jonathan Wordsworth attacked introduce evidence and opinions that may confirm or check what the poem's speaker has uttered. As David Simpson declares, in a moment where his argument gives a moral language priority over a psychological vocabulary, "The peculiar integrity of much of Wordsworth's poetry is that it records so much of the evidence that counts against its own arguments" (*Wordsworth's Historical Imagination*, 96). His poetry also preserves the ordinary names against which his imaginative transformations manifest themselves as such, the "hedgerows" against which the "little lines of sportive wood run wild" reveal themselves as the work of the speaker's desire and mind. And his accounts of his poetry, even the analysis of "hangs" of which de Man makes so much, also train his readers to take note even of the slightest transformations or substitutions as evidence of "the manner in which the mind associates ideas in a state of excitement," available at once for sympathetic enjoyment and for analytic contemplation. We have seen how a poem like "The Sailor's Mother" corrects a vision while calling attention to the motives that make the vision that replaces it pleasurable. A poem like "Resolution and Independence" involves corrections not only of the speaker's tragic vision of himself but also of his tragic vision of the prosaic old man who helps him to correct it. Though there may be moments in the poetry in which "poetic persuasion" escapes the counterpoint of such moments of "analytic rigor," it is hard for me to see how the collapse of this distinction could be the most important effect of the work of a poet who has cultivated it and embodied it so repeatedly in his work, knowing, as he did, that to do so would provoke the resistance of many of his readers and call his knowledge of his art into question.[28]

One line of defense of de Man's work has portrayed de Man, too, as a cultivator rather than as a destroyer of the distinction between aesthetic pleasure and philosophical rigor. Christopher Norris, who organizes his recent book on de Man around the theme of de Man's "critique of aesthetic ideology," writes,

Like Kant, [de Man] is concerned to set limits to the play of seductive metaphors and analogies that characterize aesthetic understanding; that he sees a real danger in the various moves to extend or annul those limits, to apply aesthetic notions *directly* to other domains of knowledge; and that this is what leads him to treat such attempts with an unrelenting suspicion.[29]

But the passage of de Man's from which I began at least flirts with the collapse of the distinction between poetry and philosophy in an argument that dwells upon an aspect of language in Wordsworth's poetry that defies this distinction, and what Hertz shows about the way de Man combines the pathos of "lurid figures" with the tone of analytical rigor confirms my own view that de Man's writing repeatedly "tempts fate" in its combination of authoritative academic assertions with seductive visionary violence.

28 Frank Lentricchia, also contrasting Wordsworth's habits of mind with de Man's, characterizes Wordsworth as "a writer for whom there are real questions, real conflicts, a writer for whom at enormous psychic cost, nothing is 'entirely' this way or that way. One could argue that it was lucky for poetic history that Wordsworth was not as sure as de Man is about the nature of selfhood" (ANC 294).

29 Christopher Norris, *Paul de Man: Deconstruction and the Critique of Aesthetic Ideology* (New York and London: Routledge, 1988), 48.

Lindsay Waters offers a portrait of a more radical and recalcitrant de Man committed to an ascetic rather than a critical standpoint, though Waters describes the goal of that asceticism in terms that a Baconian or Wordsworthian might acknowledge: "If he can be sufficiently ascetic, if he can get to the plain sense of things, then he is to be valued. If not, his work should be discarded" (*Critical Writings*, lxiii). De Man's lurid vision, however, colors Waters's reading of "the 'plainness of plain things'" through Wallace Stevens as "'a savagery'" and so begs the critical question Wordsworth and Bacon at their best leave open to inquiry and argument (*Critical Writings*, lx). Perhaps also the action that Waters says should follow if de Man's work fails to get to "the plainness of plain things" is too extreme. In the case of de Man's readings of Wordsworth, I think it is fair to say that de Man has not gotten to the plainness of Wordsworth's plain texts, even if those texts are not always as plain as they may at first appear. I would not urge that his works on Wordsworth be discarded, however, only that they be read closely with the texts they purport to represent close at hand. De Man's words need to be examined more carefully and contextually than he frequently examines the words of the texts he discusses. His texts, in my view, cannot provide a model for a literary critical practice or an agenda for a literary critical enterprise, but their power makes them important objects upon which such a practice in such an enterprise must work.[30]

30 This conclusion is consistent with O'Hara's remark that "such sublime irony [as de Man's] can only compose an eccentric, provisional style incapable of being formulated into a program or method and thus passed on to others, without travesty" (*Romance of Interpretation*, 234–35) and with his reading of de Man as a "creative" critic (4).

❖❖

7

The revival of rhetoric and the reading of Wordsworth's *Prelude*

❖❖

If readers have been reluctant to link Wordsworth with the classical past, it is only because the revolutionary aspects of his contribution, above all his expressive theory of poetry as "spontaneous overflow," has [*sic*] remained predominant in their minds. But it would be far more accurate to see Wordsworth, and above all the Wordsworth of *The Prelude*, as standing at a sort of meeting-point between two views of literary form: the modern view that the form of a work results from the demands and rhythms of personal vision, and the traditional view of objectively existing styles and structures to which the writer accommodates his personal interests.

Herbert Lindenberger, "*The Prelude* and the Older Rhetoric,"
in *On Wordsworth's "Prelude"*

If, despite my reservations (and his own),[1] de Man's work has provided a model and an agenda for other critics of Wordsworth and Romanticism, the phenomenological and rhetorical phases of his work have inspired different critics to different projects. Tilottama Rajan, who finds the early phenomenological criticism "more useful," identifies her own *Dark Interpreter* and Helen Reguiero's *The Limits of Imagination* as works which, though powerfully influenced by the early de Man, "show a reluctance to assimilate his recent work wholesale and turn to some alternative voice in romantic or contemporary criticism to provide a counterweight to his rhetoric of

---

1 See his ambivalent introduction to the special issue of *Studies in Romanticism* on "The Rhetoric of Romanticism," 18 (1979): 495–99, and Lindsay Waters's emphatic testimony in "Paul de Man: Life and Works": "The ease with which the insights he had earned were mimicked made him wince. He told me so" (*Critical Writings*, ed. Waters, lxi). On the other hand, for a *prediction* that the application of his deconstructive techniques to the "whole of literature … will in fact be the task of literary criticism in the coming years," see *Allegories of Reading*, 16–17. Whatever the tone of this remark (see Lentricchia, ANC 284), it is not programmatic.

demystification." Karl Kroeber adds Margery Sabin's *English Romanticism and the French Tradition* as another book that acknowledges Paul de Man as its "original inspiration" but counters de Man's tendency to "conflate Rousseau and Wordsworth."[2]

The followers of de Man's rhetorical period who have written on Wordsworth and Romanticism have generally repeated his themes and strategies of reading, even his choices of texts and citations, more religiously than his phenomenological followers. Either situating their arguments, as de Man situated "Time and History in Wordsworth," as extensions and corrections of Geoffrey Hartman's argument in *Wordsworth's Poetry*, or self-consciously imitating de Man himself without reference to any prior critical situation, Cynthia Chase, Timothy Bahti, Andrzej Warminski, and Cathy Caruth have presented rhetorical readings of Wordsworth in a special issue of *Studies in Romanticism* introduced by de Man, in an anthology of critical essays on *Romanticism and Language*, edited by Arden Reed, and in a special issue of *diacritics* edited by Chase and Warminski and headed by the posthumous publication of de Man's "Time and History in Wordsworth."[3] In addition, J. Douglas Kneale has presented himself as a follower of de Man in his book-length *Monumental Writing*:

2 Rajan, "Displacing Post-Structuralism," 451; Kroeber, "Wordsworth," 338. See also Tilottama Rajan, *Dark Interpreter* (Ithaca: Cornell University Press, 1980); Helen Reguiero, *The Limits of Imagination* (Ithaca: Cornell University Press, 1979); and Margery Sabin, *English Romanticism and the French Tradition* (Cambridge, Mass.: Harvard University Press), 1976. Cyrus Hamlin, too, finds "de Man's single most important and lasting contribution to literary criticism in America" in the "essays from his middle period" culminating in "the brilliant achievement of 'The Rhetoric of Temporality.'" See his "Literary History After New Criticism: Paul de Man's Essays on Romanticism," 133–48.

3 Cynthia Chase, "The Accidents of Disfiguration: Limits to Literal and Rhetorical Reading in Book V of *The Prelude*," *SiR* 18 (Winter 1979): 547–66; "Monument and Inscription: Wordsworth's 'Lines,'" *diacritics* 17 (Winter 1987): 65–77; "The Ring of Gyges and the Coat of Darkness," *Romanticism and Language*, ed. Arden Reed (Ithaca: Cornell University Press, 1984): 50–85. Chase's essays from *SiR* and *Romanticism and Language* are reprinted in her *Decomposing Figures* (Baltimore: Johns Hopkins University Press, 1986). Timothy Bahti, "Figures of Interpretation, the Interpretation of Figures: A Reading of Wordsworth's 'Dream of the Arab,'" *SiR* 18 (Winter 1979): 601–28; "Wordsworth's Rhetorical Theft," *Romanticism and Language*, ed. Reed, 86–124. Andrzej Warminski, "Facing Language: Wordsworth's First Poetic Spirits," *diacritics* 17 (Winter 1987): 18–31; see also Warminski's "Missed Crossing: Wordsworth's Apocalypses," *MLN* 90 (1984): 983–1006. Cathy Caruth, "'Unknown Causes': Poetic Effects," *diacritics* 17 (Winter 1987): 78–85.

Aspects of Rhetoric in Wordsworth's Poetry, though his rhetorical resources go beyond his explicit de Manian definition of rhetoric as "figural language, indeed language itself."[4] In this recent revival of rhetoric, *The Prelude*, with its questions of voice, writing, auto-biography, self-division, and reading, has been the principal text whose "key words" and "famous" passages have provided de Manian critics the materials from which they have constructed the "rhetorical structures," "tropological systems," and "allegories of reading" that reveal, in Cynthia Chase's revoicing of Wordsworth's words, "a voiceless 'language unremittingly and noiselessly at work...to vitiate and dissolve' the condition of the possibility of meaning."[5]

Toward a more resolute focus on rhetoric

In the previous chapter, I have followed closely the de Manian arguments from which Chase derives this vision of language vitiating meaning, and I will leave it to others to read his followers with the rigor de Man says they deserve to have applied to them; they themselves have read (publicly at least) only one other critic of Wordsworth with anything approaching that rigor.[6] I am more interested here in pursuing a possibility opened by de Man's and their identification of their inquiries with "rhetoric" – the possibility of recovering rhetoric as an instrument of critical inquiry into Wordsworth's poetry, especially *The Prelude*, and advancing that inquiry beyond the few tropes and figures and topoi de Man and his disciples have repeatedly documented and enacted.

Jonathan Arac has recently reminded us that all the other major American critics of Wordsworth's *Prelude* of de Man's generation also "located Wordsworth in the history of European rhetoric" made available to us by "the German philological tradition" (*Genealogies* 71, 74). Arac recalls that "Hartman dedicated his book to the memory of Erich Auerbach; Abrams' essay ["English Romanticism: The Spirit of the Age"] drew on Auerbach for its climactic argument; and Lindenberger related *The Prelude* to topoi studied by E. R. Curtius,"

---

4 J. Douglas Kneale, *Monumental Writing: Aspects of Rhetoric in Wordsworth's Poetry* (Lincoln and London: University of Nebraska Press, 1988), xv.

5 Chase, "The Ring of Gyges," 85.

6 See de Man, "Introduction," *SiR* 18 (1979): 499. Bahti's reading of Hartman in "Figures of Interpretation, Interpretation of Figures" is the exception, 601–07.

as did de Man in "The Rhetoric of Temporality." In addition, "Hartman began by isolating the romantic figure of 'surmise,' derived from the classical *'fallor ... an'* construction. Lindenberger devoted his first chapter to *'The Prelude* and the Older Rhetoric' and went on to define Wordsworth's new 'rhetoric of interaction.' Abrams connected the sublime to the matter-of-fact in Wordsworth through the Christian rhetoric of *sermo humilis"* (71).

These initiatives kept a number of rhetorical categories in play in subsequent discussions of *The Prelude* even before the de Manian revival of rhetoric and have influenced participants in that revival,[7] but the problems with their German philological sources that Arac touches on are not the only problems that have limited the fruitfulness of their influence. Arac notes that "the multiple approaches of Lindenberger's book have prevented it from con-solidating a clear position in the critical tradition" (72). Lindenberger's book is doubly rhetorical, limiting itself to readily available resources ("whatever resources I can find available to the modern literary historian" [viii]) and drawing from sources in the rhetorical tradition, and it does not open an inquiry into other rhetorical sources that are not immediately to hand. I would add that Abrams and Hartman are equivocal rather than uninquisitive about the rhetorical tradition. While Abrams's *Natural Supernaturalism* and the essays leading up to it drew upon rhetorical sources to illuminate Wordsworth's poetry, *The Mirror and the Lamp* and its preparatory essay "Wordsworth and Coleridge on Diction and Figures" presented a Wordsworth who "rejected the long-enduring rhetorical understructure of poetic theory" and a Coleridge who supplemented that necessary but inadequate "rhetorical analysis" "by reference to the powers of the human mind."[8] Abrams's version in those earlier works of a Wordsworth associated with the "spontaneous overflow of powerful feeling" contributed, as Herbert Lindenberger notes in the epigraph to this chapter, to a reluctance to link Wordsworth to the classical past and its rhetorical forms.[9] Hartman's reading of Wordsworth has

---

7 Bahti's essay in *SiR* is more openly indebted to Hartman than to de Man, for example.

8 M. H. Abrams, "Wordsworth and Coleridge on Diction and Figures," in *English Institute Essays, 1952*, ed. Alan S. Downer (New York: AMS Press, 1965), 184, 200.

9 Herbert Lindenberger, *On Wordsworth's "Prelude"* (Princeton: Princeton University Press, 1963).

been informed throughout by his schooling in Auerbach's "Figura" in both the classical and Christian senses, but his turn in *Wordsworth's Poetry* to reinterpret rhetorical figures as phenomenological "structures of consciousness" (414–15), like Coleridge's reinterpretation of rhetoric in terms of the imagination, again cut off connections between Wordsworth's poetry and classical rhetoric. De Man, as some of his students have recognized, propounded an idiosyncratic version of rhetoric, and the manner in which he propounded it has provoked very little historical curiosity about what else the art might ever have meant to its other professors and practitioners.[10]

Despite such problems, Arac calls for a "more resolute focus on rhetoric" (75) and a repluralizing of the figures (78), not only to improve our criticism of Wordsworth's poem but to revise the "fundamentals of critical practice and principle" (70) that have been at stake in that criticism. He is right to think that the field, as our chief authorities have defined it, is too constraining, but the reach of his proposals to expand the field is still too limited. Arac repluralizes the figures by adding irony to the already proposed figures of metonymy, synecdoche, and metaphor to account for the overall organizing principle of *The Prelude* (74). He is not satisfied with what he sees as the New Critical reduction of all rhetoric to metaphor or with Jakobson's restoration of metonymy to our repertoire of figures (78) or with de Man's idiosyncratic interpretation of metonymy (252), but Arac's restriction of his purview to the de Manian conception of "rhetoric (in its largest sense of how words work to different effects

10 There is a telling moment in Barbara Johnson's recent book *A World of Difference* (Baltimore and London: Johns Hopkins University Press, 1987) when she lists two definitions of rhetoric in addition to her own de Manian definition – one from I. A. Richards and one from Aristotle's *Rhetoric*. A footnote thanks John Schilb for calling these alternative definitions to her attention. What is remarkable to me is that Johnson, one of our subtlest rhetorical critics, introducing her second book concerned with rhetoric, has only lately discovered Richards's and Aristotle's definitions of rhetoric and realized that her school's notion of it is not the only one (5, 6, 213 n. 3). Cynthia Chase acknowledges that "de Man's usage of *prosopopoeia* is distinctive and unfamiliar," even idiosyncratic. See *Decomposing Figures*, 83–84. See also my review of Brian Vickers's *In Defence of Rhetoric*, *College English* 51 (March 1989): 325–29, for comments on de Man's appropriation of Nietzsche's lectures on rhetoric. The recent publication of those lectures in English, however, may also be attributed, in part, to de Man's interest in them. See *Friedrich Nietzsche on Rhetoric and Language*, ed. and trans. Sander L. Gilman, Carole Blair, and David J. Parent (New York and Oxford: Oxford University Press, 1989).

from those of grammar or logic)" (73) still leaves out too much of the conceptual repertoire that is available even in Auerbach and Curtius, let alone their classical sources.[11]

Even Auerbach's essay "Figura," which sketches the history of uses of the word *figura* in pagan and Christian Latin culture, would not sustain Arac's definition of rhetoric "in its largest sense" as a concern with "how words work," for Auerbach notes Quintilian's division of "figures into those involving content and those involving words (*figurae sententiarum* and *verborum*)" (26). A quick review of Curtius's *European Literature in the Latin Middle Ages*, especially Chapter 4, "Rhetoric," would recover not just rhetorical topoi (which are much more central to rhetoric for Curtius than figures) but also the five divisions of the "system of antique rhetoric" (*inventio, dispositio, elocutio, memoria,* and *actio*), of which only the third concerns itself with how words work. Arac examines Auerbach's and Curtius's differences over literary modernism (74–75) but does not examine their differences over rhetoric or gauge their fruitfulness for the "more resolute focus on rhetoric" he calls for.

His call is nevertheless worth heeding with the recognition that the project will require the contributions of "joint labourers in the work" (*Prelude* 1850 XIV, 443). Lindenberger's incomplete deployment of Curtius's rhetorical terms at least avoided the massive and potentially deadening single-handed production of an authoritative, magisterial account of every rhetorical form or figure or topos in *The Prelude*, and the subsequent gestures of various critics toward occasional figures or topoi with occasional bows to Curtius or Auerbach or Quintilian have left open the possibilities of more thorough and critical excavations of the rhetorical tradition and of better informed rhetorical inquiries into Wordsworth's *Prelude* (and his other poems as well). Theresa M. Kelley's recent *Wordsworth's Revisionary Aesthetics* has reminded us that from Longinus to Wordsworth "aesthetics and rhetoric are presented as parallel inquiries" and has reopened fruitful inquiry into "the rhetorical competition between sublime and beautiful figures" and "the role of places" or topoi in Wordsworth's poetry;[12] J. Douglas Kneale's recent *Monumental Writing: Aspects of Rhetoric in Wordsworth's Poetry* has recovered more aspects of rhetoric than its

11 Erich Auerbach, *Mimesis*, trans. Willard Trask (Princeton: Princeton University Press, 1953). Ernst Robert Curtius, *European Literature in the Latin Middle Ages*, trans. Willard Trask (New York: Harper, 1953).
12 Kelley, *Wordsworth's Revisionary Aesthetics*, 4, 1, 43.

avowedly de Manian premises would have led me to expect and has provided the richest and most thorough commentary on the rhetoric of *The Prelude* we have to date; Susan Wolfson's *The Questioning Presence* and L. J. Swingle's *The Obstinate Questionings of English Romanticism* have revived the question, rhetorical and otherwise, as a significant device; but none of these critics has pretended to or achieved exhaustiveness.[13] In the remainder of this chapter I shall offer my own limited contribution by exhuming three sets of rhetorical distinctions that have not yet been used to inquire into *The Prelude* – the division of parts of the classical oration, the distinction between tropes and figures, and the category of figures of thought. I hope that my demonstration of their fruitfulness in reading the first book of the poem will indicate possibilities for digging deeper into the remains of the rhetorical tradition, thinking harder about it, and looking further into Wordsworth in the light of it.

The invention/disposition of *The Prelude*, Book I

It is interesting, and perhaps characteristic of his emphasis on rhetorical content over rhetorical form, that Curtius places under invention the commonplace division of parts of the classical judicial oration that most historians of rhetoric place under disposition. This division of the "disposition" into "1. introduction (*exordium* or *prooemium*); 2. 'narrative' (*narratio*), that is, exposition of the facts in the matter; 3. evidence (*argumentatio* or *probatio*); 4. refutation of opposing opinions (*refutatio*); 5. close (*peroratio* or *epilogus*)," Curtius claims, "was already anticipated in the five parts or sections of an oration, which for their part provided the clue to 'invention'" (70–71). Curtius goes on in a subsequent chapter to enumerate "topics of the exordium" and "topics of the conclusion" (85–91) that would provide the writer or speaker with matter appropriate to these parts of the oration, justifying his sense that the matter is not generated separately and subsequently distributed to the parts but rather generated to fit the functions each part prescribes.

13 Susan J. Wolfson, *The Questioning Presence: Wordsworth, Keats, and the Interrogative Mode in Romantic Poetry* (Ithaca: Cornell University Press, 1986). For an exemplary instance of a resolute focus on rhetoric concerned mainly with Coleridge's theory and practice (though with important remarks on Wordsworth and other Romantic poets), see also Susan Wolfson's "'Comparing Power': Coleridge and Simile," in *Coleridge's Theory of Imagination Today*, ed. Christine Gallant (New York: AMS Press, 1989), 167–95.

The placement of the divisions of the oration under "invention" or "disposition" warrants further inquiry and reflection, but the division itself must be recognized in either case as a commonplace rhetorical pattern widely disseminated (with variations) in pedagogy and widely practiced in formal argumentation. Lee M. Johnson has discovered a version of the pattern operating in Wordsworth's adaptation of the Miltonic sonnet, and Richard E. Matlak has recently argued that another version shapes the discourse of both Coleridge's "Eolian Harp" and Wordsworth's "Tintern Abbey."[14] That pattern has not, however, been commonplace for most modern readers of Wordsworth, who have felt compelled to place his poems in new genres like the greater Romantic lyric or to declare them generically anomalous.[15]

The first book of *The Prelude*, too, has thus regularly confounded the generic expectations of readers and baffled their attempts to describe or account for its parts. Geoffrey Hartman nicely declares the difficulty from the point of view of readers with narrative expectations of the epic sort: "No poem of epic length or ambition ever started like" *The Prelude*. Lyric expectations aroused by the first fifty-four lines of present-tense celebration and self-questioning also founder on the subsequent passage that places them in quotation marks as the beginning of a past-tense narration. David P. Haney offers "autobiography" as a genre "midway between" lyric discourse and epic narrative, but the term applies only with dialectical distortions to the two main parts of the book, even as it illuminates the function of

14 See Lee M. Johnson, *Wordsworth and the Sonnet* (Copenhagen: Rosenkilde and Bagger, 1973), 42–44, and Matlak, "Classical Argument and Romantic Persuasion in 'Tintern Abbey.'"

15 Johnson follows a three-part pattern, *narratio*, *propositio*, and *peroratio*. The "Ciceronian pattern of argumentation" Matlak uses differs in some respects from Curtius's paradigm and from the one I shall follow. Matlak lists "five or six functional parts – the *exordium*, or introduction; the *propositio*, or view to be maintained, which often contains a *partitio*, or division of the proposition; the *narratio*, or presentation of experiences and facts that lead to the proposition; the *argumentatio*, or confirmation of the proposition through arguments of reason and emotion and which sometimes offers a refutation of contrary arguments; and the *peroratio*, or exhortation to the audience to adopt the speaker's position" (99). Following Richard Lanham, I adopt a version of this model that places the *narratio* before the *propositio* and that includes an *expositio* between them. But as Matlak's proximate source Hugh Blair says, "I do not mean, that each of these [parts] must enter into every Public Discourse, or that they must enter always in this order." See *Lectures on Rhetoric and Belles Lettres*, ed. David F. Harding (Carbondale: Southern Illinois University Press, 1965), II, 157.

the question – "Was it for this...?" – that links them. John F. McCarthy attempts to read everything after that question as a "continuous narrative unit," yet he must acknowledge that "the significant link between the episodes of the first section is not chronological but typological." The thematic paragraphs that at first seem to punctuate the narrative later seem to govern it. Timothy Bahti, too, divides the book at the question "Was it for this...?," preceded by a "negative situation...of a poem beginning without either an ontologically stable speaker or an unvexed scene of its own creation" and followed after some "two hundred-odd lines" by "the actual beginning of the poem's autobiographical narrative," which is itself characterized by "inarticulateness or blockage of narrative representation." Michael G. Cooke comes closest to recognizing the rhetorical form of the poem, but he finally declares that "it is not a thing of argument, with a systematic assemblage of topics disposed in keeping with proper rhetorical principles...Rather it incorporates argument in its own lyrical-epical system."[16]

Though Romantic and deconstructive readers have found their highest expectations – that the poem would somehow defy conventional expectations – satisfied in these accounts, all the anomalies their generic hypotheses have produced can be accounted for with the seven-part variant of the classical model of the oration. All the divisions noticed by previous critics and a couple of crucial divisions they have failed to notice take their place in conformity with this paradigm, and only one part is missing, replaced by an authorized optional part. Every school-boy, including Wordsworth, used to know that the standard oration begins with a proemium, proceeds to a narration and sometimes an exposition, states a proposition, offers a confirmation of it, presents a refutation of other views, and concludes with the necessary conclusion.[17] *The Prelude* Book I lacks a

---

16 Hartman, *Wordsworth's Poetry*, 38; David P. Haney, "The Emergence of the Autobiographical Figure in *The Prelude*, Book I," *SiR* 20 (Spring 1981): 34; John F. McCarthy, "The Conflict in Books I–II of *The Prelude*," *MLQ* 30 (1969): 370, 375, 373; Bahti, "Wordsworth's Rhetorical Theft," 91, 110; Michael G. Cooke, "The Mode of Argument in Wordsworth's Poetry," in *Acts of Inclusion* (New Haven: Yale University Press, 1979), 204.

17 See John R. Nabholtz, "Romantic Prose and Classical Rhetoric," *WC* 11 (Spring 1980): 119–26. See also his *My Reader My Fellow-Labourer* (Columbia: University of Missouri Press, 1986) for suggestive connections between Romantic prose and classical rhetoric. Jane Worthington notes one reference to Quintilian in Wordsworth's letter to Charles James Fox of January 14, 1801, and two copies

refutation but replaces it with a digression, which sometimes appears before the conclusion, according to Lanham.[18] Wordsworth realizes this pattern in a discourse so rich in figures of thought that it does not immediately impress its argumentative pattern upon us, but I shall show how those figures generally function in relation to the aims of the parts in which they appear. There is more to this book of *The Prelude* than its conformity to this pattern, but our recognition of the pattern can avoid unnecessary bafflements and free our attention for other more appropriate and fruitful inquiries. I regret that I cannot enter the whole first book of the 1805 *Prelude* here into my own text or quote the whole of each section I shall now analyze, but the analysis follows the order of the book's unfolding and introduces line numbers so that readers may, if they wish, keep track of it in their own texts.[19]

Following Wordsworth himself, we have learned to call the opening section of *The Prelude* I (lines 1–54) the "glad preamble" (VII, 4), but we do not commonly ask what functions a rhetorical preamble serves, what forms it can take, what topics it touches on, or what decorum it observes. The terms "preamble," "proemium," and, indeed, "prelude" all name the opening or introductory move of a discourse. Quintilian links the term "proemium" with the Greek tradition of lyric poetry, in which it named the musical preludes composed by lyre-players to precede their sung poems and win the good will and attention of their listeners.[20] Wordsworth himself describes his preamble as having been sung "aloud in dithyrambic fervour" (VII, 5), and Hartman names it with a phrase from Book V as "'an Ode, in passion utter'd.'"[21] Tradition advises speakers in their proems to express hope, prayer, anxiety, and lack of self-assurance to conciliate their hearers' good will, and it recommends presenting extraordinary or important matters to arouse their attention (Cousin,

---

of Quintilian in his personal library in *Wordsworth's Reading of Roman Prose* (New Haven: Yale University Press, 1946), 76–77.

18 Richard A. Lanham, *A Handlist of Rhetorical Terms* (Berkeley: University of California Press, 1968), 112.

19 I will be following the text of the 1805 *Prelude* except where otherwise noted. The divisions I am discussing remain in the 1850 text, except that the section I call the proposition no longer stands apart as a separate verse paragraph.

20 Jean Cousin, *Etudes sur Quintilien* (1935; reprint Amsterdam: Verlag, 1967), 211–12.

21 Geoffrey Hartman, *Unremarkable Wordsworth* (Minneapolis: University of Minnesota Press, 1987), 99.

Etudes, 220, 224). It allows the speaker to speak about himself, especially in those cases where ties of friendship exist between him and his subject or his auditor.[22] It permits both apostrophe and prosopopeia as appropriate figures of thought, but it warns that the appearance of spontaneity must be especially observed in an opening when the judge's impression of the speaker is on the line (Cousin, *Etudes*, 224–25).

Wordsworth's "glad preamble" takes the form of an extended prosopopeia or self-impersonation, which is revealed as such only at the end when he declares that he has been recording his own previous spontaneous utterance. His opening paean turns quickly to an apostrophe of welcome to the gentle breeze to whom he narrates his situation as a recent escapee from the city, declares his problem of choosing a habitation, and asks where he should go.[23] Rather than answering, he turns to elaborate his freedom, celebrate it ("I breathe again" – the very figure of simulation, Kneale notes, that Quintilian points to as an example of the type [37–38]), and return to asking – this time not where he ultimately should go but just where he should turn next. Again avoiding a direct answer, he declares the sufficiency of his freedom even without a chosen destination and then corrects his initial account of his situation by finding in it not merely the joy of freedom but a "gift that consecrates [his] joy" (I, 40); Curtius lists the "topos of dedication" which the Romans commonly called "consecrations" as one of the topics of exordium (86–87). His expressions of uncertainty and hope display the required lack of self-assurance, even as his final self-correction reveals that what is at stake here is more important than the speaker's own freedom and joy – there is promise too of serious contribution to an honorable field of endeavor. The preamble is itself a partial mini-oration with its own proem, narration, proposition, and conclusion; every move in it has a Latin or Greek name in the list of rhetorical figures of thought and forms of argument; its lyric mode recalls the traditional lyric associations of the proem; and even its pose of recorded spontaneity

22 Elnora Carrino, "Conceptions of Dispositio in Ancient Rhetoric" (Ann Arbor: University Microfilms, 1959).

23 Alistair Fowler, who recognizes that the opening of *The Prelude* meets "proemial conventions...in a deeply implicit form," assimilates the apostrophe to the gentle breeze to an epic invocation of the muse, but the oratorical proemium is a more capacious genre that allows a greater variety of figures than the epic opening and need not be reduced to it. See Fowler's *Kinds of Literature* (Cambridge, Mass.: Harvard University Press, 1982), 102–03.

(which from compositional evidence we know to be a pose) satisfies the demands of art. This spontaneous overflow of powerful feeling has been carefully poured into a traditional mold.

Critics have called the preamble by its proper rhetorical name, but they have not known what to call the second part of *The Prelude* I (lines 55–271). John F. McCarthy thus calls it a "post-preamble" (371). David P. Haney recognizes that "we enter the world of narrative" (38–39) at this point in *The Prelude* I, but he sees the shift as part of an elaborate dialectical "series of discursive and narrative divisions which follows the preamble" (40). The dialectical epicycles of his deconstructive analysis can be simplified by the recognition that we here enter the second part of the formal oration, the *narratio* or narration. This part, as Lanham says, "tells how the problem at hand had come up ... [and] gives the audience, as it were, the history of the problem" (68). Adopting the classically recommended manner of laying out the events leading up to the problem in chronological order without digressions, this section places the utterance of the preamble as the first event in a chronological series of hopes, disappointments, and self-absolutions that leads to the speaker's present impasse. There is no mystery about shifts of tense from past to past perfect to present in such a narration (see Haney, "Emergence," 42–43).

The narrative section is also marked by repeated addresses to the speaker's friend that bring him into the position from which he can learn what has happened to the speaker, by a single self-impersonation of the speaker's past words, and by figures of complaint, wish, and confession that declare the speaker's present difficulty. The narration concludes with another partial mini-oration that declares the proposition that the speaker has many of the requisites for undertaking a "glorious work" (I, 158) but cannot single out "time, place, and manners ... with steady choice" (I, 169–71). His review of the alternative times, places, and manners confirms their plenitude, but the figure of aporia in which he enumerates them enacts his doubt. This subordinate argument concludes not with a choice but with a confession of inability to choose and a wish to escape the issue altogether. The narration ends by confessing that the problem it has traced persists.

All readers of *The Prelude* recognize that Book I takes its most important turn at this point with the question "Was it for this...?" Wordsworthians and users of a now out-of-date edition of the *Norton*

Anthology know that the poem began in its two-book form with this question and that the parts I have so far examined were later added to it. Some rhetoricians might recognize that this question begins the exposition (lines 272–304), the part that introduces the issue to be proved.[24] The question opens an inquiry or quaestio that asks whether the problem the narration has presented (the antecedent of "this") is the appropriate and necessary outcome of a previously unmentioned cause – the River Derwent's (and, more broadly, Nature's) nurturance of the speaker in his childhood (the as yet undeveloped "it"). The question also opens a vein of recollection that does not directly answer it but does begin to amplify the "it" of the question in a way that leads to a claim about it.

That claim appears in the next and briefest verse paragraph of Book I (lines 305–09), the formal proposition to which all the rest of the argument pertains. Again following its classical role as a brief, formal declaration and division of what is to be proved, the proposition succinctly declares a two-part claim: "Fair seed-time had my soul, and I grew up / Fostered alike by beauty and by fear." This claim is not a yes-or-no answer to the question posed in the exposition by the phrase "Was it for this…?" Rather it is a claim about the part of that question that has not yet been examined – the "it" whose bearing on "this" is still uncertain. Nature has fostered him, he claims, both through beauty and through fear.

The vivid accounts of hunting woodcocks, stealing from the raven's nest, stealing a boat, and skating that follow are all introduced to confirm this proposition (lines 309–570) – particularly the part that claims that the speaker was nurtured by fear. And the passages that John F. McCarthy identifies as "three separate paragraphs of reflection and self-congratulation" (373) that "punctuate" those vivid accounts in fact connect those accounts to the proposition that McCarthy does not notice. The elaborately described scenes have occasioned much commentary, but each of the three paragraphs that attempt to subordinate them to the function of confirming the proposition deserves scrutiny as well. The first, following the descriptions of hunting woodcocks and robbing the raven's nest, briefly widens the claim from what fosters the speaker to what fosters the mind of man, but it quickly returns its focus to the speaker and

24 Lanham identifies this third part of the oration and its function, though it is not as widely recognized by the rhetorical tradition as the two that precede and the four that follow it.

reformulates Nature's framing the mind of man as Nature's framing the speaker as "a favored being" (I, 364–65). Nature fostered him, he suggests, for a special purpose, not, he implies for "this."[25] The second connecting paragraph is the familiar apostrophe to the "Wisdom and spirit of the universe" (I, 427) that follows the boat-stealing passage. It draws the first direct consequence of the confirming evidence not just for the proposition it confirms but also for the question "Was it for this...?" You did not just foster me, you fostered me "not in vain" (I, 431), the speaker declares. And not stingily either, he adds. The third connecting paragraph follows the skating scene. It directs a rhetorical question to the "presences of Nature" to confirm again not just *that* the presences of Nature fostered him but that they did so with more than "a vulgar hope," that they ministered to him for something more than "this" (I, 490–93). The proposition formally governs each of these confirmatory summations but the question "Was it for this...?" haunts them all as well.

The next two verse paragraphs (lines 501–70) turn to confirm the other half of the proposition, the claim that the speaker was fostered by beauty (or, as he reformulates it in his conclusion, by "pleasure and repeated happiness" [I, 632]). They enumerate some of the changes "of exercise and play to which the year / Did summon us in its delightful rounds" (I, 503–04) both outdoors and within the "lowly cottages in which we dwelt" (I, 526), though they turn at the very last to end the confirmation of the proposition with one more reminder of its fearful side.

The two parts of that proposition, however, have not exhausted all that the speaker has found to say about how Nature fostered him in his childhood, and he adds in the next two paragraphs a formal

---

25 Bahti, who reads everything following "Was it for this?" as an autobiographical narrative rather than as an exposition, proposition, and confirmation, diminishes this passage as "twenty lines of reassuring teleology: talk of 'harmony' and the 'reconciling' of 'discordant elements,' summed up in the exclamation 'Praise to the end!'" with no sense of its argumentative function. He thinks its purpose is to "account for the parenthetic 'surely I was led by her [nature],' which introduces the scene of Wordsworth's stealing the boat. This opening line thereby qualifies this theft, too, as an engagement of the persona with nature, even though the specific object of the theft is a boat, rather than birds or eggs," "Wordsworth's Rhetorical Theft," 112. Bahti ignores the apostrophe to the "Wisdom and spirit of the universe" that follows the boat-stealing passage, and his theme of "theft" permits him to ignore the skating scene and the passage that follows it as well.

digression from the proposition that nevertheless serves the larger purpose of showing how well he has been fostered. "Other pleasures" (I, 575) besides those connected with either beauty or fear have been his, he declares, and he goes on to recall occasions of those pleasures and to call on natural forms to bear witness and confirm his experience of them.

At this point the speaker begins his conclusion (lines 609–674). First he concludes the digression by bringing it, too, to bear on the question "Was it for this...?" and asserting that the pleasures it points to were "not vain / Nor profitless" (I, 619–20). Next he opens the conclusion of the whole argument by summarizing point by point, as the canons of conclusion require, not only the two parts of the proposition but also the digression he has confirmed.

> And thus
> By the impressive discipline of fear,
> By pleasure and repeated happiness –
> So frequently repeated – and by force
> Of obscure feelings representative
> Of joys that were forgotten, these same scenes,
> So beauteous and majestic in themselves,
> Though yet the day was distant, did at length
> Become habitually dear, and all
> Their hues and forms were by invisible links
> Allied to the affections.   (I, 630–40)

He turns then to confess his weakness and to appeal to his friend for sympathetic indulgence – another hallowed topos of rhetorical conclusion. He then oddly transforms the other common concluding topos of showing indignation toward one's opponent by declaring that he has hoped to invigorate and reproach *himself* with his own argument.

This turn makes the absence of the expected refutation understandable, for the speaker here clarifies that he has made his argument in opposition to himself; the whole argument from "Was it for this...?" to the conclusion has been an indignant self-refutation. His proposition has been confirmed and expanded to outweigh the problem his narration has presented, to convince him that *it* is sufficiently powerful and good *not* to have been for *this*. But the qualification that follows this passage still allows the possibility that his hopes might be vain and appeals once more – this time with a rhetorical question – for the sympathy and indulgence of his friend.

The speaker declares at the beginning of the next-to-the-last paragraph, "I began / My story early" (I, 641–42), but we have seen that, except for the narration section itself and perhaps the boat-stealing passage as well, there has been no story here but rather an argument. Even the other vivid descriptions were not presented as episodes or single events but as accounts of repeated kinds of experience, and the overall arrangement of the first book was governed not by a chronological sequence of events but by a formal rhetorical model. Nevertheless, the speaker's sense of having begun a story leads him to declare in the final paragraph his decision to continue telling one and to "bring down / Through later years the story of my life" (I, 666–67). He determines here the issue that he had left in suspense in the aporia of his narration and chooses to make the times, places, and manners of his own life his subject. Though he has not yet fully convinced himself that it was not for this, he has discovered a purpose and the beginnings of a story in the act of trying to persuade himself. The end of his oration marks the formal beginning of his tale, but we should not forget that the end of his oration also marks the end of his oration, and that the narrative expectation projected retrospectively onto Book I cannot account for its argument.

Neither will it do to read backwards from the conscious beginning of the narrative at the end of Book I to take the preceding Book, even in its 1799 version, as a "lyric retrogression" finally transformed into a "narrative progression."[26] Book I of the 1799 *Prelude* already contains the outlines of the oration I have just presented. Though it lacks the opening proemium and narration and the formal proposition, all the other parts are in place. Despite the absence of the divided proposition, the two parts of the confirmation already show how Nature impressed the speaker's mind with "beautiful or grand" (line 378) forms, and the digression already adds the impact of "other pleasures ... / Of subtler origin" (lines 380–81). The vivid descriptions and their thematizing paragraphs are already in place, though some of their figures differ from those of the later version. The conclusion offers the same summary and the same gestures, lacking only the declaration to "bring down / Through later years the story of my life" (1805, I, 666–67).

26 Paul D. Sheats, "Wordsworth's 'Retrogrades' and the Shaping of *The Prelude*," *JEGP* 71 (1972): 477.

The crucial difference in Book I of the 1799 text is its insertion of three famous anecdotes, all of which are moved to other places in the later expanded poem – the anecdotes of the drowned man, and the two "spots of time" of coming upon the hanged man's grave and waiting for the horses before Christmas vacation. Wordsworth placed these anecdotes at the end of his enumeration of the changes "of exercise and sport to which the year / Did summon us in its delightful round" (lines 200–01), that is, after the confirmation and before the digression. The passage that introduces them makes clear that they, too, are a digression.[27] He writes:

> All these [changes of exercise and sport], and more, with
>   rival claims demand
> Grateful acknowledgment. It were a song
> Venial, and such as – if I rightly judge –
> I might protract unblamed, but I perceive
> That much is overlooked, and we should ill
> Attain our object if, from delicate fears
> Of breaking in upon the unity
> Of this my argument, I should omit
> To speak of such effects as cannot here
> Be regularly classed, yet tend no less
> To the same point, the growth of mental power
> And love of Nature's works.   (247–58)

Wordsworth implies here that the effects he has treated thus far have been "regularly classed" – the effects, I have argued, of fear and of pleasure and repeated happiness (or beauty). It appears, however, that the three anecdotes make a more intrusive digression than the digression that follows on "other pleasures... / Of subtler origin,"

---

27 Claims for the superiority of the "imaginative writing" of the 1799 text hinge upon these anecdotes, and claims for the centrality of what I am calling here a digression depend upon the thematic remarks about "spots of time" that come between the "Drowned Man" anecdote and the other two anecdotes in the passage as a whole. The arguments Jonathan Wordsworth and Stephen Gill have made for the 1799 text as a separate and superior poem do not show how this passage integrates into the argument of the rest of the poem but rather how it stands out from the rest of an argument that, in their view, revolves around it. Wordsworth would appear to have preferred, in the end, to preserve the unity of his argument from the disorienting and distracting power of this passage. See Jonathan Wordsworth and Stephen Gill, "The Two-Part *Prelude* of 1798–99," *JEGP* 71 (1973): 503–25, and Jonathan Wordsworth, "The Two-Part *Prelude* of 1799," *The Prelude: 1799, 1805, 1850*, ed. Jonathan Wordsworth *et al.*, 567–85.

for it not only violates this regular classification but it also gets no acknowledgment in the summary of topics offered by the opening of the digression that follows or in the summary offered in the book's conclusion, even though that final summary does include the topic treated in the second digression.

The very intrusiveness of this digression does provoke Wordsworth to declare, however, that he sees himself as constructing a unified argument.[28] Despite his closing (and conventional) apologies for self-indulgence in remembrance of things past, he has been purposefully pursuing an argument in answer to his opening question. Though he has not yet made a "resolute commitment to narrative progression," he is already writing a formally disciplined discourse that pursues an "'appointed task'" and knows when it digresses from that task (Sheats, "Wordsworth's 'Retrogrades,'" 478). His ultimate removal of the three digressive anecdotes and of this passage of apology for them, as well as his formal completion of the classical oration in Book I of the 1805 text, fulfills the formal intention already evident and self-conscious in 1799, a rhetorical generic intention reducible to neither "narrative progression" nor "lyric retrogression" (Sheats, "Wordsworth's 'Retrogrades,'" 477).

Sheats's (and Haney's) dialectical opposition between narrative and lyric in *The Prelude* I derives its plausibility from the presence in the text of parts that relate actions and parts that enact figures. Mary Jacobus, too, finds "a division...between discursive time and narrative time – a radical discontinuity which ruptures the illusion of sequentiality and insists, embarrassingly, on self-presence and voice...[an] incompatibility between the lyric voice of *The Prelude* and its much-desired, 'distracting' epic progress."[29] We have already seen, however, that the narrative parts function in a generic whole not definable as a narrative. The *narratio* tells a story to set up the question "Was it for this...?," and the boat-stealing passage tells an anecdote to confirm the proposition that the speaker was fostered by

28 The editors of the Norton *Prelude* gloss the word "argument" in this passage as "theme, as in *Paradise Lost*, I, 24: 'the highth of this great argument,'" but I think the better gloss is "connected series of statements or reasons intended to establish a position" (OED, sense 4). The digression violates the *form* of the argument Wordsworth has otherwise established but in fact treats the same theme or subject matter, or as he says, "the same point, the growth of mental power / And love of Nature's works" (257–58).

29 Mary Jacobus, "Apostrophe and Lyric in *The Prelude*," in *Lyric Poetry: Beyond New Criticism*, ed. Hošek and Parker, 172.

fear, but *The Prelude* I does not tell a story, though it does discover the beginning of one and the intent to tell it. In a similar way, the early apostrophe to the gentle breeze provokes lyric expectations in those who identify lyric with apostrophe,[30] and the succeeding apostrophes to the river Derwent, the Wisdom and Spirit of the Universe, and the presences of Nature revive those expectations in the midst of other sorts of discourse. But the book as a whole does not develop as a lyric or sustain the elevated tones of its apostrophic passages, and the somewhat arbitrary association between apostrophe and lyric diverts attention from the many other figures that constitute the discourse and the many other genres and parts of genres in which apostrophes function. Like the vivid spots of time, the elevated apostrophes attract our attention at the expense of the other figures that environ them and distort our apprehension of the functions all those figures serve and of the genres they work in.

Our rhetorical tradition, as Genette has shown, is so drastically reduced "within the figurative domain itself" that we do not recognize the range of figures or kinds of figures that the tradition once identified, nor do we recall the canons of decorum that once regulated the use of different sorts of figures in different genres of composition.[31] Culler's identification of apostrophe with lyric exemplifies the collapse of the distinctions between figures and tropes, between figures of thought and figures of speech, and among apostrophe, invocation, and anacoenosis (communication or taking counsel with), and it ignores the role apostrophes play in the several parts of other than lyric kinds of discourse, e.g., in the proemium, narration, and conclusion of the classical oration. Culler's version of the dialectical opposition between lyric and narrative works only so long as these reductions go unquestioned and the distinctions we have recovered in this section go unremembered. There is little to be gained beyond a dramatic conclusion in collapsing the "entire poem," as Jacobus does in the end, into "an apostrophe or 'prelude'" (181), if we have workable notions of apostrophes, preludes, and their correlative figures and counterparts. The vertigo produced by such

---

30 See Jonathan Culler, *The Pursuit of Signs* (Ithaca: Cornell University Press, 1981), 137, 149, whose account Jacobus follows.

31 Gérard Genette, *Figures of Literary Discourse*, trans. Alan Sheridan (Oxford: Blackwell, 1982), 107. For another valuable account of the collapse of rhetorical categories – focused on Hayden White's four-trope Viconian system – see Wallace Martin, "Floating an Issue of Tropes," *diacritics* 12 (1982): 75–83.

collapsing distinctions in some recent rhetorical criticism may come from its falls into the gaps, even the abysses, in its knowledge of rhetoric.

Trope, see figure: figure (or trope)

Those gaps or abysses run deep, however, and have long imperiled travel in what Schwarz and Rycenga called "the province of rhetoric," especially in the area mapped by the terms "trope" and "figure."[32] A pair of index entries in Gérard Genette's *Figures of Literary Discourse* epitomizes an important stage in his narrative of the collapse of classical rhetorical distinctions: "Trope, *see* Figure," "Figure (*or* Trope)" (303, 298). Genette tells a story in which the classical art of rhetoric is reduced to style, style to tropes and figures, tropes and figures to tropes (which are usually called figures), and tropes (or figures) to smaller and smaller numbers of devices, until metaphor alone remains as the last remnant of the art. This last stage in the history of disappearing distinctions is itself something of a hyperbole, but the stage in which "trope" and "figure" collapse into near synonyms does represent the current state of the art for many of its diverse professors.

Thus Richard Lanham's *Handbook* entry on "Figure" sends us to "Trope," where the distinctions between the terms break down, collapse, and depend on undefinable categories. Edward P. J. Corbett's index in *Classical Rhetoric for the Modern Student* sends us from "trope" to "figure of speech," a generic head under which "tropes" are distinguished from "schemes." Corbett adopts Quintilian's definition of "figure" to encompass "trope" without noting that Quintilian sets these two categories up on different footings, not as genus and species. Kenneth Burke indexes neither term, though he treats four master tropes in an appendix to his *Grammar* and enumerates traditional figures as "rhetorical devices" in a section of his *Rhetoric* on "Formal Appeals." Perelman and Olbrechts-Tyteca conduct their entire discussion of such devices under the heading of "figure," identifying metaphor alone as a traditional trope.[33]

32 John Arthur Rycenga and Joseph Schwarz, *The Province of Rhetoric* (New York: Ronald, 1965).
33 Edward P. J. Corbett, *Classical Rhetoric for the Modern Student* (New York: Oxford University Press, 1965), 459–95, esp. 459–61; RMGM 503–17, 589–93; Ch. Perelman and L. Olbrechts-Tyteca, *The New Rhetoric: A Treatise on Argumentation* (Notre Dame and London: University of Notre Dame Press, 1969).

Literary scholars, too, perform similar identifications and subsumptions: Rosemond Tuve parallels Corbett's subordination in her entry on "Figures (tropes and schemes)."[34] Curtius observes that

the study of figures has never been satisfactorily systematized. Besides figures of language and thought, grammatical figures (that is, figures occurring in the exegesis of poets) and rhetorical figures have been distinguished. Furthermore, antique and later textbooks commonly call many figures of speech *tropoi* ("turns"), *tropi*. This lack of settled terminology, and, in short, the endless variations in enumerating and defining the figures, are to be explained historically by contacts between various schools. (45)

Theresa Kelley subordinates tropes to figures but does recognize "tropes in the strict sense of the term (i.e., 'turnings' from literal meanings)" (69).

Among recent theorists, the case is the same. Jonathan Culler can call metaphor a figure and apostrophe a trope without any cognitive dissonance caused by Quintilian's opposite placement of these devices, and Paul de Man slips from calling metaphor a trope to calling it a figure without problematizing the distinction between the terms: "figural" and "tropological" appear to be synonymous among his followers. Roland Barthes offers the most circumspect recent account of the distinction, placing both "Tropes" and "Figures" under the broader heading of "Colors" or "Ornaments," noting the reductions necessary to set the "Tropes" and "Figures" in opposition to one another, and exploring diverse oppositions in terms of which these distinctions have been determined through history.[35] Barthes, however, like many other modern summarizers of the rhetorical tradition, is insufficiently historical and excessively systematic in ultimately opposing the figured to the proper, when Quintilian, whom Auerbach identifies as author of "the fundamental work on the subject" on which "all later efforts were based" (25), explicitly opposes tropes, which deviate from the proper, to figures, which, though they do nothing improper, nevertheless do something interesting.

It may appear quixotic, faced with this terminological meltdown, to propose to desynonymize "trope" and "figure" through an

34 Rosemond Tuve, *Elizabethan and Metaphysical Imagery* (Chicago: University of Chicago Press, 1947).
35 Roland Barthes, *The Semiotic Challenge* (Oxford: Blackwell, 1988), 84–90.

examination of the divergent historical institutional contexts in which Quintilian constructs his distinction between these terms. I believe, however, that a reconstruction of those contexts would reveal that the two categories of rhetorical devices need not be identified or systematically opposed to one another within some single frame of reference or single binary opposition of terms, but may instead be understood as analogous rhetorical exploitations of two distinct sorts of expectations, both of which are produced socially by historically specific institutions that regulate verbal practices. Tropes, "the artistic alteration of a word or phrase from its proper meaning to another," are constructed against the background of a prescriptive grammar that defines proper usage. For Quintilian, this grammar was formalized and taught by grammar school teachers, who would have sensitized the language users they trained to register departures from propriety and note them as either errors or as licensed artistic devices. Tropes, for Quintilian, are licensed deviations from grammatical norms of naming, categorizing (e.g., animate/inanimate, or human/non-human), and the like.[36]

Quintilian was already aware that "many authors have considered *figures* identical with *tropes*," while others "call *tropes figures*" (IX.i.2), but he goes on to argue that, unlike a trope, "a *figure* does not necessarily involve any alteration either of the order or the strict sense of words" (IX.i.7). The question is, what do figures depart from? A worked out answer would require some interpretation of the several ways in which Quintilian describes them, of his differentiation of his account of them from Cicero's, and of his analysis of the figures themselves, but I suggest that figures depart artificially not from a naturalized ordinary language or from a normative grammatical standard but from a logical or dialectical or philosophical ideal of direct, transparent discourse focused on the subject at hand. Figures of thought diverge from that ideal to call attention to the speaker, the judges, other persons, or to the text of the utterance itself, whereas figures of speech enhance the unadorned form of direct subject-centered declarations, without necessarily departing from grammatical propriety. Figures diverge from what Quintilian calls "the direct method of statement" (IX.ii.1), from "reference to the matter" (IX.iii.100), and from "direct and simple language" (IX.iii.3). They mark a rhetorical departure from an ideal of neutral, objective

---

36 Quintilian, *Institutes of Oratory*, VIII.vi.1.

philosophical style that takes no account of "the requirements of time, place, and character on each occasion of speaking" (IX.iii.102). Tropes violate "proper" usage; figures modify and embellish unobtrusive and declarative style.

In these terms, we may wish to reconsider both Wordsworth's pronouncements on poetry and his poetic practices. He does not appear to use the word "trope" or develop an explicit distinction between tropes and figures, though in the 1802 Preface to *Lyrical Ballads* he does twice use the phrase "metaphors and figures" (255), which hints at such a distinction. He would appear, however, to be preoccupied in the Preface and Appendix to *Lyrical Ballads* with issues of diction that mainly concern what Quintilian calls tropes, that is, departures from literal or proper usage. The so-called "figure of speech" – "personifications of abstract ideas" – that he singles out for blame (250) violates the grammatical line between animate and inanimate beings, and the lines he objects to in Cowper's poem are "an instance of the language of passion wrested from its proper use" (*Prose* I, 164). His objection to "a large portion of phrases and figures of speech which from father to son have long been regarded as the common inheritance of poets" (LB 251) may be understood as an objection to the formation of a separate language community in which the rules of usage make what was once an effective violation of propriety into a required proper use. Metaphors read as the marks of poetic diction are not, for the community of poets, tropes at all, but marks of proper conformity to the usage of their professional community. Paradoxically, for Wordsworth the "proper use" of metaphors – which by definition violate the grammatically proper usage of "the real language of men" – is as expressions of "the language of passion" provoked by moving occasions, and the improper use of them is as lawful signs of poetic propriety. Wordsworth even allows himself the use of personifications when they are "occasionally prompted by passion" and so felt as violations of the grammatical propriety of the "language of men," but not when they are "foolishly repeated" (LB 250–51) in conformity to the grammatical propriety of the "particular language" (LB 260) of poets.[37]

---

37 Barbara Johnson explores this issue in terms of the opposition of "natural" and "mechanical" devices of style rather than in terms of the differences between the "language of men" and the "language of poets." See her "Strange Fits: Poe and Wordsworth on the Nature of Poetic Language," in *A World of Difference*, 92–97.

Tropes, then, as Quintilian's definition lets us see, are relative to the grammar of the community of their use; the same expression may be a trope in one community and a proper use in another. Wordsworth's issue with poetic diction in these terms is really a question of whether poets should conform to the norms of their own autonomous community or whether they must write in relation to (though not necessarily in conformity with) the norms of a generic human community unmarked by professional diction, whether of the poet or of the lawyer, physician, mariner, or natural philosopher.

It remains a serious question, however, whether any such generic or common language exists or whether the poet, as I have suggested in Chapter 3, must represent the interplay of diverse social languages and the consequent conflict over what is proper and what is a trope in their divergent grammars. We may also wonder with Roger Murray whether the peculiar convictions of an individual poet, such as Wordsworth's conviction of the "one life" in all things, may issue in an idiosyncratic grammar in which the widely enforced distinctions between animate and inanimate beings literally do not apply.[38] Even such a usage would depend for its poetic effect, however, on the reading of readers who, not fully sharing the conviction that all things are alive, could recognize the poet's subtle, consistent violations of their categorical expectations and imagine the possibility of a person for whom those expectations literally did not apply. To imagine the possibility of such a person would be not just to appreciate a particular trope from the point of view of "common sense," but to recognize, as Murray does, the possibility of another language whose alternative grammar structures another world. To recognize these possibilities would be, not just to live within a single language that structures the world and lets us know a trope when we see one, but to discover a radical alternative version of the world in dialogic competition with "common sense."

Rethinking figures of thought

If, as I have just suggested, Wordsworth's long-debated pronouncements on what he and we have usually called "diction and figures" are mainly concerned with what Quintilian would call tropes, we may

---

38 Roger N. Murray, *Wordsworth's Style: Figures and Themes in the "Lyrical Ballads" of 1800* (Lincoln: University of Nebraska Press, 1967).

ask what his theory and practice can tell us about his attitudes toward and uses of what Quintilian would call figures of speech and figures of thought. I think it will be evident to anyone who peruses, say, "Simon Lee" and the "glad preamble" of *The Prelude* with an eye for artful arrangements of words, an ear for elaborated but not improper forms of language, and a hand on a book like Arthur Quinn's *Figures of Speech* that Wordsworth uses figures of speech frequently and without apology.[39] Take, for example, the polysyndetons of "from the green fields and from the clouds / And from the sky" or "And he is lean and he is sick"; the brachylogia of "Pure passions, virtue, knowledge, and delight" or "Men, dogs, and horses"; the anadiplosis "hearts unkind, kind deeds" and the polyptoton "free, enfranchised." "Dearly loves" and "green fields" both fit Quintilian's description of phrases that involve "addition, which, although the words added may be strictly superfluous, may still be far from inelegant" (IX.iii.18).[40] My point, however, is not to find Latin names or classical precedents for these stylistic devices (and there are many others for which this could be done), but to indicate that figures of speech in this sense seem to have been acceptable to Wordsworth in ballad experiments and elevated blank verse alike. Their use was never an issue for him, and the resources for recognizing them are still at hand for us.

The case of figures of thought is more difficult to assess because this category of devices has been almost completely lost to us with the exception of a few undeveloped and idiosyncratic mentions of it, nor is it clear to what extent Wordsworth himself recognized the category. Genette shows how Fontanier, a crucial authority in the

---

39 Arthur Quinn, *Figures of Speech: 60 Ways to Turn a Phrase* (Salt Lake City: Gibbs M. Smith, Inc., 1982).
40 Kneale observes the "anadiplosis of 'free / Free'" and the "triple anaphoric scheme" repeating the word "shall" at the beginning of lines 11, 12, and 13 in the 1850 text, *Monumental Writing*, 37. Bahti notes recurrences of litotes in Book I, though he does not distinguish this device as a figure of speech as opposed to a trope, "Wordsworth's Rhetorical Theft," 90–91. Bahti and other de Manian critics also frequently note repetitions or echoes of words, often at greater distances from one another than the classical definitions of figures of speech, which pay attention to repeated beginnings, middles, and endings in poetic lines or prose sentences, can describe. There is no rule by which we can decide how far apart repeated words can be and still be described as related to one another in a figure of speech, but I would suggest that the further apart they are, the greater the probability that the critic who notes the repetition is constructing a figure like *accumulatio* in enumerating them together in his or her prose.

development of French rhetoric, excluded figures of thought as
figures altogether because they are "contents, not modes of
expression" (53, 105), in effect, because they are *not* the figures of
speech from which Quintilian distinguishes them. Auerbach preserves
them under the same division of "figures into those involving content
and those involving words (*figurae sententiarum* and *verborum*)" and
offers a helpful, brief list of them that closely follows Quintilian (26).
Roger N. Murray includes an interesting footnote that revives
Quintilian's distinction in relation to Wordsworth's art as a category
of figures that "have to do with the 'matter'; in oratory, they might
be designated as figures expressive of appropriate passion or figures
requisite to the adumbration of ideas or logical thought development;
in poetics, they might be designated as having thematic interest," and
he concludes with the observation that, in order to avoid devices that
will be recognized as such, Wordsworth strives to turn all of his
figures "into what Quintilian calls 'figures of thought,' as distinct
from figures of language, speech, or what not."[41] But Murray's only
example of such a figure is the thematically consequential repetition
of a single word – a device Quintilian does not include in this
category, and his "or what not" suggests that he has not worked out
the distinctions he has nevertheless suggestively revived. Curtius,
too, appears to be impatient with the category and careless in
enumerating its members when he writes, just before he notes the
"endless variations in enumerating and defining the figures," that
"figures of thought are litotes, metonymy, allegory, and many
others" (44–45), though Quintilian lists none of these as figures of
thought. Jacques Lacan interestingly revives the category as an
enumeration of "mechanisms of defense" in "the rhetoric of the
discourse that the analysand utters," but he, too, adds to the
confusion by enumerating "periphrasis, hyperbaton, ellipsis, sus-
pension, anticipation, retraction, negation, digression, irony" as
"Quintilian's *figurae sententiarum*," though the first three devices are
not on Quintilian's list, and he compounds the difficulty by calling
them "figures of style."[42] Wordsworth may or may not have the
category of figures of thought in mind when he speaks of

41 Murray, *Wordsworth's Style*, 37 n. 3, 135.
42 Jacques Lacan, "Agency of the Letter in the Unconscious," in *Ecrits: A Selection*,
   trans. Alan Sheridan (New York: W. W. Norton, 1977), 168. Vincent Leitch's
   Deconstructive Criticism: An Advanced Introduction (New York: Columbia
   University Press, 1983), 13, called this passage to my attention.

"Imagination as it deals with thoughts and sentiments" in his Preface of 1815 (*Prose* III, 34), but I think there will be no question, once we recall them to our own minds, that he used them frequently and varied them effectively. If we take them in the broader of the two senses I shall now present, we will have to say that they are the elementary units of utterance from which he constructed larger parts and wholes of his poems.[43]

Quintilian's account of figures of thought acknowledged an already longstanding dispute over their definition and enumeration. His own definition requires that they depart from the direct method of statement, and his enumeration of them includes the *question*, when not asked to get information, the *reply*, when one question is asked and another answered, the *confession, self-correction, hesitation, simulation of emotion* or *exclamation, impersonation* of speech to display inner thoughts, the *apostrophe*, or diversion of address from the judge, the *interruption, vivid description, irony* (which may also be a trope), and the *hidden allusion*, among others. He reports that Cicero, who requires only that the move be striking and affecting, offers a looser and longer list that includes the formal gestures of *summarizing, digressing, declaring propositions*, and the like, as well as *wishing, warning, entreating, supplicating*, and *execrating*. Quintilian says that *communicating* with one's opponent is a figure of thought, but Cicero allows that *communicating* with the judge is also a figure.

This list enumerates some of the many things we do in discourse. The verbal forms characterize discursive actions and the nominal forms the products of those actions as they are found in discursive artifacts. Quintilian's list emphasizes gestures that are artful departures from a posited artless norm of statement, while Cicero's includes ordinary and extraordinary moves alike. Both lists are helpful, for we need names for both the artful departure and the common practice. Even those moves that are not fancy and therefore not on Quintilian's list of figures are part of the speaker's and writer's repertoire of discursive gestures or speech genres and should be part of the listener's or reader's repertoire of recognizable moves. We cannot describe all the gestures of any extended discourse without

---

43 James Fairhall, then a graduate student at SUNY-Stony Brook, first called my attention to rhetorical figures in *The Prelude* in a seminar report on the eleventh book of the poem. Drawing on Renaissance rhetorical sources, he called attention to anthypophora, apostrophe, interrogatio and metabasis — all figures of thought, though he did not then class them as such.

identifying the ordinary as well as extraordinary ones. Having taught a graduate seminar on the Romantic long poem several years ago in which I assigned students to outline a book of *The Prelude* by listing the sequence of "gestures" the speaker makes, and having lacked at that time knowledge of the figures of thought, I can testify to a shock of more than mild surprise when I recognized, upon reading Quintilian, that *these* were the very things we had been trying to talk about. While I am in a testimonial vein, I might add that my discovery of the conformity of *The Prelude*, Book I, to the pattern of the seven-part oration emerged, not from an attempt to fit the book to that pattern, but from an attempt to work through the book naming each of its figures of thought. When the declaration of a proposition appeared in the middle, set apart in the 1805 text in its own unusually short paragraph, the rest of the pattern began to crystallize around this seed.

In my account of how Book I fits the pattern of the formal oration, I described in the vocabulary of figures of thought many of the gestures that make up the parts of *The Prelude*'s first book; here I shall illustrate the precision and usefulness of that vocabulary by comparing two versions of a brief passage from the 1799 and 1805 texts in its terms. The first is a relatively straightforward statement of beliefs, the second a more figured passage. Both passages immediately follow the recollections of hunting woodcocks and plundering the raven's nest and precede the boat-stealing recollection. The 1799 passage reads:

> The mind of man is fashioned and built up
> Even as a strain of music. I believe
> That there are spirits which, when they would form
> A favored being, from his very dawn
> Of infancy do open out the clouds
> As at the touch of lightning, seeking him
> With gentle visitation – quiet powers,
> Retired, and seldom recognized, yet kind,
> And to the very meanest not unknown –
> With me, though rarely, in my boyish days
> They communed. Others too there are, who use,
> Yet haply aiming at the self-same end,
> Severer interventions, ministry
> More palpable – and of their school was I.   (67–80)

Here is the 1805 passage:

> The mind of man is framed even like the breath
> And harmony of music. There is a dark
> Invisible workmanship that reconciles
> Discordant elements, and makes them move
> In one society. *Ah me, that all*
> *The terrors, all the early miseries,*
> *Regrets, vexations, lassitudes, that all*
> *The thoughts and feelings which have been infused*
> *Into my mind, should ever have made up*
> *The calm existence that is mine when I*
> *Am worthy of myself. Praise to the end,*
> *Thanks likewise for the means!* But I believe
> That Nature, oftentimes, when she would frame
> A favored being, from his earliest dawn
> Of infancy doth open out the clouds
> As at the touch of lightning, seeking him
> With gentlest visitation; not the less,
> Though haply aiming at the self-same end,
> Does it delight her sometimes to employ
> Severer interventions, ministry
> More palpable — and so she dealt with me.
>
> (I, 340–71 italics mine)

Both passages open by declaring a general proposition that is a figure of thought only in Cicero's broad sense of the term, but neither can be described without noting it. The first passage moves directly from that general declaration to state a personal belief connected with it, while the second passage first elaborates the general proposition and then defers the statement of belief with two figures of thought that both my authorities would recognize — the exclamation that interrupts line 355 and continues to line 361 and the *eucharistia* or thanksgiving that immediately follows. The exclamatory figure of thought calls extra attention to itself through the figures of speech that give it shape — the opening asterismos, "Ah me," the triple anaphora "all...all...all," the brachylogia "miseries, / Regrets, vexations, lassitudes," perhaps even — forgive my enthusiasm for these new toys — a polyptotonic epanalepsis, "mine when I am worthy of myself." The figure of thanksgiving, in contrast, is shaped as an isocolon, which avoids anaphora by substituting "thanks" for "praise" in the second phrase and avoids epistrophe by ending in opposite words instead of the same words (end...means) — there must be a name for this, too. As figures of thought highly wrought with contrasting figures of speech, both the exclamation and the thanksgiving call attention to themselves as the proposition and credo that frame them do not, but clearly the force of the figurative departures from direct statement depends in part on the statement they interrupt. Indeed the interruption transforms the credal declaration from a direct and unproblematic consequence of the proposition to an exception to the exclamation that must introduce itself with a "but." The application of the credo to the speaker's own case that simply followed in the first version becomes, because of the improbable reversal at which the exclamation wonders and for which the thanksgiving gives thanks, an unlikely and surprising belief that he *has* been improbably favored and musically formed.

Timothy Bahti, who finds in the passage "reassuring teleology ... summed up in the exclamation 'Praise to the end!,'" seems to think that it would require considerable critical exegesis to show "how problematic this reassuring pause ... actually is – how tenuous its propositions, how qualified its self-conviction" (112). We can see, however, through comparative analysis of these two versions of the passage (Bahti offers such analyses in the case of other passages to which he attends more closely) that there is no hidden complication here that only a critic can discover under the reassuring surface of the passage. Wordsworth has deliberately and openly turned a relatively unproblematic passage into a problematic one by inserting two artfully heightened figures of thought into the middle of two ordinary figures of thought. He has altered the force and tone of his confession of faith by elaborately calling attention to his awareness of the circumstances that made it unlikely, thereby increasing both the force of his affirmation and our awareness of his awareness of the powerful resistance to it. This passage does not show us "'language unremittingly and noiselessly at work ... to vitiate and dissolve' the condition of the possibility of meaning" – to recall Chase's concluding use of Wordsworth's words from the *Essays upon Epitaphs*;[44] it shows us a poet rather noisily at work to call attention to his speaker's doubts in order both to strengthen his affirmation of meaning and reveal the tension inherent in making it.

The rhetorical vocabulary of figures of thought offers a precise instrument for describing significant features of passages like these and distinguishing their effects. Like Bahti's imprecise labeling of the

---

44 Chase, "The Ring of Gyges," 85.

passage as "reassuring teleology," McCarthy's characterization of the 1805 passage as one of three "paragraphs of reflection and self-congratulation" (373) cannot distinguish it from the 1799 passage or from the other two thematic paragraphs, whose figurative workings are significantly different. Our usual emphasis on tropes would also direct our attention to other features of the passage – the simile (not technically a trope but just an ornament) that compares the framing of the mind of man with music or the metaphor and simile that make the dawn of infancy like the opening of the clouds, but that focus would probably not make the gestures I have highlighted objects of scrutiny. Even the deconstructive rhetoric that calls our attention to the unresolved tension between apparent reassurance and actual uncertainty in the 1805 passage would benefit from identifying and analyzing the nameable gestures that it often mystifies in order to demystify them.

To identify such figures – even to discover an instance in which Wordsworth appears to employ them artfully and deliberately – is not, however, to settle the question of how to interpret them, but to open it. The same figure – the exclamatory interruption I have just discussed, for example – may be taken in at least three ways: rhetorically, in Quintilian's terms, as an artful revision of the poet's; psychologically, in Lacan's terms, as a defense mechanism of the poet's or the speaker's; and dialogically, in the terms I have used in Chapters 3, 4 and 5, as a sign of the speaker's response to "other people's views."

The particular figure I have just analyzed, in fact, closely resembles the "If this / Be but a vain belief, yet, oh! how oft" lines from "Tintern Abbey" I discussed in Chapter 3 as a sign of the poem's speaker's dialogic responsiveness to another skeptical voice he cannot ignore. And the commands on which I placed so much weight in my readings of "Beauteous Evening" and "Solitary Reaper" could also be identified as figures of communication with an auditor that in both these poems may lead us to imagine an auditor where there is otherwise no sign of one. The long quotation of the words of the sailor's mother's I discussed in Chapter 3 is technically a prosopopeia, and the addresses to the reader I will highlight in my reading of "Simon Lee" in Chapter 9 are again communications; both are figures of thought. So too are the self-corrections I repeatedly highlight as a characteristic gesture of Wordsworth's poetry. Similarly, the allusions to Milton and Coleridge that J. Douglas Kneale documents under the label "trope of collaboration" (69) might be distanced from what for me is a confusing use of the category "trope" and brought into both the classical context of figures of thought and, so, too, into the purview of dialogic analysis of the interplay of voices.[45]

Whatever the motivation our arguments may ascribe to the use of such devices – whether we imagine them as artful moves, involuntary defenses, as the dialogic responses I prefer to imagine, or even as evidence of the silent working of language itself – I would submit that we can learn to discriminate and describe them more precisely with the help of Quintilian's definition and elaboration of figures of thought. I would even venture the suggestion that, for the reading and teaching of Wordsworth's poetry (as opposed to the history or theory of his critical thought), Book IX of Quintilian's *Institutio Oratoria* would be a far more fruitful assignment than Book II of Coleridge's *Biographia Literaria*. The latter has narrowed our expectations of what poetic discourse can do; the former would expand and sharpen them.

45 See Kneale's Chapter 2, "The Rhetoric of Intertextuality."

8

Theoretical commitments and Wordsworthian pedagogies

The most important development in the study of literature over the past few years is that once again pedagogy is no longer a dirty word. One of the things that made New Criticism genuinely new, at least from I. A. Richards's *Practical Criticism* to Brooks and Warren's *Understanding Poetry*, was its concern with teaching ... Some literary theorists have realized that the recent wave of theoretical inquiry has implications for teaching and that these implications should be pursued. It is acceptable once again to devote energy to thinking about what we do and should do in the classroom.

> Reed Way Dasenbrock,
> "What to Teach When the Canon Closes Down"

Reading poetry seems an inevitable sequence of incomprehension followed by instruction; the classroom becomes the necessary adjunct ... Wordsworth ... among all his contemporaries, and perhaps more than any poet before or since, would not be entirely dismayed by our present literary situation, where reading poetry is largely a formal classroom experience.

> Kenneth R. Johnston, "On First Looking into Wordsworth's *Prelude*"

My raising the question of assignments at the end of Chapter 7 recalls my argument to the educational context that has been, since Plato, the ultimate context of justification for literary study. Wordsworth himself, in choosing not to gratify the given taste of his readers but to provoke them to achieve more worthy and enduring tastes, founded the modern constitution of literature as an educational enterprise, not an entertainment industry. In that educational project, questions of literary theory have never been far from questions of "the present state of the public taste ... and ... how far this taste is healthy or depraved" (LB 243) and what pedagogical steps might be taken to improve it. And such questions have not been far from what I. A. Richards called the "large and awkward question" of "how far insensitiveness, poor discrimination, and a feeble capacity to understand poetry imply a corresponding inability to apprehend and make use of the values of ordinary life" (PC 299–300).

I have registered in Chapter 1 the coercive accents such formulations might ring with in Clifford Siskin's ears or F. R. Leavis's mouth and have examined in Chapter 2 the tensions between Wordsworth's distaste for popular entertainments and his efforts to educate and elevate his readers' tastes through the representation of "low" subjects and language. I have also argued, as I believe Wordsworth ultimately did, that the real educational issue with which poetry is concerned is not the inculcation or gratification of passive and constrained tastes but the provocation of active, free thought in response to perceived likenesses in difference and differences in likeness. In doing so I have argued not only for a critical practice free, in principle, from linguistic and political imperatives but also for a liberal literary education that does not automatically reinforce or oppose established cultural values and attitudes but does oppose what I. A. Richards called "mental inertia" through the cultivation of active critical thought (PC 295).

Richards's own project for literary education reaffirmed in *Principles of Literary Criticism* Wordsworth's commitment to "'the widening of the sphere of human sensibility'" through the powerful agency of the arts (133) and went on in *Practical Criticism* to call for "the critical reading of poetry" as a liberal intellectual discipline suited to strengthen the judgment and clarify the powers and limitations of human choice (328–29). Richards's collection of student reading "protocols," however, put him in a position to inventory, as Wordsworth could not, the "present state of the public taste" or, as Richards put it, "the current state of culture" (PC 291). The modern institutionalization of "English" provided Richards with experimental subjects in the "undergraduates reading English with a view to an Honours Degree" (PC 4) whom he taught as a lecturer at Cambridge; no such social subjects as students or teachers of English existed in Wordsworth's time or under his control, and he could not elicit, collect, analyze, and publish, as Richards did, reading "protocols" that were, at the same time, products of the English Apparatus and evidence of the need to reform it. Neither could Wordsworth turn to an audience of English teachers – provided to Richards by the same educational apparatus – who were in a position to heed proposals for educational reform, invent textbooks and pedagogies to enact or oppose those proposals, test the books and methods in their own

English classrooms, and theorize the interpretive principles entailed by their teaching.

Wordsworth could imagine a program of English literary education in an institutional situation still dominated by classical literary education for the few and no formal literary education for the many, but Richards brought forward his interconnected literary theory and pedagogical proposals at a moment when institutional structures were in place and eager young English educators were ready to put them into practice or invent their own answering programs, making even antitheoretical pedagogies like Leavis's theoretical in the broad sense of being explicit and reflective about their aims and methods. Cleanth Brooks, who testifies to the influence of Richards while Brooks was a Rhodes Scholar at Oxford, conducted cultural polemics, ventured poetic theories, and produced textbooks that all played parts in what came to be called the New Criticism. Reuben Brower – a crucial, though frequently unmentioned, New Critic and teacher of New Critics who studied with Richards at Cambridge – exerted his influence through his teaching at Amherst, his supervision of graduate instructors of a Harvard undergraduate course in "The Interpretation of Literature," and his published work.[1] M. H. Abrams, who also studied with Richards at a formative moment in his intellectual career, combined his scholarly and theoretical labors with editing the most influential and widely used undergraduate literature anthology in America.

The English Apparatus elaborated by these (and other) theoretical pedagogues or pedagogical theorists sustained an intensive theoretical discussion during the past two decades in which some critics ignored the pedagogical implications of their inquiries, while others continued to wonder about those implications.[2] The return of

---

1 See Paul de Man's testimony that his teaching in Brower's course inaugurated his own "awareness of the critical, even subversive, power of literary instruction" in "Return to Philology," 23. See also Richard Poirier, "Hum 6, or Reading before Theory," *Raritan* 9 (1990): 14–31. Poirier questions "New Critic" as the label for Brower and his Amherst and Harvard colleagues and students, who learned from Frost and Kenneth Burke and Leavis to recognize "that no matter how powerful the writer or the reader may be, his or her relation to words on the page is of necessity dialogic, a recognition that scarcely awaited the current Bakhtinian hoopla" (28). To echo a phrase of Frost's that Poirier approvingly quotes, "scarcely awaited" for "whom, where, and when is the question."

2 See, for example, Cary Nelson, ed., *Theory in the Classroom* (Urbana and Chicago: University of Illinois Press, 1986), and Bruce Henrickson and Thaïs Morgan, eds.,

theorists to pedagogical questions, which Dasenbrock observes in my first epigraph, marks not just an important new fashion among a number of literary theorists but a homecoming to the combination of interests that has built the institution of literary studies in England and America and sustained many of its most successful and worthy careers. To proceed, as Robert Scholes does in *Textual Power*, on the assumption that "literary theory and classroom practice really do have something to say to one another" (x) is to reassert one of the fundamental tenets of the constitution of literature.

The conversation between literary theory and pedagogical practice, however, is another that has taken place only piecemeal. The various available accounts of pedagogical theory and practice have been published for our edification without being juxtaposed to related accounts, scrutinized for consistency or fruitful inconsistency, or made the objects of sustained critical discussion. Almost all of them report a particular teacher's creed or course without taking alternative practices inspired by the same theory or other practices sustained by other theories into account. It is characteristic of the genres of personal pedagogical narrative and credo that the contributions to the 1986 MLA volume *Approaches to Teaching Wordsworth's Poetry* (including my own) do not engage with the contributions to the 1978 *Wordsworth Circle* special issue on teaching Wordsworth but instead tell their own stories as if each were a first-born birth and none had lived before them.

Nevertheless, their dissimilitudes in similitude or similitudes in dissimilitude are provocative of further thought, revealing alternative practices within apparently common theories and common practices under divergent theoretical banners and in diverse theoretical styles. Further, these narratives represent diverse dialogic relations among speaker (teacher), hero (Wordsworth), and listeners (students) in registering or suppressing voices other than the teacher-narrator's own. Like critical readings of poems and essays about poems, critical readings of these narratives may reveal possibilities for our choice and limitations in our habitual self-understandings as teachers, leading us to think further about our theories, our practices, and their complex interrelations.

Reorientations: Critical Theories and Pedagogies (Urbana and Chicago: University of Illinois Press, 1990). In 1990 several conferences and calls for papers on this topic appeared in the U.S. and Australia.

Tragic and picaresque responses to changing critical paradigms

It is striking that both the *Wordsworth Circle* special issue "On Teaching Wordsworth" and the MLA *Approaches to Teaching Wordsworth's Poetry* open with autobiographical essays by mature professors who look back on how their teaching of Wordsworth changed with changes in the dominant paradigms or methods of criticism during their careers. The *Wordsworth Circle* reprints Frederick A. Pottle's recollections, as he approached retirement in 1961, of his conversion from historicist to New Critical teaching of Wordsworth and ultimately to a combination of the two that acknowledged primacy of reading from the point of view of the present but recognized the small but distinctive contribution of scholarly contextual annotation. The MLA volume opens with Herbert Lindenberger's recounting from an earlier vantage point in his career (mid-fifties rather than mid-sixties) his passage through more than one revolution in the dominant literary critical paradigm; having encountered Wordsworth under an Arnoldian literary discipline in elementary school and a positivist/appreciationist historicism in college, he himself has taught Wordsworth as a New Critic, a comparatist "intertextualist" *avant la lettre*, a deconstructionist in spite of himself, and now a New Historicist, anticipating still another paradigm in the last decade of his career.[3] Pottle writes with the awareness that his synthesis of the two methods compels the present moment to recognize its own tragic participation in "special insights and ... special blindnesses" (330) that any moment in history is subject to as only one moment among others; Lindenberger presents himself as a cheerful picaresque hero who has turned with the winds of change before (his trope) and looks forward to moving with them again. Not situated between two antithetical possibilities that admit an eclectic if limited synthesis, Lindenberger does not write of using the insights of one paradigm to correct for the blindness of another but of the wearing out of critical languages, their loss of "vitality" once their "most talented practitioners have had their essential say" (38).

Both Pottle and Lindenberger confess that their students produced

---

3 Frederick A. Pottle, "A Method of Teaching," *WC* 9 (1978): 328. Herbert Lindenberger, "Teaching Wordsworth from the 1950s to the 1980s," in *Approaches* 32–38.

surprisingly sophisticated or brilliant papers with critical paradigms that they themselves distrusted. Though he himself was "antagonistic" to *Understanding Poetry*, Pottle's freshmen wrote papers "far more sophisticated ... than those we had received in the course before we introduced Brooks and Warren" (327), and Lindenberger's graduate students took deconstructive topoi of which he was suspicious and "achieved a brilliance that can occur only when a group of talented students confront an idea whose moment has come" (36–37). Pottle was moved by this experience to what he describes as painful awareness of the inadequacies of his own earlier position that led him to make himself (again his own tragic locution) confront facts of his experience that he had previously denied. Lindenberger read the results not in terms of his own limitations but in terms of the "fit" between "the skepticism central to" deconstruction and "students whose view of the world had been shaped by the late '60s and early '70s" (37).

However characteristically they responded to their students' success, what is remarkable to me is that their different ways of holding and changing the critical methods or paradigms they brought to the teaching of Wordsworth nevertheless produced similar pedagogical results. Pottle's dutiful commitment to "play fair" (326) with a critical method he opposed and his serious self-criticism and self-correction in light of its success and Lindenberger's easy openness to embrace "with varying degrees of intensity" the diverse critical paradigms that have come his way over the years both introduced students to more than their teachers knew or believed and permitted those students to do better work than their teachers had reason to expect. The students seem to have found their own power where their teachers, impressed but not persuaded by New Critical voices and unsure of themselves, introduced those new voices into their classes.

Logocentric mystagogy and student powerlessness

Two senior men from the generation between Pottle's and Lindenberger's contribute to the *Wordsworth Circle* issue in the form of pedagogical credos rather than autobiographical narratives, and the creeds they profess are remarkably similar. Geoffrey Durrant declares himself for the teaching of a Wordsworth poem "in its uniqueness as an illumination of mind," one instance of "the recurring miracle of illumination." Newton P. Stallknecht locates "Wordsworth's greatest gift as a poet" in "his power to share with his more sympathetic readers moments of awareness that seem miraculously complete."[4] Both teachers find such miracles of illumination in "The Solitary Reaper" and "Westminster Bridge" as well as other poems, and both induce their students to share in those moments through their own impassioned readings aloud of the poem. Durrant declares that he must "speak it for the students so that it becomes to some degree what most of them unaided cannot make it – living speech" (352), and Stallknecht declares that the students' feeling the power depends "upon our willingness not only to read aloud but to read *viva voce* with full attention to the living sound of words spoken in intimate reaction with one another" (382).

Deconstructionists, New Historicists, and dialogic critics alike, struck by this privileging of speech over writing, of poetry over history, and of unity over diversity, might be moved to declare in one unexamined voice, "'Tis against that / Which we are fighting'" (1805 *Prelude* IX, 519–20), but I would remind them (and myself among them) that these voices of logocentric aesthetic Wordsworthianism and others in harmony with them do not dominate the teaching collections I have surveyed and that they have not dominated Wordsworth criticism, if they ever did, for at least the past twenty years.

I would also note one important difference between Durrant's and Stallknecht's accounts of their teaching with these convictions and ask after its significance. The difference is already evident in the two formulations with which these two teachers justify their recourse to *viva voce* presentation of the poems: Stallknecht emphasizes the reading as necessary to realize the full meaning of the words, whereas Durrant introduces the reading as also necessary to compensate for the inadequacies of his students. In the two essays, Stallknecht gives no indication of the assumptions about students that inform his teaching. Durrant, on the other hand, elaborates his vision of students who cannot read the poem for themselves, students

for whom poetry – and especially metrical poetry – is more than ever a foreign tongue... children of a world so far removed from Words-worth's, ... victims of a culture steeped in sensationalism beyond the poet's

4 Geoffrey Durrant, "An Elementary Strategy for Teaching Wordsworth's Poetry," *WC* 9 (1978): 352–53. Newton P. Stallknecht, "Wordsworth's Poetry of Participation," *WC* 9 (1978): 382–83.

worst nightmares, many of them barely capable of a literate sentence in English, or of reading aloud a single line of poetry without stammering and blundering ... [for whom the poem is] nothing more than marks on the page, or at best English words strung unaccountably together.　　　(352)

This nightmare vision of illiterate, indeed mindless, students, disabled by their culture for any independent intellectual effort gives Durrant the justification he needs to assume the role of mystagogue, initiating these benighted souls into the sublime presence of the poem through his own voice and putting off the invitation to "critical thought" until the poem is "there ... held in the mind as an autonomous thought ... [that] perform[s] its magical transformation of the natural world" (352). Since Stallknecht does not mention students, it remains an open question whether the teacher who takes the poet, the poems, and himself as he and Durrant do also must imagine the students as Durrant does. Teachers of Wordsworth who remain committed to teaching what Stallknecht calls, following J. A. Stewart, the "'Transcendental Feeling'" of "the Wordsworthian experience" (383) might ask themselves. They and others might also wonder how strong is the correlation between this pedagogical orientation and the choice of lyric poems like "The Solitary Reaper" and "Westminster Bridge" that can be read for what Langbaum called "epiphanic" moments. On the evidence of available pedagogical writings, it would appear that such poems attract not only believers in Wordsworthianism but also those who would deconstruct or historicize their idealized vision and the poems that support it.[5] Whether these atheists from the Wordsworthian Church view their students differently than the true believers is also a question worth asking, but one that the available evidence does not let us decide.

Experimental poems and student autonomy

There is a strong, though not universal, correlation between teachers who give accounts of teaching Wordsworth's experimental poems from *Lyrical Ballads* and those who hold a higher estimation of their students' powers than Durrant expresses. Laraine Fergenson tells how she "presented Wordsworth as a reward" to remedial English

5 See Spencer Hall's and Francis Russell Hart's accounts of their respective deconstructive and historicist readings of "Westminster Bridge" in *Approaches* 73, 127.

composition students tired of grammar exercises and invited them to write in response to "We Are Seven." Its "easy diction and structure," she reports, were "well within the comprehension of the students," and the papers many of them wrote were "perceptive" and responsive to what one student she quotes recognized as "'two different views of death'" and the question "'is death real?'"[6]

Peter Manning and Eugene Stelzig identify their students' difficulties with these simple poems as functions not of students' illiteracy but of what Stelzig sees as their conditioning to expect "that a poem is a series of edifying sentiments to be taken to heart with downcast eyes and pursed lips" and Manning sees as their having acquired "from high school or elsewhere... the notion that poetry should be poetic, not plain and awkward."[7] Stelzig invents an exercise to get "students to go beyond a sentimental or unreflecting taking-in of Wordsworth's poetry" and Manning sees himself as an uncomfortable "agent" of the educative process by which the experimental poems "show students the inadequacy of [their] understandings" and the shallowness of their sympathies "on the generous assumption that the reader is educable" to better understandings and sympathies. Both presume with Wordsworth that there is nothing wrong with the students' powers themselves but that the problem is to activate those powers and to avoid preempting their exercise by, as Manning says, substituting "a deceptively inclusive lecture for the labor of wrestling with the poetry" (41).

Jared Curtis, who aims to "free students to move from the periphery of the hermeneutic circle, as receivers of approved wisdom, to the center, as the active subjects of their own (and Wordsworth's) experiments in linking ordinary experience with literary experience," assigns "Anecdote for Fathers" and quotes a lengthy passage from a student's response to the poem. My own contribution to the MLA *Approaches* volume, which draws most of its examples from *Lyrical Ballads*, adopts John Danby's understanding of Wordsworth's attempt to confront his reader "'with the need to be aware of what he is judging with as well as what he is judging'" and further imagines that students and their teachers can reflect theoretically upon and take responsibility for "their expectations in the constitution of their

6 "Teaching Wordsworth in the Open Admissions Classroom," *WC* 9 (1978): 334.
7 Peter J. Manning, "On Failing to Teach Wordsworth," in *Approaches* 39–42. Eugene Stelzig, "Beyond Simplicity: Three Strategies for Teaching Wordsworth," *WC* 9 (1978): 356–59.

poetic (and other) experiences." John T. Ogden opens several sophisticated lines of inquiry into *Lyrical Ballads* in the expectation that students can understand and pursue them. Donald G. Priestman assigns to his undergraduates topics "which have also claimed the attention of Wordsworth scholars in the past" such as "the manipulation of the narrator's role in *Lyrical Ballads*" and notes that "although they bring less experience to bear on a text, their responses are generally sound and even tend to reproduce the different interpretations observable among professional critics."[8]

The confidence these teachers declare in Wordsworth's experimental poems and in students' ultimate ability to respond to them and to their own responses complicate the teachers' conceptions of their own pedagogical roles. Manning makes the most of this problem in recognizing his discomfort in allying himself with poems designed to enlarge "the sympathies of ... readers by disclosing their shallowness" and his ultimate dispensability in a situation where the "understanding of [Wordsworth] develops largely in the solitude he prized" and "the truest teaching occurs long after the teacher's voice is heard no more." My own contribution is more committed to a public inquiry into the laws of the art of Wordsworth's poetry that makes explicit the premises of its reading and reflection on their adequacy. Manning expects his readers to reproduce the sensations of "strangeness and awkwardness" Wordsworth expected his readers to feel upon reading the poems, whereas I would replace the poetic premises that produced those sensations with other Wordsworthian and Bakhtinian premises in terms of which the poems are normal and interesting. Whether I spoil the reading of the poems by naturalizing them or whether he repeats the history of taste when he should change it are questions open for more thought.

Feminist silenced voices

Anne K. Mellor narrates her "Teaching of Wordsworth and Women" with an active-voiced, first-person directness that calls to my mind the last stanza of "The Solitary Reaper." An elided version of her essay

8 Jared Curtis, "Teaching Wordsworth by Response," in *Approaches* 50–53. Don H. Bialostosky, "Teaching Wordsworth's Poetry from the Perspective of a Poetics of Speech," in *Approaches* 153–56. John T. Ogden, "'Was it for This?,'" *WC* 9 (1978): 371–72. Donald G. Priestman, "Comparing Wordsworth's Poems with Their Origins and Intentions," *WC* 9 (1978): 350–51.

that emphasizes her pedagogical actions and her students' reactions will exaggerate this aspect of her account but not, I think, seriously misrepresent it:

What questions do I, as a feminist critic teaching Wordsworth's poetry, wish to pursue? First I ask my classes to analyze Wordsworth's conception of the female ... Second, I raise the issue of Wordsworth's personal relationships with women ... And finally, we try to determine the extent to which sexuality or gender as such is central to Wordsworth's creative processes. Finding it necessary to begin with a working definition of feminist criticism, I propose ... In teaching Wordsworth's poetry and life from a feminist perspective, I typically focus on a few representative texts ... I begin by asking the class to explore the following text for what it reveals of Wordsworth's concept of the female ... My students quickly recognize ... We go on to point out ... But in Wordsworth's case, I suggest ... I then ask the class to analyze the consequences of Wordsworth's identification of nature as the mother or female ... My students usually interpret the "Nutting" episode as a rape of nature by the male poet ... More critically sophisticated students here often ... argue that Wordsworth substitutes the linguistic creations of his own imagination for a genuine participation in nature or in the female ... If nature is female, is the converse also true? Are women identified with nature in Wordsworth's poetry? ... My women students frequently comment that Wordsworth never presents his female figures as distinct individuals with complex, changing personalities ... At this point I make the polemical feminist argument that Wordsworth ... has denied to the female both her own language and the opportunity to speak ... When my male students protest that Wordsworth's masculine figures are also nonindividuated projections of his own ego, anxieties, mental states, or philosophical concerns, I emphasize that Wordsworth's male characters are literally permitted to speak ... But his women – Lucy, Margaret, Martha Ray, Dorothy – do not speak *in propria persona*; the words assigned to them are literally spoken by male narrators. Turning now to the topic of Wordsworth's relationships with women, I rely on biographical and historical evidence to support the assertion ... Placing a passage from Dorothy's journal beside a poem by Wordsworth based on that passage ... When my classes have compared these two texts, they readily acknowledge Dorothy's gift for precise vivid description. But in contrast to Wordsworth's poem, Dorothy's observations do not reveal the significance of what she sees ... While we must give Wordsworth full credit for genuinely loving and respecting Dorothy and his wife, I end the class by reminding students that he entirely dominated his own household.[9]

Mellor presents herself here as a teacher with an announced standpoint and agenda. She knows what texts she will read, what

9 Anne K. Mellor, "Teaching Wordsworth and Women," in *Approaches* 142–46.

questions she will ask, what responses her students (male and female) will make, what answers she will make to their objections, what unanswerable evidence she will cite, and what judgments she will conclude with. Her students "recognize" and "acknowledge" what she expects them to, and they appear to "interpret," "argue," "comment," and "protest" at predictable places in recognizable ways.

One moment in the narrative has special interest for me, because I want to protest again after she has quelled the protest of her male students with the argument that Wordsworth's "women – Lucy, Margaret, Martha Ray, Dorothy – do not speak *in propria persona*" (145). My margin lists the Sailor's Mother, the Mad Mother, the Female Vagrant, Goody Blake, the child in "We Are Seven," Betty Foy, the Forsaken Indian Woman, Nature, the Maiden in "The Pet Lamb," Joanna (admittedly not speaking but manifestly voiced), and Alice Fell among Wordsworth's female characters with voices of their own (for I do not hold that narrated voices are not permitted to speak), and I am tempted to go back and object to what her women students declared without argument from her about the absence of "female figures as distinct individuals with complex, changing personalities" when I think of Margaret or the Female Vagrant.

But these silenced voices in Wordsworth's poetry – voices Mellor's students are not invited to hear – seem less important than the silenced voices of Mellor's students themselves as she portrays them, compared, at least, with another feminist account of teaching Wordsworth in which the fostering of student voices is part of the project and the representation of student voices part of the pedagogical text.[10] Deanne Bogdan presented her students in a graduate seminar in women's literature and feminist criticism with William Wordsworth's "I wandered lonely as a cloud," Dorothy Wordsworth's related journal entry, Joyce Peseroff's parody of the poem, "Adolescent," and William's Preface to *Lyrical Ballads*. In a sequence of assignments, Bogdan invited her students to respond in their journals to combinations of these texts and to their own previous responses. Bogdan's paper reports and frequently quotes the

---

10 Deanne Bogdan, "Feminism, Romanticism, and the New Literacy in Response Journals," in *Response to Literature*, ed. M. Hayhoe and S. Parker (Milton Keynes, England: Open University Press, 1990). I read this essay in manuscript and have not seen the pagination of the publication. I am grateful to Deanne Bogdan for permission to quote from the MS.

diversity of students' responses – Clare's, Ruth's, Gayle's, Liz's, Jane's, Marion's and Karen's – no more or less condescended to in this familiar first-naming than Dorothy, William, and Joyce.

Bogdan's class shared one assignment with Mellor's – the comparative judgment of William's "I wandered lonely as a cloud" with the entry from Dorothy's journal on which he based it – but the two instructors report different results in their different styles. After noting that her classes "readily acknowledge Dorothy's gift for precise, vivid description: she makes you see what she has seen," Mellor shifts to declaring general propositions, attributed to neither students nor teachers, that declare the superiority of what William has wrought:

But in contrast to William's poem, Dorothy's observations do not reveal the significance of what she sees. She does not mention her emotional or intellectual responses to her observations, nor does she generalize from this particular event to universal meaning. Wordsworth in contrast brings to the scene a charged imaginative realization of what it means ... Wordsworth adds to what Dorothy sees the presence of a self-conscious human mind, judging, evaluating, treasuring, mourning. Dorothy is a tourist, recording her travels; William is a poet, creating meaning through language. Dorothy explicitly wrote her journals for William's pleasure and benefit, and he repaid her devotion by using her eyes to write some of the finest poems in the English language. (145–46)

Bogdan, however, reports

a lack of agreement as to whose writing, William's or Dorothy's, was the more successful in achieving the goals stated in William's "Preface" ... Jane's examination of William's "Preface" led her to prefer his poem. While she challenged his assumptions that "'the language of men,' 'common life,'" and transcendent experience produce timeless poetic truth, she nevertheless luxuriated in precisely the kind of aesthetic pleasure that William's poetic method intended to evoke ... Liz blamed William's failure to engage her on the self-consciousness he brings to the poet's mandate to engage through the deliberate act of remembering ... [Marion] saw William's poem as an exhalation whereas "Dorothy's daffodils draw air into the lungs; they inspire and conspire to cut cleanly through the persona of the poetic genius looking down at himself as poetic genius."

These students have not only diverse opinions but reasons of their own pertinent to the reasons Mellor declares for her preference of Wordsworth's poem over Dorothy's prose. Bogdan, whose Women's Studies course was taught to an interdisciplinary group of students, observes that the English specialists tended to prefer William, and those who were "other," Dorothy. I think I can safely say that professional literary conditioning affects how readers are engaged by writers ... Karen, an English specialist, found William's poem more imaginatively satisfying and emotionally intense than Dorothy's "drawn out and uninspiring" prose ... Liz, a non-specialist, rendered Dorothy's daffodils more vivid and immediate. Their specificity was a product of simple memory or direct observation rather than the long reflection recommended by William.

It may be that Mellor and all her students shared the specialist predispositions that Bogdan identifies, or it may be that Mellor's own commitment to inculcating those predispositions prevented her from registering student voices that did not share them. The contrast between these two accounts of feminist pedagogy should demonstrate, in either case, that the feminist question of silenced voices applies not just to poets' representations of their female (or male) characters but also to teachers' attention to and representation of their students, male and female, and that feminist theory admits significant variations in pedagogical practice.

Deconstructionist self-division

It is fitting that the one avowedly deconstructive account of teaching Wordsworth I have found should be a voice divided against her own task, a voice who from the start is two voices in one, rejecting a widely received version of deconstruction and practicing in the name of deconstruction what many of its professors would not call deconstruction at all. Tilottama Rajan resists from her first paragraph what she calls the "grammatological and linguistic" as opposed to the "ontological and psychological" account of the text.[11] She turns for Romantic anticipations of deconstruction to Nietzsche and De Quincey, who translate deconstructive concerns into "mythological and psychological rather than purely semiotic terms" (157). Her focus on "the intersection of voices" in the various versions of Book I of the *Excursion*, her critique of "attempts at unified self-representation" (158) in *The Prelude*, her interest in "the dialogizing of poetic voice," "the differences between ... voices," "utterances as dialogically addressed to another person," "the larger problem of whether the

---

11 Tilottama Rajan, "Deconstructing Wordsworth," in *Approaches* 157–62.

conversation of text and reader in that poem will necessarily be a communion between like minds" in that poem – all these emphases outweigh her attention to "the disruption of the relation between voice and word, the possibility that the text of the self may become no more than a collection of signs, a grammatological construct" (160–61). She has a powerful investment in phenomenologically exploring "a being enmeshed in language," in affirming the possibility that "'original voice is already double'" and in resisting the possibility "that voice and origin are fictions" (162). She is interested in teaching Wordsworth along dialogic lines that attend to the divisions in his voice and between his voice(s) and the voices of others, more than she is interested in dwelling on the materiality of the signs in his poetry and the discontinuities produced by their uncontrolled and uncontrollable repetitions.

I would claim Rajan as an ally for the dialogic perspective I have elaborated in this book and in the essay that precedes her own in the MLA *Approaches* volume, but I suspect that readers of the two essays would be more impressed by our differences. Her starting point in the tradition of Derrida and Heidegger makes her arrival at a dialogic perspective sound against a different dialogizing background and in different theoretical diction than my own profession of dialogics, starting, as it does, from Wayne Booth, the Aristotelian Chicago School, and Wordsworth's poetry and prose. I cannot write of "the truth of being" whether single or "always different from itself" or say that the blind beggar's placard "speaks as an emptiness and dis-closes a being grounded in nothingness" (162), but my talk of always already deconstructed entities such as speakers, heroes, and listeners or "the human" in general must be equally unspeakable from her mouth (or pen). Nevertheless, I think she resists the same sort of deconstruction I do out of an interest in the same sort of poetic features that interest me, and we even use the same word, "dialogic," to describe them, but these similarities will never be identities, and our differences will always call for further thought and discussion.

New Historicist imaginations

In *Radical Literary Education* Jeffrey Robinson presents a book-length account of his attempt to invent a New Historicist classroom practice. Robinson tells how he tried to help his students "develop and exercise a historical imagination in the presence of literature" by teaching a semester-length introductory literature course focused on Wordsworth's Intimations Ode in its several historical contexts.[12] Robinson's syllabus begins with a close reading of the poem and goes on to place it in a "chronologically ordered selection of odes from Pindar and Horace ... to ... Keats and Shelley," to study its manuscript revisions in connection with "discussion of biography and English and European history," to read its nineteenth-century reviews by critical contemporaries including Coleridge and especially Hazlitt, to examine eighteenth- and nineteenth-century texts about topics broached by the poem, including "childhood, human development, [and] the place of passion and sex in human life," and finally to contextualize the poem in relation to other poems and prose of Wordsworth (18–19). Robinson's book fleshes out this syllabus with autobiographical reflections, speculations on adolescent socio-psychological development, reports of student writing, summaries of lectures and lines of classroom inquiry, and polemics in defense of his project.

As a pedagogical work of the New Historicism focused on one of Wordsworth's major lyrics, Robinson's book bears comparison with Marjorie Levinson's *Wordsworth's Great Period Poems*, a collection of New Historicist essays on four of Wordsworth's major poems, including a chapter on the Immortality Ode. Levinson presents her project, too, as provoked by the needs and interests of her undergraduate students and conducted in the name of the "historical imagination" (11), though she writes not a narrative of classroom work but a series of critical arguments contextualized by and addressed to fellow critics of Wordsworth. Both Levinson and Robinson, whose books appeared within a year of one another without mutual influence, associate the historical imagination with political consciousness, both revive Hazlitt's readings of the Immortality Ode, and both read the internalized poem against the world it silently shuts out. But Robinson's account of his course omits the historical and political center of Levinson's argument, and Levinson deprecates the psychological emphasis that shapes Robinson's course.

Robinson entitles one section of his book "Biography and History," but the section is in fact devoted exclusively to reporting

12 *Radical Literary Education: A Classroom Experiment with Wordsworth's Ode* (Madison: University of Wisconsin Press, 1987), 3.

his summary of Wordsworth's biography. Levinson's emphasis on the history Robinson omits supplements Robinson's work but also highlights his omission of contemporary history and politics in a project ostensibly committed to historical and political reading. Levinson calls attention to political events at the times of the Immortality Ode's composition. She shows how its key terms and images resonate with the political language and symbolism of the French Revolution, associating Wordsworth's "single tree," for example, with the tree of liberty, and his "single field" with the Champs de Mars. She traces, as Robinson does in an earlier essay, the common language of Wordsworth's political sonnets and the Immortality Ode.

For Levinson, politics is a matter of wars, revolutions, and allegiances; for Robinson, it turns out to be a matter of libido, repression, and human development. Her politics affiliates her with McGann, Jameson, Thompson, and Marx; his links him to Trilling, Freud, and Blake. The Hazlitt essay she cites applies the language of the ode to the French Revolution, while the Hazlitt Robinson cites criticizes Wordsworth's model of human development in the ode, especially his neglect of the passion of love. Levinson sees the "developmental and psychological themes [of the ode] as a device for (dis)figuring a specifically treacherous [political] vision" (97); Robinson invites his students to engage those themes and criticize the poem from the standpoint of their own adolescence.

Robinson's perception of his students as adolescents interested in their own psychosocial development shapes his pedagogical emphases, and his own participation in psychoanalysis allows him to imagine himself in the same developmental scheme. Wordsworth, too, he argues, could have realized the same scheme but chooses not to. Levinson's image of her students as "practical and empiricist" and "more worldly" than she is (ix) does not so readily explain her political emphases or connect them with her students' interests. Though she says that her inquiries started not from Freudian or Marxist theories but from undergraduates who had not learned not to ask why there is no abbey in "Tintern Abbey," she does not explain how such literal-minded empiricism constitutes her students as citizens or the classroom as a civic context in which their practical bent might express itself in political interests. In addition, in claiming that Wordsworth's political interests are alien to her own and her students' interests, she produces another distance that must be mediated; in order to mediate her construction of Wordsworth's politics with her students' interests, she must supply students with both the historical information and the political standpoint from which her criticism of the poem operates. Robinson, on the other hand, does not appeal to a reconstructed history or a contemporary political standpoint but identifies himself, his students, and Wordsworth with a shared human nature that authorizes his own and his students' critiques.

Robinson thus short-circuits historicist pedagogy and circumvents its most difficult and dangerous necessity – the background lecture that provides the historical information necessary to discover the historical significance of the work. In its place Robinson turns, as Wordsworth himself did, toward a generic and natural human knowledge rather than toward a knowledge specific only to biographers or historians. Thoroughgoing historicists would see claims for such generic knowledge as a mystification of specific, class-bound or culture-bound knowledge, but students can at least judge for themselves whether they know this generic knowledge, whether they share the limitations and the resources that constitute it. The historicist's reconstruction of background knowledge, on the other hand, is the result of specialized research, and undergraduates are in no position to check the lecturer's selection or interpretation of facts. As Pottle observed of the Old Historicism, "the method of contextualism has the bad pedagogical effect of making it appear that you can't read Wordsworth without being a Wordsworth expert."[13] Students in the one case may mistake their own participation in a truth for its universality, but students in the other case must take their instructor's account of the truth for the truth itself, for they do not participate in its ground at all. It would be regrettable if the students' critical liberation from the authority of the poem had to be purchased at the price of uncritical submission to the authority of the instructor.

The question of the students' access to the instructor's community of knowledge arises in Robinson's course in another way. Robinson organizes his course around Wordsworth's Immortality Ode because that poem has a special place in one line of Robinson's tradition of criticism, and he historicizes the poem because other critical voices to which he is responsive object to placing the poem on a pedestal, reading it as a thing in itself, and taking consolation from its

---

13 Pottle, "A Method of Teaching," 328.

argument. Robinson engaged the conflict between these voices before he invented the course in an article that defends Lionel Trilling's social and psychological reading of the Ode against Helen Vendler's aesthetic reading. Robinson's syllabus, however, has no place for either of those essays or for any other voices that might have shaped his syllabus and his teaching themes.[14] His bibliographic essay offers his readers a rich context for his course, but the readings in that essay are not on the syllabus. Robinson is the lone representative in his course of the conflicts of contemporary criticism, and he does not place himself in a historical context or give his students an indication of what is at stake for him in his course's organization and themes. I have declared elsewhere that the instructor may most appropriately stand and speak for the critical community at the introductory level where Robinson teaches this course and less appropriately do so at higher levels of college and graduate work,[15] and Robinson's practice seems to correspond to this policy, but the historicist program of his course would seem to require a different practice. If, as Robinson says, "in order to discover a work of literature as an event both making and made by various histories and contexts readers must discover themselves in something like a comparable history" (3), then teachers must place themselves in such a history for the benefit of their students or, better still, share with their students the formative contexts of their own interests.

This legitimate and, from Robinson's principles, necessary contextualizing of the course, however, leads me to ask whether Robinson's course belongs where he placed it as an introduction to literary analysis called at the University of Colorado "Writing about Literature." This curricular placement suggests comparison of his course both with conventional courses of this designation and with other innovative courses with the same function like the one laid out by Scholes, Comley, and Ulmer in their new *Text Book*. Robinson contrasts his principle of choosing a single major canonical text and building around it a series of generic, historical, biographical, and authorial contexts with the conventional series of writing assignments "covering the major accepted literary genres" and "classic examples

---

14 See Jonathan Ramsey's account of a unit on the Immortality Ode based on the juxtaposition of these critical essays, "Contexts for Teaching the Immortality Ode," in *Approaches* 96–99.

15 "Teaching and Research in Literary Criticism," *ADE Bulletin* 86 (Spring 1987): 1–3.

of literary criticism" (17). It also contrasts with Scholes's and his co-authors' innovative presentation of "literary language" in the contexts of related non-literary genres and theoretical essays.

Like Alan Liu's historicist reading of "Westminster Bridge," Robinson's pedagogical model must grant the canonical poem on which it focuses immense authority and representativeness before it can bring the poem down into relation with the other texts that historicize it. Robinson posits a dominant cultural ideology associated with the poem (though not necessarily embodied in it) against which he works to show what the text excludes or hides or overcomes. Robinson, like many other New Historicists, associates cultivating the historical imagination with cultivating "critical consciousness" because history for him includes what the work excludes and therefore necessarily offers a perspective outside the work from which it can be judged. Pedagogically, this position requires the production at the outset of sublime or mystifying readings of eloquent and difficult texts that can then be demystified or desublimated through the discovery of explanatory traditions, biographical and historical motivating contexts, and alternative accounts of the poem's theme or topic. In bringing such art back into history his course brings it down to earth and back into what Bakhtin calls the "zone of contact."

Scholes, Comley and Ulmer proceed in the opposite direction: they start from the "zone of contact" in ordinary language and common speech genres and move toward more complex and self-conscious literary elaborations; they begin with intelligible conceptual frameworks and move to more problematic applications of those terms to difficult texts. They use, for example, a speech-act analysis of oral story telling to derive a conceptual model of narrative that they then invite students to apply to literary narratives that do not entirely fit the model. They approach intertextuality not as a specialized way to demystify a text worshiped for its autonomy but as a commonplace and public way to produce texts, from bumper stickers to epic poems. They invite students to handle and to imitate other people's verbal works. Instead of leading students to question the authority of cultural monuments, they let students climb on them and show them how to make their own. They cultivate students' intellectual power not as a mobilization of historical knowledge to counteract the sublime power of the text but as a practical competence, gained through ordered literary experience, cultural knowledge, and conceptual reflection, to read and write more and more powerful texts.[16]

The contrast between *Radical Literary Education* and *Text Book* clarifies the relatively unreflective practices of the conventional "Writing about Literature" course and poses important questions about its aims and methods. Do we want such a course to humble students before the sublimity of great works and increase their sense of the distance between the literary texts they read and the critical texts they write? Do we want it to produce the effect of sublimity in reading a great text but to use other texts to reduce that effect by historicizing our central text? Do we want to teach the genres and criticism of literature apart from non-literary genres as a matter of pure literary competence, or do we wish to engage literary texts in a semiotic domain that naturalizes them and cultivates general verbal competence?

For an introductory course, I would follow Scholes *et al.* rather than Robinson because they move in what seems to me the right direction for such a course. They start in ordinary language and work toward literature, whereas Robinson begins caught up in literature and helps students to get out. His project is more appropriate for advanced English specialists who, like him, need to get some distance from over-valued literary and aesthetic experience or over-valued traditional and critical authority. I cannot escape the impression that Robinson's course acts out his own conversion from New Critical sacralism (not formalism) to historicism and reinforces his new convictions while preserving the power and centrality of his old object of worship. I believe him when he writes at the beginning of his autobiographical chapter, "I find the power of art mysterious" (22), and I understand how he might believe this when I read a pedagogical essay like Durrant's or Stallknecht's. But I am not convinced when he says that his students, though most of them lack the peculiar aesthetic education he received in an artistic family and a Harvard New Critical training, still experience art as something "sacralized out of the arena of the fantasy life and reified beyond the

16 See Robert Scholes, Nancy R. Comley, and Gregory L. Ulmer, *Text Book* (New York: St. Martin's Press, 1988). For my own elaboration of a compatible Bakhtinian pedagogy, see "From Discourse in Life to Discourse in Poetry: Teaching Poems as Bakhtinian Speech Genres," in *Practicing Theory in Introductory College Literature Courses*, ed. James M. Cahalan and David B. Downing (Urbana, Illinois: NCTE, forthcoming).

life of the mind" (171). I am more inclined to share Robert Scholes's assessment in *Textual Power* that we and our students start from a "loss of faith in the scriptural status of literature" and aim to give our students "knowledge and skill that will enable them to make sense of their worlds, to determine their own interests, both individual and collective, to see through the manipulations of all sorts of texts in all sorts of media, and to express their own views in some appropriate manner" (15–16). "The worst thing we can do," Scholes goes on, "is to foster in them an attitude of reverence before texts" (16), but Robinson's course presumes that reverence as a starting point – and must produce it where it does not already exist – if it is to have its proper effect of demystification. Instead of re-enacting the loss of reverence for the sacred text, I would begin, with Scholes, to cultivate critical and secular understanding of human verbal products.

The part of Robinson's course most compatible with the introductory instructional program of Scholes and his co-authors is his placement of Wordsworth's Immortality Ode in the tradition of the classical Horatian ode. In this unit, Robinson offers a theoretical proposition about the function of the ode, a classical model of that function, and a question that asks students to consider Wordsworth's ode in the light of this fundamental generic pattern. Following his teacher Allen Grossman, Robinson presents the ode as acting out a "commitment to the acknowledgment of the person by the community of civilization" (69) and presents Horace's ode *In praise of magistrate Lollius* as exemplifying it. He elaborates both the characteristics of the ode and the responsibilities of its readers, traces developments in the English ode before Wordsworth and asks finally of Wordsworth's ode, "Whose image does the poet wish to conserve and praise?" (105).

The confusion and effort he reports his students undergoing in response to this question strike me as the intellectual high point of the course, more important than what Robinson calls his "biggest discovery…that the adolescents studying Wordsworth with me found so compelling Hazlitt's criticism that the 'Ode' has substituted childhood…for its real subject adolescence" (163–64). This latter discovery was set up by Robinson's own master theme, and I cannot say that I am surprised that his students found compelling what had been compelling him throughout the course. But the former confusion and struggle arise from a plausible question with no set answer or pre-established theme. If Wordsworth called it an ode, it should have something to do with what we know about odes, and now we know quite a lot. But still it is not what we would expect. The dissimilitude in similitude created by setting Wordsworth's ode in this context of odes provokes thought whose outcome cannot be foreseen.[17]

Such thought does not consist in moving from a given standpoint to another predictable standpoint outside it, a movement too easily identified with raising "critical consciousness." Rather, such thought proceeds from an informed confusion to an active discovery of new relations and to a critical examination of its own terms in as yet unformulated terms. The idea of the hero of the ode has to be radically reconstrued or rejected in Wordsworth's ode; the civic occasion too comes into question. Indeed, Wordsworth himself seems to be raising these questions instead of always appearing to evade questions. Robinson has shared enough of the ode tradition with his students to enable them to recognize the need for these reconsiderations, but he did not (and did not wish to) predetermine what they would discover. This moment, more than any other Robinson reports, exemplifies his best formulation of the good at which his teaching aims, "*the thinking subject*, aware of its limits yet trusting its available power" (15). This formulation calls into question our images of our students as adolescents, practical empiricists, historical class members, critical or uncritical consciousnesses, men or women, and it calls into question our related images of ourselves and our authors as well. To function as thinking subjects, we, our students, and the writers we read must explore the limits of such images, even as we produce and experience their power.

17 For a richer generic and intertextual context in which to consider Wordsworth's Ode, see Ruoff, *Wordsworth and Coleridge.*

❖❖

9

Wordsworth, Allan Bloom, and liberal education

❖❖

At its best a liberal education ought to be a moment of transformation in the life of a growing mind – a moment in which it becomes conscious of itself and its powers as such and of the problems of assessing their fruitfulness and their limits, as well as their relation to the human enterprises they both constitute and serve. The stabilization of that moment of transformation as one to which the mind may fruitfully return as its powers are exercised and expanded is an essential part of the objective.

> Charles Wegener, *Liberal Education and the Modern University*

Why turn to Wordsworth in the current controversies over liberal education? He was a poet, after all, who was not a serious student during what he calls the "deep vacation" (*Prelude* III, 542) of his own university days. Of his time at Cambridge he confesses,

> The thirst of living praise,
> A reverence for the glorious dead, the sight
> Of those long vistos, catacombs in which
> Perennial minds lie visibly entombed,
> Have often stirred the heart of youth, and bred
> A fervent love of rigorous discipline.
> Alas, such high commotion touched not me;
> No look was in these walls to put to shame
> My easy spirits, and discountenance
> Their light composure – far less to instil
> A calm resolve of mind, firmly addressed
> To puissant efforts. (*Prelude* III, 343–54)

Instead of submitting passionately to the discipline of the great minds and great books, Wordsworth and his casual friends "sauntered, played,...rioted,...talked / Unprofitable talk at morning hours, / Drifted about along the streets and walks, / Read lazily in lazy books, went forth / To gallop through the country in blind zeal / Of senseless horsemanship, or on the breast / Of Cam sailed boisterously, and let the stars / Come out, perhaps without one quiet thought" (III, 251–58). Writing some eighteen years after he matriculated at Cambridge, he cannot persuade himself to believe his compensatory fantasy of a university that would "have bent [him] down / To instantaneous service" and "made [him] pay to science and to arts / And written lore ... / A homage frankly offered up" (III, 382–86). The awe-inspiring sanctuary of learning that he conjures here is too good to be true and he knows it. The golden age of poor dedicated scholars reading "by moonshine through mere lack of taper light" (III, 490) suggests moonshine in more ways than one.

Why, then, turn to Wordsworth at a time when a new wave of gurus on liberal education command general attention in America? Allan Bloom, conspicuous among them, would appear to have attended the university that Wordsworth fantasized, where, as Wordsworth puts it, youth was "awed, possessed, as with a sense / Religious, of what holy joy there is / In knowledge if it be sincerely sought / For its own sake" and where "the passing day should learn to put aside / Her trappings ..., should strip them off abashed / Before antiquity and stedfast truth / And strong book-mindedness" (III, 396–404). Bloom declares that in his undergraduate days he fell "in love with the idea of the university" at the University of Chicago and found his life in it. He discovered a higher and more serious world than he had previously known in his Chicago high school, a world of knowledge sought for its own sake, of great old books that revealed the present day to be a pale reflection of their glory:

The substance of my being has been informed by the books I learned to care for. They accompany me every minute of every day of my life, making me see much more and be much more than I could have seen or been if fortune had not put me into a great university at one of its greatest moments. I have had teachers and students such as dreams are made on. And most of all I have friends with whom I can share thinking about what friendship is, with whom there is a touching of souls.[1]

If we want our authorities on liberal education to identify themselves with the university and to warrant their claims with testimony of their own ideal educations, Bloom would appear to be our man.

1 Allan Bloom, *The Closing of the American Mind* (New York: Simon and Schuster, 1987), 245.

The critical poet and the enthusiastic philosopher

Bloom's differences from Wordsworth are striking.[2] At Cambridge Wordsworth was an outsider whose imagination had previously attached itself to natural "shapes sublime" (III, 102) from which friends and professors alike were distractions; the substance of *his* being was informed by his experiences of beautiful and sublime natural forms. At the University of Chicago, Bloom was a convert who found a worthy object for his "youthful and enthusiastic imagination" (245) in the sublime shapes of the great books and the great men who wrote and taught them and the great university that sustained that teaching, and he identified himself with friends who defined their friendship, indeed their very beings under the powerful influence of those great books and great men. Wordsworth was an onlooker at the university who celebrated the power of books only as an afterthought to his celebration of the power of nature in his education. Bloom was and is a true believer in an idea of the university who finds the only nature worthy of notice in the great books themselves. For Wordsworth, who writes "I was the dreamer, they the dream" (III, 28), Cambridge and its academic inhabitants were insubstantial compared to his earlier life in nature. For Bloom, the university, compared to his high school years, was a dream become real where he had, as he says, "teachers and students such as dreams are made on."

Paradoxically, however, we must turn to Wordsworth, the poet, for a critical account of university education, while the philosopher Bloom enthusiastically offers us an idealized university education. Our poet is critical of his own superficial undergraduate experience, of the university he attended, and even of the university he projects

---

2 He has, however, recently been linked to Wordsworth in an article that came out after this chapter was completed. Karen Swann, who concedes that "Wordsworth's romanticism is powerfully anti-elitist in its effort to claim the high literary significance of the customary, the common, even the low," nevertheless traces Bloom's attack on the vulgarization of culture back to Wordsworth's 1800 Preface to *Lyrical Ballads*. See her "The Sublime and the Vulgar," *College English* 52 (1990): 8. Swann's argument, which invokes "Wordsworth" in alliance with Edmund Burke as well as Allan Bloom on the basis of a different passage from those I have highlighted here, leaves me unsure as to our agreements and disagreements. She appears to hear the same Leavisite accents in Wordsworth that Siskin does, but does she or does she not hear in Wordsworth's call to cultivate the "discriminating powers of the mind" a critical antidote to the sublime mystifications she opposes?

as an ideal. Our political philosopher takes his own education and the university he attended as magical fulfillments of the ideal in comparison with which today's students, teachers, and universities appear degraded and demoralized.

The contrast between the critical poet and the enthusiastic philosopher is equally apparent in the tone and manner of their writing. Our poet hesitates after grand assertions, questions his own formulations, corrects his overstatements with alternative claims, checks his interpretations of his own earlier thoughts, and reflects on the limitations in his evidence and distortions in his point of view. Our lover of Socratic philosophy, on the other hand, asserts himself without hesitation or qualification, offers interpretations even of the most difficult philosophic texts without argument or citation, and celebrates greatness and condemns triviality with equal self-assurance.[3] Wordsworth tells the story of his own life with a critical self-consciousness that is utterly absent in Bloom's story of the decline of Western culture. Wordsworth is less sure of a tale he should know first-hand than Bloom is of a story that someone has had to construct from difficult and controversial texts.

How, we might ask, has a philosopher come to be sure of so much and a poet of so little? What has enabled the philosopher to tell his tale with such inspired confidence, while the poet struggles visibly to hold his story together? The sources in the Great Books to which Bloom directs our attention would have led us, after all, to expect inspired but unselfconscious poets declaring unquestioned maxims and telling powerful stories while critical philosophers subjected maxims and stories alike to rational scrutiny. Plato's Socrates opens the inquiry of the *Republic*, for instance, by questioning the meaning of a maxim which Polemarchus attributes to the poet Simonides, and he later leads his interlocutor Adeimantus through a critical revaluation of the content, form, and music of Homer's and Hesiod's tales. He interrupts the poets' declarations and narrations with awkward questions that refuse to take the meanings of words and the pleasures of stories for granted, and he judges the poets' tales by

---

3 See Martha Nussbaum, "Undemocratic Vistas," *The New York Review of Books*, November 5, 1987, 23. This review is reprinted, along with a remarkable array of essays and commentaries on Bloom's book, in *Essays on "The Closing of the American Mind*," ed. Robert L. Stone (Chicago: Chicago Review Press, 1989). For another critique of Bloom's scholarly and critical practices, see George Anastaplo, "In re Allan Bloom: A Respectful Dissent," in *Essays*, ed. Stone, 267–84.

moral criteria that spoil the stories and the storytelling. Socrates' philosopher critically examines the limits of his own and other people's claims to knowledge; his poet produces unsubstantiated, magical tales that the unphilosophical take for knowledge. How, again, have Wordsworth and Bloom managed to reverse these classical roles?

Education for the guardians and education for the philosophers

To answer this question, we must briefly review the classical models of education in relation to which the roles of poetry and philosophy have been defined. In the city that Plato's Socrates guides his interlocutors to invent, the distinction between two kinds of education defines distinct roles for poetry and philosophy. On the one hand, there is the musical or poetic education of the guardian class, which is also the elementary education of the philosophic class. On the other hand, there is the higher education of the philosophers, which has no use for poetry.

The *Republic*'s first extended analysis of poetry arises in the service of the first sort of education, the education of well-trained high-spirited soldiers who will obediently defend the state against its enemies and gently rule the passions of its citizens. In their education poetry serves as a powerful instrument of implanting in their souls the right opinions, and it can serve this function only if it is carefully screened by philosophic critics who see that it conforms to those opinions. The songs the guardians sing, the music they march to, the heroes they imitate, and the gods they worship must be selected by their teachers to train them to courageous self-discipline on the battlefield and loyal gentleness in the city. Poetry helps to fix this cultural and behavioral repertoire in their souls.

Philosophic and unphilosophic natures alike undergo the discipline of this training, but the philosophic natures reveal themselves by their dissatisfaction with it, their unsuppressed desire to know the meaning of the words they have been trained to recite and the idea of the good they have been taught to serve. In their higher education, poetry has no further function, for it offers only a simulacrum of true knowledge and a seduction from rational thought. Mathematical disciplines wean the philosophic soul from sensory appearances and accustom it to seek rational forms to resolve contradictory appearances. Those mathematical and abstract studies also prepare the philosophers after long study for a return to the analysis of words in dialectic, a discipline which inquires into the rational forms that resolve the contradictions between conflicting premises and which follows out the logical consequences of its discoveries even when they contradict accepted opinions and arouse feelings of resistance. The philosopher thinks beyond conflicting appearances and traditional premises to truths that can stand the tests of reason. Poetry, which imitates those appearances and fixes those premises in the soul, is an obstacle to such inquiry.

These two stages of the philosopher's education, which are at the same time two kinds of education, one for philosophers and the other for guardians, are also paradigms for the two principal kinds of liberal education that Bruce A. Kimball presents in his recent history of this idea, *Orators & Philosophers*.[4] The education of the guardians is a prototype for what Kimball calls the oratorical ideal of liberal education, with one important modification. We must substitute the orator for the guardian as the type of person to be produced by this education. The orator is to the exigencies of public leadership what the guardian is to the exigencies of war and the maintenance of public order, a well-trained man (typically a male in the classical tradition) whose character provides him with the virtues and competencies necessary for his public role. In both cases the role "implies the prescription of values and standards for character and conduct" and a concomitant "respect for commitment" to those prescribed values and standards, and the means for inculcating those values is "a body of classical texts" that provides ethical and stylistic models for those selected to serve in the role. In both the education of the guardian and the liberal education of the orator, the standards by which these models are selected are taken for granted by those who are trained to conform to them. As Kimball puts it, "the task of liberal education is to inform the student about the virtues rather than, as the Socratic tradition held, to teach the student to search for them" (37–38). Kimball's oratorical ideal of liberal education thus presupposes an already established tradition of classical texts and trained orators to pass on the virtues they embody; it lacks any place for a committee of philosophers to sift through the classics and separate their virtue-

4 Bruce A. Kimball, *Orators & Philosophers: A History of the Idea of Liberal Education* (New York: Teacher's College Press, 1986).

promoting aspects from their vice-engendering ones. This ideal is characteristic of Plato's timarchic or timocratic constitution, in which unphilosophical virtuous men uncritically transmit the songs and stories that shaped their virtues to the next generation. We may also note that poetry, taken as a memorable and soul-stirring repository of models and maxims of virtue, enjoys high prestige in this model of liberal education.

Kimball's second principal model of liberal education takes up what he calls the Socratic or philosophic tradition and follows, up to a point, the pattern of Plato's philosophic education, though it does not presuppose participation of the philosopher in the more elementary training of the guardians. Kimball's philosophical ideal begins where Plato's philosophical inquiry begins, in a freedom to inquire beyond "a priori strictures and standards." Informed by a commitment to rational intellect modeled on mathematical reasoning, it practices a critical skepticism of traditional certainties and toleration of diverse hypotheses. In the modern world where Kimball identifies its full emergence, this ideal diverges from Plato in positing a fundamental equality among men rather than a fundamental diversity of human natures, and it sanctions the free intellectual inquiry of individuals over "the obligations of citizenship" found in the oratorical ideal and in Plato's imposition on philosophers of the obligation to rule the city (119–22).

Like Plato's philosophical education, the philosophical model of liberal education has no place for poetry, which either perpetuates uncritical traditional beliefs or encourages imaginative gratification of desire at the expense of realistic attention to facts. At best, as Bacon suggests, poetry might provide evidence for inquiries into the operations of the passions, but poets themselves would be disqualified from conducting this inquiry by their habits of indulging the passions and encouraging the imagination. Philosopher-scientists accustomed to controlling their passions and suppressing their imaginations would be better able to discover what the poets reveal about human nature than the poets themselves.

Wordsworth as Baconian philosophical poet

It will help us to understand how Wordsworth has become a self-critical or philosophical poet if we recognize that he has accepted these terms of the philosophical model of liberal education and tried to make a place for poetry within them. His Cambridge education may indeed have had a more profound effect upon him than he admits in *The Prelude*, for he is a poet who feels compelled to make his poetry answerable to the scientific spirit epitomized there by the statue "of Newton with his prism and silent face, / The marble index of a mind for ever / Voyaging through strange seas of Thought, alone" (1850, III, 61–63). Wordsworth declares not only that "Poetry is passion" but at the same time that "it is the history or science of feelings" (*Wordsworth's Literary Criticism*, ed. Owen, 97). Poetry is not merely "the spontaneous overflow of powerful feelings," an involuntary expression provoking an irrational response in others, but also the conscious tracing or illustrating of emotions, the thoughtful study of emotions inciting others to similar thoughtful study. Wordsworth presents his poetry as "an experiment" that traces "the primary laws of our nature: chiefly as far as regards the manner in which we associate ideas in a state of excitement" as those laws reveal themselves in the utterances of subjects chosen from "low and rustic life" (LB 241–45). He has "at all times endeavoured to look steadily at [his] subject" (LB 251) and to refrain from substituting the work of "his fancy and imagination" for the emanations of "reality and truth" (LB 257).

Even when he acknowledges that he deliberately indulges his own pleasing passions and dutifully serves his readers' pleasure, Wordsworth does not allow that the dignity of his vocation is inferior to that of the "Man of Science," the paragon of the philosophical ideal. Exaggerating Aristotle's remark that poetry is more philosophical than history, he claims that "Poetry is the most philosophic of all writing" and further declares that Aristotle is correct about poetry: "Its object is truth" pursued by the poet "under one restriction only, namely that of giving immediate pleasure to a human Being possessed of that information which may be expected from him ... as a Man." This restriction, Wordsworth goes on, is not to be "considered as a degradation of the Poet's art" because the poet's commitment to give immediate pleasure is grounded in "the grand elementary principle of pleasure," a fundamental truth that underlies not only the poet's participation in the pleasures of his fellow humans but also the man of science's isolation in specialized pursuits of knowledge (LB 257–58).

Both the poet and the man of science are motivated, on Wordsworth's account, by a common principle of pleasure, and both of them are dedicated to discovering the truth. The poet, however, restricts himself to revealing and celebrating the truth of the pleasure he shares with all human beings in common experience, whereas the man of science avidly pursues the uncommon truths of "those particular parts of nature which are the objects of his studies." They differ, then, neither in the ends they pursue (truth) nor in the pleasurable interests with which they pursue them, but rather in the relative commonality of their objects and communicability of their findings (LB 257–59). Scientists have more specialized interests than poets and address themselves to other scientists rather than to "all human beings." But they are not for Wordsworth, as they are for Bacon, heroes of truth who achieve knowledge only by denying their pleasures, while poets are indulgers of pleasures contrary to truth, seducing themselves and others away from knowledge. Bacon and the tradition he fostered oppose the scientist to the poet on the premise that "so differing a harmony there is between the spirit of man and the spirit of nature" (*Advancement* 133). Wordsworth denies this premise, asserting that "the mind of man is naturally the mirror of the fairest and most interesting qualities of nature" (LB 258–59).

On Wordsworth's premise the poet is simultaneously an inquirer into the mind's interactions with nature, a mind that itself interacts with nature, and a celebrant and teacher of the mind's interactions with nature. His research and teaching, we might say, are more closely connected to one another than those of the man of science because the poet specializes in what all human beings share as passionate, articulate, thinking beings involved with the objects of common human experience, "with the operations of the elements and the appearances of the visible universe; with storm and sun-shine, with the revolutions of the seasons, with cold and heat, with loss of friends and kindred, with injuries and resentments, gratitude and hope, with fear and sorrow" and the like (LB 261). What distinguishes poets from other human beings for Wordsworth is not a distinctive sort of experience or a distinctive language for communicating it, but a cultivated and self-conscious interest in common experiences and the workings of mind they exemplify.

Poets, then, can claim to teach others because poets have observed closely and "thought long and deeply" about the workings of *their* minds and the minds of others. They can claim a privileged place in the curriculum of the philosophical liberal education because they know their own minds and can teach others to know their minds with pleasure. Such knowledge potentially unites the whole human community in the consciousness of its intellectual powers and limitations, but it also has an indispensable role in the education of specialized inquirers. Without such knowledge, the whole project of the advancement of specialized learning and the philosophical ideal it promotes may founder on their overreaction to what Bacon calls the idols of the tribe or "fallacies of the mind of man" (*Advancement* 132). In their attempts to expose or suppress the mind's tendencies to distort its perceptions of nature, these philosophical projects lack the self-critical consciousness which Wordsworth sets out to cultivate, overreacting to the mind's inevitable contributions to what it sees and understands. In their uncritical suspicion of the mind's perceptions, they may fail to recognize those cases in which nature *conforms* to the mind's hypotheses, and in their uncritical suppression of passion and imagination, they may open themselves to dangerous encounters with (to use Emerson's phrase) the alienated majesty of those powers of mind they have struggled to suppress. Only a self-conscious, critical habit of taking into account the mind's contributions to its perceptions can both warrant the fruits of inquiry and teach us to recognize their inherent limitations. Only a pleasure in that self-conscious critical habit can sustain it. Poetry, as Wordsworth theorizes and practices it, cultivates this self-conscious critical habit and sustains it with pleasure.

Poetry in a philosophical liberal education

Poetry that does what Wordsworth says his does would be an indispensable part of a philosophical liberal education. It would meet the thoughtfully derived criteria for such an education presented by another University of Chicago writer on the subject, Charles Wegener, who has not been as widely read and discussed as Allan Bloom, but who deserves the attention of anyone concerned with the subject his title announces, *Liberal Education and the Modern University*.[5] In this book Wegener arrives at a formulation of the purpose of liberal education that epitomizes the function of poetry I have drawn from Wordsworth and generalizes it to the educational enterprise as a whole: "A liberal education...should be an effort to

5 Charles Wegener, *Liberal Education and the Modern University* (Chicago: University of Chicago Press, 1978).

create a *habit* of reflection as an integral part of the life of the mind" (94). Wegener goes on to elaborate this purpose in terms that might be taken as a reading of Wordsworth's *Prelude* from the point of view of liberal education. He writes:

At its best a liberal education ought to be a moment of transformation in the life of a growing mind — a moment in which it becomes conscious of itself and its powers as such and of the problems of assessing their fruitfulness and their limits, as well as their relation to the human enterprises they both constitute and serve. The stabilization of that moment of transformation as one to which the mind may fruitfully return as its powers are exercised and expanded is an essential part of the objective. (94–95)

The famous "spots of time" in Wordsworth's *Prelude* exemplify and stabilize such moments of transformation, revealing the mind to itself upon reflection as the source of their extraordinary power, and allowing Wordsworth to recognize in them that power as the source and servant of the human enterprise of poetry. The narration of these moments preserves them, as Wordsworth says, "for future restoration" (XI, 342) or, as Wegener puts it, as moments to which the mind may fruitfully return. Wordsworth emphasizes, as Wegener does not, the pleasure of returning to those moments, and he also reminds us that the mind may have recourse to the record of their occurrence not only "as its powers are exercised and expanded" but also as the "hiding-places of [its] power" close (XI, 335). To recognize upon reflection these moments in which "we have had deepest feeling that the mind / Is lord and master, and that outward sense / Is but the obedient servant of her will" (XI, 270–72) is not, however, to become addicted to them and seek to repeat them or to mystify them as manifestations of some great power beyond the mind. It is rather to take them into account, to trace the mind's workings in other less powerful experiences, and to dedicate the powers thus disclosed to human enterprises that are worthy of them. One expression of this dedication is to teach in a way that makes such moments likely or that provokes reflection on such moments as have already taken place; to teach others how, as Wordsworth declares in the closing lines of *The Prelude* "the mind of man becomes / A thousand times more beautiful than the earth / On which he dwells" (XIII, 446–48).

Such teaching is not aimed, however, at inspiring worship of those powers, which are, after all, our own, but at provoking the exercise and recognition of them. It does not lie, as Wordsworth puts it in his Essay Supplementary, "in establishing that dominion over the spirits of readers by which they are to be humbled and humanised, in order that they may be purified and exalted" but rather in provoking the reader – or the student, I would add – to "the exertion of a co-operating *power*" in his or her own mind. The poet or teacher is not to overpower but "to call forth and to communicate *power*" or "call forth and bestow power, of which knowledge is the effect" (ES 80–82). Poets or teachers may lead, may goad, may set occasions for the reader's or student's exertion and recognition of his or her power, but if they arrogate the power to themselves or assign it to Great Minds and Great Books alone, they mystify it and unjustly exclude their students and readers from recognizing, cultivating, and exercising it themselves.

How might a poet write if he wished to provoke readers to exert and discover and enjoy their own mental powers, and what might a poet do to avoid the danger of overwhelming readers with his own power? He might, as Wordsworth does, interrupt his own eloquent exertions with questions, qualifications, reinterpretations, and explanations. He might challenge the evidence for his own assertions and call attention to the wishful exaggerations and mistaken readings to which his own imagination led him. He might trace the manner in which his own mind and the minds of others associate ideas under the influence of exciting passions and call attention to the difference between a neutrally reported "hedgerow" and an imaginatively transformed "little line of sportive wood run wild." In all this he would be careful not just to demystify his readers' pleasurable fantasies but also to please his readers by leading them to discover their minds' contributions to their perceptions.

Reading "Simon Lee" and "Tam o' Shanter"

Perhaps I can illustrate the working of such a poetic liberal education with a poem that proceeds not only by exposing the failure of its poet-narrator to control his tale but also by directly inviting its readers to discover the story that the poet-narrator cannot tell. The 1798 version of "Simon Lee" (LB 60–63) – a poem L. J. Swingle has called a "touchstone for considering Wordsworth's artistic designs" (99) – exhibits the "strangeness and awkwardness" that Wordsworth expected his readers to find in his lyrical ballad experiments.[6] The

6 For extended readings of this poem and responses to a number of its other critics, see *Making Tales* 51–54, 74–81.

poem directly confronts its readers with the question of how they should read it and how they should judge its narrator and hero — questions that could, if they were taken seriously, provoke the sort of reflection on reading itself that might permanently transform the reader's relation to all subsequent reading. After eight and a half stanzas of confusing descriptions of his hero, Wordsworth writes:

> My gentle reader, I perceive
> How patiently you've waited,
> And I'm afraid that you expect
> Some tale will be related.
>
> O reader! had you in your mind
> Such stores as silent thought can bring,
> O gentle reader! you would find
> A tale in every thing.
> What more I have to say is short,
> I hope you'll kindly take it;
> It is no tale; but should you think
> Perhaps a tale you'll make it.

Readers who put themselves in the position of the addressee of this utterance are bound to wonder not only what to make of "Simon Lee" but also why the making of it should fall to them. Why won't the narrator, or why can't he, tell the tale? Why should he have knowingly led us to expect a tale only to frustrate our expectations and leave the making to us? For that matter, what do we expect when we expect a tale, and why should it be a problem to expect one?

To help us answer this last question, we can turn to a generic model of the tale that Wordsworth might himself have turned to. Burns's "Tam o' Shanter" calls itself a "tale" and a "tale o' truth" without narratorial coyness or embarrassment.[7] Like "Simon Lee" it takes its name from its hero and relates, as Wordsworth puts it, "an incident in which he was concerned." Burns's narrator first identifies himself as one of many Scotsmen who love to sit and drink on market day, avoiding their disapproving wives for as long as possible, then introduces Tam o' Shanter directly as one more such man, ignoring one more such wife. Introductions completed, the narrator abruptly turns to tell the tale of Tam's drinking one market night to the point of transcendence ("Kings may be blest but Tam was glorious, / O'er a' the ills of life victorious"). Having reached this height, Tam takes

---

7 Robert Burns, "Tam o' Shanter: A Tale," in *The Poems and Songs of Robert Burns*, ed. James Kinsley, vol. II (Oxford: Clarendon Press, 1968).

to the road to return home on a preternaturally stormy night and on his way happens upon a dance of witches and warlocks. Made courageous by drink, he watches their capers, focusing on a scantily clad younger witch in a "cutty sark" or short skirt, whose movements are so bewitching that he shouts out his approval. Immediately the witches set out in hot pursuit of him, and he is saved by the leap of his wonderful horse Maggie, who loses her tail to the pursuers. Burns's narrator concludes with a cautionary moral addressed to "each man and mother's son" about the dangers of strong drink and short skirts, pointing to Maggie's missing tail to conclude Tam o' Shanter's marvelous tale.

If we read Wordsworth's "Simon Lee" expecting some such tale as Burns's to be related, we are indeed likely to feel some strangeness and awkwardness. Wordsworth's narrator, we will discover, is not, like Burns's, one of the guys, enjoying national, gender, and class solidarity with his hero and his readers. Wordsworth's narrator is instead an outsider to Simon Lee's community who depends partly on hearsay for his present knowledge of Simon. He is an outsider also to the world of hunt and hall in which Simon lived in his youth and with which he still identifies himself. The narrator, it turns out, is an intruder as well into the present world of Simon's struggle to survive, a stranger who, without so much as a howdy do, has taken Simon's mattock out of his hands and done him an unasked for kindness. Wordsworth's narrator is also an awkward intruder in the world of his "gentle" readers. He rudely confronts them by making an issue of the literary expectations he might have silently gratified, and he creates further awkwardness by appealing to them to take his tale kindly and make up for its deficiencies. The unanimous masculine "we" Burns constructs in his first stanza against an excluded "her" breaks down for Wordsworth into a strange and awkward "you," "they," and "I," in which Simon Lee and his wife Ruth are bound together in common labor and pain, while the narrator and his "gentle" but ungendered readers are estranged from one another and from the hapless Lees.

The characterization of Simon Lee in Wordsworth's poem is also strange and awkward compared to Burns's presentation of Tam o' Shanter as a boon companion inspired by John Barleycorn and a "cutty sark." Wordsworth's descriptions vacillate even within the same stanza between inconsistent portraits of Simon Lee. For a moment Simon appears as a helpless old man with swollen ankles who was once, in a distant past, a consummate athlete of the hunt;

but then he appears as a rosy-cheeked old man who, though pitifully reduced from his youthful strength and prowess, still takes pride and pleasure in his former profession. Any good teacher of writing who reads the first eight and a half stanzas of the 1798 poem with red pen in hand will mark shifting emphases and subordinations that reveal a narrator who has not decided what his point is about Simon Lee. In concluding comments that teacher might ask, "Is the point that he appears to be poor but is really still proud or is it that he appears to be proud but is really miserably poor? Is he isolated from the now dead world of hunt and hall that ruined his eye and his legs, or is he still, despite his decrepitude, living in that world, keeping up his livery coat, lying about his age, and exulting in the cry of the hounds that still chimes in the countryside? What are you trying to prove?"

Wordsworth's narrator knows that a tale like Burns's would also lead his readers to expect that the description of his hero should be followed by the tale they have been waiting for, perhaps even a tale like Burns's that will take them from the familiar world they share with the hero and narrator to a supernatural world of exaggerated fears and fulfilled wishes. A dream vision of the hunt or a meeting with a ghost of Simon's former master might have filled the bill, but instead of leading us the merry chase we might have hoped for, Wordsworth's narrator breaks into his confused description of Simon and Ruth Lee with the direct address to the reader I have already quoted and follows that address with a personal anecdote of his own encounter with Simon Lee. Here are the last three stanzas of the poem:

> One summer-day I chanced to see
> This old man doing all he could
> About the root of an old tree,
> A stump of rotten wood.
> The mattock totter'd in his hand;
> So vain was his endeavour
> That at the root of the old tree
> He might have worked for ever.

> "You're overtasked, good Simon Lee,
> Give me your tool," to him I said;
> And at the word right gladly he
> Received my proffer'd aid.
> I struck, and with a single blow
> The tangled root I sever'd,
> At which the poor old man so long
> And vainly had endeavour'd.

The tears into his eyes were brought,
And thanks and praises seemed to run
So fast out of his heart, I thought
They never would have done.
— I've heard of hearts unkind, kind deeds
With coldness still returning.
Alas! the gratitude of men
Has oft'ner left me mourning.

We can recognize in these stanzas that the awkwardness of the earlier description has its origin in the awkwardness of the speaker's encounter with Simon Lee. It was awkward to see the old man struggling to do what he (the narrator) could easily do, but also awkward to accept the outpouring of gratitude for help that meant too little to him and too much to the man he had assisted. By associating the "old man" with the "old tree" and the sudden severing of the root with the sudden outflow of thanks and praises from Simon's heart, the narrator suggests that he has cut the vein of Simon's self-respect in acting upon the impression of his helplessness. The language of his moral, too, may be taken to imply that the gratitude of this man pains the narrator because Simon returns the narrator's unkind deed with such excessive kindness.

The anecdote reveals that the narrator has acted on a simpler impression of Simon Lee than the confused impression he has presented at the beginning of the poem. The impression on which he acted took into account Simon's present helplessness but neglected his former prowess, his present attempts to keep up appearances, and his continuing pleasure in thoughts of his younger, stronger self. In restoring these complications in his description of Simon — even at the price of sacrificing a coherent description and an acceptable tale — the narrator puts his readers in a position to judge differently than he did and at the same time to judge how he might have judged as he did, to understand the narrator's mistake and to know what might be necessary in order not to make it. There is a tale in Simon's well-kept livery coat and in his lies about his age and in his love of the sound of the hounds, just as there is a tale in his swollen ankles and his missing eye. There is a tale, too, in the severed root, but the narrator is too embarrassed, and perhaps too kind, to tell it. The tale is more strange and awkward than Burns's tale of Maggie's lost tail, but for Wordsworth the community we discover among ourselves, the narrator and the Lees as we make that tale is more worthy of us than the community we might take for granted in enjoying Burns's untroubled tale, and the power we exert in thinking out the tale for ourselves is more worthy of us than the tears we might have shed had the poet overwhelmed us with a sentimental telling of it.

By a long route, we have answered, I think, one-half of the question from which we began. Our poet Wordsworth presents himself as hesitant and self-critical, sometimes even as incompetent, partly out of a consciousness of the limits of his mental powers and partly out of a wish to provoke his readers to discover the strength of their own powers. He tells awkward stories of himself and others in order to provoke and share moments of reflection that reveal how the mind exerts its power, sometimes to the glorification of ordinary experience, sometimes to the cruel neglect of its complexity. He exposes his self-consciousness and his anxiety over the evidence for his claims because he has reflected on the dangers of unchecked imagination and reason. He deliberately fails to tell a tale that would render a consistent vision of Simon Lee because he has heard the voice of Simon Lee himself but has heard it too late to respect the dignity it affirms. Our philosophic poet has forged an account of poetry and a poetic practice that can serve the philosophical ideal of liberal education and perhaps also check its uncritical faith in the free intellect.

Bloom's education

What then of the self-assurance of our contemporary philosopher and what of his unselfcritical confidence as a storyteller? What sort of liberal education does Allan Bloom envision and what sort of community does he offer to the readers of his tales? Bloom's vision of liberal education fits neither of Kimball's models, and it modifies Plato's two-stage and two-type model as well. Though Bloom approaches the oratorical ideal in his emphasis on teaching the classical texts to a leisured elite, his Great Books-centered liberal education magnifies the greatness of the books beyond the status of the traditional classic and equivocates between the ends of training citizen-orators and attracting converts to the philosophical life. Though he approaches the philosophical ideal of liberal education in identifying with philosophic inquiry as exemplified by Socrates, Bloom describes a Socrates who can be all things to all people and leaves us unsure about which Socrates is divinatory of *his* longings and necessary to *his* self understanding (281–82). Bloom seems to follow Plato in distinguishing the philosophic education of an intellectual elite from that education "rather more poetic or rhetorical than philosophic, the purpose of which is to temper the passions of gentlemen's souls" (281), but he makes no clear distinction between educational programs for these kinds of students and seems to recommend the "good old Great Books approach" for both alike (344). Does he imagine that these books, like the figure of Socrates, will be different things to different students, confirming some in the "prevailing moral taste of the regime in which they [find] themselves" and leading others "to the Elysian Fields where the philosophers meet to talk"? (283). If so, he would be following his master Leo Strauss, who, in teaching the same texts, taught "some of his students to be statesmen and gentlemen while teaching others to be philosophers."[8]

Bloom certainly places himself among the philosophers and identifies himself with the philosophic "community of those who seek the truth...the true friends" (381), but he sometimes describes that community in another less philosophical way: the university "contained marvels," he writes, "and made possible friendships consisting in shared experiences of those marvels" (244). These marvels reappear when his account of liberal education bemoans the contemporary university's failure to give its young student the "intimation that great mysteries might be revealed to him, that new higher motives of action might be discovered within him, that a different and more human way of life can be harmoniously constructed by what he is going to learn" (337). Whether Bloom hopes to initiate his students into the community of philosophical friends or the community of gentlemen friendly to philosophy, he emphasizes the Great Books as profound, powerful, marvelous objects that will excite students, "thrill" them, even, and open what he calls "the royal road to students' hearts" (344). Himself an initiate in the community that shares Leo Strauss's esoteric wisdom, Bloom intimates mysteries that will attract new initiates and magnifies power that will subdue those who are not worthy of the full freedom of the philosophic community.

This is not the place to probe those mysteries or to trace the sources of that power, though I strongly recommend Shadia Drury's

---

8 Shadia B. Drury, *The Political Ideas of Leo Strauss* (New York: St. Martin's Press, 1988), 188.

recent book, *The Political Ideas of Leo Strauss,* as a guide to such inquiries.[9] If we still wonder, however, where Bloom gets his confidence as a commentator and narrator, we may recognize his identification with an exclusive male community of friends not unlike the one to which Burns's narrator belongs. Bloom's disapproval of feminist violations of "human nature" is notorious, and the exclusive masculinity of the Straussian community is evident. Even the intoxication of Burns's hero and his glory "o'er a' the ills o' life victorious" have their equivalents in Strauss's philosophical community in the intoxication of the philosophical *eros* and the philosopher's superior ability to "withstand the deadly truth," as Drury shows (170–81). Self-assurance in both cases depends upon an unquestioned sense of belonging to a community of men who know above all else that they are superior to those whom they exclude and who enjoy together the fulfillment, in fantasy or in philosophic conversation, of their erotic longings.

The one thing such a community must exclude more than any class or gender of others is the reflective moment that might call its status into question and, in effect, liberate its members from their belief in its exclusive hold on excellence and truth. Bloom unquestioningly takes Strauss's notion of philosophy as philosophy itself and is contemptuous of the discipline that calls itself philosophy today. A reader of Drury's book will also recognize that Bloom similarly accepts Strauss's story of the history of philosophy and repeats it without question. Wegener, however, notes

the serious risk of confusing the character of [an] activity with the way in which it is carried on by a particular person or persons – even, perhaps, a school or a tradition, whether of fly-fishing or physics. The liberating power of explicit and communicated reflection lies not only in its ability to refine and reinforce an activity by directing attention to its essential features but also in its necessary component of separating the generic condition of the activity from its particular occasions and exemplifications ... To recognize a personal or traditional style of fly-fishing is to face the possibility of others; to recognize that one does a certain sort of history is to recognize that history is not thereby exhausted. Of course, it is always possible that one has been fortunate enough to encounter the ideal or complete style of fly-fishing or of history, but it is a possibility to be subjected to skeptical

9 Drury is cautious in reconstructing a political philosophy close to Bloom's from Strauss's writings in the history of political philosophy, but one should also note Anastaplo's effort to distinguish Bloom from the more scholarly and circumspect Strauss in "In re Allan Bloom: A Respectful Dissent."

consideration, and it can be subjected to such examination only in the context of reflection.   (93)

Bloom's immunity to such reflection is evident not only in his belief that he has been fortunate enough to attend the ideal university with ideal teachers and fellow students but also in his inability to distinguish philosophy generically from its exemplifications in particular Great Books and in his ability to assert dubious pronouncements and to tell questionable stories without doubts or questions. Bloom offers a liberal education that promises to some students the same unreflective certainty and to others the unreflective thrill of humility before greatness, but he cannot lead them to know their own minds because he does not appear to know his own. Even in his identification with what he takes to be greatness, he is the mouthpiece of a power outside himself. He tells his story with such confidence because it is someone else's story that has taken him for its own.

It is tempting to conclude that our philosopher is a rhapsode possessed by the Straussian muse, our poet a self-critical and self-possessed intellectual. Such a philosopher could teach his students to sing or at least to admire the powerful and mysterious song that possesses him; such a poet could perhaps provoke them to think for themselves, know their own minds, and take interest in the minds of others.

But my own mind has too easily accepted its own paradoxical premise and too neatly mobilized "Wordsworth" and "Bloom" as antithetical figures of its argument. I must confess that I could construct from Bloom's text a brief for reflection, a preference for "humanizing doubts" over "impoverishing certitudes" (239) and an association between "self-consciousness" and "poetry" (298) that might at least destabilize the portrait I have drawn of him, even if it does not displace it. Wordsworth, of course, has been read for generations as an exemplification, even a pathological case, of the imaginative power of which I present him as the self-conscious critic.[10] Like poor old Simon Lee, these writers present aspects that

10 For a recent account of Wordsworth that reaffirms this position and stands sharply against the argument I have made here, see Charles J. Rzepka, *The Self as Mind: Vision and Identity in Wordsworth, Coleridge, and Keats* (Cambridge, Mass.: Harvard University Press, 1986). Rzepka writes that "instead of placing itself among things and others that demand a reply, and thus enforce self-consciousness, Wordsworth's visionary mind tends to embrace all things" and that Wordsworth "does not recognize...the workings of his own mind" in its

tempt me to conflicting constructions; like the narrator of Wordsworth's poem, I can only make those constructions, act on them, reflect upon my own constructions and actions, and submit them to my readers' reconstructions and judgments.

It is not just Great Books or Great Minds that we must read carefully and self-consciously. The discrepancies in the texts of a poor old huntsman's clothing and a best-selling professor's book can become the occasions for critical reflection or thoughtless self-congratulation, just as discrepancies in Wordsworth's or Plato's texts can. Only readers with habits of reflection, sustained by self-critical practices and by constitutions which provide for review of their own provisions, can hope (they cannot guarantee) to read any of these texts for the good.

"visionary effects" (37–38). His reading of "Simon Lee" (in a later version substantially different from the one I examine) is in keeping with his account of the poet (52–55).

Index

abaser (tapinosis), *see* tropes and figures, repluralized

Abrams, M. H., 21, 22, 24, 39, 50–51, 55, 114n, 153, 168–69, 187, 191; and humanism, 15; and I. A. Richards, 234; and John Stuart Mill, 47; criticized by Arac, 10; misreading of Wordsworth's Essay Supplementary, 12–14; on greater Romantic lyric, 80; on J. Hillis Miller, 119; on rhetoric, 202–03; on transition from pragmatic to expressive orientation, 45–46; on Wordsworth's expressive art, 56, 60

Amherst College, 234

Anastaplo, George, 258n, 273n

Apollodorus, 84

Approaches to Teaching Wordsworth's Poetry, 235–54

Arac, Jonathan, xvi, 29, 46, 47, 49, 56, 57, 91, 127, 152n, 153–54; and Baconian literary history, 22; and critical discipline, 8–11; and New Literary History, 2; as critic of Coleridge's authority, 23–25, 37; on agreement to ignore important work, 80; on history of discussion of lyric, 81; on rhetoric, 9, 202–05; on Romantic constitution of literature, 3; on women and literature, 18–19; on Wordsworth's Essay Supplementary, 11; on Wordsworth's poetry as social or metaphysical, 134; power and knowledge in, 14–18; program for constitutional review, 20; views compared to Siskin's, 9–11

Aristotle, 35, 38, 39–40, 61, 98 n. 18, 103, 204n, 246, 262

Arnold, Matthew, 2, 9–10, 50, 125, 152n, 236; and imperative to "make us feel," 4; as authority for Arac, 10; as unsatisfactory authority on Wordsworth, 47; "Dover Beach," 116; on high seriousness, 43; on "The Sailor's Mother," 58; on Wordsworth's naturalness, 60

Auerbach, Erich, 202, 220, 225; *Figura*, 203; on figures, 205

Auerbach, Nina, 19

Augustine, St., 41

authorship, bourgeois, 26–28

Babbitt, Irving, 50

Bacon, Francis, 48, 199, 263–64; *Advancement of Learning*, 21, 193–94; as alternative authority to Sidney, 43–45; literary history in, 21–22; *New Organon*, 194, 196–97

Bahti, Timothy, 201–02, 208, 213n, 224 n. 40, 229–30

Bakhtin, M. M., 22, 48, 102, 241, 251; and Chaucer, 43n; and Julia Kristeva, 81–82; and novelized poetry, 66; anticipated at Amherst, 234 n. 1; on dialogic discourse theory, 82–83; on dialogic figure of the speaker, 91; on dialogic poetics, 35–36, 57, 65–78; on dialogic relations between utterances, 79, 84; on dialogizing background, 91–92; on discourse oriented to other discourse, 87; on hero as participant in discourse, 110; on heteroglossia, 56; on hidden dialogue, 121; on ideological horizon, 110; on loopholes, 9; on lyric poetry, 84; on non-verbal context, 106–07; on

277

Index

Index

Mill, John Stuart, 47, 50
Miller, J. Hillis, 80n, 83, 128, 130;
  ethics of reading, 118, 122–27; on
  "Westminster Bridge," 118–24;
  rationale for New Critical essay, 82
Milton, John, 180–81, 183–84, 207,
  230; *Paradise Lost*, 190
Modiano, Raimonda, 28
Molesworth, Charles, 83, 115, 122,
  128; and Liu, 130–31; on
  "Westminster Bridge," 108–14
Montefiore, Jan, on Wordsworth and
  feminist poetry, 19
Moorman, Mary, 117 n. 36
Morgan, Thaïs, 234 n. 2
Murphy's law, 195
Murray, Roger N., 223, 225
Myerson, George, 104 n. 24

Nabholz, John R., 208 n. 17
Napoleon, 147
nationalism, 113, 131, 147n, 151
Needham, Lawrence, 27n
Nelson, Cary, 234 n. 2
New Criticism, 44, 47–48, 51, 124,
  153, 234, 236; American versus
  British, 63–64, 89–90n; American,
  versus European dialectical criticism,
  158; and Alan Liu, 129, 130; and
  Coleridge, xiii, 36–38; and David
  Ferry, 123; and rhetoric, 204; and
  Russian formalism, 95–96; and
  Wordsworth's sonnets, 85–90;
  criticized by Crane, 97; genres of,
  80–81, 125; sacralism versus
  formalism, 252
New Historicism, 2–3, 57, 138, 238;
  and dialogics, 128–33; and teaching,
  236, 246–54; and "The Solitary
  Reaper," 145–51
New Literary History, 2–3
New Rhetoric, *see* Rhetoric, New
Newton, Sir Isaac, 262
Nietzsche, Friedrich, 10, 245; on
  rhetoric, 204n
Norris, Christopher, 198–99
novelization, 66
Nussbaum, Martha, 258n

O'Hara, Daniel T., 186n, 199n; on
  women and literature, 19
Ogden, John T., 241
Olbrechts-Tyteca, L., 219
Olson, Elder, 98 n. 19
Owen, W. J. B., 30, 110n
Oxford University, 234

Page, Judith W., 83, 130 n. 50; on
  "Beauteous Evening," 114–18
paradox: and double-voiced discourse,
  89; Christian, 12–13; dialogical
  view of, 86–88; in Miller's and
  Ferry's readings of "Westminster
  Bridge," 124; language of in Brooks,
  86–90
Parker, Patricia, 80
Parrish, Stephen Maxfield, 35, 50, 60n;
  on Wordsworth's dramatic art, 63
Pater, Walter, 47
Payne, Robert O., 48; on medieval
  rhetoric, 41–43
Perelman, Ch., 219
Pericles, 72
Perkins, David, 138n, 145
Peseroff, Joyce, 243–44
philosophy: versus poetry in
  Wordsworth and Allan Bloom,
  257–59, 274–75; versus poetry in
  Wordsworth and de Man, 193–99
Pindar, 247
Plato, 35, 38, 40, 179, 232, 275;
  poetics of speech in, 98 n. 18;
  Republic, 258–61; *Symposium*, 83, 84
pleasure: grand elementary principle
  of, 50, 68–69, 262
poetics: dialogic, 35; dialogic or
  sociological, 138; expressive, 60; in
  Aristotle, 39; of speech, 35, 39–40,
  57, 98 n. 18; Russian formalist, 95
Poirier, Richard, 47, 158, 234 n. 1; on
  Wordsworth's Essay Supplementary,
  11n
Pope, Alexander, 175, 184
Pottle, Frederick A., 134, 137, 249; on
  teaching, 236–37
power: and knowledge in Foucault and
  Wordsworth, 14–18; as a good, 17;

283